Cash on the Table

Publication of this book and the SAR advanced seminar from which it resulted were made possible with the generous support of The Paloheimo Foundation and The Brown Foundation, Inc., of Houston, Texas.

School for Advanced Research
Advanced Seminar Series

Cash on the Table

Contributors

Peter Benson
Department of Anthropology, Washington University

João Biehl
Department of Sociology, Princeton University

Avery Dickins de Girón
Center for Latin American Studies, Vanderbilt University

James Ferguson
Department of Anthropology, Stanford University
Department of Sociology and Social Anthropology, Stellenbosch University
Department of Social Anthropology, University of Cape Town

Edward F. Fischer
Department of Anthropology, Vanderbilt University

Robert H. Frank
Johnson Graduate School of Management, Cornell University

Jonathan Friedman
Institut de recherche interdisciplinaire sur les enjeux sociaux, L'École des hautes études en sciences sociales
Department of Anthropology, University of California, Santa Barbara

Matthew Grimes
Business School, University of Alberta

Stephen Gudeman
Department of Anthropology, University of Minnesota

Stuart Kirsch
Department of Anthropology, University of Michigan

Deirdre N. McCloskey
Department of Economics, University of Illinois at Chicago

Natasha Schüll
Program in Science, Technology, and Society, Massachusetts Institute of Technology

Jonathan A. Shayne
Shayne and Company

Jesse Sullivan
Artist

Anna Tsing
Department of Anthropology, University of California, Santa Cruz

Bart Victor
Owen Graduate School of Management, Vanderbilt University

Caitlin Zaloom
Department of Social and Cultural Analysis, New York University

Cash on the Table

Markets, Values, and Moral Economies

Edited by Edward F. Fischer

School for Advanced Research Press

Santa Fe

School for Advanced Research Press

Post Office Box 2188
Santa Fe, New Mexico 87504-2188
www.sarpress.org

Managing Editor: Lisa Pacheco
Editorial Assistant: Ellen Goldberg
Designer and Production Manager: Cynthia Dyer
Manuscript Editor: Sarah Soliz
Proofreader: Kate Whelan
Indexer: Catherine Fox
Printer: Versa Printing

Library of Congress Cataloging-in-Publication Data

Cash on the table : markets, values, and moral economies / edited by Edward F. Fischer.
   p. cm. — (Advanced seminar series)
 Includes bibliographical references and index.
 ISBN 978-1-938645-00-6 (alk. paper) — ISBN 978-1-938645-07-5 (e-book)
1. Economics—Moral and ethical aspects. 2. Economics—Sociological aspects.
I. Fischer, Edward F., 1966- editor of compilation. II. Shayne, Jonathan A. Bezzle and sardines.
 HB72.C385 2013
 330—dc23

            2012041370

Cover illustration: *Traders at the Chicago Mercantile Exchange*, © 2010 by Simone Perolari/
LUZphoto.

*The School for Advanced Research (SAR) promotes the furthering of scholarship on—and public
understanding of—human culture, behavior, and evolution. SAR Press publishes cutting-edge scholarly
and general-interest books that encourage critical thinking and present new perspectives on topics
of interest to all humans. Contributions by authors reflect their own opinions and viewpoints and do not
necessarily express the opinions of SAR Press.*

Contents

Figures and Tables

Preface

This volume is the result of a School for Advanced Research advanced seminar held in Santa Fe, New Mexico, in May 2009. Peter Benson and I organized the seminar with the aim of bringing together anthropologists, economists, and business scholars who are working on similar issues from different disciplinary perspectives. The benefits of such interdisciplinary collaboration are widely acknowledged even if the practical difficulties of working across distinct vocabularies, analytic paradigms, disciplinary politics, and academic incentive structures are underplayed. We hoped to realize some of the untapped potential (what we referred to in the seminar as the "cash on the table") in the overlap among these fields.

We chose the theme "markets and moralities" not because of its alliterative allure but because the issues of moralities and values provide us with a fruitful area of intersection between anthropology and economics. By *moralities* we do not refer to the moral code of a religious tradition or legal ethics or to any absolute sense of virtue, but rather to an anthropological understanding of culturally contextualized values. In this light, and following Arthur Kleinman (2006), we define moralities very broadly as "what matters most" to people in particular times and places. Moralities, in this sense, overlap significantly with cultural processes, but we thought it useful to isolate their emphasis on value judgments. Economics is all about value judgments, if of a very particular sort, and ethnography, too, is centrally concerned with how values are played out in daily life.

Our seminar was organized around a sustained discussion of how markets are imbued by particular value systems. We examined the values implicit in dominant paradigms within economics and business and in the actual workings of particular markets, and we looked at what ethnographic and anthropological approaches bring to economic and business models in terms of understanding both market systems and individual behavior.

Cultural anthropology and economics represent an especially deep epistemological divide. In the end, given the exigencies of weather and illness, the anthropologists far outnumbered the economist and business professor around the living room table where we held our recorded discussions, although we are able to present a more complete representation in the chapters that follow.

The points of view represented in the group were diverse, sometimes directly opposed. And although we experienced no moment of epiphany and complete mutual understanding, the discussions and presentations sharpened positions and revealed some surprising areas of agreement and complementarity. As David Stark has observed, the very dissonance and friction of diverse value systems can make for creative and productive encounters. We agreed that markets are contrivances, social constructions, but differed over the values they embody and the potential they hold. Markets may be seen as channels of power, but this power is manifested and perceived in very different ways (widely distributed, as with the power exercised by consumers, or concentrated, as in the hands of corporations). In this view, markets themselves are neither good nor evil but are conduits for a wide range of prosocial and self-interested, democratic and authoritarian, hegemonic and subaltern processes, all justified by certain moral stances. It also follows that since markets are constructed, they may be reconstructed, through regulation and social norms, as we see fit. Rather than displace tough moral and political debates onto the supposedly neutral forces of the market, we need to have more open and honest debate about how markets and the economy can best serve us all.

This volume is intended to be read as a conversation, and we attempt to capture the dialogue between divergent perspectives by juxtaposing styles and points of view. The volume is divided into three sections composed of edited dialogues from the seminar discussions, short interventions, and longer scholarly articles. We present not a simple linear narrative leading up to a singular conclusion but rather a collection of perspectives that together offer a multifaceted view of anthropological engagements with issues of economics and moral projects.

The first section defines some key terms of debate and represents two points of surprising convergence between the anthropologists and economist and students of the market. The opening dialogue (chapter 2) shows that all the seminarians accepted the very anthropological observation that markets are contrivances. The surprise comes because much of popular and textbook economics likens the market to a natural force we have to deal with, like the weather. Yet, our participants, along with many academic economists and business scholars, agree that markets are historically specific, social constructions built upon particular legal, political, and social structures and imbued with certain moral valences.

The other surprising consensus in the chapters of this section is a view of markets as obfuscating. One may fruitfully view markets, as many economists do, as flows of information, with prices and behaviors representing this information. But even if the authors differ on particulars, they all show how the market obfuscates, as well as informs.

Jonathan Shayne (chapter 3) offers the perspective of "financial Platonism," in which the representations we have to work with are but imperfect reflections of the underlying material reality. Moreover, our financial system's normal workings actually depend on such virtualization (to use James Carrier's term), and the system is vulnerable to failure when the derivative representations become too far removed from reality.

Anna Tsing (chapter 4) also focuses on the obfuscating nature of the market, but from a more ethnographic perspective. She unpacks the values embedded in the material goods we consume, looking not to Plato but to Marx to find the humanity that is often obfuscated by the fetish of the "thing." Tsing reminds us what anthropology brings to the table: a careful consideration of what people tell us—in this instance, what folks tell us about value in the context of the Matsutake mushroom trade. As Tsing points out, the unitary value of price is misleading. While power structures become encoded in supply chains (see the illustrated piece by Anna Tsing and Jesse Sullivan [chapter 5] showing how supply chains—value chains—treat and mistreat labor), values are nonetheless debated and negotiated constantly by actors all along the commodity chain and along a number of axes.

Both Anna Tsing and Jonathan Friedman are concerned with theories of value and the ways these become obscured. Friedman (chapter 6) cautions us not to confuse economic and moral values and to remember that "price and value are not the same." Friedman would agree with Oscar Wilde that one may know the price of everything but the value of nothing. He shows the ways in which concepts and key words have been fetishized and the ways moral discourses have been grafted onto their usage. He locates the 2008 financial crisis in a much broader cycle of increasing investment in fictitious capital and Western hegemonic decline and points to the Kafkaesque nature of moral representations of the market: morality emerges from the social order—including both internal and external critiques—while justifying that same order. Although he is concerned with the *longue durée*, Friedman sees the current system as suffering from an imbalance of greed over generosity and reciprocity, what Deirdre McCloskey terms P and S variables in the next section.

João Biehl (chapter 7) reminds us of the promise and commitment of ethnography. Biehl calls for putting people first, for living up to the commitment to individuals as human beings, which is all too often forgotten in technocracies (of economics and development). He relates that in public health discourse (indeed, in much of the public sector), "value" is the new rubric for understanding and evaluating interventions. The discourse of value, as it turns into practice, treats patients as a market segment, imposing a particular moral structure in governing the human relations. The quest for value also leads to a disproportionate focus on magic bullet solutions, but, as Biehl shows, this approach fails to account for the messy, complicated, on-the-ground realities permeated by desires and moral valences.

The second part of this book looks at the ways that moralities and rationalities converge on market discourses and practices surrounding values and choice. Economics is the study of choice. Ethics, too, is the study of choice, of moral choice. Yet, as subjects of study, the two rarely meet.

Deirdre McCloskey (chapter 8), a Chicago-trained economist, makes a powerful case that the discipline of economics needs to move away from a singular reliance on the explanatory power of what she terms "P variables" (price, profit, property, power—in sum, Prudence and the Profane). She argues that the P variables explain only part of human behavior and, to get the full picture, we must also account for "S variables" (sympathy, sociality, solidarity, soul, spirit, shame—the Sacred). McCloskey's attention to S variables is very anthropological, although she maintains that we cannot ignore P variables and the forces of supply and demand. In the end, she takes a more optimistic view of market virtues than most anthropologists, arguing that the market encourages, facilitates, and even demands certain prosocial virtues.

Where McCloskey calls on economists to embrace the social, James Ferguson (chapter 9) encourages anthropologists to reconsider the role of cash. Noting that anthropology tends to be critical of the influence of cash economies and commodification on mechanisms of social solidarity and mutuality, Ferguson provocatively argues that, far from being separate and opposed logics, the market and the social are shot through with each other. Indeed, he shows how cash can actually facilitate and encourage the very social bonds it is thought to destroy. He concludes by offering guaranteed cash transfer schemes as a possibility not only for economic development but also for opening new spaces of political expression by historically marginalized peoples.

Cash transfers facilitate market choices, and in the dialogue on "value machines," seminar participants debate the nature and role of choice. What conditions our choices? Psychology? Society? The laws of supply and demand? An emerging subfield of economics examines choice on the neurological level, as described by Natasha Schüll and Caitlin Zaloom (chapter 10). In some ways, this field converges with a common view of humans as value machines, constantly faced with choices and decisions over values.

The problem with biological reductionism and methodological individualism is that considerations of choice are most often decontextualized, ignoring both institutional structures and social contexts. Indeed, as Schüll and Zaloom (chapter 11) show, neuroeconomics understands "the social" in terms of information feedback loops. The neurology of choice is revealing and uses modern imaging techniques to map reward mechanisms along broad synaptic pathways in the brain. Nonetheless, this process fails to capture the Durkheimian superorganic quality of social contexts, in which the sum is greater than its individual parts.

Avery Dickins de Girón and I (chapter 12) present an ethnographic case study using methods borrowed from experimental economics to get at the balance of McCloskey's P and S variables, the rational and the social, in two Maya communities. We report on playing the Ultimatum Game in two very different Maya towns in Guatemala. In one, participants played exceedingly cooperatively, and in the other, much more self-interestedly. We explain this difference by looking at the particular histories and current social structures of the two towns, showing how social contexts influence economic rationalities.

The third section of the volume presents views on how markets actually embody and deploy moral discourses, playing at the intersection of "is" and "ought." Can markets promote moral values? To what extent does corporate moralization reflect cynical moves to increase market share? Here we present several divergent views of how the market, especially large corporations, does act and how it could or should act. As Bart Victor remarks in chapter 2, we should be wary of corporations. Yet, both Bart Victor and Robert Frank offer redemptive views of corporations and markets, whereas others see less positive potential, based on actual behavior (chapter 14).

John Ruskin once remarked that the hallmark of a true profession is that it is worth dying for: doctors would rather die than kill their patients; priests would rather die than lead their congregations to hell. Then Ruskin asks what it is that the merchant will die for.

Bart Victor and Matthew Grimes (chapter 13) make the case that business, as a profession in Ruskin's sense, needs to define its moral obligations and responsibilities more broadly. They look to the literature on business ethics, find it wanting, and offer instead a fuller view of stakeholder obligations that covers a wider range of those vested in the enterprise. They apply this model specifically to those doing business at "the bottom of the pyramid," but their observations are much more widely applicable.

Stuart Kirsch (chapter 15) examines how corporations actually do interact with stakeholders other than stockholders. Among mining and other extractive enterprises, he finds that the language of corporate responsibility is often belied by actual practice. Kirsch focuses on the Ok Tedi copper and gold mine in Papua New Guinea, which has had a devastating impact on indigenous groups and the environment. He shows how indigenous peoples have been able to use international pressure and Australian courts to press their claims with substantial (if mixed) success. Mining companies have responded, and their responses often involve the language of corporate social responsibility and efforts at green-washing. Kirsch shows how companies' reactions to critiques follow a pattern of denial, then acknowledgment, then crisis management that often co-opts progressive discourse.

Peter Benson (chapter 16) takes up the case of how corporations shape public discourse, in his study of the Philip Morris Company. He examines the ethical paradoxes inherent in a tobacco company's approach to public health issues and the ways corporate power is deployed under the rubric of corporate social responsibility. Through Philip Morris's Project Sunrise, its Youth Smoking Prevention program, and its support of the Food and Drug Administration's regulation of tobacco, the company is able to adopt a language of "reasonableness" and perform a jujitsu move against its critics. Benson's piece ends by calling for more explicit discussion of how corporations shape the ethics and politics of life.

So what can we do in the face of corporate power? Robert Frank (chapter 17) proposes what he terms a "libertarian welfare state." He resolves this apparent oxymoron by asserting that the libertarian position is not to accept limitations on one's freedom unless it causes harm to others but that we should conceive of "harm to others" more broadly. He looks at a range of externalities and coordination problems (workplace safety, savings, bike helmets, even inequality and redistribution) in terms of how regulatory structures might best protect the greater good.

I then look at stated and revealed preferences in the context of buying eggs in Germany (chapter 18). In Germany, eggs are labeled with their ecological provenance, and I report on what supermarket shoppers say that they like to buy and what they actually buy. In teasing out the discrepancies, I argue that we should take stated preferences seriously in regulatory frameworks that promote overall well-being.

Stephen Gudeman (chapter 19) concludes by relating the varied contributions back to welfare economics, Adam Smith's ur-texts, and the human propensity to share, as well as compete. Calling for the inclusion of mutuality in our understanding of economic behavior, Gudeman looks at the environment, finance, and human well-being, seeing in the approaches advocated here possibilities for both theory and policy.

Taken together, the chapters in this volume eschew simple judgments, complicating and clarifying the study of markets, economies, and the human values they embody. We complicate things, following the examples set here by Tsing and Biehl, by heeding the ethnographic imperative to take seriously what the "objects" of study have to say, as well as the sensual (*sinnvoll*), lived reality of people's moral and economic worlds. We clarify—following Friedman's injunction to question key words that too easily explain away relations of power—by shining light on the often hidden world of commodity chains (Tsing) and financial derivatives (Shayne). We also question key tenets of economic models that assume humans to be rational, self-interested maximizers. (I should note that much cutting-edge economics today does not merit the brunt of this critique—but it certainly does hold for Econ 101 classrooms, think tanks of the right and the new left, and much political and public discourse, which are thus, much more than a straw man, valid objects of critique.) Humans are self-interested—but not only that, as McCloskey and Gudeman argue, they often act against their own material self-interest, as Dickins de Girón and I show. And although our choices may be based in neurology, they are also shot through with power relations (Schüll and Zaloom). This fact is demonstrated here in the chapters on the structural power and moral complexity of corporate entities. Corporations frequently act in ways counter to the greater good, yet Kirsch and Benson show how they are able to spin this behavior into a seemingly redeeming moral discourse. Victor, Frank, and I point to the potential of the corporate structure and market workings—*if* they were organized properly, which would require regulations and, even more, accepting a view of markets as contrivances pieced together to promote ends that we collectively define. This position is consistent with Ferguson's argument about the radical potential of aid programs (such as cash transfer schemes) that seek to empower agents to pursue their own socially defined and self-defined ends.

In the end, we hope that this volume leaves the reader with a more nuanced view of both the promise and the dangers of the market and the important role that the fluid and deeply meaningful values and moral projects of individuals and societies play in constructing the reality and theory of economic practice.

Köln, March 2012   *Ted Fischer*

Acknowledgments

This book is the product of the collaborative efforts of the participants in our SAR advanced seminar in Santa Fe. We were fortunate to have the support—and sage advice—of James Brooks and the whole SAR team, especially Lynn Baca and Lisa Pacheco at SAR Press.

The participants and authors represented here all committed significantly to (or invested heavily in, depending on your preferred terminology) this project, and the chapters reveal the depth and breadth of their productive engagement. I am deeply grateful for their goodwill, dedication, and openness to diverse viewpoints.

Peter Benson and I conceived of this seminar over conversations spanning several years, and his vision permeates what is good in this volume. Peter Benson and Stuart Kirsch orchestrated the dialogues included in each section. Johannes Fischer aided in the transcription of the recorded discussions from which these dialogues are extracted. Sarah Soliz carefully copyedited the entire manuscript.

Jens Beckert, Wolfgang Streeck, and the entire staff of the Max-Planck-Institut für Gesellschaftsforschung (Max Planck Institute for the Study of Societies) in Köln provided the perfect environment for me to complete the editing of this book.

Cash on the Table

1

Introduction

Markets and Moralities

Edward F. Fischer

Moral values inform economic behavior.[1] On its face, this is an unassailable proposition. Think of the often spiritual appeal of consumer goods or the value-laden stakes of upward or downward mobility. Think about the central role that moral questions regarding poverty, access to health care, the tax code, property and land rights, and corruption play in the shaping of modern governments, societies, and social movements. Think of fair trade coffee and organic produce and the thrift expressed in Walmart's everyday low prices. The moral aspects of the marketplace have never been so contentious or consequential.

Despite this relationship, the realm of economics is often treated as a world unto itself, a domain where human behavior is guided not by emotions, beliefs, moralities, or the passions that fascinate anthropologists but by the hard calculus of rational choices. The attraction of this *Homo economicus* paradigm rests in its parsimony, in the way it translates the chaos of everyday life and human behavior into a metric system complete with mathematical models based on assumptions about self-interest and maximization (see Beckert 2002; Carrier 1997; Fullbrook 2004; Stiglitz 1993). Authors of economics textbooks often liken the workings of markets to natural forces, distancing themselves from the field's historical roots in philosophy and ethics. On issues of value and morality, many economists plead agnosticism—it is not a question of good or bad, they say, but rather of efficient or inefficient (see Becker 1996; Becker and Becker 1996; Samuelson 1976). Trade restrictions, national borders, political corruption, and religious values are seen as barriers to a fluid and healthy marketplace (or "distortions"). Steven Levitt's (Levitt and Dubner 2005:13) bestseller *Freakonomics* proclaims, "Morality represents the way we would like the world to work and economics represents how it actually does work." Yet, the dominant economic paradigm itself has become a morality, laden with unchecked cultural assumptions and confident about making the world in its own secular image.

Certainly, we are driven by self-interest, but not solely, as most economists, including those represented in the chapters that follow, would readily concede. Still, best-selling books like *Freakonomics*, *Discover Your Inner Economist* (Cowen 2007), and *The Undercover Economist* (Harford 2007) convey a message of ethical agnosticism about human behavior (just letting the facts speak for themselves) that fuels the conceit of a certain brand of economics popular among policy-makers, pundits, and think tanks. This popularity comes at the very moment in which the field of economics is witnessing a proliferation of behavioral, experimental, and historical approaches that constitute a multisided challenge to the assumptions of the conventional neoclassical paradigm. Under the broad banner of "heterodox economics," we find Austrian school adherents, Marxists, and behaviorists, as well as a growing number calling for a "post-autistic" approach to economics (to use the rallying cry of rebellious French students in 2000) that moves beyond the "uncontrolled use" of mathematics and better engages with empirical realities (see www.paecon.net). More toward the mainstream, behavioral economics is working to redefine the limits of rationality and document biases that subvert rationality (see Ariely 2008; Kahneman 2011; Thaler 1992; among others). These movements in economics open the door to fruitful collaboration across traditional disciplinary boundaries.

Anthropology, too, claims to describe how the world works. But it tells a much different story about economic behavior. If anthropologists have produced any laws of their own, one is certainly that economic behavior is everywhere embedded in moral, cultural, and political systems (Gudeman 2001; Lamont 2000; Sahlins 1972; Sayer 2006; Wilk 1996). This story does not have the traction of the more parsimonious one of neoclassical economics, but it does converge with much mainstream thinking worldwide (Fogel 2000).

Anthropologists have historically tended to focus on the corrosive effects of markets on traditional lifeways and the ways in which global markets disadvantage marginalized peoples. This perspective can make engagement with economists difficult because they tend to see markets as the primary route for folks to achieve the good life as the economists themselves envision it. Instead, as we suggest in the dialogue in chapter 2, we should view markets as technologies that can be used toward various ends. It may even be the case, as James Ferguson suggests in chapter 9, that market interactions can strengthen and promote social relations, as well as erode them (see also Miller 1998a, 2008).

On the other hand, economists often have difficulty allowing that markets are embedded in particular social and political power structures and that "free" market transactions are often less free than we might think. These realities are not as neat and clean as mathematical modeling requires, but without them, we cannot expect to understand what Deirdre McCloskey calls the sacred and profane values that influence our decisions.

The title of this volume emerged from our seminar and the observation that if anthropologists could view markets a bit more ecumenically and if economists could view them a bit more politically, then great value—cash on the table—could be found in bringing these perspectives together. Much is at stake in understanding the moral dimensions of economic behavior and markets. Public debates over executive compensation, the fair trade movement, and recent academic inquiries into the limitations of rational-choice paradigms all point to the relevance of moral values in our economic decision-making processes.

This volume builds on the anthropological tradition of seeing economic activity as embedded in social worlds (Beckert 2002; Gudeman 2008; Mauss 2001; Polanyi 1944; Strathern 1988; Veblen 1899; Weber 1978). Our approach sees markets as social constructions that are shot through with values—ideas about what is good and bad, fair and unfair. Much of this approach turns on ethnographic examinations of how global economic systems touch down in local and national contexts, how moral values are marshaled by local actors to engage with and negotiate market forces and economic processes, and how moral values are deployed by global economic assemblages—international trade partnerships, structural adjustment policies, multinational corporations, and economic development organizations—in order to discipline and invite consensus among local actors and social groups.

We argue for a richer consideration of the moral and ethical values that define self-understandings, social relations, and economic behaviors in local settings. Anthropological research can make a special contribution to economics by illuminating the complex local conditions and value systems in which economic activity takes shape. This contribution includes demonstrating how economic activities are embedded in projects undertaken with moral perspectives about what is good, fair, or just and a range of possible worlds in mind. In turn, economics can explain how markets tend to promote certain modalities of behavior and how incentive structures work, along with the surprising correlations we find in actual market behavior.

MORAL ECONOMIES

All economies are "moral" in the sense that they embody and reproduce values. Economic systems are built upon assumptions—often, taken-for-granted and naturalized assumptions—about what is good, desirable, worthy, ethical, and just. These are culturally informed and historically particular assumptions, even though some actors (say, policy-makers, neoclassical economists, or human rights advocates) struggle to codify certain values as "universal."

Economic systems aggressively promote moral values as part and parcel of their normal function as evolving historical formations (Polanyi 1944; Sayer 2000; Sen 1979). Struggles over the values that are normalized and naturalized as "universal" define a dynamic arena of social practice and cultural difference. In fact, what we find ethnographically is much like the dialectical interplay Stephen Gudeman (2008) describes between market and nonmarket realms, which is at times symbiotic and at times parasitic. A key starting point for the present collaboration has been the move to historicize the moral values that underpin neoliberal free trade ideals and to parlay and contrast those values with alternative moral frameworks, such as fair trade and antiglobalization movements.

The moral economy is understood here as more than just a local tradition. This usage contrasts with the sense of the term made famous in the work of James Scott (1977, 1985), who uses "moral economy" to refer to the continuing force of localized precapitalist traditions—especially, moral values about fair prices and economic practices—in the face of capitalist development and expansion (see also Thompson 1971). For Scott, local moral values are a means of subaltern resistance to capitalism, enlivening everyday forms of resistance and thwarting the consolidation of consensual, hegemonic power.

Yet, a general valuation of all subaltern behavior as "resistance" misses nuanced aspects of how local actors negotiate societal forces (Appadurai 1996; Fischer and Benson 2006; Herzfeld 2005) and more subtle views of power as contextual and multisided (Comaroff and Comaroff 1991). Recent approaches to the study of power also rub against Scott's tendency to equate the moral with local tradition as opposed to global processes (Fox 1991; Gupta and Ferguson 1992). Moral values, in particular, take shape at the intersection of universal ethical models (such as human rights or neoclassical economics), the ubiquitous reality of uneven development and fragmented political membership, and the deeply held concerns that define ordinary life in local settings.

Adam Smith is best remembered for *The Wealth of Nations*, but his other great work, *Theory of Moral Sentiments*, opens the door to the approach we pursue here. McCloskey (2006:306) sees Smith as a "virtue ethicist for a commercial age," and, indeed, he was centrally concerned with the moral implications of economic behaviors and systems. He famously described the human "propensity to truck, barter, and exchange," but he also saw sympathy as an original part of human nature for both "the civilized and the brutish."[2] Smith was contemptuous of self-love, but, as Albert Hirschman (1977) shows, he reconciled the passion of self-love with the discipline of reason to reveal "interests," the pursuit of which is seen as mutually beneficial to both self and society.

Just as important for Smith was how the original human passion for sympathy (or "fellow-feeling") acts as a counterweight to self-love. In contrast to the post-Kantian universalizing approach to morals, Smith takes a very empirical, even anthropological approach, seeing moral values such as sympathy as arising from social interaction. For Smith, sympathy, the ability to identify with others, is both a fundamental part of human nature and what keeps self-love in check (if only, perhaps, because injury to another causes sympathetic pain in oneself). While anthropologists will contest the universal model of how basic emotions like sympathy are understood and enacted, this position remains an underappreciated aspect of Smith's work and encourages a rethinking of the latter-day moral agnosticism that has come to define the invisible hand allegory.

Living up to the moral expectations of particular value systems is in many ways the stock-in-trade of human existence, and this forward-looking, aspirational quality of the internalization of culturally produced virtues is what drives "agency." Jens Beckert (2011) writes of the power of daydreams and imaginings of the future in the construction of consumer identities, and elsewhere (Fischer and Benson 2006), I have made a similar argument for understanding the role of desire in producer identities. Although words like *morals* and *virtues* are often used in popular discourse to denote timeless, essential cultural structures, our perspective sees them as the product of ongoing processes of socially situated negotiation, continually enacted through the dialectic of everyday social life yet partially defined through presumptive continuities (Fischer 1999; see also Beckert 2002; Giddens 1984).

Alasdair MacIntyre (1981, 1988) calls attention to how virtues saturate people's everyday projects. MacIntyre approaches virtue as excellence within a given "practice," a perspective that moves away from the universality of cardinal virtues and allows for greater cultural latitude, and he writes of the fulfillment that comes from doing something well for its own sake (internal goods) as defined by a social group ("moral community"). This approach suggests an ethnographic basis for using virtues to define practices and excellence. It also suggests a public policy correlate: a social contract could introduce incentive structures to promote long-term, socially engaged metapreferences and moral stances.

That behavior is situationally dependent may invalidate the idea of absolute virtues (Appiah 2008), but it does not negate the power of normative moral ideals and individual strivings to attain a certain morally laden identity. This fact also points to the danger of our romanticizing moral communities: the consensus such communities require can as easily be oppressive as nurturing, as Jürgen Habermas reminds us, whereas social norms in local worlds can also reflect the weight of dominant ideologies, including free market principles grafted onto local value systems.

This reframing of moral economy allows for a sharpened and more specific understanding of economic globalization. It is through the prism of moral values that ordinary people engage with circulating flows of objects, images, and ideas. While moral values reflect the accumulation of historical experience, they also orient people to the future, shape a sense of how things ought to be, define what *better* means, and influence social and economic behaviors (Bourdieu 1977; Holland and Lave 2001; Rosenberg and Harding 2005). In this way, moral values serve as a fundamental linchpin linking global processes and local worlds (Ackerly 2008; Biehl, Good, and Kleinman 2007; Das 2006; Kleinman 2006).

People moralize their economic behavior and consciously so. The politics often embedded in the consumption of fair trade or "green" products does not merely evidence an individual preference; it also reflects a moral project that has likely been influenced by popular culture, governments, and corporations. To reduce moral and cultural values to an individualistic and monetary "utility" is to miss an opportunity to understand the fundamentally social and contextual dimensions of human behavior. The tenets that morality matters in ordinary people's economic decisions and attitudes and that values and norms are historically particular, however, are contradicted by market fundamentalists who view moralities and moral beliefs as superfluous, nothing more than secondary explanations that detract from an objective account of natural laws.

WORKING WITH ECONOMICS

In 1958 John Kenneth Galbraith (1998:215) presciently observed that "in the United States, as in other western countries, we have for long had a respected secular priesthood whose function it has been to rise above questions of religious ethics, kindness and compassion and show how these might have to be sacrificed on the altar of the greater good. That larger good, invariably, was more efficient production." Yet, he notes, "if the modern corporation must manufacture not only goods but the desire for the goods it manufactures, the efficiency of the first part of this activity ceases to be decisive. One could indeed argue that human happiness would be as effectively advanced by inefficiency in want creation as by efficiency in production. Under these circumstances, the relations of the modern corporation to the people it comprises—their chance for dignity, individuality and full development of personality—may be at least as important as its efficiency. These may be worth having even at a higher cost of production" (1998:213–214).

As Galbraith makes clear, these relations of production are not just a matter of economics but of morality. This approach returns to the foundations of political economy (e.g., Adam Smith, Karl Marx), a moment in which moral considerations were not separated out from more worldly political and economic concerns. Two centuries ago, the separation of moral science and political economy would have been regarded as antithetical to the ambitions of a liberal and decent society and international community.

The idea of humans as rational actors who seek to maximize utility in all areas of life can be revealing. But much rests on how utility and efficiency are defined. In dominant models of price theory and the efficient market hypothesis (see Fama 1970; Samuelson 1965), the rationality of utility maximization is most often based on immediate monetary returns from a particular transaction, leaving little room for moral considerations, the multiple values that might be at stake in a given transaction, and enduring linkages between behaviors and identity formation. What seems to be immanently empirical research turns out to elide difficult questions about subjective and experiential components of human behavior. Such an economics holds a privileged position in terms of public discourse and political influence. And such explanations have ethical and political consequences. If humans are unwaveringly driven by self-interest, then the economy is

9

best managed by monetary incentive structures and market mechanisms geared toward a very particular view of efficiency in maximizing utilities (Becker 1996; Becker and Becker 1996; Samuelson 1976).

Of course, the supposed efficiency of the free market model is, itself, a morality that embodies assumptions about who deserves what and what kinds of citizenship are valuable to the national product and national future. For all its claims to moral agnosticism, extreme economistic thinking has become a theology (Carrier and Miller 1998; Nelson 2001), laden with unchecked cultural assumptions and confident about making the world in its own secular image and converting fables about behavior's natural causes into everyday common sense.

A growing group of academic economists works on issues that touch on the role of cultural values and moral concerns. Deirdre McCloskey (1998, 2002) critiques the scientific aspirations of econometrics and the strategic uses of numbers that infelicitously seek to purify the real messiness of human values and behavior. George Akerlof (2005) and Amartya Sen (2006) write about the powerful role of identity and culture in conditioning the social networks that embed economic activity. George Akerlof and Rachel Kranton (2005) examine how identity affects commitment and performance within organizations. Robert Frank (1988) documents how economic decisions are informed by a sense of identity and narrative life history. Daniel Kahneman and Richard Thaler (1991) champion experimental methods and behavioral observation to show how psychology influences rationality. These revisions are making possible a more complicated picture of the subjective components of economic behavior that have long been bracketed in utility functions.

The notion that individuals seek to maximize utility through preferences is also being reconceived—with greater appreciation for social forces and social contexts—in terms of Max Weber's (1978) "substantive rationality." This is a framework for understanding human motivations and behaviors that eschews reduction to narrow material considerations or self-interest. Substantive rationalities are patterns of behavior that reflect the influence of cultural norms and moral considerations, as well as the way norms and values are bundled to influence senses of identity and of what kind of personhood is possible at a given moment and given place in history.

The concept of substantive rationality also calls attention to the accumulation of historical experience and the forward-looking lean of moralities in shaping behaviors. Jon Elster (1989:98) writes that "rationality is essentially conditional and future-oriented. Its imperatives are hypothetical; that is, conditional on the future outcomes one wants to realize." If anthropologists have long held that historical processes and the transmission of norms, knowledge, and expectations are crucial to cultural identities, then social scientists are also beginning to realize the relevance of cultural models of the future and the projects in which people become embroiled. Moral values propagated on a collective scale are crucial to how projects of action and identification materialize and become internalized in people's everyday lives, even perhaps just a trip to the grocery store (Fischer and Benson 2006; Miller 1998a).

Here we should consider "metapreferences," relatively long-term aspirations and goals that require a whole range of subsidiary preferences and sacrifices and are often tied to identity construction and the presentation of the self in everyday life. Harry Frankfurt (1971) posited a "meta-ranking" of preferences, and subsequent analyses by Amartya Sen (1997) and Albert O. Hirschman (1977) elucidate the powerful role of social and cultural factors in shaping preferences and the importance of seeing preferences as much more than individuated dots on an arc of behavior.

Substantive rationalities and metapreferences often hide behind seemingly irrational behaviors. For example, individuals might forgo the pursuit of immediate or short-term goals with a larger ambition in mind or instead participate in seemingly disadvantageous practices in the short term because, in doing so, they advance toward larger metapreferences. In a similar vein, Frank (1988) argues that being a trustworthy person brings material benefits and long-term trustworthiness is very hard to fake. To reap the opportunities or benefits enabled by such a presentation of self, individuals may need to give up cheating and its short-term gains in pursuit of a long-term metapreference. Such behavior relates the Prudence that McCloskey (2006) writes about—the virtue of putting off immediate pleasure for later, bigger rewards (e.g., saving money, studying, or raising children)—to questions about culture and identity.

As Kenneth Arrow (1974), among others, has shown, trust, loyalty, and honesty have clear economic value and are essential to the efficiency of the economy. Indeed, pursuit of the intrinsic rewards of a value-based system (virtues) is necessary for the workings of free and fair exchange. Businesses would crash if employees did only what they were explicitly told to do (or were explicitly paid to do); work-to-rule strikes can virtually stop production simply by following rules to the letter.

Akerlof and Kranton (2000, 2005; Akerlof 2007) observe that by focusing on monetary incentives, standard economic price theory systematically ignores important types of motivation, particularly the role of identity. In much anthropology and sociology, identity plays a central role in our understandings of motivations and actions. If preference structures are not oriented only toward immediate material rewards, we may consider a broader range of sociocultural resources and constraints. But human behavior is generally not discussed in terms of incentives and utility. In fact, many anthropologists and sociologists are suspicious of the rational, instrumental, pecuniary connotations of those terms (Sahlins 2008). Empirical research by behavioral economists like Akerlof and Kranton shows that nonmonetary motivations such as social identity are important influences on economic behavior. The extent to which these ideas challenge the methodological individualism of neoclassical economics cannot be overstated. Behavioral economists argue that utility functions can (and should) be expanded to incorporate issues of identity and culture. Even so, the definition of identity at play in this growing field has a more sociological than anthropological ring to it. For example, Akerlof (2007) asserts that identity is closely tied to social norms but that these are usually not moral or ethical views.

SOCIAL PERSPECTIVES ON THE ECONOMY

In a survey of moral views of the market society, sociologists Marion Fourcade and Kieran Healy (2007) identify three conventional paradigms for studies of economic behavior and markets. First is the view of the market as a civilizing force, an "invisible hand" that produces public goods. The market here is understood to be virtuous and harmonious as a whole, no matter how selfish its constituent parts may be—indeed, it functions because of such sentiments. Market forces are said to discourage racism, sexism, and other "nonrational" behaviors. Free market commerce is said to instill particular virtues, such as prudence, temperance, and justice (McCloskey 2006), as well as trust and cooperation (Ensminger 2004; Henrich et al. 2004; Silk 2005). Second is the view of the market as a destructive force involving coercion and exclusion, alienation and envy. This perspective is at the heart of Karl Marx's critique of capitalism. It also prevails in critical scholarship on intellectual property rights, where information and ideas are controlled by individual entities, often at the expense of a common good or well-being (Coombe 1998; Correa 2000). Third, the market may be seen as a system shaped out of cultural and institutional legacies. Different kinds of capitalism are said to exist in different regions and under different conditions; therefore, markets embody the moral values, cultural patterns, and economic rationalities of particular times and places.

Anthropologists have examined regional differences in the organization and practices of markets and corporations. This literature on vernacular capitalism follows the Polanyian tradition of understanding economic practices as culturally and socially embedded (see Becker 2009; Hall and Soskice 2001; Streeck and Yamamura 2001). For example, anthropologists have studied the cultural and economic particularities of a baby food factory in postsocialist Poland (Dunn 2004), along with other financial institutions and practices, bringing into relief the social, cultural, and moral worlds of financiers and stockbrokers in contrast to the supposedly value-neutral operation of markets (Hart 2001; Ho 2009; Maurer 2005; Zaloom 2006).

In these studies, the abstraction of a single global capitalism is usefully reconceived in terms of "global capitalisms" situated in specific settings. This literature addresses local and regional variation in order to register a theoretical and political critique of the formalist assumptions of neoclassical economics. But a substantivist focus on embedded economies can deflect attention from the fact that transnational corporations straddle multiple local worlds. These corporations strategically exploit cultural differences to gain political and economic advantages, actively constructing or objectifying differences rather than simply adapting to them (Ong 1999).

Recent work in economic anthropology relates to a fourth perspective, offered by Fourcade and Healy—the market as a set of scientific, moral, and institutional projects. Influenced by Weber and Foucault, this perspective views markets as saturated with normative moral values that are historically specific and emphasizes the importance of discourses and practices in shaping those values (see Carrier 1998; Miller 1998b). For Beckert (2002), this perspective includes a consideration of path dependencies and the structural conditions of choice, as well as a consideration of power. Anthropologists have shown that the esoteric epistemological frameworks that guide development often do not mesh with local realities, include little consideration of cultural values and the moral stakes of local communities, and even reinforce residual, usually colonial, power structures through the promulgation of elite interests (Escobar 1995; Ferguson 1990, 1999; see also Mitchell 2005). The focus on incentives in economic policy making provides a good example of the normalizing force of the market. Incentives are meant to yield "optimal" outcomes, with *optimal* often becoming a code word for *efficient*. Although a particular incentive might disadvantage particular groups or yield uneven outcomes, a generalized logic of optimization becomes normalized. Those capable of adopting rationalities of free market entrepreneurship might benefit, but others might not (Ong 2006).

Much is at stake in crafting rich understandings of the social and moral dimensions of economic behavior and markets, as well as the unchecked moral assumptions built into varieties of economistic science itself, not least because the popularity of *Homo economicus* models impacts the realm of public policy, for example, in the imposition of neoliberal economic and political reforms of market integration, liberalization, and deregulation on developing countries. This brand of knowledge production might be seen as having a "performative" rather than simply a referential function. In claiming to describe how the world works, science can also have a "looping" effect, yielding in the empirical world the very modes of thought and action said to be neutral, observable facts (Hacking 2000). The economics profession's assumption that individualistic self-interest and utility maximization drive behavior has the effect of condoning this very behavior as natural and thus encouraging (and not just describing) it. Scientific theories and concepts (e.g., rational choice) can enter the popular lexicon in such a way that over time, studies in economics are said to "discover" that people think and act in terms of economizing rationalities (see also Timothy Mitchell's [2005] argument regarding economics and "how a discipline makes its world"). Evidence for this phenomenon exists in experiments that gauge the rationality and self-interest of students from different fields: economics students tend to cooperate less with one another and scholars from other disciplines and more aggressively pursue immediate self-interested maximization (see Carter and Irons 1991; Frank, Gilovich, and Regan 1993; Marwell and Ames 1981).

Institutional frameworks also condition the expression of moral positions (Stout 2010). Caitlin Zaloom's (2006:139) study of commodity traders shows that the market itself is seen as an ethical arbiter, punishing and disciplining those who exceed its mandates: "The market is the [Chicago Board of Trade] traders' moral authority...it is both the single truth and the arbiter of a trader's work." This position is very different from an artisanal morality of work or indeed from the moralities of most professionals outside the financial industry. Richard Sennett's (2008) study of skilled work requiring years of training and practice focuses on the intrinsic rewards that come with such practices (see also Kondo's [1990] look at the construction of identity and craft in a Japanese chocolate factory). In contrast, Robert Jackall's (1988) study of corporate managers finds that company bureaucracies instill their own ethics, which are bracketed from the outside-of-work moral positions of executives, and that within this milieu, self-interested opportunism becomes habituated through repeated social interaction.

CONCLUSIONS

Understanding the empirical complexities of economic behavior in a globalized world demands an economics that is also a science of moral sentiments and a project of ethical reflection. It demands an economics that goes beyond regression analyses and moves into the real world of what people living in diverse circumstances want or do not want, how they see themselves and who they are becoming, how economic processes such as trade or health care impact their everyday lives, and how they think and feel about the structural conditions in which they live. It requires empirical study of how the world works (the "is"), but also a critical analysis of how things got that way. Despite an aversion to history built into much economics, historical processes are central to any adequate understanding of economic systems and behaviors. Furthermore, empirical and historical research on economies must be linked to moral reflection about how the world might be different (the "ought").

Ethnographic study itself can be a moral reflection or cultural critique, as when studies of beliefs about justice and equity present alternative models and reveal fractures in dominant epistemological and policy frameworks. More generally, such studies also form a basis for reflection, as when an analysis of an economic institution or a market process galvanizes imaginings about different paths and possibilities. A "conclusion" to an ethnographically grounded, empirical study of economic behavior can be expanded to include both relevant research findings and more conjectural discussion with an eye toward the future. Rather than have esoteric models inform policy decisions and public understandings of social issues, we believe, politics and civil society are best informed by empirical understanding and the prudent, grounded reflection that can come out of it.

Far from rejecting neoclassical economics, we hope to add to conversations already taking place inside and outside the academy about its limitations and policy implications. In particular, we hope to complicate the idea that economic behavior is value free and to argue that all theories and explanations of economic behavior are value laden. This is why moral reflection and epistemological reflexivity must be linked to empirical research: researchers need to apprehend what values or worldviews might be promulgated in descriptions of "how the world actually works." Ethical deliberation about values—what is the good life, what is the moral life, what are public goods—is a crucial corollary to the empirical study of economics.

In pushing for an economics that is at once inherently reflexive and more finely attuned to the empirical world, precisely because of its wariness of epistemological assumptions and established theories, we advocate a dialectical movement between what David Hume termed the "is" and the "ought." We call for greater social empiricism in economics and, simultaneously, critical reflection on the rhetorical and institutional aspects of the science of economics and the moral and policy implications of research findings.

We need a practical and integrative reframing of economics and economic anthropology because we are at a turning point, sometimes termed "late capitalism," in the development of globalized economies (Comaroff and Comaroff 2000). The moral values that could be enforced in more bounded economic systems—and the sense of community they articulated with—are often no longer viable. And while we in the North reap the fruits of global integration, elsewhere, the backlash against the moral implications of neoliberal economic models is growing.

A loud public debate about the morality of sacrificing the security of a strong social contract to the pursuit of globally competitive labor flexibility is occurring in Europe. In the United States, debates over immigration, outsourcing, and environmental issues all bring moral concerns to bear on economic behavior. Ultimately, then, we must speak to the utterly important but still understudied fact that global economic processes foster both normalizing and balkanizing tendencies across local contexts (Friedman 1994). A focus on moralities in specific cultural contexts reveals how local worlds interface with large-scale economic processes in such domains as high finance and science, shifting modes of consumption and identity, global food production, and the rhetoric and research orientations of neoclassical economics itself.

Emphasizing the centrality of values in all economic systems, we advocate studies of economic behavior that work between the "is" and the "ought," between how the world can be shown to work and how moral principles can be constituted from a discussion that arises between the competing and diverse value systems that research documents. Our emphasis on the dialogical quality of research belies the notion that academic research is simply descriptive; our emphasis on understanding moralities from the ground up counters the tendency to universalize ethical principles based on theoretical models (such as rational choice theory). The solutions to concrete problems are most effectively addressed when knowledge about diverse empirical circumstances is taken into account, even if such circumstances might muddy the neat and tidy models that sell so many books.

Acknowledgments

Thanks to Peter Benson, Bart Victor, Jon Shayne, Michiel Baud, Brooke Ackerly, James Foster, Doug Meeks, Dan Cornfield, Karl Jones, Peter Mancina, Steve Gudeman, James Carrier, and Daniel Mato for helping me think through many of these ideas. Rudi Colloredo-Mansfeld and the participants in a National Science Foundation workshop on "the commons" helped sharpen my thoughts on many of the issues touched on here. Thanks also to Jens Becket and Wolfgang Streeck at the Max Plank Institute for the study of societies, where I refined my argument. A special thanks goes to James Brooks, whose vision and support saw this project through, and to the participants in the seminar on the SAR campus in Santa Fe.

Notes

1. In using the word *moral*, I refer to Kleinman's (2006) definition of "what matters most" to people. This definition does not imply an absolute or universal morality, but rather contextualized values that orient behavior (see also Sayer 2011).

2. Quotes from Adam Smith's *The Wealth of Nations* included here come from the Wikisource online version available at http://en.wikisource.org/wiki/The_Wealth _of_Nations.

Part I
Markets
Contrivances and Obfuscations

2

Markets as Contrivances

A Dialogue

Orchestrated by Peter Benson, with James Ferguson, Edward F. Fischer, Robert H. Frank, Anna Tsing, Bart Victor, and Caitlin Zaloom

Much as with "time," we tend to talk about the abstraction we call "the market" as a thing. We are comfortable speaking about what the market is doing today, whether "it" is up or down. Indeed, we often endow the market with animate properties, as when it punishes or rewards those who engage it, as a system with its own logic, greater than the sum of its parts.

This way of talking about the market shapes how we conceptualize it. Abstracting the market as a thing unto itself, we may lose sight of all the actions—some miniscule, some profound—that make up systems of production and distribution around the world. For example, the numbers on the board at the stock exchange are more than fleeting equilibrium points of supply and demand; they also represent, if more opaquely, the qualitative realities of the movement of cash between people, the construction of factories, the extraction of resources, and various kinds of human labor.

We take a lot for granted when we talk about the market as "it." Looking at the numbers and regression lines, we may easily overlook the complex social and financial relations of the day trader, the transcontinental supply chains that bring food to the grocery store, or the treaties that have made it much more economical to produce clothes here and not there.

We need to understand the empirical processes that make up any market system. As Anna Tsing is doing with exotic mushrooms, anthropologists can document the stages of commodity chains to see what the lives of producers and consumers are like. Or anthropologists can hang out in the stressful world of day traders to see what makes them tick, as Caitlin Zaloom has done.

This is not just knowledge for its own sake, while "it" keeps on trucking. Empirical work on the functioning of markets is essential to economic policy. Important political questions need to be asked before we can understand how existing market structures came to be organized and what impact is experienced by different populations.

ZALOOM: "The market," discussed as such, often acts as a fetish. The focus on an "it," composed of qualities and tendencies, obscures the empirical relations of its production, particularly the politics. In this sense, it is useful to distinguish the technical versus political nature of the market.

TSING: One of the reasons anthropologists have been suspicious of language about markets is that markets are rarely understood as part of the larger system of provisions. Rather, they are seen as part of a self-enclosed world. Hence, markets are evaluated—the potential of markets and their ability to function as a technique of government—apart from particular political valances.

Language about "the market" tends to portray markets as apolitical systems, neglecting the fact that any market system is the product of historical relationships and human endeavors and based on particular legal and political structures. In other words, people make markets—and markets often get made in the interests of certain groups.

FERGUSON: There is a position that holds that markets are principally a good thing, and that's associated with a kind of dogmatism and political ideology. A lot of the language they use is very self-consciously neutral. It is technical, not moral, language. There are other invocations, in other languages, that talk about solidarity and citizenship and more sort of moralizing or politicizing idioms. But there is also an idea that it is somehow liberating to talk about markets in terms of techniques.

FRANK: The idea that animates this kind of discussion is the notion of an "invisible hand" as attributed to Adam Smith. But Smith was not nearly as enthusiastic a proponent of the invisible hand as many of his modern disciples are, even if the idea itself was a profound insight. Smith observed that under certain conditions, if people trade with one another for their own advantage, although they do not necessarily have any altruistic motive at all, there will be substantial gains created for everyone. Thus, individual interest, channeled through market conditions, can produce gains for society as a whole. This is the invisible hand, although Smith was clear that it did not always happen.

Indeed, Smith's argument was very much a response to the historical circumstances and power relations of a particular moment. His promotion of market mechanisms constituted a strategic attack on hereditary privilege and persistent social inequalities. As Smith well knew, how markets are organized—who owns property, who earns what in return, and who has the power to make things happen—is never a neutral outcome. We need to understand markets in terms of the concrete contexts and relationships that compose them.

That Smith now serves as the unwitting patron saint of free market economics says more about his disciples than about what he actually wrote. He did, of course, argue that competition among actors free to pursue their own self-interests can create efficiencies that benefit everyone. This argument describes the transubstantial miracle of enlightened self-interest: "led by an invisible hand to promote an end which was no part of his intention."[1] We can feel absolved from our greed, if we stop there. But we should not forget that Smith considered himself foremost a moral philosopher, and was skeptical not only of monarchical control but also of merchants and businessmen and what he saw as their conniving, monopolistic, greedy ways. He argued that just as important as self-interest is the way the original human passion of sympathy (or "fellow-feeling") acts as a counterweight to self-love.

FRANK: Let me give an example of how markets can help promote common goods. Back in the late 1960s and early 1970s, we had the first proposals to use effluent fees or pollution permits as a way of curtailing pollution from firms. The idea was to use market incentives to reward those who could clean up their act most efficiently. You couldn't pollute at all unless you bought a permit to allow you to discharge a specific amount. So you'd buy a 1-ton permit to discharge SO_2, sulfuric acid, in the air (SO_2 is the precursor of acid rain). The traditional approach was to measure how much a polluter had been producing per year and phase that down by, say, 50 percent. If you were doing 100 tons a day in 1968, by 1975 you had to get down to 50 tons. What was bad about that approach was that some firms could cut back their emissions of SO_2 very cheaply but others didn't have alternative techniques they could use and so for them to cut back would be really expensive.

Our collective interest is really not in who emits the SO_2 but how much of it is emitted—and the tradable permit system addressed this. We could specify how many tons we were willing to see discharged into the air and then let firms figure out for themselves whether they had effective and efficient ways to cut back on their own pollution. Some firms ended up polluting more, others ended up polluting much less, but the total cost of reducing SO_2 pollution was about one-eighth of what it would have been under the other system, according to one estimate.

Many on the left were angered when the trade system was first proposed. They thought it was an outrageous offense to the sensibility of the public—a proposal that would allow rich firms to pollute to their heart's content just by buying permits. But I think, gradually, people have come to see this as a misapprehension. It is naive to say that rich firms want to pollute the environment and that this is why they're doing it. The only reason there is pollution is that it is cheaper to pollute than not to pollute. And so if you make it in a firm's interest not to pollute (that is to say, they will have to incur a higher cost if they pollute), then that's the exact correct incentive to identify the ones who can cut back the most cheaply on their pollution.

It's just a way of accomplishing a goal using market-like methods. It's, in fact, creating a market where it would have been good if one had existed all along, but one didn't and so we created one. And that gave the people who could act effectively an incentive to act effectively.

FERGUSON: What is worth lingering over here is that a market in pollution credits, for example, is a contrivance. This is not a free market that somehow naturally exists. Policy-makers create a market utterly through artificial means. One sets, through nonmarket means, such as a pollution credit, a price that is then used as a mechanism to produce certain effects, such as environmental outcomes.

FRANK: All markets are contrivances. For example, unless there is a secure system of property rights at work, we do not find people organizing very effectively to produce things.

FERGUSON: If you recognize that all markets are contrivances, you need to recognize a series of political decisions about what kind of market you want to have and what kind of effects you want markets to produce.

FRANK: Exactly. The same analysis would apply to every market. It is a social decision: how do we want to regulate pollution, private property, and other domains? We answer this question in lots of interesting and different ways in different cases.

A certain strand of economics has come to trumpet a view of "the market" as an autonomous, even animate, thing (perhaps a product of human nature). Yet, Frank and many others acknowledge the constructed nature of any market. The fact that markets are always a political project—involving decisions about how to organize things, a set of rules and parameters, and frameworks of accountability—does not mean that they are inherently bad or good. A recognition that markets are historical products means that they can take on different valences and, crucially, can be changed.

FRANK: I don't think that markets are autonomous and make wealth by themselves. Markets need a lot of supervision and structure to get results that we as a collective favor.

There is a real advantage for society if a common outside force, such as a government, steps in and forces people to account for the harm they cause others. We can extend the reach of the invisible hand quite considerably, but it does not happen automatically. In making policy, there should not be any presumption that the market is an ideal instrument for distributional matters. In the case of wages, for example, the market pays the value of what you can produce in the marketplace. It does not pay you what you need. It does not pay you in any semblance guided by justice or anything of the sort.

TSING: The reason we have to think in terms of markets for the solutions we're working on is not that markets are efficient, but that markets are a political project we're stuck with, whatever our own political proclivities. The idea that the market is efficient is part of a historical ideological project that stretches across the nineteenth and twentieth centuries in its particular forms. The political project called neoliberalism has to do with the Reagan administration and the Thatcher administration and the creation of an ideology that deregulation is a good thing and giving people medical care is a kind of socialism and unfreedom. Those are the political forms through which the market can be labeled as efficient, so they're always a political project.

We have to work hard to come up with a different language because of a common sense that's been created that only markets are the legitimate way of talking about freedom. That the market is the most efficient system ever devised or can make life more efficient—this is already part of a political project in its instatement.

Here is an interesting moment in the conversation. Frank has presented a broad cost/benefit paradigm that is expansive and nimble enough to account for political, social, cultural, and moral decisions, as well as economic ones. At the same time, it is still based in a methodological individualism that anthropologists find troubling. Even if Frank puts forth an argument that does not fit comfortably with a lot of mainstream economics, it does not depart from the idea that markets are the most efficient means of conducting business. His argument is a liberal one that promotes the government as a means of regulating the social cost of externalities and sees policy as an instrument to optimize the functioning of more or less free markets while minimizing the harms related to industrial production. Despite his seemingly illiberal emphasis on regulation, Frank argues that efficiency and utility maximization are inherent to markets and are optimal social goals.

Tsing argues for a historical understanding of this standpoint as the outgrowth of particular interests and political formations. She emphasizes that the idea of efficiency has been naturalized as universal and optimal through specific political projects. Working across diverse cultures, anthropologists have found that market efficiency and utility maximization are not the natural goals of human behavior. Systems of production and distribution can be organized with other values in mind. This is not just wishful thinking: other types of systems have existed and flourished, even if they have often been overtaken by global capitalism, which is continually naturalized as the optimal and inevitable state of affairs. Tsing is arguing that the interrogation of moral assumptions, such as the idea that broad-scale utility maximization is the best a society can achieve, must be a central part of economic policy making.

TSING: The important political project about markets today is their removal from a social context. The ideological statement Bob makes is that markets in themselves produce wealth without nature or humans being involved. This is always an ideological political project, and I do not think it is a neutral project. It's this purified market that operates efficiently that is the problem, central to a particular set of ideological projects. I'm still unwilling to ever see markets as neutral—even as we pull on the politics and we make different politics out of them, they're never neutral.

FERGUSON: I'm not convinced that the efficiency framework is necessarily linked to the ideological framework you want to link it to.

ZALOOM: Adam Smith was writing to promote markets against a very specific political configuration, a monarchy. The idea was to use markets to dismantle a political system that didn't actually promote the welfare of the regular people and to spread this around. Smith was talking about the market as a mechanism, which, of course, now has hardened into an ideology.

Then there was a more modern moment, with Friedrich von Hayek, again using markets as a weapon against a system of communism and totalitarianism. Again, the market was being envisioned as an ideological weapon against some form of negative ideology. Adam Smith gets used to prop up discussions about the market as an end itself. But this nicely jumps over a whole bunch of history. It is important to see how the market has also become embedded in a left ideology. Markets are not neutral, but state redistribution is also not neutral.

In 1974 Friedrich von Hayek was awarded the Nobel Memorial Prize in Economic Sciences, which recognized his contributions to the Austrian school of economics. The Austrian school's position on free markets and free trade is perhaps best remembered through Hayek's (1944) *The Road to Serfdom*. Often forgotten is Hayek's equal disdain for blind adherence to laissez-faire principles of capitalism.

Friedrich von Hayek, Ludwig von Mises, Joseph Schumpeter, and the other Austrians' approach of methodological individualism profoundly influenced modern neoclassical economics, yet the Austrians were also equally leery of the excessive use of mathematics and skeptical of models of equilibrium. We find an anthropological kinship among the Austrians in their radical subjectivism. Hayek and others argued that social science "facts" are the beliefs of people and that "utilities" and "costs" are subjectively defined by actors. As such, attempts to impose mathematical precision on social data are futile. At the same time, this radical subjectivism underwrote a view of markets as conduits for the flow of information, with private property and political freedom seen as fundamental to market functions.

TSING: It's in the realm of economists to say, "This is just a technique and it has no politics." It's not that I think that buying and selling or having money is bad. I'm concerned with issues of the consolidation of property that are going on in the background, and I have a strong response to the ideological commitment to supposedly neutral techniques.

FERGUSON: All techniques of government come with legacies attached. This is one of the key reasons for the hostility of people like Hayek for anything that looks like redistribution (linked to a historical legacy of Soviet communism). The idea is that if you rely on those mechanisms, you are implicitly going down the road to serfdom. This is in some ways parallel to positions you hear in anthropology, that if you rely on those market techniques which are historically associated with the neoliberal project, then you're taking us down that neoliberal political road.

The discussions of neoliberalism in recent years have been highly ideological and based on a larger sense of politics. I think that the issue is not so starkly posed, if you go back a little further and look at the economic anthropology that was very interested in markets in the plural and in understanding how different kinds of trading activities were linked together with the broader set of social activities people engaged in.

VICTOR: There is a surprise alignment, or at least conviviality, between Bob's liberal position and a stronger critique of markets. There is a third element here, which I think gets muddled, and that is the corporate interest. Corporations are very much a nonmarket mechanism. They're closer to quasi-governmental organizations. Saying, "Let's get the power into the hands of more and more people"—the real threat to this is not necessarily the market but rather the concentration of control and power into fewer and fewer hands, as in contemporary corporations. Emphasizing this key difference—corporations versus markets—makes it easier to see that there can be coalition or cooperation between a behavioral economics perspective on the empirical effects of economic systems and an analysis of power.

ZALOOM: Yes, the issue of the corporation is an important counterweight to conventional criticism of "markets" per se. If we think about markets as mechanisms, then they are available to be embedded in different forms of politics. This doesn't presume that they're good or bad. It presumes that what we need to be most attentive to is the politics of the markets and the politics with which markets are being constructed. Whose interests are being served with a particular economic policy? This is always the question we should be asking.

Markets are contrivances, social constructions, Foucauldian technologies. As such, we may say that they are inherently neither good nor bad. Yet, at the same time, market relations and structures are also conduits of power: markets are always embedded in particular places and times, implicated in particular social and political projects, and endowed with certain moral valences. This means that it is incumbent on anthropologists and students of the market to understand the political valences, power relations, and structural contexts of seemingly free market relations. The idea of markets as contrivances should also be liberating from a policy perspective: folks can and should make markets work toward ends they decide are just and fair.

Note

1. Quotes from Adam Smith's *The Wealth of Nations* come from the Wikisource online version available at http://en.wikisource.org/wiki/The_Wealth_of_Nations.

3

Bezzle and Sardines

Jonathan A. Shayne

Economic reality is more than what we see around us.[1] Call me a financial Platonist.

In my day-to-day life as a money manager, I use torrents of data, and I can hardly see my desk underneath the financial reports I have stacked there. Yet, not everything that counts can be counted, as the saying goes.

In this chapter, I discuss a few important, nonmathematical ways of looking at market activities. These ideas apply particularly well to the banking system and to investing. My main conceptual tools here are"bezzle" and the humble sardine. Bezzle is the brainchild of John Kenneth Galbraith, and sardines come, of course, from the sea. Ultimately, I hope to persuade you that bezzle and sardines are useful, even necessary, in understanding financial markets and the economy generally.

BEZZLE

John Kenneth Galbraith, the late Harvard economist, wrote of the importance of undiscovered embezzlement or, as he called it, "the bezzle." Bezzle acts as a financial stimulus, he noted in his 1954 book, *The Great Crash*. To the extent that undiscovered embezzlement exists in the economy, we will feel and act richer than we are:

> To the economist embezzlement is the most interesting of crimes. Alone among the various forms of larceny it has a time parameter. Weeks, months, or years may elapse between the commission of the crime and its discovery. (This is a period, incidentally, when the embezzler has his gain and the man who has been embezzled, oddly enough, feels no loss. There is a net increase in psychic wealth.) At any given time there exists an inventory of undiscovered embezzlement in—or more precisely not in—the country's businesses and banks. This inventory—it should perhaps be called the bezzle—amounts at any moment to many millions of dollars. It also varies in size with the business cycle. In good times people are relaxed, trusting, and money is plentiful.... In depression all this is reversed. Money is watched with a narrow, suspicious eye.... Audits are penetrating and meticulous. Commercial morality is enormously improved. The bezzle shrinks. [Galbraith 1954:137–138]

Galbraith was speaking literally about undiscovered embezzlement during boom times. We have certainly seen some during our most recent boom-bust cycle. Bernie Madoff, the convicted Ponzi schemer, alone created $18 billion, or more, in now gone bezzle.[2] He was not by any means the only embezzler to have been caught, although he was the biggest.

I think the most useful application of Galbraith's term comes not when we talk about actual embezzlement, but rather when we extend his coinage to other phenomena that are aboveboard and legal yet have the same economic effect.

For example, suppose that in happy economic times, you loan me $1 million. Suppose further that I happen to be someone who is unrealistic, terrible at math, and an eager spender. I am, in the end, not going to be able to pay you back. For the moment, however, you hold what you think is money-good paper, that is, an interest-bearing claim against me.

In fact, you might feel a little *wealthier* for having made the loan, if you like the interest rate you are getting. So, feeling good about yourself for being such a clever financier and realizing you can finally swing it, you sign a contract to build a big new house. You feel good. I feel good too because I now have money to spend. The contractor starting work on your house is looking forward to sending you a big bill, so she is feeling good as well. None of us, including the contractor, will feel good, however, when I am unable to pay the loan back and declare bankruptcy.

This situation is bezzle in a broader sense than Galbraith meant.

Self-induced bezzle, if I may call it that, is even more pervasive in the economy, and important to it, than straight-up fraudulent bezzle. Universities that overspent their endowments in boom times, when markets traded at levels too buoyant, were in effect eating into principal without knowing it. The situation is the same with homeowners who took out home equity loans at inflated values. Their assumption, apparently shared and perhaps fostered by bankers, was that housing prices could only go up.

When looking at fictive, "bubblicious" economic activity, those who have not been initiated into the mystery cult of bezzle will make the mistake of thinking that the activity can be sustained. But economic activity we can see and measure should not always be taken at face value. Positivism is well and good, but it can also become a self-deception.

MONEY AND BANKING

Money and banking are centrally important concepts that most of us take for granted. I will demonstrate that banks create bezzle too, but first we need to look at what money and banks actually are.

So what is money? The classic definition is a medium of exchange and a store of value. Gold can be used as money, and so can silver. In prisons, cigarettes have served the purpose. In the United States, we use tokens, or more specifically, paper currency, as money. Our currency consists of pieces of paper with elaborate printing and security features. At the top is the text "Federal Reserve Note." The currency also says, "This note is legal tender for all debts, public and private." Furthermore, it reminds us, "In God We Trust."

The federal government does not give us a right to redeem its currency for gold or silver, so faith is, actually, important here. However, any court in the land would hold that a debt paid back with US dollars, in paper or electronic form, has been satisfied. In the end, the authority of our currency comes from the power of our courts and our moral sentiments.

Some people think that gold is real money and everything else is a weak substitute. I question this belief. What if someone found a way to synthesize gold cheaply by rearranging the right number of protons, neutrons, and electrons from other elements? The atomic weight of gold is 79, so it is a big atom, but nuclear reactors do rearrange subatomic particles. I am not predicting that someone will do it but am just imagining a scenario in which the utility of gold as money could disappear. Gold is *used* as money and has proved a stable store of value over time, but it is not money itself.

No, money is ultimately an idea. Like the idea of energy in physics and chemistry, it is a "conserved quantity": no one can touch it physically, no one knows what it really is, but it is nevertheless central and, like energy, must be tracked if we want to understand what is going on. There is something Newtonian about the idea that for every debit, there is an equal and opposite credit.

Moving on, what is a bank? I will try to keep things basic. The conclusion here will be that banks create a form of bezzle, and even if you miss a point or two (or simply skip to the next section), you will have the spirit of it if you keep this proposition in mind.

At the most basic level, banks are in the business of liquidity transformation. Generally speaking, their business is to mediate the flow of funds from depositors, whose time frame is short, to borrowers, whose time frame is long.

Suppose you have a certain amount of money in paper US dollars. You do not need the money right now but want to keep it available at a moment's notice. Ideally, you would like to earn interest on it. Mr. Borrower, on the other hand, would like to start a business. He needs the money locked up for several years as he builds his new store and develops his clientele. Let us agree, for the sake of argument, that Mr. Borrower will be able to pay back the loan over time, with interest, but that he will not be able to pay back the principal for a few years.

You have money and would like interest. Mr. Borrower needs money and is willing to pay interest. The problem is that you insist on liquidity, and Mr. Borrower insists on permanence, that is, repayment of the loan over time.

At this point, the bank steps in. Upon start-up, the bank—let us call it Galbraith Bank & Trust—has some money of its own from its shareholders as capital. The bank management wants to amplify returns by taking deposits at a low interest rate and then lending them out to borrowers at a higher rate. It is a business of spread. You deposit your money. The bank loans most of your money to Mr. Borrower. And, of course, the bank conducts business with many depositors like you and many borrowers like Mr. Borrower. The bank keeps about 10 percent of its checking deposits in reserve to handle withdrawals and other transactions. But the vast majority of the deposit money is lent out and therefore illiquid.

Galbraith Bank sends you a statement each month showing you how much money you have "on deposit." The implication of the word *deposit* is that your money is just sitting there at the bank. Of course, very little of it is there, so if you take it literally, you will be misled. Mr. Borrower has your money. When the bank says you have $1,000 on deposit, this is really just an IOU from the bank. *Deposit* is a euphemism for *IOU*. Generally, deposits in the United States are backed by an agency of the federal government up to certain limits.

Banks create money. Mr. Borrower will count his loan proceeds as money because they are. You will count your deposits at the bank as money, too. Your deposit is doing double duty, monetarily speaking, like bezzle. The money supply has expanded because of the bank's operation.

The reason we and other countries have central banks is that there might be a run on any ordinary (i.e., other-than-central) bank. If you and others like you demand all your money back at once, your bank will be unable to pay. The Federal Reserve System, the central bank in the United States, stands ready to loan Galbraith Bank money against good collateral in order to alleviate liquidity crises. In our example, collateral against which the Fed would lend would be the loans that Galbraith Bank made to Mr. Borrower and those like him. The Fed knows that the Galbraith Bank is good for these extensions of credit from the central bank because Mr. Borrower will be paying back the bank over time.

I am speaking about classic central banking and assuming that Galbraith Bank is sound. If the bank has instead made bad loans and can-not repay its depositors in full, we will have a problem more severe than a liquidity crisis, and that is a solvency crisis. If the central bank provides cash to Galbraith Bank under those circumstances, it is handing out a subsidy that is coming from someone else in the society.

An honest version of bezzle occurs when banks make bad loans but no one yet knows they are bad. During bad times, the loans sour, banks fail, and this banking-related bezzle shrinks, along with the classic Galbraithian (Madoffian) bezzle from actual embezzlement.

Nonbank banks, or as some call them, shadow banks, are institutions that are functionally similar to banks. They include hedge funds and investment banks. Like traditional banks, they borrow short-term money and lend it out or invest it for longer terms. They are therefore subject to runs, which come from creditors.

Let us look at money market funds, the simplest type of nonbank bank. When you put money into a typical money market fund, the fund uses your money to make very short-term loans, usually lasting about ninety days, to businesses. Once you buy the shares in the fund, your *money* is gone, strictly speaking. You now own shares of a fund, not money. The fund temporari-ly has your money, but it then passes your money along to businesses in exchange for their short-term corporate IOUs (largely, commercial paper and bank deposits). You own, through the fund, IOU paper. Your money market fund shares are almost as good as money, but they are not money, if you define the term strictly enough. If you have faith in the fund, you will believe, and act, as if you still have your money. If you and others begin to lose faith that the companies can make good on their IOUs, you will not think of your money market fund shares as *money* anymore. The fund will take a loss when some of the companies cannot pay off their debts. Normally, there is no federal guarantee or backing for money market funds.

The point is that banks, and nonbank banks such as money market funds, expand the money supply during good times. During good times, people accept bank IOUs and money market fund shares as money. During bad times, people get worried and lose their faith, reducing the money supply. The bezzle shrinks. If the cycle is bad enough, we experience deflation and deleverage.

During the crisis of 2008 and 2009, the federal government moved to backstop banks, investment banks, and money market funds. Without these programs, we would, fairly obviously, have been at severe risk of another Great Depression as bezzle of all kinds, and our spirits, would have fallen even further than they did.

INVERSE BEZZLE

I have tried to illustrate, through the idea of bezzle, that psychology and confidence, though difficult to measure, matter greatly in economics. I have also explained what central banks, like the US Federal Reserve, do.

Paul Krugman, the Princeton professor, recipient in 2008 of the Nobel Memorial Prize in Economic Sciences, and controversialist, has an idea about intentional laxity in central banking that is subtle, non-obvious, and true. In fact, although Krugman does not say it, he has come up with an inverse bezzle that helps us think about central banking.

Krugman (2000, 2008) argued that the Federal Reserve has to make us think it is crazy enough to create excess inflation, even if it will not really do so. His wording was more genteel; he wrote that a central bank must "credibly promise to be irresponsible" or, in other words, promise to violate expectations by continuing to create inflation even after a recession is over (2008). Fear of inflation can drive people to spend and invest in real assets, which is actually what policy-makers want after a crisis. Confidence in low inflation or deflation, on the other hand, can lead people to hoard dollars, which can cause deflation. If you think your dollars will buy more next year, not less, then there is no rush to spend them.

The Federal Reserve created new, fiat dollars by the trillion during the financial panic of 2008 and its aftermath to buy mortgage bonds and US Treasury debt. In part, sellers of these securities accepted the payments in created-by-fiat dollars because they and the public trusted that the Federal Reserve would pull the newly created dollars out of circulation in time, if inflation were to heat up enough. The Fed would do this by selling off, for cash, some of the securities it bought. As dollars are turned back in to the Fed, they cease to circulate and thus go out of existence.

Our faith in the Fed's long-term responsibility actually makes us less worried about holding cash. We feel no rush to spend because we trust the Fed to be careful and to prevent inflation by mopping up the extra dollars it made ("printed") after times improve. Yet, spending is what the Fed wants. Our confidence in the institution actually works against its purpose. Krugman's idea could backfire easily if investors factor in too much future inflation. But at least in the short and intermediate term, it is hard to argue with his logic.

Sometimes, then, the Fed might be able to use our unwarranted doubts about its inflation-fighting resolve. This situation is an inverse bezzle in that the Fed does not want us to believe we have money that is not actually there, but rather to have doubt about the soundness of money we actually *do* have.

SARDINES

Canned fish provide one more important, hard-to-quantify way of piercing the economic veil.

There is an old Wall Street story that money managers like me, oriented to financial fundamentals, love to tell. It starts with a young man who gets his first job trading sardines on the floor of a commodity exchange near Monterey, California, many decades ago. One of the old traders mentors him. The old trader warns that trading is a very difficult business and that making money during the first month or two, in particular, is almost impossible. So the mentor advises the novice to be very careful and to keep his first trades small.

In the tale, things do not go as badly as they might have. At the end of week two, after the day's trading has closed, the novice runs a tally and realizes that, against all the odds, he actually has made a modest profit. He is exhausted but very happy. He sits down on a crate of sardines to catch his breath. Realizing that he has never actually tasted a sardine before, he pulls back one of the wooden slats, feeling entitled now to take a can, and opens it.

As soon as he tastes one of the sardines, he spits it onto the floor. "These are awful," he says to no one in particular. His mentor is nearby and says, "What are you doing! Those aren't eating sardines. Those are trading sardines!"

Anyone involved in markets, or affected by them, needs to learn to ask whether an asset being traded is valued at a price justified by fundamentals or is, instead, being viewed by the market participants mainly as a "trading sardine." Sometimes people running even very large and seemingly sophisticated operations forget this lesson or choose to ignore it in order to be able to keep their jobs. On July 9, 2007, just a few weeks before the credit crisis kicked into gear, the chief executive officer of Citigroup at the time, Chuck Prince, explained to the *Financial Times* why his huge bank was continuing to lend, even in bubbly conditions: "When the music stops, in terms of liquidity, things will be complicated. But as long as the music is playing, you've got to get up and dance. We're still dancing" (Nakamoto and Wighton 2007). As we know, the financial crisis came hard and fast, and Citigroup would have gone bankrupt if not for federal rescue. Citi had been making loans with the mentality of a sardine trader. It would have been a mistake to read its financial statements literally, as if it were making loans because it believed them to be sound fundamentally.

CONCLUSION

I have laid out some thoughts on bezzle, money and banking, and sardines. We first discussed bezzle, which describes any wealth we think we have but do not. As yet, undiscovered embezzlement is the paradigmatic example. We then moved on to money and banking, which, like bezzle, rest on belief or, more precisely, on the social grounding of our legal system. And finally, the sardine story about traders in Monterey illustrates the idea that some financial professionals, like the former CEO of Citigroup, care only about how others bid on the instruments or commodities they are trading, not about what they themselves think of the value.

The most practical feature of these conceptual tools is that they can help prevent us from getting caught up in manias and panics. But in the broader context of this volume, they also illustrate how social beliefs underlie some phenomena that traditional neoclassical economics would mistake as fundamental. There is a reality to our economy; it is not all smoke and mirrors. But what appears to be happening, that is, what we can see readily and measure, may differ significantly from the underlying reality.

Alfred North Whitehead (1978) famously described Western philosophy as a series of footnotes to Plato. In *The School of Athens*, the early sixteenth-century painting by Raphael, Plato stands in the center, gesturing upward. He is calling our attention to all-important, pure forms that Aristotle, beside him and pointing out into the world, will miss. The deepest issues seem to persist across epochs, and we must realize that there can be important, unquantifiable social phenomena that an empirical, neoclassical approach to economics will overlook.

Notes

1. This chapter makes use of parts of a talk I gave to the Old Oak Club in 2009.

2. If we subtract the amount that Madoff's investors put into his vehicles, $36 billion, from the amount they *thought* they owned based on their statements, about $65 billion, the bezzle comes to $29 billion. More conservatively, we could call the bezzle simply the amount of the losses investors incurred against their original investment, about $18 billion ("The Madoff Scam: Meet the Liquidator," *CBS News*, June 20, 2010 [quoting Irving Picard, the court-appointed trustee overseeing the Madoff liquidation and his chief counsel]).

4

How Do Supply Chains Make Value?

Anna Tsing

So much of what we use and eat every day is drawn from far-reaching supply chains stretching around the world. Each bit entangles us, inside and out, in social and ecological processes scattered across every continent and about which we know so little. Our own essence, forged in increasingly fragmented and cosmopolitan consumption habits, becomes a mystery. The moment I taste a bite or touch a key, questions proliferate. What worlds are we making through the objects we use? What kinds of riches should count as socially productive value in today's world? In this gale of urgent questions, I tackle one small but pertinent mystery: How do continent-crossing supply chains make value?[1]

Value is a term most commonly used not in ordinary life but in abstract discussions of the economy. The most powerful theories of value in the economy these days hold that value is created by competition in markets. When sellers offer something buyers want, at a price that buyers are willing to pay, it has value. Recent ideas about value created by information, design, innovation, and networking are ornamentations on these more fundamental theories of value; they do not change the assumptions of the theories but elaborate on the kinds of things that are given value in markets.

Yet, adherents of these market theories are always working to elude other important theories about value. Two opposing theories have been particularly convincing. Marxist theorists (drawing from classical political economy) hold that value is created by human labor in the transformation of nature. Labor cannot be treated as just another cost in preparing goods for market, they explain; labor makes value. Meanwhile, environmentalists argue that value is created by the regeneration of the natural world, so often taken for granted by both Marxist and neoclassical economists. Without the regeneration of nature, the economy would fall apart. Market-competition theorists assert their power by either translating labor and the environment into their own terms or sweeping them under the rug. Their goal is to stand uncontested. But they cannot close the questions alternative theories raise, in part because the discussion of value is based on propositions rather than observations of the world.

What if we take discussions of value into the world? To avoid policing the meaning of *value*, we might listen to what people tell us. Since people rarely talk about value per se, we would need a generous interpretation of what might count. Then it becomes clear that discussions of value are everywhere. Which economic activities are useful, and which ones get in the way? Everyone has an opinion. These opinions matter because they have an effect, however small, on what seems reasonable and possible as livelihood and wealth. My phrase "socially productive value" signals these conversations about what kinds of value ought to count for something.

What processes, then, make commodities valuable? People disagree. If we are interested in how their disagreements help shape the world of commodities, we might begin by investigating commodity processes in which disagreement stands out starkly. The continent-crossing commodity chains that bring to us so much of what we use today are a good place to begin. Such chains, in management jargon, are "supply chains."

Supply chains, by definition, connect varied enterprises. The current fascination with supply chains is based on the notion that *differences* among these enterprises can create a profit, at least for those with the best position on the chain. This idea is why entrepreneurs with some power try to create chains involving enterprises that are as different as possible—for example, located in countries with much less international clout, using employees whose differences make it difficult for them to demand a living wage, and exploiting environments with different, that is, fewer, legal protections. Difference—as disadvantage—is built into the system by the businessmen at the top. But difference has implications beyond disadvantage. It means, for example, that the people associated with the varied enterprises of the supply chain rarely agree about the purpose and the importance of the work they do. Their theories of socially productive value are incommensurate. The negotiation and translation of theories of value becomes a major element of the work of the chain. Tensions need not be fully resolved for the goods or services to be delivered. The fizzing, bubbling instability of such tensions *is* the chain. Only the haunting presence of force, congealed in historical memories and renewed in political frameworks of law, policy, and convention, holds the chains, in their agitated asymmetries, for a time.

Consider an example from my ethnographic fieldwork.[2] To see how difference works in the chain, I bypassed better-known products traveling to the United States and turned to one of Japan's globalized chains. Matsutake are aromatic wild mushrooms gathered in forests around the Northern Hemisphere for export to Japan, where they are highly valued. The matsutake supply chain has many levels of independent enterprise. In the US Pacific Northwest, for example, mushrooms are gathered by proud-to-be-independent pickers, who imagine themselves as entrepreneurs rather than laborers. Independent buyers buy the mushrooms and sell them to bulkers who sell them to Canadian exporters who sell them to Japanese importers who sell them at auction to intermediate wholesalers who sell to grocery stores and restaurants who offer mushrooms to consumers. I picked this supply chain because participants all along the chain recognize the importance of cultural expression. Pacific Northwest buyers, for example, endorse American freedom by rough, exaggerated performances of competition in which they aim to put the other guys out of business by any means possible. This practice creates value, they say. In contrast, Japanese high-end retailers court wealthy and aristocratic customers through intimate diplomacies and performances of finesse. This practice creates value, they say. These examples are just the tip of the iceberg: at each link, chain participants explain that the value *their* work adds to the product is the key to the chain as a whole.

How are cultural differences and incommensurable theories of value negotiated on the matsutake supply chain? Japanese traders have a long history of imagining trade as a form of translation, that is, the management of difference. Japanese traders do not try to make their partners Japanese. Instead, they aim to use difference as an aspect of the trading business. Matsutake importers I interviewed in Japan chuckled at what they called the "psychology" of US buyers, showing me their tourist photographs of the exotic "Wild West" competitions that brought forth mushrooms. They expected their suppliers to be different. The role of traders, they explained, is to work across global differences to get the right goods to the right customers.

But how did Japanese traders—in contrast, say, to American exporters —gain the power to define this framework of chain translation? In part, their power is due to the fact that matsutake is an insignificant product in American eyes, slipping through the cracks of North American imperial power. For the moment, here, Japanese trading standards rule. But this tentative hegemony is in play within a history of political interactions between Japan and North America, in which the United States currently strives for—but never fully achieves—the upper hand in setting standards. Negotiations of value in supply-chain capitalism everywhere depend on such shifting political dialogues, with their backdrops of force held back, extended, or remembered.

The idea that trade is translation in Japan goes back to nineteenth-century Meiji period initiatives in which trading companies, with government backing, sent young men abroad to study both language and trade in Western countries (Yoshihara 1994). Traders were expected to gain the skills necessary to mediate between Japan and other places. By the twentieth century, such skills enabled Japanese trading companies to organize extensive supply chains across the globe to bring materials to Japan. In the 1970s and 1980s, Japanese trading companies became some of the most powerful companies in the world because of the continent-crossing supply chains they initiated and abetted (Yoshiro and Lifson 1986). The endorsement of a supply-chain model of capitalism in the United States in the 1990s, which upset the mid-twentieth-century model of the corporation through downsizing and outsourcing, responded directly to the challenges of Japanese competition organized through supply chains.

Japanese supply chains have responded to pressures from the United States from the first. Meiji period trade initiatives were responses to US commodore Perry's "black ships" in Tokyo Harbor. After World War II, US occupation forces dismantled Japan's conglomerates, opening the field to competition, but US quotas limited Japanese exports to the United States. To get around these quotas, Japanese trading companies sponsored production in Korea (Castley 1997), forming an influential supply-chain model of Japanese economic control. In the 1970s, Japanese supply chains spread across Asia and into Latin America—particularly after the United States forced the revaluation of Japan's currency, making Japanese products too expensive to export. The worldwide supply-chain economy that ensued was a model of success for those who would reap profits without paying any costs for labor or natural resource management. It was this model of success that US entrepreneurs reshaped in the 1990s with designers and retailers in charge, rather than traders. The "finance-driven" world economy they created, in turn, caused worldwide crises, including the 1997 Asian financial collapse in which Japan's economy was badly hit. US financial experts rushed to Japan afterward to reform the Japanese economy using American standards but without any consciousness of how Japan's pioneer supply chains had shaped US history. But US reformers could not be everywhere, and Japanese trading schemes continued to flourish in many corners of the world, including the matsutake supply chain. Perhaps US matsutake buyers perform "the American spirit" so passionately, in part, because they have so little influence on the US apparatus of international coercion.

By focusing on a product outside global institutional debates, I am able to examine supply-chain negotiations of value without the blinders of currently powerful economic ideologies, with their insistence that only one imperial formula for value can exist at a time. Such ideologies never fully achieve the dominance they seek, and it is important not to be blinded by their claims. Without their blinders, the active interplay of varied understandings of value making becomes clear. Varied theories and practices of making value are established across most any supply chain, and these do not disappear in the global connection. A successful chain creates a moment of traction that allows commodities to be passed along—but without resolving differences across chain nodes.

The question of socially productive value is a public issue and should be debated and determined by active public discussion. Why should we take for granted the terms and conditions for generating wealth? Economists and officials continually try to take the issue of value away from the public, telling us that questions of value can be decided only by carefully trained technicians and accountants working for private, state, and imperial institutions. Systems of making value, and its playmate, wealth, are out of our control, they tell us; we can only do our best to succeed within them. This is because the problem of value has one correct answer and they know it and we do not. But the world shows them wrong. Many answers exist, and they are actively in play—within the constraints of political force—all the time in every supply chain. Disagreements and negotiations concerning socially productive value matter for those of us who care about the conditions under which people live and work, as well as life on earth, from which resources for the economy are continually mined. At the very least, negotiations of value help us understand the heterogeneous social and environmental forms our supply-chain-laden lives are creating. They also sometimes offer leads not just to understanding the world but to changing it.

Notes

1. This chapter derives from a longer paper, "Value Added," presented at the SAR advanced seminar "Markets and Moralities," Santa Fe, April 2009. During the seminar, participants decided to forego composing a volume of academic papers because our discussion mainly revealed intellectual and political differences and did not "add up" in any way to an approach to understanding markets. We agreed to write five-page papers on our research rather than full-length academic reports; these short papers would form part of a volume that would also include creative work. I was sorry to hear that these plans were later dropped. I offer my short essay and collaborative cartoon in the spirit of the open-ended volume we originally planned.

2. My fieldwork has proceeded through many layers of collaboration. The Matsutake Worlds Research Group includes Shiho Satsuka, Michael Hathaway, Miyako Inoue, Lieba Faier, and Tim Choy. In my Oregon research, I collaborated with Hjorleifur Jonsson, Lou Vang, and David Pheng. For more on the research and the mushroom, see Tsing 2009.

5

Profits of Diversity

Anna Tsing, with illustrations by Jesse Sullivan

Remember the nineteenth century? As Europeans encircled the globe, natural resources were up for grabs. Native labor was yoked to white profits. Finance ruled.

In the twentieth century, people reacted to the unruliness of finance, giving rise to the world we imagine as "modern." Nation-states and corporations

ruled had in hand. Modernization and development shaped dreams across the globe.

The "shareholders revolution" at the end of the twentieth century put finance back in charge. Corporations became "lean and mean," outsourcing everything. Subcontractors outsourced to smaller and shadier

subcontractors, driving labor cost and environmental risk to those regions with the least regulation.

Pundits proclaim that the economy has entered a new "knowledge" era beyond labor and natural resources. But people do not eat knowledge.

Supply chains transform raw materials into the products that sustain our lives and then bring these products to us as the consumers.

Supply chains are often ignored because they outsource labor and natural resource management to the people unrecognizable to pundits and
perhaps to the twentieth-century architects of modern capitalism.

Yet, continent-crossing supply chains have become the ideological center of contemporary global capitalism. Follow the path of your food, of your
clothes, of your computer.

Through outsourcing, profits have come to depend on diversity. Diverse workers and resources are mobilized for global capitalism.

Often this diversifying causes the worst kinds of exploitation. Workers in dangerous conditions are paid a pittance. Natural resources are plundered. Because only small subcontractors are liable, no one with power takes any responsibility.

Supply chains create profits from diversity; they are also diverse. Every now and again, diversity-based supply chains offer opportunities for combining income with cultural empowerment, on the one hand, or environmental protection, on the other.

Pay attention to the supply chains you use, so that you can tell the difference. Supply-chain capitalism opens whole new economic processes for becoming human, nonhuman, and inhuman. Watch out, it is coming for you!

6

Capitalist Markets and the Kafkaesque World of Moralization

Jonathan Friedman

In this chapter, I locate the current economic crisis within two larger contexts. The first is the real material process that connects declining hegemony in the global system to credit bubbles and crunches, neoliberal flexibilization, and the cyclical logic of capital accumulation as a time-space phenomenon. The second embeds such crises within an ideological space that becomes increasingly a *moral* space in periods of desperation like the present. Thus, we are dealing with a powerful material logic on the one hand and on the other an accusatory moralism that spans the gamut from hunting devils to castigating the system itself.

In 2008 the neoliberal *shock doctrine* came home to roost in the form of the so-called financial meltdown in the American economy and large segments of the world economy. A sense of moral indignation surrounded the entire affair, and the media hunted for the culprits who "got us into this mess." The interpretations of the cause vary from one end of the political spectrum to the other.

Yet, little attention has been paid to the overall scale and dynamics of capital accumulation and the various cycles that are packed into it, from shorter business cycles to longer cycles (including hegemonic cycles). (Of course, such considerations are not part of the immediate reaction to losing one's savings, pension, house, or livelihood.) Consciousness has tended to be short term, and in large parts of the Western world, this short-term thinking was for a time reinforced by a myth that somehow business cycles were over, that growth had become a permanent state.

Elsewhere, I have written about the cyclical nature of global systems, in which we currently see a decline of Western hegemony and a shift of accumulation to elsewhere (see Ekholm and Friedman 1980; Friedman 1992, 2000, 2004). Now we see a widespread recognition that the rise of parts of the developing world comes with a parallel decline in the developed world. Indeed, this rise and decline is a systemic process we find across the entire history of commercial civilizations (back to at least the third millennium BCE) founded on the accumulation of wealth in relations of competition. If this story has a "moral," it is that we have been participating in a gigantic civilizational repetition compulsion from the very start. Marx and Freud can again be understood as that odd couple in the study of humanity.

The following discussion deals with the articulation between the dynamics of economic value and moral values. These two sorts of values are distinct and autonomous yet connected in the larger reality of experience and its conditions. I examine the discourses around current moral reactions against markets and analyze the circumstances that produced the crisis as part of a more general structural expression.

AGAINST KEYWORDS

We have an excessive, almost obsessive, contemporary tendency to label reality rather than try to account for its genesis and dynamics. Terms such as *globalization*, *millennial capitalism*, and *neoliberalism* are used as causal and definitive rather than as objects to be deconstructed and deciphered, skewing discussion in the direction of labeling and categorizing rather than analyzing. These words take on moral connotations, part of the ahistorical, almost visceral reaction to the rapid transformations of the past decades, as if capitalism was the work of bad guys and required a Rambo of the left to set things straight.

The term *globalization* itself has been, for quite a few years, a way of designating the nature of the contemporary condition, a stage in history unlike anything we have seen previously. The discontinuity embedded in its usage is also a prophetic statement about the new enlightened elite, who demand a rethinking of anthropology through a barrage of critiques of "the old school," in which "culture" was assumed to be bounded and essentialized: before, we were local, but now we are global; specific cultures do not exist anymore—all are globalized and hybridized and thus need to be rethought in such terms even if, once upon a time, they were in fact local.

The vocabulary of this shift is what I (Friedman 2000) refer to as trans-x (where *x* represents *national, local, gender,* etc.) discourse. In its heyday, globalization discourse made assumptions about a coming world of happy fusions, at least in cultural terms ("we'll all be culturally free" [Appadurai 1996:23]). Soon this image was confronted by the contradictory processes actually occurring in the world, with all their fragmented violence and class polarization. More recently, *globalization* has been modified if not replaced by the word *neoliberalism,* with a new focus on the "bad side" of globalization.

In all these cases, the words contain a certain magic. Globalization is the cause of increasing sorcery accusations in South Africa and the emergence of xenophobic movements seemingly equivalent to sorcery in Cameroon (Geschiere 2009) and Europe. But on the basis of what we know of the materiality of globalization, we have reason to be skeptical concerning the power of these terms to explain anything.

Of course, words are used to capture a certain aspect of reality, and *globalization* and *neoliberalism* refer to real objects, but they have also taken on a magical explanatory value rather than needing to be explained themselves. They have been used as such, metonymically, to be generous, as symbols of larger-scale yet more specific phenomena, but this usage endows them with powers they do not have. They are not autonomous realities, but aspects of larger logics or processes. Globalization is a moment within an already constituted global system, and "neoliberalism" is a historically specific structural adaptation to the declining profitability of a former corporate structure of accumulation (Friedman 2000; Harvey 2005). Discourses associated with this neoliberal politics (and it is politics and not economics) include those by such famous characters as Friedrich Hayek and Milton Friedman, but these are not implementations of particular policies, only their rationalization. And in all of it, we discover that presidents such as Reagan, who was supposed to be an icon in this respect, are better categorized as Keynesians, military Keynesians, for reasons of necessity within the logic of capital accumulation in a particular historical situation.

GLOBALIZATION AS A HISTORICALLY SPECIFIC MOMENT WITHIN GLOBAL SYSTEMIC CYCLES

I suggest that many of the aforementioned keywords are used in a way that directs attention toward products and away from driving strategies. Globalization is not a stage of history, but a historical phase of capitalist processes of long-run expansion and contraction. Today's globalization of wealth and decentralization of world accumulation is related to declining hegemony, and this occurrence is not the first. It happened as recently as a hundred years ago as part of the decline of the United Kingdom. The crisis emerges from the linked properties of hegemonic decline and a shift in capital. Capital is either exported on a massive scale or invested in a growing finance sector oriented to other, nonproductive sectors such as real estate and various forms of speculation that produce a bubble economy at the same time that a consumption economy in which the balance of trade is increasingly negative runs up enormous debt.

This shift of capital investment is termed "financialization." Financialization—part of the shift from Fordism to post-Fordism—occurs simultaneously with the contraction of large firms into a financial core and the decentralization and fragmentation of capitalist production and services into a network of subcontractors who are often globalized. *Financialization* refers to that part of the capital that remains at home in the financial cores of the system. Thus, globalization, financialization, and post-Fordism are aspects of a single process. Neoliberalism is a product of a unitary financialization/globalization/decentralization (post-Fordist) process. This process does not create an assemblage because the separate strands are not autonomous domains with their own internal logics. On the contrary, they are very much mutually constitutive.

Thus, we may understand globalization as a period of hegemonic decline in which capital accumulation within the larger system is rapidly decentralized and potential new centers of world accumulation begin to rise to dominance (see also Arrighi 1994; Braudel 1977, 1979). The internal logic of centuries of global expansion and contraction is as follows:

1. A state begins to expand within a pre-existing global system or co-extensively with the formation of the latter. Warfare usually plays a crucial role in this initial process as a major form of "primitive" accumulation of wealth, thus making possible the following processes.

2. A hegemonic economic position forms in which a center becomes a "workshop of the world" and produces a large percentage, even a majority, of the final consumption goods of the larger world.

3. The accumulation of wealth leads to increasing costs of reproduction in the hegemonic center as the immediate product of this accumulation. These increasing costs are the result of the translation of increased wealth into higher standards of living and higher levels of consumption.

4. Following step 3, the center becomes relatively more expensive to reproduce than other regions of the system.

5. This expense leads to a gradual process of capital export (which takes many different forms) to areas that are more profitable for investment.

    a. In this phase, capital (accumulated wealth) cannot profitably be invested in local production. Instead, it is both exported and invested locally in luxury consumption and various forms of fictitious accumulation that tend to proliferate exponentially via chains of packaging, securitization, and sale. In the contemporary version of capitalism, these investments lead to the emergence of hedge funds, referred to as casino capitalism, and, in the final instance, to phenomena described as "naturally occurring Ponzi processes" (Schiller 2001:78).

    b. This phase is equivalent to the general shift from industrial to financial dominance in the accumulation process.

6. The center loses its productive activities to other areas of the world at the same time as it becomes a major consumer (based on credit) of the products of its own exported capital.

7. New centers emerge, former recipients of capital investment from the now declining center, which becomes a major global debtor after having been the major global source of credit (Braudel's [1984:64] thesis of the autumn of hegemony).

Steps 4 to 7 correspond to the period of "globalization." This use of the term is specific and is clearly distinct from a use that refers to expansive periods of colonization and empire formation in which capital is exported but primarily for the extraction of raw materials and people rather than the development of competing industrial activities. Whereas cultural diffusion is plentiful in periods of expansion, the globalization referred to in contemporary discussions is typical of hegemonic decline.

NEOLIBERALISM AS A SPECIFIC HISTORICAL CONJUNCTURE

Just like *globalization*, *neoliberalism* can be understood as a cover term for a set of transformations in governance that accompany declining hegemony. A logical relation exists between globalization and the complex of processes referred to as neoliberalism.

The transition from Fordism to flexible accumulation is an expression of the declining profitability of vertically organized, capitalist production (found in classical analyses of modern corporate capitalism). The Fordist model is one in which the chain of production leading from raw material extraction to the final product is incorporated within the vertical hierarchy of corporate structure. This model has been replaced by a double process: the contraction of formerly productive units into a financial hub surrounded by a slew of competing, flexible (replaceable) subcontractors and a diversification into activities that need not have anything to do with the original productive activity (e.g., real estate [hotels, golf courses, casinos] and derivative markets [General Electric becomes GE Money, General Motors becomes General Motors Acceptance Company]). Finance is thus freed up from the production process, leading to periods of massive expansion of finance capital relative to industrial capital. Flexible accumulation also implies flexible labor that is likewise hired on uncertain short-term contracts in the wake of the gradual dissolution of labor unions. The proportional increase in the power of finance capital is a periodic phenomenon in the long cycles of capitalist accumulation, what can be understood as a historical moment in the cycle of hegemony.

In the model I suggest, the rise of any hegemonic center implies an increase in its trade surplus and in wealth levels, which leads to internal class conflict and redistribution of income that in turn is translated into rising social costs of production. The center thus enriches itself using its formerly competitive position, and capital moves to more lucrative areas. The portion of capital that does not move is invested in the nonproductive sectors where money can readily and directly be turned into more money, thus creating the bubble phenomenon. The so-called shift from industrial to finance capitalism is the logical outcome of the center's previously established superiority, one that is expressive of the decline itself. Thus, a temporal logic connects hegemony to massive capital export to financialization and speculation. This process is one in which production in the center becomes increasingly uncompetitive and is replaced by imports from cheaper industrializing areas that often are, themselves, organized in regulated, centralized, and Fordist structures. The flexibilization of central economies, like their neoliberalization, is a product of this pressure that leads to declining profit levels. Flexibility and deregulation are strategies that work to counteract this downward trend by separating financial hubs from decentralizing productive activities, by diversifying in the direction of strictly financial investments, and, last but not least, by flexibilizing the workforce, thus re-creating a lumpen proletariat.

The globalization I refer to (once celebrated, now not so celebrated) is a product of a certain phase in the transformation of the global system's hegemonic structure, in which former monopolistic production centers begin to export massive amounts of capital to more profitable production areas (not just to avoid labor costs but also to seek more profitable conditions generally) at the same time as there is a reversal of the mass migration that results from the dislocations of a fragmenting global system (i.e., in those areas not privy to such capital export, itself an aspect of the decentralization of capital accumulation that fosters the generation of

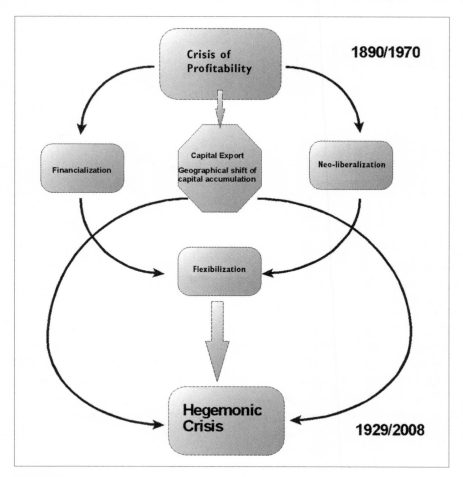

FIGURE 6.1

Historical logic of two kinds of crisis.

global underclasses or flexible labor pools). (This is not the whole story, of course. The process also entails a reconfiguration of identities as a result of both fragmentation and opposition to former hegemons.)

G. Duménil and D. Lévy (2004, 2010) show that hegemonic crises ensue upon profitability crises after a period of financial expansion. If we add a geographical dimension, we can see how a global systemic analysis can link this process to hegemonic shift. Figure 6.1 shows a single complex set of relations linking the cycle of crisis to the transformation of the global arena. In other words, globalization is an aspect of a broader shift in the global system rather than an evolutionary stage of its own. While massive

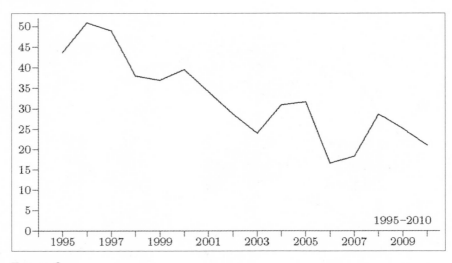

FIGURE 6.2

New capital raised by US corporations (percentage of the total of such capital raised worldwide). Courtesy of Gérard Duménil and Dominique Lévy.

amounts of capital were transferred to East Asia over the past decades, capital accumulation in the United States was declining rapidly (fig. 6.2). This model implies that globalization is logically connected to decline in the former hegemon and that the decline takes the form of neoliberalization, financialization, and flexibilization. The long cycle of crisis leads from a crisis of declining profitability of capital to a crisis of hegemony resulting from the strategies that necessarily intervene to counteract the first decline.

One important lesson to be drawn from this discussion is that *globalization, neoliberalism,* and related assemblage terms are not, as I have already suggested, indicators of some general development, a social evolution. On the contrary, they are crisis phenomena typical of end-of-hegemony scenarios.

DISCOURSES AND MORALITIES

> We need to get people back to what they were doing before and away from finance.
>
> *—Discussion of the transformation of industrial companies into financial companies, CNBC Squawk Box, March 3, 2011*

The thinking expressed in this quote indicates the dislocation of reactions to the crisis. The speaker does not ask why finance became the dominant market operator but instead declares that it was wrong to do X and that we should return to Y without examining the conditions of implementation of such a strategy.

If I am an investor, I believe that with the right strategy, I will make money in this business. When the speculative bubble was expanding, I was right there making millions at no cost. Every penny of the capital was borrowed. I became used to an expanding market. It can only go up, after all. It is in the nature of things. When the bubble burst, I could not understand what had happened, not at first. After a time, I realized that of course it was all stupid, that I was living in a casino or a pyramid scheme. After all, how does the market expand like a bubble if not by attracting new buyers who can invest because they have borrowed money. The idea is to keep the high rollers coming, no matter the asset values involved. The work of turning money into more money would appear to constitute a world of its own, one related to production only in the form of potential stimulus and not as a moment within the larger process of economic reproduction. The autonomy of different economic spheres is, of course, an immediately experienced reality even if a misrepresentation of the economy as a whole.

The American consumer, the world's consumer of last resort, plays a magnified role in the contemporary world economy, which is propped up by a now failed credit bubble, the backside of Marx's fictitious capital accumulation. This role is neither a mere assemblage nor a product of neoliberalism or of any other singularity in the history of the global system we inhabit. It is merely the working out of the logic of the system. As David Harvey himself admits, neoliberalism, although linked to the names of Hayek and Friedman, is not an imposition of a particular market ideology, but something that became a necessity in the crisis of capital accumulation that afflicted the 1970s. The solution has been interpreted as a restoration of the power of the capitalist class and of its income advantages (Duménil and Lévy 2004), because the postwar period saw a steady decline in the Gini index income differentials between the wealthiest and poorest segments of the population in most Western countries. Neoliberalism in this sense is really a return to the traditional liberal regimes that characterized the imperial centers before the Great Depression. And if one considers the class conflict implied in this analysis, the current phase can be understood better in cyclical rather than in linear terms.

Harvey links globalization and neoliberalism to the same historical shift cited at the start of this chapter. I argue here that the two phenomena are elements of a single logic of transformation in which the decentralization of production in geographical terms is simultaneously a decentralization and fragmentation of economic activity in organizational terms. So the short cycle itself is arguably more significant than the approach of any particular school of economics. This significance accounts for Richard Nixon's stance (borrowing a phrase from Milton Friedman) that "we are all Keynesians now," compared with the clearly neoliberal policies of respective Labour and Democratic party heads Tony Blair and Bill Clinton.

The point is not that keywords should be eliminated. On the contrary, they refer to tangible realities, but they have no explanatory value. Instead, they ought to be *objects of* explanation.

THE KAFKAESQUE WORLD OF MORALIZATION

I am concerned here with the embeddedness of discourses, whether practical, political, or moral, in the category sets within which they are conceived and that make them very much products of what they seek to criticize.

The economic crisis has led to numerous reactions, a great many of them moralizing. I use the word *morals* here in the emic sense only. Whether an etic morality exists is questionable, even if we hope so, but as anthropologists, the only morality we can study is existing morality. And because our practical lives are embedded in our material existences, which are constituted within social reproductive processes governed by the logic of capitalism, we should expect that our moral discourses are generated within the same fields of material existence.

If one is a "liberal," then the market is good by definition, and evil is the product of deviations from true market morality: cheating in the form of pyramid schemes or bad loans. This belief has produced a flurry of accounts about how X screwed up a perfectly "good" economy through irresponsible behavior and whether X should be put in jail or at least relieved of his enormous bonuses and parachutes. Occasionally, as I have suggested, it is revealed that the designated evildoers were only doing their jobs, that in a speculative system in which markets have become casinos, a pyramid scheme is not necessarily an anomaly.

For others, the evil is capitalism itself, and this system has no apparent alternatives nowadays. Attac International and alternative globalization movements are primarily Keynesian, as Keynesian as George Soros and the Democratic Party at this particular moment, unlike under Clinton, who was a neoliberal. The resurgence of Keynesianism, clearly reflected in the choice of Paul Krugman for the 2008 Sveriges Riksbank Prize in Economic Sciences, is also the expression of the moral critique of capitalism. But this critique is very much expressed in terms of the "excesses" of the economy, *capitalism gone wild*, which leads to chaos and unemployment and impoverishment. So we need more regulation and, of course, we need to bail out the big shots, which is painful yet necessary. Nationalization is on the agenda but as a short-term solution, in order to pay off/wipe out accumulated "toxic," *dirty* debts. The dirty part of capitalism is here understood as clutter in the free flow of capital, which, since we are all liberals now, is good, if not entirely natural. Thus, as is well known, nationalization is not a socialist revolution, as some American conservatives claim, but a necessary intervention to save capitalism.

MORALITY WITHIN THE SYSTEM

The discussion of the social consequences of capitalism is as old as capitalism itself. Much of the discourse is produced from the *alternative* position and includes an array of more or less radical critiques that, I argue, are generated from within the categories of the capitalist order. However, a more pedestrian stance is limited to the morality of particular capitalist actors. It assumes that some practices are legitimate and morally acceptable and some are beyond the threshold of immorality. Thus, trickery, stealing, and ponzi schemes define the limits of the legitimate.

The internal critique posits a set of behavioral rules adapted to what is assumed to be a well-functioning economy. When seen from the "alternative" position, selfishness, competitiveness, unfairness, and other traits usually assumed to be negative outgrowths of capitalism are understood as normal and as ways of differentiating the successful from the unsuccessful. This interpretation is based, of course, on a pure market model in which all are equal at the start of the process.[1] All the specific institutional and other processes that reinforce hierarchy are understood in this approach as impurities in the system, immoral impurities. Honest businessmen do exist, just as some institutions are conducive to the maintenance of maximum competition.

The internal critique—internal, that is, to the principled interpretation of capitalism—is focused on corruption and other activities that derail the ideal of economic activity. The Madoff affair is a case in point. Ponzi schemes are considered to be immoral, even if on closer scrutiny the differences between such schemes and the new speculative economy are not as great as might be assumed. Hedge funds depend to a large extent on attracting investors primarily because the "values" in play have nothing to do with the asset values they supposedly represent. In a scheme in which only price-based transactions occur, no fundamental difference exists between speculation as a general category and what we might call the "necessary" material processes of social reproduction. Thus, what Marx (in volume 3 of *Capital*) called fictitious capital—the accumulation of which is the final interlude in the cycle of investment, growth, and decline—is also the principal *operator* of accumulation. It does not support the growth of production or services, not the turning of cars into more cars, but the turning of money into more money—the expansion of speculative and other forms of fictitious accumulation in periods of real decline.

Price and value are not the same and need not even be related in the sense of *linked*. What a commodity fetches in the market is not based on mechanisms related to value in the Marxist sense. The latter refers to the "social cost" of reproduction, which is different from market value simply because it is arrived at by a different kind of calculation. The capitalist system, like all commercial systems, is based on price or market value alone. Value enters in a partial way, first, as a limiting factor and, second, as an issue of direct cost as it is filtered through the reproductive process. Prices have a lower limit that is based on costs of production, but costs of production in terms of price. This is an effect of real value, but not value in itself. Value in itself is simply a measure of the real social costs of the reproduction of a population, costs that would have to be calculated in terms of real expenditures of energy in different activities. I refer not to *subsistence* (which refers to a particular level of reproduction), of course, but to *social* reproduction in general. These costs are distributed among the various economic activities that are part of the reproductive process. Marx's analysis does not consider the speculator because speculation is "unnecessary" for the reproductive process, although it is part of the logic of the system.

Here is the crucial problem with value theory: it can be seen in terms of added costs of reproduction that could be eliminated without any deleterious effect (since such elimination would increase profitability), but it need not be dealt with in moral terms. That is, fictitious capital is capital that redirects income to the holders of such capital, but it does not create wealth in the ways production and services that enhance the reproductive process do. Fictitious accumulation is immoral accumulation, and here is where the internal critique overlaps with the external critique: the net effect of fictitious accumulation is the transfer of a portion of the total wealth rather than the increase of that wealth. And here the Marxist joins the liberal and even the conservative critiques. For all, moral representations are based in the same categories that constitute the social order more generally, which accounts for the similarity of so-called external moral critiques and internal critiques. This similarity leads to the Kafkaesque nature of representation, interpretation, and practice with respect to "the economy" that makes it the proper domain of anthropological analysis.

I am not making a mechanical Durkheimian argument here; I do not argue for a reflexive or causal relation between the social order and its forms of representation. Rather, as Claude Lévi-Strauss argued in a different context, reacting, interpreting, and acting involve enormous creativity, which produces a plethora of variations grounded in a set of invariants, what he called the "social armature." Such a perspective differs from rational actor theory since it never posits anything like an autonomous subject, not even when the subject is a physically autonomous individual. Nor is it like the more Freudian statement that man has free will but the will is not free, although this is also largely true. It is, instead, a situation in which intentionality is not its own source in terms of content. In crises like the present one, what becomes even clearer is to what extent our reflections on reality are not autonomous, even if our immediate experience might have us believe so. What is Kafkaesque is the blindness of action with respect to its own conditions of existence. Or, as Lewis Carroll put it in a different context and lighter format, when you do not know where you are going, every road takes you there.

CONCLUSION

The morality related to capitalism as a system is already embedded within that system or, better, its set of logics. Thus, the immorality of capital accumulation stems from greed associated with the rationality of accumulation (although this is a greed by implication, i.e., capitalists can be very generous outside their necessary activity of accumulation). This kind of critique, that of Marcel Mauss and Karl Polanyi, is not a critique of capitalists, but of the logic of capitalism. The two should not be confounded. The behavior of capitalist actors is rational within the system and is necessary for success or even survival within that system. On the edge of this position are works such as the recent *Freefall* by Joseph Stiglitz (2010), who criticizes the Obama administration for having continued to let the financial sector run wild. He does not ask why it happens but takes an essentially normative stance in which runaway financialization as such is understood as an aberration with negative implications: we have to stop the bad guys, the evildoers whose greed is deleterious to the (good) market system.

The moral judgments concerning the capitalist market or system are of the following sorts, which correspond to the different levels of the system:

- The problem is the greed of certain capitalists and their cheating of others, especially in the financial sector. The market system is fine, but certain of its actors have ruined it for the rest of us.

- The immorality of financial speculation is undermining the market system. This problem is systemic and requires regulation so that "Main Street" is not undermined by Wall Street.

- The major contemporary problems are neoliberalism and neoliberal globalization—which have, via deregulation, enabled maximum profit taking at the expense of ordinary people—but also the extremes of exploitation that result from post-Fordist methods of production. Neoliberalism is the problem, not capitalism, which is often not mentioned or, if mentioned, is referred to as a regulated Fordist capitalism of the previous period.

- Fernand Braudel (1979) also makes a more general distinction between the market and capitalism. The market was a zone of small-scale trade and relatively limited profits over medium distances in which single or small-scale entrepreneurs dominated a relatively transparent process. Capitalism, in contrast, was almost opposed to the market since it consisted of monopolies of long-distance trade in which large amounts of capital were needed, as well as an alliance with the state. Capitalism is thus opaque with respect to the populations on which it feeds and quite opposed to market principles as well. The market (the pure market) is only approximated in small-scale producer societies in which the profits of trade do not exceed wages by a great margin. Though this situation is not necessarily moral, Braudel implicitly and sometimes explicitly saw the market as liberating and progressive, whereas capitalism was a colossus based on autocratic power, an alliance of great wealth, and massive state power (Wallerstein 1991).

- Finally, for Mauss and others, the root of the problem is the market system because it promotes selfishness, which does not lead to the highest good for all, but to maximum inequality. It is, therefore, basically an immoral system and opposed to one based on true reciprocity.

The moral reactions span a gamut from individual accusation to a general critique of the system couched in moral terms, even if based on the supposed consequences of the system, which are deemed to be evil. And the evil is paramount even at the systemic level. It is greed, as opposed to generosity and reciprocity. The lines of division, of course, vary with both scale and the way the situation is defined. For Mauss, the evil is the market, but for Braudel, the market as a small-scale network of trade is still on the side of social security and the real evil is the loss of control over conditions of existence, due to the encroachment of large-scale capitalism (which is what capitalism *is* for Braudel).

The reality of global process, best revealed in crisis periods when one can clearly see the contradictory tendencies involved, generates interpretations that are quite critical but still rooted in the properties of the world that is critiqued. This contradiction produces the Kafkaesque effect that structures much of the moral discourse in response to the crisis. Now some might object that my own analysis is also embedded in these categories, and this might indeed be the case. This would make my analysis part of that which I seek to critique. However, I have not argued that the relation is deterministic, even if it can easily become so in the absence of a clearly reflexive stance (which is why I can feel some sympathy with the witch hunting, even if I disagree with the interpretation). Not to fall victim to the tendencies, one has to maintain a self-reflexive position that allows one to distance oneself from the larger phenomenon. This reflexivity is the value of anthropology, which has such distancing as its basic methodology. But it is never a sure-fire methodology, especially when dealing with ones' own experiential world, so I proffer this work as hypothesis to maintain an open-minded sanity.

Note

1. Consider Braudel's (1979) distinction between market and capitalism, in which the latter was not merely a mechanism for the exchange of goods and services but an articulation of state and capital in a large-scale process of predation. Markets were only part of a larger process of expansion of wealth, which was essentially an opaque, secretive "antimarket" ruled by powerful elites.

7

Patient Value

João Biehl

"PHYSICALLY WELL YET...ECONOMICALLY DEAD"

"Today is another world," Luis Cardoso told me as he looked at the portrait that photographer Torben Eskerod had made of him in March 1997 (fig. 7.1), when he was beginning to take AIDS therapies. It was now December 2001 and I was back in Caasah, a community-run AIDS-care facility in Salvador, the capital of the northeastern Brazilian state of Bahia. I wanted to know what had happened to the AIDS patients we had worked with in 1997. "One Luis has died, and another has emerged," the thirty-six-year-old man continued. "My family and friends discriminated against me. For them, AIDS was a crime. A doctor sent me to Caasah.... Here people supported me. I got used to the antiretrovirals. Medication is me now."

Caasah was also a changed institution. It was founded in 1992 when a group of homeless AIDS patients squatted in an abandoned hospital formerly run by the Red Cross. Soon after its founding, Caasah became a nongovernmental organization (NGO) and began to receive funding from a World Bank loan disbursed through the Brazilian government. By the mid-1990s, the unruly patients in Caasah had been evicted, and a smaller group was undergoing an intense program of resocialization run by psychologists and nurses. "With time, we domesticated them," recalled Celeste Gomes, Caasah's director. "They had no knowledge whatsoever. We showed them the importance of using medication. Now they have this conscience."

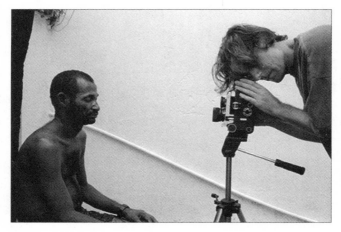

Figure 7.1
Luis and Torben at Caasah, 1997. Photograph by the author.

Figure 7.2
Luis, 1997. Photograph by Torben Eskerod.

Luis was one of the few who got that chance (fig. 7.2). He and his fellow "AIDS citizens" (as many in Caasah called themselves) knew all too well that inequalities of power, ranging from economic destitution to racial discrimination, determined who had access to what services. They had to take up a new patient identity, and this newly learned ability to "accumulate" health at Caasah was also a highly competitive enterprise.

With antiretroviral therapies (ARTs) more widely available, healthy residents like Luis had been asked to move out of Caasah. And in the past year, Caasah itself had moved to a new state-funded building. It had been redesigned as short-term recovery facility for patients sent by hospitals' AIDS wards and a shelter for orphans with HIV. Maintaining the institution was a daily struggle, Celeste told me: "This is a beautiful building, but that's all the state gave us. We owe more than $1,000 to local pharmacies. Our patients come from the hospital with their ARTs but nothing else. No vitamins, no painkillers, no Bactrin to treat opportunistic infections." Celeste remarked, "We now have this paradox that the poor AIDS patient is physically well yet he is economically dead." Disturbingly, as I would find out, the state AIDS unit and Caasah made no systematic effort to track patients and their treatments once they left.

SUBJECTS OF RIGHTS AND INTERESTS

Via pharmaceuticals and at the mercy of a volatile economy, Caasah's patient-citizens live in flux. Like millions of other poor AIDS patients worldwide who now have access to treatment, they struggle to move out of the stream of history and into a technologically extended life (Fassin 2007; Hunter 2010; McKay 2012; Nguyen 2010; Reynolds Whyte et al. in press). As they scavenge for resources and care, their lives reveal desperate and extraordinary efforts to swerve around and exceed constraints of all kinds.

As these new subjects of biomedical rights try to undo social death, they also express world-altering desires. Luis was happy to show me the photograph of Davi, the three-year-old boy he had informally adopted. "His parents died of AIDS. He was living here in Caasah. I now pay his grandma to care for him. All expenses are on me. I love him." The disability pension and salary he earned as Caasah's office assistant enabled Luis to pay his bills and save for the home he dreamed of owning.

AIDS therapies have opened up a space that did not exist before. But they alone cannot explain everything that has happened to Luis. This chapter is about Luis and the social fields that the new people of AIDS invent and live in. I am particularly concerned with how subjects of biomedical rights (as in the case of Brazil's AIDS citizens) struggle to become

FIGURE 7.3
Luis, 2001. Photograph by Torben Eskerod.

Homo economicus—the values they espouse and the ways they speak of state and society. As I show throughout the chapter, the world-altering desires and doings of these ambigious political subjects upset probabilities, bias estimates, and expand the limits of what can be known and acted on in the new world/market of global health (fig. 7.3).

Caasah's initial collective arrangement replaced the absent family and enabled Luis to access medical and psychological care. "Here I stopped blaming others for what was happening to me. Self-pity and hatred keep you imprisoned, don't let you live the present. I learned that the AIDS patient has the right to struggle for a future like any other human being. I always look first at what is up to me to do. I must have this conscience...to have to take food and medication and to sleep at the right time, to always be alert to my symptoms and to the weather, to schedule my medical appointments. I am the effect of this responsibility." Treatment regularity occasioned a previously unknown gratification. Luis said, "I gained another body. But it is a mistake to think that one can put the guards down."

This novel engagement with technology is lifelong and involves constantly challenging and interrogating the self. It requires personal virtue, Luis insists, a new way of claiming actuality and existing beyond immediacy. "If one wants to have a real life one must make medication a routine and…know what is good for oneself, beyond the moment. The world presents all possible paths. It is a school in getting lost. But it is up to me to take life forward. I know that beyond the immediate pleasure of a drug or of alcohol, there are grave consequences. So I chose to do what is best for me, and I don't counsel anyone to take the easiest route."

Luis is an amazing person: hardworking, wise, witty, and masterful at moral discourse. He spoke of a new moral economy (Fassin 2008) organized around AIDS therapies. And he himself was the dominant human form that emerged from this economy. "I face my problem. I take advantage of the help I get. I struggle to live." He was indeed the representative of a new medical collective and subject position, and his discourse conveyed the present-day forms and limits of society and state. "I have nothing to do with society," he said. "From my perspective, society is a set of masters deciding what risk is and what is bad for them. I have never participated in that. As for the government, I must say that I am thankful for the medication."

The new Luis spoke as if the paradigm of an activist civil society was vanishing and, in its wake, a conjoined subject of rights/interests had emerged in relation to medical technology. "People fought a lot, and we are now a country in which the AIDS therapies have not been missing. This is the good aspect of the state. The rest is for me to do."

Luis had harsh words for those who threw medication away: "It's a crime." A crime against the state and the person himself, Luis reasoned. "The government is paying a lot for medication. To keep the person hospitalized would be even more expensive. People don't sell the antiretrovirals, for no one would buy them. Many people with AIDS already gave me their drugs, and I brought them to Caasah. Tell me, what is the point of dying in a hospital bed? I must follow the medication regimen rightly."

Luis made adherence to treatment seem too easy. As much as I admired his resilience and uplifting presence, I also found his righteousness quite disturbing. For him, individual conscience was the foundation of a healthy existence, and mourning a loss, any kind of loss, was a defect to be overcome. Moreover, his overemphasis on individual responsibility was self-serving. It clearly reflected Caasah's house-of-passage modus operandi and, more broadly, the hegemonic discourse that one has to be evermore self-conscious, in control of oneself, upbeat, and forward looking. The institutional and interpersonal forces that threw Luis into action in the first place were by and large absent from his life-extending account, particularly as he spoke of noncompliant *marginais* (marginals). It was evident from his recollection of the recent past that without belonging to Caasah, he would not have benefited as he had from the AIDS therapies and that he kept harnessing strength from being the object of regular public attention (as the "good" AIDS patient, volunteer, and peer educator).

Yet, in Luis's technocratic moral discourse, social abandonment exists in a vicious cycle with self-created risk and the possibility of self-destruction. His pharmaceutical subjectification had indeed led to salutary effects, yet it was built upon the exclusion of those who cannot conform and who remain at the pheriphery of this local economy of salvation. "It is not a matter of getting the street patients help, for they already have medication. They use their social condition as an excuse to keep their habits…. It is a question of self-destruction. As I see it, these people are more for death than for life. But I also know many people who struggle to live and to earn their money honestly and don't surrender…. It is your mind that makes the difference."

NEW FORMS OF THEORIZING AND RECONSTRUCTING WORLDS

Antiretroviral treatment rollouts are matters of intense negotiation; their local realizations are shaped by contingency and uncertainty. As I show throughout this chapter, such realizations encode diverse economic and political interests, as well as the anxieties and desires of groups and individuals. Drawing from my long-term study of the Brazilian therapeutic response to AIDS, I explore the limits of the vertical-technical-fix approach in global health and the feasibility of people-centered initiatives. Broadly speaking, I am concerned with (1) the arts of government that accompany pharmaceutical globalization, (2) the remaking of people as market segments (specifically, therapeutic markets), and (3) the articulation of para-infrastructures for everyday living.

Several questions guide this chapter: When and under what conditions are marginalized people accounted for as population subjects in new biomedical regimes? How do social projects (such as Caasah) become integral to novel state–market formations (such as the AIDS policy)? In which ways can patient-citizens draw resources from social projects and governments as they negotiate the vagaries of the market and survival? How can anthropology map these precarious para-infrastructures and think through the ambiguous political subjectivities that crystallize amid the blurring of distinctions among populations, market segments, target audiences, and collective objects of intervention or disregard?

Ethnographic evidence consistently dies within dominant frames of knowledge production in global health (Biehl and Petryna in press). People are put into preconceived molds, and the multiplicity of realities and lines of flight that ethnography makes available has nowhere to live in the counting of drugs delivered, in the dire and faulty statistics of mortality, or in the biased selectivity of randomized experiments. Moreover, policy and popular accounts tend to cast people as helpless victims, overdetermined by environment, history, and power, or as miraculous survivors who bear witness to the success of external aid. Details are suspended. Broken infrastructures, rifts that deepen, and larger political economies in which these lives unravel seem peripheral to both analysis and activism. But in our anthropological works, we must continue to challenge orthodoxies of all kinds and seek original ways to communicate the categories that are significant in human experience—which the powers that be dismiss as anecdotal, nongeneralizable, and inherently impractical—to the worlds of science, policy, jurisprudence, and caregiving. If this kind of engagement leads to the subtraction of quick-fix theories and policies and to the addition of new forms of theorizing and reconstructing worlds, so much the better.

OPEN-SOURCE ANARCHY

Brazil accounts for 36 to 57 percent of all HIV/AIDS cases in Latin America.[1] An estimated 630,000 Brazilians in the fifteen to forty-nine age group are living with HIV/AIDS. The prevalence of HIV infection in the population at large has remained stable at around 0.6 percent since 2004; among women, the rate of infection is 0.4 percent and among men, 0.8 percent (Szwarcwald et al. 2008). But social epidemiological studies show considerable heterogeneity in HIV infection rates, with large numbers infected among vulnerable groups such as men who have sex with men, commercial sex workers, and injecting drug users. Brazil is indeed known for its stark socioeconomic inequalities and for its persistent development challenges. Yet, against all odds, Brazil invented a public way of treating AIDS.

In late 1996, groundbreaking legislation guaranteed universal access to antiretroviral therapy. This policy resulted from potent rights-based social mobilization, legal activism, and novel public–private partnerships. The democratic constitution of 1988 granted the right to health to all citizens and mandated the creation of a national health-care system—AIDS activists were the first group to effectively equate this right to access to medicines. Some two hundred thousand Brazilians currently take antiretroviral therapies paid for by the government. The government managed to reduce treatment costs by promoting the production of generics and also negotiated substantial price reductions from pharmaceutical companies.

According to the Health Ministry, both AIDS mortality and the use of AIDS-related hospital services have fallen by more than 50 percent. Perhaps even more impressive is the steep decline in mortality during the first year after diagnosis, signifying the transformation of HIV/AIDS from an acute to a chronic disease. Brazil's bold, multi-actor, large-scale therapeutic response to AIDS has made history. The country empirically challenged the economic and medical orthodoxies that treating AIDS in resource-poor settings was infeasible and that poor patients could not adhere to complex drug regimens—as a result, Brazil has been a leader in the struggle to universalize access to AIDS therapies.

Yet, I wondered, what would be the effects of the universal treatment policy on the country's poorest and most marginalized citizens, among whom HIV/AIDS is spreading most rapidly? How would people such as Luis and Salvador's "street patients" transform a death sentence into a chronic disease? What social innovation could make such medical transformation possible?

For more than ten years, I have explored the impact of the AIDS treatment rollout on Brazil's government, its health systems, and individual lives. I have interviewed policy-makers and health professionals and carried out a long-term study of marginalized AIDS patients in Salvador. In charting the lives of poor patients before and after they had access to ARTs, I (Biehl 2007) wanted to open a window into the real-life outcomes of novel national, international, and corporate policies.

In my ethnographic work, I also engaged nongovernmental and pharmaceutical communities as they took up the call for responsibility and care in the face of AIDS. Until recently, global health initiatives were the domain of states through the coordination of specialized international bodies such as the World Health Organization (WHO). In the past decade, however, a complex matrix of partnerships (state and nonstate actors that include philanthropic organizations, nongovernmental organizations, and pharmaceutical industries) has arisen and is shaping health interventions worldwide, increasingly under the framework of security—the field of global AIDS treatment is paradigmatic of this trend.

Public–private partnerships in global health come in multiple forms, and they have diverse interests, ranging from the Bill & Melinda Gates Foundation to corporate drug donation programs to PEPFAR (the US

President's Emergency Plan for AIDS Relief) to myriad small and hopeful pilot projects. These various actors set goals and new norms for institutional action and sometimes fill voids in places where national systems and markets are failing to address public health needs or have been absent altogether. Whatever ideological differences exist across corporate, activist, and state public health agendas, the imperatives of "treatment access" and "saving lives" appear to reconcile these differences and fold them into an ethos of collective responsibility in the face of "crisis." Arguably, players can become impervious to critique as they point to crises and dire statistics and their essential duty to act on health in the name of humanitarian reason or as an instrument of economic development, diplomacy, or national security (Fassin 2011; Fidler 2007; Sachs 2005a; Singer 2009). We are left with an "open-source anarchy" around global health problems (Fidler 2008)—a policy space in which new strategies, rules, distributive schemes, and practical ethics of health care are being assembled, experimented with, and improvised by a wide array of deeply unequal stakeholders.

So far, few if any institutions are in place to monitor this burgeoning and somewhat disordered "public goods" field (Adams, Novotny, and Leslie 2008; Biehl 2008; Samsky 2012). In practice, the interests and concerns of donors, not recipients, tend to predominate, and the operations of international organizations tend to reinforce existing and unequal power relations between countries (Banerjee 2005, 2007; Epstein 2007; Ferguson 2006; Ramiah and Reich 2005). Moreover, initiatives tend to be disease specific and are increasingly dominated by scientifically based measures of evaluation revolving around natural experiments, randomized controlled trials, statistical significance, and cost-effectiveness (Duflo, Glennerster, and Kremer 2008; Todd and Wolpin 2006)—a technical rhetoric aligned with the demand of funding organizations for technical solutions. Traditional public health initiatives are now categorized as "nonscience," and this "scientific preoccupation" tends to overlook the on-the-ground dynamics of programs—assuming that other settings are replete with distinct institutions, practices, and rationalities—not to mention the more intractable failures in the infrastructure of receiving countries (Adams in press; Deaton 2010).

Indeed, much is sidestepped and remains unaccounted for in this global form of governance and medical experimentality (Petryna 2009; Whitmarsh 2008). Magic bullet approaches have been the norm in international health for decades now—that is, the delivery of health technologies (usually, new drugs or devices) that target one specific disease regardless of myriad social, political, and economic factors that influence outcomes.

A growing number of social scientists and health policy advocates has been cautioning, however, that a narrow focus on technology delivery, the basic science of disease, and patient compliance, as important as they are, is inadequate by itself. They argue that we need to better attend to a wide array of structural and social determinants of health and find ways of integrating them into delivery and care (Farmer 2004, 2010; Freedman 2005; Hahn and Inhorn 2008; Singer and Hodge 2010). Moreover, extreme inequalities in the distribution of risk and disease remain structured into the current international order, and unintended consequences are unleashed by even the most carefully designed interventions.

What happens concretely when new treatments are introduced into epidemiologically diverse and variable social worlds? How is care organized by providers and state and nonstate institutions, and by what struggles and mechanisms is care acquired—or not—by the people who desperately need it?

LOCAL ECONOMIES OF SALVATION

The ethnography of AIDS after the introduction of antiretroviral therapies illuminates processes of individual and group becoming, as Luis suggests, taking place through medicines and multiple sites, relations, and intensities—fields of immanence. It is within this circuitry, as it unequally determines life chances, that AIDS survivors articulate their plastic power (instead of a given truth or life form) and invent ties and temporary medical collectives that enable a domesticity and health—a plateau of sorts—to live in and by.

The day after I talked to Luis at Caasah in December 2001, he joined me on a visit to Rose. She had been a founding member of Caasah and, like Luis, had also been asked to move out as she "gained body." I would have never found Rose's place on my own. No traffic signs guide you through these labyrinthine favelas-turned-commercial-districts. Houses and informal businesses blur in an unplanned and overcrowded way. Luis did not use the words right or left, and after missing a few exits and having to make some dangerous turnarounds, we finally reached the bumpy highway that connects southern and northern Brazil. Five miles north, we turned right onto an unpaved road and into the heart of Salvador's misery: the Cajazeiras district.

Rose was waiting for us. "It's a poor shack, but it is mine." She introduced us to Jessica, her one-year-old daughter, and Ricardo, her eleven-year-old son, who had previously been under the care of "Professor" Carlos, the man who had been Caasah's head nurse for several years until health authorities found out that that he had forged his nursing diploma (he was now Caasah's operations manager). At any rate, Rose's kids kept watching television as we sat to talk.

She immediately made fun of her new hairdo. "It's modern. I straighten it and put some color in it. Men will be knocking at my door.... For someone who passed through hell, I am in good shape. I am strong and conscious, right, Luis?"

Tearful, she recollected the death of her partner Jorge from AIDS-related diseases a few months before Jessica was born. "He wanted this child so much." Rose knew that Jessica's HIV-positive status could still change. "She has never been ill, and we hope for the best. This is how I lead my life...always struggling to pay the bills, raising my children, for I am mother and father."

Rose had given birth to another daughter in 1993 in Caasah. Rose gave her up for adoption to Naiara, Caasah's associate director. I also learned that Ricardo's father lived in the streets and also had AIDS—a word Rose did not utter.

"Life continues. When one has the 'girl' [*menina*], one must have the responsibility. I can do everything, but within my limits. I am not a fanatic patient. There are people who think about *it* twenty-four hours a day and who live in hospitals. I live a normal life. I know to have fun, too." As Rose used the word *menina* and the pronoun *it* to refer to AIDS, she gesticulated to convey that she was talking in code because of the kids and the neighbors. "They don't know I have the menina. It's tough to go about life without *it*, and if you have *it*, oh Lord, no one wants anything to do with you."

"The first time we met in Caasah—it was 1995, right?—we were all losers there," Rose continued. "If I look back, I consider myself victorious. I am thankful to the government for the medication and to Dr. Nanci [her physician]. She is a blessing, a mother to me. I never had another doctor, and I never had this problem of having to change treatment. People fight to have Dr. Nanci as their doctor. We are siblings in Christ and in doctor, right, Luis? When the antiretrovirals first came in, we were among those she gave priority."

Like Luis, Rose spoke of being medically conscious and responsible. Yet, in her account, new life was anchored in the experience of being saved *by* Caasah. Like most poor AIDS patients, Rose had experienced cruel forms of abandonment and self-abuse and had no family, no one to count on. "I had no support. I was lost in the world. The world was the only school I had, and it ended in what it did." Death by AIDS, she meant, a destiny she escaped. "We were lucky to get disability pension before the medication. We are the founders of the old institution. Caasah was my salvation. The majority who now applies for disability does not get it. We had everything done for us, food, medical appointment.... That routine helped."

To adhere to ARTs, to make a child, and to take on maternity/paternity in such vulnerable and precarious conditions—"life is on a hanging thread"—was already the effect of something else, evidence that a change had taken place. Caasah made it possible for Rose and other socially dead subjects to reconstruct themselves from ashes. In her account, "salvation" had to do with distancing oneself from and elaborating upon losses and failures, with finding a place for death other than in one's body. "One was the mirror of the Other. This proximity and constant interaction made one reflect on what had passed." In this intervening grassroots space—which redefined what family is—a discourse of morbidity was channeled into agency and labor vis-à-vis the newly available medical technologies.

Caasah remained a foundational reference (material and symbolic) to the AIDS- and class-defying, breadwinning mother Rose had become. "I know that they have financial difficulties there. It is a big operation. And they have the children now. But I am glad I can count on them. When Celeste and Naiara see that I have a serious problem, they say, 'Come here and we will see what we can do.'" Rose confided that Professor Carlos, informally, kept playing nurse to her. "He helps me a great deal. I don't care what people say about that creature.... Whenever I need a drug I cannot buy or I have a wound that won't heal, I can count on him."

She complained bitterly about the lack of medicines for opportunistic diseases in the hospital and local health post and told me how she herself had become a proxy-physician/pharmacist, recycling available medications through trial and error. "The basic pharmacy program and health post is just facade. A few weeks ago, Jessica got this horrible scabies. I couldn't get a specialist in this end of the world. So I had to tell Dr. Nanci about it. She gave me a prescription but had no samples. The medication was too expensive. I couldn't buy it. Carlos had given me a medication. So I used it in Jessica. Thank God, it worked."

Rose's powerful discourse of salvation from the world, from herself, and from social AIDS—"I am a new creature. You can write my story"—was matched by an equally powerful account of the ways she was able to establish and sustain transference with people standing for state and medical institutions and thus realize her new life. The actions she microscopically alluded to reflected long-lasting social and subjective forms based on *apadrinhamento*—the practice of godfathering, as revealed by the canonical works of Gilberto Freyre (1987) and Sergio Buarque de Holanda (1956). Pragmatically, to have one's child adopted by someone powerful greatly helps one to traverse institutions and to access goods. This engineered kinship stands for and does the welfare work of the community and neighborhood and, ultimately, also makes the vision of social mobility possible.

Rose went to the kitchen to brew coffee. Quite poignantly, she served us *cafezinho* on a tray. She was proud of her well-cared-for home, urbane manners, and children—"The boy is my right arm"—and she was always captioning her moves. "Who would have imagined that Rose, from the Pelourinho, would be giving interviews, telling the professor from the United States what life is all about, huh? I tell you, I want to be alive to see a cure. In the name of Jesus, I want to be a guinea pig when they test the vaccine."

Rose also made it evident that she was expecting some financial aid at the end of our session. "Any aid is welcome, my brother. You know that I limp, from those mad times [intravenous drug use]. I need help to buy Voltaren [a painkiller]. The other day, the pharmacist sold me five tablets. I didn't have enough money to buy the whole box. And I couldn't buy meat that week. It's not easy."

HOMO ECONOMICUS AND THE INTENSITY OF SURVIVAL

We have no easy way of understanding how a technologically prolonged life may be achieved in Brazil or in the growing number of other poor countries where AIDS is finally being treated through an unprecedented array of public- and private-sector initiatives. More than 25 million have died of AIDS to date, and an estimated 33 million people are living with HIV worldwide, about two-thirds in sub-Saharan Africa. Some 15 million people are in need of antiretroviral therapy. The battle for access has been hard fought, and nearly 6.6 million are now on treatment in low- and middle-income countries.[2]

Global AIDS treatment rollouts rightly open the door to medicinal access, but they also exemplify the inadequacies of a magic bullet approach to health care. Disease is never only one thing, and medicines are ancillary to care and well-being over time. Not money or medicine or a sophisticated pilot project can alone guarantee success. Healing, after all, is a multifaceted concept, and *healing* is no more synonymous with *treatment* than *treatment* is with *medicines*. Statistical strategies and profit motives hover above, by and large missing the interpersonal networks that link patients, doctors, and governments and are especially important in resource-poor settings where clinical infrastructures are not improving. AIDS deaths and HIV infections continue to increase among the destitute. An estimated 2.6 million people become newly infected each year. For them, HIV/AIDS is one tragedy among many others.[3]

These realities are not reducible to the critical theories we bring to the field. Numerous anthropologists have been using Michel Foucault's (1980, 2007) formulation of biopower— how the naturalness of population became central to Western techniques and conducts of government—to assess emerging assemblages of technology, medicine, and governance, particularly in the face of HIV/AIDS (Comaroff 2007; Fassin 2007; Nguyen 2010; Robins 2006). Yet, the Foucauldian biopolitical maxim *making live and letting die* deserves deeper probing because it might assume transcendent forms of power, along with homogeneous people and overly normalized populations (Biehl 2005; Biehl and Locke 2010; Biehl and Moran-Thomas 2009; Deleuze 2006). It has to be tested against the intense political-economic-experiential fields that Luis, Rose, and millions of other poor AIDS patients now on ARTs traverse in their quest for survival. Here the absoluteness of neoliberal principles in health-care delivery goes hand in hand with a surprisingly absolute juridical subject of rights, and we also witness the power of biotechnology to remake human and social worlds, opening up new spaces of contestation, resistance, and ethical problematization.

As I have been arguing, the Brazilian AIDS policy is emblematic of novel forms of state action on and toward public health. Pressured by activists, the democratic government was able to negotiate with the global pharmaceutical industry to make ARTs universally available to its citizens and also to open up new market possibilities for that industry. The policy's sustainability has to be constantly negotiated in the marketplace, and one unintended consequence of the AIDS treatment ramp-up has been the consolidation of a model of public health centered on pharmaceutical access. This intervention gains social and medical significance by being incorporated into infrastructures of care that are, themselves, being reshaped by state and market restructuring.

In 1978–1979 lectures at the Collège de France, Foucault (2008:2) aimed to retrace "the rationalization of governmental practice in the exercise of political sovereignty" from the principle of right and law to an age of critical governmental reason. "Political economy made it possible to ensure the self-limitation of governmental reason" (2008:13), and liberalism tells the government, "I accept, wish, plan, and calculate that all this should be left alone" (2008:20). Interestingly, Foucault (2008:19) puts a pause on the analytics of biopower (particularly on the power/knowledge apparatus that marks that which does not in reality exist—"madness, disease, delinquency, sexuality, et cetera"—and submits it to "the division between true and false"), which was supposed to be fully spelled out in these lectures. We can adequately analyze biopolitics only when we understand the economic truth within governmental reason, he stated. "Only when we know what this governmental regime called liberalism was, will we be able to grasp what biopolitics is" (2008:22).

After all, the market is the "site of veridiction—falsification for governmental practice" (Foucault 2008:32). In this reality, the possibility of the collective good as an object of governance or as an interest guiding individual lives is excluded. The imperative to pursue economic self-interest without interference from the government means that *H. economicus* cannot become aware of the ways in which he functions to support the advantages of others within a system. This situation implies a departure from the biopolitical model of governance in which population well-being is the object of administration and regulation. Foucault actually ends the *Lectures* with the surprising notion of civil society as a "transactional reality." Because there is "no localization, no territoriality, no particular grouping in the total space of the market" (2008:301), it is "the idea of society which permits the development of a technology of government based on the principle that it is already in itself 'too much'" (2008:319). Civil society works as "the medium of the economic bond" of subjects of interest and is "a permanent matrix of political power" (2008:303). This concept-work unleashes a myriad of questions about present-day crises in the apparatuses of governmentality and the concrete actuality of liberalism among us and how we apply a liberal politics to ourselves today (Berlant 2011; Biehl and McKay 2012; Povinelli 2011).

The travails of Caasah's AIDS survivors introduce us to contemporary linkages that, somewhat and for some time, connect the rights of people with the utilitarian calculus that presumes independent, rational choice–making economic subjects. Traversing worlds of risk and scarcity, constrained without being totally overdetermined, people create small and fleeting spaces, through and beyond classifications and apparatuses of governance and control, in which to perform a kind of *life bricolage* with the limited choices and materials at hand (including being the subjects of rights and pharmaceutical treatments made available by state and nonstate actors). Scholars and policy-makers are challenged to respect and to render publicly intelligible, without reduction, the angst, uncertainty, travails, and passion for the possible that people like Luis and Rose, amid lifesaving interventions, are left to resolve by themselves and, too often, at the expense of others.

When I returned to Salvador in August 2000, I worked with the roughly thirty homeless patients under the care of a nurse called dona Conceição (Biehl 2007). They were living on a concrete platform adjacent to the city's main soccer stadium. Many looked undernourished, had skin lesions, and complained of flu-like symptoms. But Carisvaldo philosophized, "We push life forward anyway." Several said that they had begun picking up free anti-retrovirals at the hospitals but that they had stopped using them. Roberto declared, "Medication alone will not solve anything." His friend Jair said that he did not believe in the efficacy of the drugs. "My medicine is food, beans in my belly." A culture of "compliance" was far from here.

At the end of that week, I went to Brasília, where I met with Dr. Paulo Teixeira, then coordinator of the National AIDS Program. "The success of the Brazilian AIDS policy is a consequence of the activism of affected communities, health professionals, and government," he told me. Two years later, I would hear a similar explanation from Fernando Henrique Cardoso, Brazil's former president: "Brazil's response to AIDS is a microcosm of a new state–society partnership," he told me.

The AIDS policy emerged against the background of neoliberalization, and the politicians involved with it were consciously articulating a market concept of society. For Cardoso, citizens are consumers who have "interests" rather than "needs." In the words of economist and former health minister José Serra, whom I also interviewed in 2003, "the government ends up responding to society's pressure. If TB had a fifth of the kind of social mobilization AIDS has, the problem would be solved. So it is a problem of society itself." In this rendering, the government does not actively search out particular problems or areas of need to attend to—that is the work of mobilized interest groups. In practice, activism has enhanced the administrative capacity of the reforming state.

Luis's and Rose's trajectories, like those of many others, show how empowering pharmaceutical access can be but also how much additional effort is required to transform medicines that are "accessible" into medicines that are effective in the everyday lives of poverty-stricken patients. A vertical, top-down, mass campaign against a disease, although valuable, leaves unaddressed the social realities that co-construct health outcomes. Health policies need to be directed at *people*, not simply disease.

ANTHROPOLOGY OF THE MEANTIME

For more than ten years, I have chronicled life in and out of Caasah. By repeatedly returning to the field, one begins to grasp what happens in the *meantime*—and I like to think of this work as a study of the meantime—the events and practices that enable wider social and political change, alongside those that debilitate societies and individuals, dooming them to stasis and intractability. In such returns, entanglements and intricacies are revealed.

We witness how policies unfold over time—and the literalness of becoming, as AIDS survivors transition from patienthood back into personhood. I say *becoming*, for we have a responsibility to think of life in terms of both limits and crossroads, where technologies, interpersonal relations, and imagination can sometimes, against all odds, propel unexpected futures (Biehl and Locke 2010).

AIDS therapies are now embedded in landscapes of misery, and hundreds of grassroots services have helped to make AIDS a chronic disease even among the poorest in Brazil and beyond. These services are not a top-down, biopolitical form of control. The government is not using AIDS therapies and grassroots services as "techniques...to govern populations and manage individual bodies" (as anthropologist Vinh-Kim Nguyen [2005:126] has framed the politics of antiretroviral globalism). Based on my study of Caasah, I am arguing that the question of accountability has been displaced from government institutions and that poor AIDS populations take shape, if temporarily, through particular engagements with what is made pharmaceutically available. The political game here is one of self-identification. Proxy communities, often temporary and fragile, and interpersonal dynamics and desires are fundamental to life chances, unfolding in tandem with a state that is pharmaceutically present (via markets) but by and large institutionally absent. Against the backdrop of a limited health-care infrastructure and economic death and through multiple circuits of care, individual subjectivity is refigured as a *will to live*.

The anthropologist, upholding the rights of micro-analysis, brings into view the fields that people, in all their ambiguity, invent and live by. Such fields of action and significance—leaking out on all sides—are mediated by power and knowledge, and they are also animated by claims to basic rights *and* desires, as Rose affirms. It is not enough to simply observe that complicated new configurations of global, political, technical, and biological (and other) segments exist or are the temporary norm. We must attend to the ways these configurations are constantly constructed, undone and redone by the desires and becomings of actual people caught up in the messiness, the desperation and aspiration, of life in idiosyncratic milieus. Nor is ours necessarily a choice between primarily "global assemblages" (Collier and Ong 2005) and principally local "splinters" of a "world in pieces" (Geertz 2000). At the horizon of local dramas, in the course of each event, in the ups, downs, and arounds of each individual life, we can see the reflection of larger systems in the making (or unmaking). And in making public these singular fields—always on the verge of disappearing—the anthropologist still allows for larger structural processes and institutional idiosyncrasies to become visible and their true impact known. Thus, what we find is a movement from collective epidemic to personalized disease; from public health to the pharmaceuticalization of health care; from governmental distance to the industrialization of the nongovernmental sector and to a privatized politics of survival.

Critical questions abound: Can we think of the biopolitical as a multi-scale battle over the utility of government by private and public stakeholders? Does the "futility" of the biopolitical rehabilitation of surplus poor and diseased subjects (as in Luis's rendering of death-driven street patients) speak to the waning of civil society as a viable "transactional reality" for social justice? Might the subject of rights and the economic subject actually be included or excluded according to shared or similar logics, practices, technologies, and knowledges? And might inclusion in the name of rights, as we see in the world of global health and humanitarian interventions, be a key means by which one becomes part of a market segment? Is the market, then, what must be and is ultimately always produced both in government and by people?

PATIENT VALUE

The most prominent proponent of an approach that innovatively blends vertical technological intervention with a horizontal focus on making health systems work is anthropologist Paul E. Farmer (2001, 2004, 2010). Farmer and Partners In Health, the organization he cofounded with Jim Y. Kim, are especially interested in understanding diseases as nexuses of biological and social determinants of health, as well as revealing the structural conditions that make diseases possible and perpetuate them. Partners In Health works with local communities in Haiti, Boston, Peru, and now Rwanda. Each local clinic becomes a nexus of care, integrating HIV/AIDS treatment and prevention activities, for example, while also attempting to address coinfections and the new medical problems AIDS patients face as they age. Accounting for individual trajectories and staying with patients through the progression of the disease and treatment (the work of paid *accompagnateurs*) is considered as important as tackling the economic and social factors that impact their families and mitigating the demise of clinical infrastructures.

As part of his push for the best available care for the world's neediest people, Farmer (2008) urges the elimination of superficial metrics of "cost-effectiveness" that focus on particular interventions and shortsighted measurements of profits. His argument, however, is not a call to reject economics (in fact, it is this discipline's pragmatism that Farmer says others should emulate), but instead to incorporate different values and temporalities into the evaluation of initiatives that affect public health. In this way, Farmer is able to reject structural adjustment programs that demand the elimination of health expenditures in the name of economic development (increases in gross domestic product per capita that seldom make their way back to those most afflicted by austerity measures and budget cuts), which result in sicker populations with even slimmer chances of finding care in now crumbling public health systems (Pfeiffer and Chapman 2010). He also rejects the limitations of wraparound services imposed by cost-effectiveness benchmarks that fail to take into consideration the longer-term and far-reaching social, economic, and medical benefits of providing such services.

In an interesting convergence, Farmer and Kim have been collaborating with business scholar Michael E. Porter on the articulation of a science of global health delivery (Kim and Porter n.d.).[4] According to Porter (2009; Porter and Teisberg 2006), current systems of health-care delivery in the United States and globally rely on very narrow measurements of efficacy that concentrate exclusively on the intervention level and can only assess discrete preventative steps, drugs, or services. "Global health is stuck in an access and volume mindset, rather than focusing on the value delivered to patients" (Kim and Porter n.d.:4). For patient value to be achieved, interventions should be informed by a strategic framework that would orient the design and operation of health delivery systems as a whole instead of the discrete-component approach currently in use.

A more holistic understanding of health is called for, and interventions should be evaluated at the level of medical conditions. "the set of interrelated patient medical circumstances involving the full disease cycle" (Kim and Porter n.d.:11). In order to create such a framework, numerous and diverse disciplines (including anthropology) must be engaged, each producing knowledge at a different scale and perspective that can be integrated into a workable knowledge regarding the complexities of the context and content of interventions. At stake in the process is also changing the epistemic framework that informs donors' priorities and funding decisions, as well as global health evaluation schemes.

Meanwhile, the magic bullet approach, with its focus on drug delivery and supply chain management, stretches far beyond the antiretroviral rollout. Many tropical diseases have also been subject to blanket treatment approaches, including childhood malaria, river blindness, and parasitic infections. But as historians of the fight against syphilis and malaria remind us, eradication is an elusive target (Brandt 1987; Cueto 2007). Just as medical know-how, international political dynamics, and social realities change, so are biological systems in flux—bugs grow resistant, new infections appear. A more complex model of this flux of people–disease–policy *and* market dynamics is needed and requires innovative partnerships and methods as suggested by Farmer, Kim, and Porter.

Consider the widely cited study by economists Michael Kremer and Edward Miguel on curing worm infections in rural Kenya. Kremer and Miguel found that treating Kenyan schoolchildren with extremely cheap deworming medication increased their school attendance by some 10 percent. A *New York Times* op-ed heralded the study as "landmark" (Kristof 2007): with just a bit of cheap medication, poor countries could increase school attendance by leaps and bounds. Given the affordability and stunning success of the treatment, many commentators suspected that families who had not benefited from treatment during the study would very happily adopt this new technology.

But Kremer and Miguel (2007) then observed a puzzling turn of events when they followed a group of families outside the original study (their ethnographic turn) after the trial had ended. Among these families, those who were friendly with families in the treatment group were *less* likely to treat their children than those who were friendly with families in the control group. They were also less likely to deem the medication effective at improving health. If deworming medicine is the panacea for anemia and school truancy, then why were better-informed families not treating their children?

Here again we have a case in which the interpersonal relations and needs of people on the ground elude controlled studies. With their strict methodological imperatives, global health scholars, experts, and planners often sacrifice existing ethnographic evidence or counterknowledge as experiments and interventions (ever more closely linked) unfold—at the expense of better understanding and, ultimately, more meaningful and long-lasting outcomes.

The question of how to bring local communities into the very design and implementation of feasible (rather than technology-enamored) interventions is a continuous challenge. With international and national health policy success being largely reframed in terms of providing and counting the newest technology delivered, what space remains for the development of low-tech or nontech solutions (such as the provision of clean water) and the strengthening of public health systems and preventative measures that could prove more sustainable—and ultimately more humane?

FRAGILE ISLANDS OF HOSPITALITY

"If you look carefully, nothing has changed," a tired Celeste told me during my last visit to Caasah in August 2005. Caasah was still the only place in Salvador that provided systematic care to poor AIDS patients who had been discharged from public hospitals. "Some patients return to their families. Others go back to the streets. Disease keeps spreading, and the government pretends not to know."

At the state's AIDS ward, Dr. Nanci lamented, "We are still full of wasting patients. The difference now is that they come from the interior, where no new services have been created. Access to therapies has been democratized, but health has not." Many doctors do not put drug addicts and the homeless on antiretroviral therapy. They say that there is no guarantee that these people will continue the treatment and that they are concerned about the creation of viral resistance to ARVs. Thus, against an expanding discourse of human rights and pharmaceutical possibilities, we are here confronted with the on-the-ground limits of infrastructures wherein a new life with AIDS can be realized, but only in a limited way.

We can understand the conflicting effects of late liberal governance only by looking at the materiality of policies and related individual and communal struggles for survival. By ethnographically charting the ways policies and people operate at the margins, we can also illuminate political rationality in the making. Politics here is not a sphere, but a lack, a technology, and a process all at once. In the case of the AIDS policy, medication makes people equivalent—difference lies in laboratory testing and viral loads—and grassroots work must address the social determinants of patients' conditions or make those markers invisible. From the perspective of an outsourcing state, grassroots entities such as Caasah are important, if transient, social instruments of remediation. Yet, for AIDS patients, they become proxy families and communities, providing the context necessary to make ARVs work. Here medical commodities are used in tandem with other ways of claiming citizenship, and desperate and creative interactions occasion novel public sites in which rights and health are privatized alongside the emergence of novel political subjectivites.

Out of the initial group of twenty-two Caasah patients with whom I had worked in 1997, seven were still alive in 2005—among them, Luis and Rose. Their added life was obviously a result of technological advancements, argued Celeste, "but it would not have happened if they had not learned to care for themselves." In the end, treatment adherence, she stated "is relative to each person. It requires a lot of will." Yet, far from representing a natural vitality, this *will to live* has to be fabricated and asserted in the marketplace and in local medical worlds by those with the means, as limited as these are, to do so. Political subjectivity is here articulated through pastoral means, disciplinary practices of self-care, and monitored pharmaceutical treatment.

The politically ambiguous AIDS survivors with whom I worked had all engineered fragile islands of hospitality in which they could inhabit their unexpected lives. To have someone to live for and to be desired by was also a constant thread in their accounts. They all had a place they called home, some form of labor, a small, steady income, and a social network of sorts. In a pinch, they could still resort to Caasah. This institutional tie, as tenuous as it now was, remained vital to them. These AIDS citizens are active in the pursuit of health, although few are activists.

I also met Luis during that August 2005 visit. He was still working at Caasah. He was in charge of the institution's fund-raising activities. "I am not concerned with HIV. If there is medication, let's take life forward." In the preceding year, Luis had experienced kidney failure and had been hospitalized for two weeks. "Work keeps my mind occupied, and one needs projects and objectives to meet—if not, life has no meaning." "Becoming a father," he said, "is the best thing that ever happened to me." Davi, his adopted son, was now a happy seven-year-old. "He is my passion. He makes it all worthwhile."

Rose was doing great, as were her children. I was particularly happy to learn that her daughter had turned HIV-negative. Ricardo, her fifteen-year-old son, was helping two workers to finish the house's second floor. "It is my skyscraper. Water was infiltrating, and in the long run, I plan to rent it out." Rose intelligently navigates the local circuits of AIDS care. She had garnered the support of several NGOs, opened up a little business called Rose Tem de Tudo (Rose Has It All), and also devised a way of raising funds among religious philanthropists. She was proud of having been able to enroll her son in the project Teenage Citizen, which dona Conceição was running with World Bank funds.

Later that week, I met with dona Conceição. She was proud of her new project, which employed 120 children of AIDS patients in local industries, but she also regretted that hers remained the only institution to address AIDS in the streets. Her funds from a World Bank project would last only a year, and she still cared for some two hundred homeless families living with HIV/AIDS. "We cannot meet all the demand for help. It's a disgrace."

Without a doubt, Brazil has experienced a striking decrease in AIDS mortality. Seen from the perspective of the urban poor, however, the AIDS treatment policy is not necessarily an inclusive form of care. Local AIDS triage services and social and economic rights for the poorest are sporadic at best. Brazil, which has innovated in making access to treatment a human right, must more fully define and implement a right to health that transcends medicines and individual demands and must ensure that primary health care and prevention are sufficiently robust to reduce vulnerability to disease (Biehl et al. 2009). Also at issue is a reconsideration of the systemic relations among pharmaceutical research, commercial interest, and public health care. We should think about more sustainable solutions to the obstacles posed by patentability and business control over medical science and care on the ground. Part of the solution may lie in comprehensive information and technology sharing among Southern countries—a paradigm that would enable poorer countries to develop health technology assessment programs, pool their manufacturing know-how, and unite in the fight for fair pricing.

Caasah's former residents are the new people of AIDS. They have by all standards exceeded their destinies. Now receiving treatment, Luis, Rose, and many others refuse the condition of leftovers. And they face the daily challenge of translating medical investments into social capital and wage-earning potential. Thus, from their perspective, health in a time of global health is a painstaking work-in-progress by monadic patient-citizen-consumers in relation to therapeutic markets, ailing public health infrastructures, and improvised medical collectives. They live in between-moments, between-spaces, scavenging for resources. At every turn, they must consider the next step to be taken to guarantee life. Theirs is the force of immanence. From these people, as poet João Cabral de Melo Neto (2005:82) puts it, "you can learn that the human being is always the best measure, and that the measure of the human is not death, but life."

Acknowledgments

I am deeply grateful to Adriana Petryna, Tom Vogl, Sebastian Ramirez, Adriana Petryna, Joseph Amon, Amy Moran-Thomas, Alex Gertner, Ari Samsky, Peter Locke, Ramah McKay, Mariana Socal, Raphael Frankfurter, Edward Fischer, and Peter Benson for their comments and help. Research and writing have been supported by Princeton University's Health Grand Challenges Initiative and the Woodrow Wilson School of Public and International Affairs.

Notes

1. See http://www.unaids.org/en/Regionscountries/Regions/LatinAmerica/, accessed April 29, 2012.

2. See http://www.who.int/hiv/topics/treatment/en/index.html, accessed April 29, 2012.

3. See http://www.usaid.gov/our_work/global_health/aids/News/aidsfaq.html, accessed April 29, 2012.

4. See http://www.hbs.edu/rhc/global_health.html, accessed April 29, 2012.

Part II
Choices

Values and Rationalities

8

Not by P Alone

Deirdre N. McCloskey

My friend the noble and Nobel-worthy economist Bob Frank will try to persuade you that apparently imprudent behavior such as anger can arise nonetheless from prudent sources—not from an immediately calculating source, perhaps, but from behavior evolved in human society for a rational purpose.[1] Economists specialize in such reasoning. What morality a market has, they declare, has rational causes, by which they mean another tale in the adventures of Max U whom only an economist could love. I propose here to argue against Bob and against many other of my beloved economist colleagues.

Now Prudence is the *central* virtue of the bourgeoisie, in the way that Courage is of the aristocrat-hero or Love is of the peasant-saint. But the point is that Prudence is not the only virtue and to turn, as Bob does, to evolved rationality misses the point. Mothers love. Fathers have courage. *That* is where a theory of markets and morality should start, not at just-so stories about evolved behavior depending entirely on Prudence.

In Adam Smith's (1776) book about Prudence, *An Inquiry into the Nature and Causes of the Wealth of Nations*, he embedded it among the other virtues, such as Justice and, especially, Temperance. Smith (1982) himself provided the embedding in his only other book (in some ways a better one), *The Theory of Moral Sentiments* (more people nowadays are reading Smith this way, as an ethical philosopher; see McCloskey 2008).

If Smith had been also a modern econometrician, he would have put it this way: Take any sort of willed behavior you wish to understand—browbeating an enemy, say, or brooding on a vote or birthing children or buying lunch or adopting the Bessemer process in the making of steel. Call it B for behavior. Brooding, buying, borrowing, birthing, bequeathing, bonding, boasting, blessing, bidding, bartering, bargaining, baptizing, banking, baking. It can be put on a scale and measured or perhaps seen to be present or absent. You want to give an account of B, a little story about what causes it to happen, with quantitative weights on the causes, if your ambition is scientific rather than philosophical.

What the Prudence-Only fellows, from Machiavelli to Judge Posner of the United States Court of Appeals for the Seventh Circuit, are claiming is that you can explain B by Prudence Only, the P variables of price, pleasure, payment, pocketbook, purpose, planning, property, profit, prediction, punishment, prison, purchasing, power, practice—in a word, the Profane.

Adam Smith and John Stuart Mill and John Maynard Keynes and Joseph Schumpeter and Albert O. Hirschman and quite a few other economists have replied that, no, you have forgotten Love and Courage, Justice and Temperance, Faith and Hope, that is, social Solidarity, the S variable of speech, semiotics, society, sympathy, service, stewardship, sentiment, sharing, soul, salvation, spirit, symbols, stories, shame—in a word, the Sacred. The two-level universe of the axial religions are these, the Profane and the Sacred. The two summarizing commandments, I have noted, refer to the two levels: (1) love God, and (2) love your neighbor. As the historian of religion Mircea Eliade (1959:14) wrote, "sacred and profane are two modes of being in the world."

Or at least they are two modes of being in a God-haunted world, especially the places that trace their religions to Abraham. A world without al-Lah is magical or materialist, merging the sacred and the profane into a single plane of technical tricks. The shaman's tent and the local Brookstone store have a lot in common. In both, you get gadgets for dealing with life piecemeal, trick by trick (McCloskey 1991). The special holiness of a YHWH separated from mere human tricks and gadgets is reflected in the Christian Lord's Prayer, "Our Father who art in heaven, *hallowed* be thy name," and in every other bit of monotheism.

The gods of polytheism are less sacred and less set apart from us because they are competitive. In the Cantonese Temple of the Five Hundred Gods, which was destroyed in the Cultural Revolution, a supplicant could choose from a diverse portfolio of gods to whom she could offer incense, the way one lights a candle before the shrines of the Blessed Virgin *and* Saint

Thomas *and* Saint James (Stark 2001:20). The Protestants were protesting such residual polytheism among the Romans—"the Romish doctrine concerning...worshipping and adoration...of images as of relics, and also invocation of saints,...a fond thing vainly invented, and grounded upon no warranty of scripture; but rather repugnant to the word of God," as the Anglicans put it.[2] It is repugnant to the word of al-Lah, the One, *echad*.

The Japanese, lacking gods, especially a single jealous, monopolizing God, mix the sacred and the profane in ways that startle a Westerner accustomed by a monotheistic culture to a strict separation (Bellah 2003:13). Favors of friendship or clientage in the West are supposed to be granted with the free hand of a proud aristocrat or a charitable Christian. They have value precisely because they are *not* accounted for in a bourgeois way. Ruth Benedict (1989:61) claimed to see in Japanese life up to the American occupation a "postulate of indebtedness" that reduced the sacred to the profane. The Japanese, she said, view favors as exchanges, for which written records are kept and even a species of interest charged if the redemption is long in coming. "Americans are not accustomed to applying these financial criteria to a casual treat at the soda fountain or to the years' long devotion of a father to his motherless child," but "in Japan they are regarded quite as financial solvency is in America and the sanctions behind them are as strong as they are in the United States behind being able to pay one's bills" (Benedict 1989:142–143). The truly virtuous in Japan, she claims, are those who pay their ethical bills, "like our stories of honest men who pay off their creditors by incredible personal hardships" (1989:142–143, see also 121, 113, 115).

Whether this description of the Japanese is accurate (and we have, in fact, considerable doubts) is not here important. It is in any case a tale of P taking over from S. Economists have specialized in the profane P, anthropologists in the sacred S. But most behavior, B, is explained by both:

$$B = \alpha + \beta P + \gamma S + \varepsilon$$

To include both P and S is only sensible, and sociologists call it a "multiplex" calculation. However, it is not wishy-washy or unprincipled. The economist Amartya Sen (1987:71) is not abandoning economics when he calls for "a remedial expansion of the set of variables and influences that find room in economic analysis." In an analysis of the bargaining power of women in various times and cultures, for example, one may admit as simply true, without betrayal of one's identity as a quantitative social scientist, that norms, laws, and the obligations of love matter. Nor, on the other side, is it a betrayal of the interpretive turn to admit that the relative economic productivity of women and the relative physical strength of men mediated through sanctions on wife beating matter, too. Both work. Of the neorationalist claim that everything can be reduced to P, the philosopher Jerry Fodor (1998) remarks: "I suppose it could turn out that one's interest in having friends, or in reading fictions, or in Wagner's operas, is really at heart prudential. But the claim affronts a robust, and I should think salubrious, intuition that there are lots and lots of things that we care about simply for themselves. Reductionism about this plurality of goals, when not Philistine or cheaply cynical, often sounds simply funny. Thus the joke about the lawyer who is offered sex by a beautiful girl. 'Well, I guess so,' he replies, 'but what's in it for me?'"

The equation including both P and S is a figure of speech, not a program for actual quantitative research. I do not mean to suggest by it that the Sacred can be made into the same units of influence on B as the Profane. Identity is not the same as prudence, and recent attempts to absorb the sacred into the profane as a sort of exalted commodity are of limited value, limited by the very sacredness in question. There are *some* prices at which *some* women might be induced to become prostitutes. But we are not talking here only about the price. As Immanuel Kant said, "in the realm of ends everything has either a *price* or a *dignity*. Whatever has a price can be replaced by something else as its equivalent; on the other hand, whatever is above all price, and therefore admits of no equivalent, has a dignity" (McClay 1993:397).

On the other hand, I do not wish to offer comfort to the followers of Karl Polanyi, such as the late great classical historian Moses Finley, who believe that because the ancient world had views of S that devalued businessmen, it was not subject to the ordinary economics of supply and demand. That is mistaken, too, serving merely to exempt the substantivists—the economic anthropologists rejecting modern economics—from having to learn the wearisome mathematics and statistics that go along with P factors in the economy. Modern economies are just as imbued with multiplex virtues as were ancient ones. John Stuart Mill (1909:2) wrote that "the creed and laws of a people act powerfully upon their economical condition; and this again, by its influence on their mental development and social relations, reacts upon their creed and laws." Any society operates with both P and S variables:

Prudence	Solidarity
Price	Sympathy
Payment	Service
Pocketbook	Soul

Purpose	Spirit
Planning	Sentiment
Property	Stewardship
Profit	Salvation
Prediction	Semiotics
Punishment	Shame
Purchase	Symbols
Private	Society
Power	Speech
Practice	Stories

Let me use the metaphor of an equation, nonetheless—though I do realize that it will tempt some of my economist colleagues to put S in dollar terms. I just want to remind them of a technical point. It is that, econometrically speaking, unless the P and S variables are orthogonal, which is to say unless they are entirely independent, or unless the covariance of P and S is zero or unless there is reason to believe that a variable such as PS multiplied together has no influence, an estimate of the coefficients α and β that ignores S or PS will give biased results. An increase in sample size will not solve the problem. Technically, the estimates will be inconsistent. The bias and inconsistency are important if the S variable is important. The experiment is not properly controlled. Its conclusions are nonsense.

A career in business must have a transcendent goal. Economics professors who doubt this should ask themselves why *they* work. If solely for the paycheck, perhaps they should seek another line of work. They are unlikely, with such a utility function, to perform well the Alasdair MacIntyrean (1981:187) practice of being an economics professor—*practice* in this sense being "any...co-operative human activity through which goods internal to that form of activity are realized...with the result that human powers to achieve excellence...are systematically extended." In business, the case is the same.

The pseudo or actually transcendent goal can be as profane as merely keeping score in a macho game of acquisition. He who dies with the most toys wins. But it can also be devotion to workmanship, a duty, a calling— being an apartment manager who provides the tenants with a decent place to live or a dentist who fends off gum disease in her patients. Or providing goods for poor people in Walmart. Or enlarging the life opportunities for one's family. These are devotions, too. We Christians say that unless the transcendent reaches to God, you are liable to be indulging in idolatry of things in this transient world and will be gravely disappointed. But a desire for the transcendent is (an evolved?) characteristic of human beings, which social scientists ignore at their peril.

A particular sacred goal will commonly change the workings of prudence. This is what is right about Moses Finley's view of the ancient economy—though contrary to his view, the market for grain in ancient Greece and Rome would still have worked, and did in fact work, pretty much as it does now, with or without a change in the workings of prudence. Again, the modification of pure prudence has been discovered to be powerfully influential in laboratory experiments, as Elizabeth Hoffman (Hoffman and Spitzer 1985) and Robert Frank himself and many others have noted.[3] If you allow the subjects to talk to one another, or even recruit subjects who are already friends, the P-Only behavior falls toward zero. People cooperate "irrationally" in aid of sacred solidarity.

The economist Frank Knight (1997:306 n.) noted in 1935, "Rigorously speaking, there is no such thing as an economic interest, or a material interest," no human with P-Only motivations, because "economic interest is never final; it is an interest in the efficacy of activity, and the use of means, in promoting…final interest. And these final interests do not inhere in particular physical things…but are all, at bottom, social interests. Even the food interest, the 'most' material of all, is in concrete content overwhelmingly a matter of social standards." Knight, who was philosophically sophisticated for a modern economist, would have been aware that *final* is the Latin for the Aristotelian "having to do with the *telos*, the end or purpose." The professor of law James Boyd White (1990:70) notes that "'exchange,' upon which economics focuses too much, is a secondary rather than primary mode of life. It presupposes another world, in which it is embedded and which it can strengthen or weaken." The economic historian John Nye (1997:132 n.) explores the logic of P-Only in the last thousand years of ruler and ruled in Europe—but he starts, as any discussion of literal or tax slavery must, at the S value of freedom: "Individuals value that freedom more than anyone else" and therefore are willing to make deals with their ruler to buy it. We desire, said Aristotle (1934) at the beginning of the *Nicomachean Ethics*, some ends for their own sake, some S. It is mistaken to think that P-Only can be a life for a human.

But the myth of *Kapitalismus*, to use the German word in honor of its heavy German usage, is that it consists precisely of the absence of any purpose other than accumulation "for its own sake." Thus, the late and princely Robert Heilbroner (1999:201) said, "Capitalism has been an expansive system from its earliest days, a system whose driving force has been the effort to accumulate ever larger amounts of capital itself."[4] Thus, Max Weber (1958:53), too, in 1905: "The *summum bonum* of this ethic [is] the earning of more and more money.... Acquisition...[is] the ultimate purpose of life." These descriptions are straight Marx, money to capital to money.

At the level of individuals, there has never been any evidence for it. The chief evidence Weber gives is his humorless and literal reading of *The Autobiography of Benjamin Franklin*. Of course, Weber (1958:51) modified the pointlessness of the Marxian impulse by claiming that "this philosophy of avarice" depends on a transcendent "*duty* of the individual toward the increase of his capital" (italics added). But his Franklin, who after all was no Calvinist, at age forty-two abandoned forever the life of "endless" accumulation and devoted the rest of his long life to science and public purposes. So much for "ever larger amounts of capital itself."

Many fine scholars believe this claim that modern life is unusually devoted to gain. They are mistaken. "The unlimited hope for gain in the market," writes the otherwise admirable political theorist Joan Tronto (1993:29), "would teach people an unworkable premise for moral conduct, since the very nature of morality seems to dictate that desires must be limited by the need to coexist with others." Running a business, though, would teach anyone that gain is limited. Dealing in a market would teach that desires must be limited by the need to coexist with others. Scarcity, regard for others, and the liberal values of a market society work as the tuition of an ethical school. Pagan or Christian preachments, absent capitalism, did not.

Even so fine an anthropological historian as Alan Macfarlane (1987:226) believes the Marxist/Weberian lore. "The ethic of endless accumulation," he writes, "as an end and not a means, is the central peculiarity of capitalism." If it were, the miser would be a strictly modern figure and not proverbial in every literature in the world. In China, the poet Tang Bo Ju-yi (772–846 CE) complained of the salt-tax monopolist (the Chinese state sold and resold to the bourgeoisie the right to buy and sell salt): "The salt merchant's wife / has silk and gold aplenty, / but she does not work at farming [in Confucianism the only honorable source of gain for the non-elite], /... Her gleaming wrists have gotten plump, / Her silver bracelets tight" (Owen 1996:501). Or Liu Zong-yuan (773–819 CE), in a parable comparing the miser to a pack beetle: "Those in our own times who lust to lay hold of things, will never back away when they chance on possessions by which to enrich their household [just like the beetle, carrying on his back whatever useful thing he encounters, even twice his weight]. They don't understand that it encumbers them, and fear only that they won't accumulate enough" (Owen 1996:617–618).

Accumulate, accumulate. "In this consists the difference between the character of a miser," wrote Adam Smith (1982:173) in 1759, "and that of a person of exact economy and assiduity. The one is anxious about small matters for their own sake; the other attends to them only in consequence of the scheme of life which he has laid down for himself."

At the level of the society as a whole, we *do* see "unlimited" accumulation. Corporations with supposedly infinite lives—though in truth 10 percent, such as Kodak, die every year—are indeed machines of accumulation. The individual economic molecules that make up the river of capitalism may not always want more, but the river as a whole, it is said, keeps rolling along. True, and to our good. The machines and improved acreage and splendid buildings, and so forth, that we inherited from an accumulating past are good for us now.

But no evidence exists for accumulation being peculiar to capitalism. Infinitely lived institutions like "families" or "churches" or "royal lineages" existed before modern capitalism and were sites of accumulation. Thus, the improved acreage spreading up the hillsides under the pressure of population before onslaught of the Black Death. Thus, the splendid building of the medieval cathedral, a project of centuries. Accumulation is not the heart of modern capitalism, as economists have understood at least since the calculations by M. Abramowitz and R. Solow in the 1950s and before them the calculations by G. T. Jones in 1933.[5] Its heart is innovation.

Judge Posner has long advocated "wealth maximization" as the standard for good law. If judges arrange the laws of liability so that the economic pie is made as large as possible, then our wealth—*our* meaning the society's as a whole—is maximized. Good. You can see the merit of his argument, a utilitarian one. It goes along with "unlimited" accumulation. But in 1980 Posner was checkmated in two moves by another eminent legal scholar, Ronald Dworkin (1980), who made the same observation as Knight had, that wealth is a means, not an end in itself.[6]

The observation is ancient. Aristotle (1934, vol. 1:8) said in the *Nicomachean Ethics*, "Clearly wealth is not the Good we are in search of, for it is only good as being useful, *a means to something else*" (italics added). The ends of justice, in and of themselves or for the sake of love or faith or hope, can be served by greater social wealth, to be sure. But they can be corrupted by greater social wealth, too. Whether the historical balance has been positive or negative is an empirical matter. And in any case, an economist would recommend that if you want justice or faith to prosper, you should pursue them directly, not indirectly and uncertainly through another, allegedly correlated, means, such as the accumulation of wealth.

Bob Frank (1988:211) has shown in detail that "the most adaptive behaviors will not spring from the [direct, simple, short-run] quest for material advantage." By this statement, he means that people love or leave tips or build reputations because of their character and that what is "adaptive" about it is not instant profit, but our very long-term survival. In some ways, his is also the vision of Adam Ferguson and David Hume and Adam Smith: we build a successful *commercial* society out of love and justice, too; trust spreads, as it in fact did in the eighteenth century. The contractarian philosopher David Gauthier is the modern master of this sort of sweet reasoning.

Yet, I doubt that Bob is right to cling to "survival" as the goal of human life and therefore the just-so stories of evolutionary psychology. What about human flourishing, beyond bread alone? What about the spandrels of San Marco and other accidental results of evolution that Stephen Jay Gould and Richard Lewontin showed can undermine the retrospective claims of functionality? Love is surely not *only* a "commitment mechanism," a way of keeping people from wasting time looking for new mates when the one they have is pretty good already. Bob's argument is cute and parallels nicely, as he points out, the requirement of a lease in rental property. Swell. But he would not say, I think (and *never* to his wife), that it is a full account of love (see Frank 1988:196 nn.).[7]

In any case, "the self-interest [P-Only] model," Frank (1988:256) argues, with numerous tests and examples, "provides a woefully inadequate description of the way people actually behave." Frank's (2004:26) most amusing and persuasive case in point is the following: "When a man dies shortly after drinking the used crankcase oil from his car, we do not really explain anything by asserting that he must have had a powerful taste for crankcase oil." Amartya Sen (1987:13) puts it so: "If a person does exactly the opposite of what would help achieving what he or she would want to achieve, and does this with flawless consistency,...the person can scarcely be seen as rational." Making "empathy" or "a powerful taste" or "consistency = rationality" into an all-purpose motive that explains everything else is unhelpful. We have renamed love "empathy." And for what scientific gain? *Alors? Nu?*

But further, Love is not love—not the best sort of love for another human and certainly not Aristotle's or Jesus's or C. S. Lewis's highest sort of agape—if it is utilitarian. In *The Maltese Falcon*, Brigid O'Shaughnessy almost runs out of arguments to persuade Sam Spade to let her go:

> She put her hands up to his cheeks and drew his face down again. "Look at me," she said, "and tell me the truth. Would you

> have done this to me if the falcon had been real and you had
> been paid your money?"
>
> He moved his shoulders a little and said, "Well, a lot of money
> would have been at least one more item on the other side of the
> scales."
>
> She put her face up to his face. Her mouth was slightly open
> with lips a little thrust out. She whispered: "If you loved me you'd
> need nothing more on that side." [Hammett 1984:215]

That is right. Orderings and trade-offs of material things are irrelevant to
True Love. It is not for sale.

But Spade will not be persuaded. "Dreading the role of the chump,"
says Bob Frank (1988:xi) in making a point about the general case, "we are
often loath to heed our nobler instincts." Or more exactly, we let one nobil-
ity trump another. Loyalty to his profession as a detective, Faith in his identity as a nonchump, Spade says, wins against putative Love. True Love—or
True Patriotism or True Courage or True Faith or True Anything—is not
an input into something else, or else it is not True.

"It is in the nature of loving," the philosopher Harry Frankfurt (2004:42)
observes, "that we consider its objects to be valuable in themselves and to be
important to use for their own sakes" (compare Aristotle's notion of friendship). So says theology, literature, Patsy Cline, and any characterization of
humans that is not based on an analogy with accounting—one more item
on this side of the scales—that is, Prudence. "If a strength [of character,
one of the twenty-four they identify] is recognized only when it produces
a payoff," the psychologists Christopher Peterson and Martin Seligman
(2004:19) argue, "we do not need the notion of good character to account
for human conduct. We can return to a radical behaviorism and speak
only of prevailing rewards and punishments, in the style of Steven Levitt
of *Freakonomics* fame (Steve claims implausibly, from a tenured post at the
University of Chicago, to be therefore a 'rogue' economist; some rogue).
But as Aristotle and other philosophers concerned with virtue persuasively
argue, actions undertaken solely for external reasons cannot be considered
virtuous, because they are coaxed or coerced, carroted or sticked."

The compulsion to find some Prudential seed for so-called virtues is
modern. Benjamin Franklin himself claimed famously to be governed by
Prudence Only, a rhetoric popular by the time he composed the first part
of his *Autobiography*. Alexis de Tocqueville (1954:130) said, "In the United
States as...elsewhere people are sometimes seen to give way to those disinterested...impulses...; but the Americans seldom admit [it]...they are more

anxious to do honor to their philosophy than to themselves." Like that of his countrymen, and Steve Levitt and Robert Frank, Franklin's rhetoric was self-deluded. In his life, he was a good friend and a good citizen, just and courageous, hopeful and temperate. Carl Van Doren noted that people "praise his prudence. But at seventy he became a leader of a revolution" (Lepore 2008:82). He was not perfect, but he was not a Prudence-Only machine, a goyisher kop, not at all. Max Weber, D. H. Lawrence, William Carlos Williams, and even the perspicacious Alasdair MacIntyre, raised in Scotland, fail to grasp this characteristic of their "pattern American."

Even very sensible philosophers want nowadays to deny such observations by reducing every virtue to Prudence. In his last book, Robert Nozick (2001:244) tried to argue that "ethics exists because at least sometimes it is possible to coordinate actions to mutual benefit." Or "ethics arises when frequently or importantly there are situations offering opportunities for mutual benefit from coordinated activity" (2001:246). And a utilitarian—which Nozick was not—would say that "since cooperation to mutual benefit is the function of ethics, the only thing that matters is...the size of the social pie" (2001:256).

But after sixty-four closely reasoned pages, Nozick is left worrying that ethics must have something more. The reason he gets into trouble is that he makes the characteristically modern philosophical mistake of simply defining ethics as "concerning interpersonal relations" (Nozick 2001:248). That is, his main argument has no place for the virtues of self-improvement or of devotion to a transcendent. It is a middle-level ethics, neither at the Hope–Faith–Love transcendent and Sacred top or the Temperance–Courage workaday and Profane bottom, but aimed at Justice implemented with Prudence. It is entirely about economics, that is, "Pareto optimality" or mutually beneficial deals. The ethical object is the other people in the deal, not ever oneself as Profane or God as Transcendent.

But I said Nozick was sensible. And I can hardly imagine a more intellectually honest person. So, occasionally in his book, he breaks into praise for the alternative ethical objects, as though realizing uneasily that his reduction to prudent deals has not sufficed. He distinguishes four "levels or layers of ethics," referring to a treatment in his semipopular book *The Examined Life* (1989; see Nozick 2001:280, 1989:212–215). The first, or lowest, is the mutual benefit on which Nozick spends most of his analytic effort in the book, Pareto optimality, the ethic of respect. The next highest is an ethic of responsibility, discussed also in his earlier book *Philosophical Explanations* (1981:499–570).[8] The next is an ethic of caring, Nozick's version of love. And the highest is an ethic of Light, "truth, goodness, beauty, holiness," or, in other words, the ethics of faith, hope, and transcendent love (1989:214).

Nozick admits that he has no account of how the levels relate or why he should always refer to the ethics of respect as basic—except on the not unreasonable political grounds that it is the least controversial. He has no acquaintance with the virtue ethicists. They are never referred to by this most ethically obsessed of the analytic philosophers—the two references to Bernard Williams in *Invariances* (2001) are on matters of metaphysics, not ethics. Aristotle is discussed only briefly as an ethical theorist; Saint Thomas Aquinas is not mentioned in any work of Nozick, nor are any other virtue ethicists (see Nozick 1981:515 nn.). He appears not to have read with any care Smith's *The Theory of Moral Sentiments*. His 2001 book speaks of Smith's favorite book as holding a theory of the "ideal observer," a misquotation placed in quotation marks—the phrase is the "impartial spectator," not the "ideal observer." And the passage construes Smith's notion as being about "moral" matters having to do with other people, not the self-shaping temperance that is the chief theme of *The Theory* (Nozick 2001:288). Nozick, like Frankfurt and other mainline English-speaking analytic philosophers, finds himself trapped at the bottom of a Kantian well, unable to clamber up to the virtue-ethical fields of flowers lying round it.

Bob Frank (1988:258) wants to offer a "friendly amendment" to P-Only, namely, that people commit at a higher level to having a good character S-style, which is then advantageous. I am not so sure his suggestion is "friendly" to the belief of most economists that P-Only Rules. If one admits S in the thorough way Frank does and as a few economists such as George Akerlof and Bruno Frey do, one ends like Adam Smith, speaking of the values and relations of a particular form of life, that is, the transcendent and the self-disciplining. One does not stay, like Jeremy Bentham or Gary Becker or Richard Posner, fixated on the single virtue of prudence for pleasure.

The sacred and the profane are woven together. Take, for example, the characteristically transcendent commodity of modernism, the Sacred Work of High Art. Olav Velthuis (2005), a young Dutch scholar and journalist who worked with Arjo Klamer of Erasmus University, has studied the pricing of first-time sales of high-art paintings in New York and Amsterdam and interviewed hundreds of dealers. Among art dealers and among the economists watching the art dealers, Velthuis notes, prudence has a rhetoric. The economist-observer would wish to find that the pricing of art is profane, a matter of wealth maximization. Yet, the dealer-participant wants to play both roles, *both* sacred and profane. He or she wants to be the Pater- or

Materfamilias in a sacred imitation of the family *and* the Smart Cookie in a profane imitation of the stock exchange. P and S, both, rule.

How dealers in the first-time purchase and sale of art negotiate such a contradiction with their *talk* is crucial: "The highly ritualized way in which contemporary art is marketed is not just a matter of cultural camouflage but is the heart of what the art market is about. Therefore it makes sense to study how dealers talk when they do business" (Velthuis 2005:52). Indeed it does. Economists and some sociologists want to stick with an eighth-floor view. Velthuis (2005:28) also wants to get down into the rhetoric of the lifeworld, "to supplement Bourdieu's structural reading of the market for symbolic goods with a symbolic reading." It does seem natural to read symbols symbolically. Late Pollocks and the market talk *about* late Pollocks and anything to do with late Pollocks are certainly symbolic.

But the economist wants to read any price as Prudence and the anthropologist wants to leave *that* to the economist. The anthropologist want to read High Art as Solidarity, and the economist wants to leave *that* to the anthropologist. But all this leaving-of-*that* to the other leaves the first-time pricing of art underexplained.

The avant-garde circuit that is the focus of Velthuis's research creates two spaces: the front room of the private art gallery in Soho in New York or the Museum Quarter in Amsterdam and the back room—the sacred museum out in front and the profane office behind. He contrasts the dual ritual of the avant-garde circuit with a third "commercial" circuit of more accessible art, sold at high prices on Michigan or Seventh Avenues or at lower prices on Hilton Head Island or at still lower prices off a truck at the local mall. The dealers on the commercial circuit "bring out their own straightforwardness and honesty" (Velthuis 2005:52). The commercial dealer is bourgeois, the avant-garde aristocratic, and each defines herself by contrast to the other. The reigning duchess of the avant-garde circuit, Marian Goodman, prefers to be called a "gallerist" rather than a "dealer." She was asked by a journalist what the difference was, but she would not say. The journalist speculated, "The French-sounding 'gallerist' signals... an old-fashioned cosmopolitan ethos, for which the Atlantic Ocean is a lake shared by aspirants to transnational culture" (Schjeldahl 2004:41).

The avant-garde dealers give the art museums discounts precisely because the work will not therefore enter into the profaning world of auction houses or commercial dealers. The auction price is higher, but the gallerist spurns it. The gaps Velthuis observes between gallery and auction prices are large and explained by the steady effort of the gallery owners to keep their circuit separate from the other. From an economist's P-Only point of view, their efforts are crazy, as though sellers of wheat in Chicago just *detested* the idea that some of their lovely red winter product would end up getting sold in, of all vulgar places, *Liverpool*. "Dealers actively seek to control the 'biography' of artworks that leave their gallery," and "selling to the highest bidder was considered 'immoral,' 'very unethical,' and 'extremely controversial'" (Velthuis 2005:81). Getting a higher price is "controversial"? We are not in a bourgeois ethical world after all.

In particular, for S reasons, the dealers want their artists to have shapely careers with an impoverished bohemian beginning, a vigorous middle, and an honored and wealthy old age, in the style of Monet. One dealer put it this way: "Young artists deserve a grace period in which what they do can be viewed as a work of art, not a price tag" (Velthuis 2005:89). The price for the same work is about the same across the various avant-garde galleries but insulated from commerce, family style. The gallery owner is "an educator and confidant" (Velthuis 2005:95). Marion Goodman declared that "the choice of whom to work with goes to one's spiritual core. It starts with intuition, but it's important to reflect on how deep a commitment one feels before one gets involved" (Schjeldahl 2004:41). The Profane is enabled by the Sacred, but the Sacred is the end. The Marxist cycle of Money–Capital–More Money is not correct. What is correct is the cycle of Sacred–Profane–More Sacred.

Arjo Klamer himself gives another example of how P and S interact. The charitable organization Doctors Without Borders (Médecins Sans Frontières [MSF]) was asked whether it would accept a large cash contribution. Well, why not? The P-Only logic of economics says that a contribution relaxes the budget constraints, making more of the organization's good works possible by paying more doctors to work for it. But in fact Doctors Without Borders turned down the contribution. The problem was that the very meaning of the organization was the grace of the gift *from the doctors*. To make them into merely paid employees would transform the enterprise into just another hospital. Likewise, a couple of weeks after the Indian Ocean tsunami, the organization outraged some people by turning down further contributions to its relief work. "As you know, it is very important to MSF that we use your contribution as you intend it to be used," Médecins Sans Frontières said on its website. "This is why we want to let you know that at this time, MSF estimates that we have received sufficient funds for our currently foreseen emergency response in South Asia."[9] Some doctors laboring in the same needful fields sneer at such purity, pointing out that MSF therefore puts its or its contributors' sacred identity rather than the health of patients at the center of its concern. But the sneer itself is an expression of sacred identity: we are not those moral aesthetes at Doctors Without Borders, but practical, high-volume care providers who understand that money is money.

Similarly, the National Baseball Hall of Fame and Museum in Cooperstown will only accept *donations* of memorabilia—it never buys them. The Salvation Army in Naples, Florida, returned a $100,000 donation from the winner of the $14.4 million Florida Lotto jackpot in 2002 since it believes that gambling is a sin. The Salvation Army will not employ even highly competent gays and lesbians, if they are out, since it believes that homosexuality is a sin on the sacred grounds of two misread prohibitions in the Hebrew Bible and one in Paul's letters. The Salvation Army and the conservative Anglicans unhappy with the gay bishop of New Hampshire and the parents who push gay children out onto the streets follow strictly these two thou-shalt-nots in Leviticus 10:13 and 20:13 and the five in the Ten Commandments. They do not follow the 358 other thou-shalt-nots of orthodox Judaism. Whether this odd selection has any rationale, the gift or the principle or the identity is Sacred. *Sacred* here does not mean "admirable" or "following Jesus's example of love" or even "based on competent biblical scholarship familiar with Hebrew and Aramaic and Greek." The point is that the Salvation Army's beliefs on these matters are not for sale.

Klamer draws out the moral with a personal example. Suppose you go in distress to a good friend, who spends an hour over coffee comforting you. At the end of the hour, the friend says, "All right, time's up. That'll be $100, for counseling." Because the consultation happened as part of "friendship," such a demand is impossible, friendship destroying. As the sociologist Allan Silver put it, "friendships are diminished in moral quality if terms of exchange between friends are consciously or scrupulously monitored" (Pahl 2000:62).[10] Yes, or at any rate, in an axial culture maintaining a large gap between the Sacred and the Profane. Never mind that the counseling services would be more prudently allocated among competing uses if a price system were introduced, as it already has been in the allocation of donuts and movie tickets. Friendship at Aristotle's highest level is transcendently Sacred. At its lower levels, it is more like trade, accepting each other in spite of what we know. Yet, it has an element of transcendence in that it goes beyond Prudence or Justice and is something higher than literal, priced trade.

Likewise, you would not run your home entirely on prudential principles, requiring your children to pay for their meals. *This does not mean that P variables play no role whatever in friendship or in families.* As Sen (1987:19) puts it, "normal economic transactions would break down if self-interest played no substantial part at all in our choices." Instead, *both* P and S are at work. *Of course* the S variables are the conditions under which the P variables work, and *of course* the P variables modify the effects of S variables. "The confounding of the sacred and the profane," says the literary critic Stephen Greenblatt (2004:112), "are characteristics of virtually the whole of Shakespeare's achievement as a dramatist." No wonder. It is the human condition. The store clerk from whom you buy your glazed donut every morning can become a "friend," then a friend, then perhaps a Friend.

John Stuart Mill put it well in a classic definition of political economy as "the science which traces the laws of such of the phenomena of society as arise from the combined operations of mankind for the production of wealth, *in so far as those phenomena are not modified by the pursuit of any other object*" (1874:Essay V, v.39). Yes, P-objects are the usual focus of economic analysis, but the analysis is modified by S-objects, such as an imprudent love for Harriet Taylor or a disinterested and highly unpopular advocacy of rights for women or a high-minded sentiment of unity and solidarity with other human beings. For the same reason we have star-crossed lovers and political martyrs.

In the wider view, as I have already noted, there is no such thing as a pure P production phenomenon. At about the time of Mills's last edition of *Principles of Political Economy*, the younger economists decided that whatever value a product has depends on S variable tastes. No labor resides in a commodity and explains its value. Taste value, and the opportunity cost of being unable to have some other taste value, such as amaretto if you select chocolate this time, is all the economy runs on, said the generation of 1871.

David Hume had hinted at a similar consumption-oriented economics in 1751 when forces were gathering in Scotland to constitute the non–French Enlightenment. P variables—that is, self-love, rationality, utility, labor costs, and production—he argued, come to be experienced only because of the exercise of an S variable. "If I have not vanity," he wrote, "I take no delight in praise…. Were there no appetite of any kind antecedent to self-love, that propensity could scarcely ever exert itself because we should…have felt few and slender pains and pleasures" (Hume 1751:301). Before Hume, Bishop Butler (1736:351) had noted that "the very idea of an interested pursuit necessarily presupposes particular passions or appetites…. Take away these affections and you leave self-love absolutely nothing at all to employ itself about." And before him, Cicero (1938:189) had written that "everyone loves himself, not with a view of acquiring some profit for himself from his self-love, but because he is dear to himself on his own account." The P variable of profit means nothing without an S variable of Sentiment.

The S variables themselves are more than vanity of vanities. You do, of course, get some ponderable and perhaps vain pleasure from your family. True. And you get ponderable pain as well. But the family sprung in the first instance from Love. Given love, a child is to its parent a unit of pain or pleasure in a calculus. But neither would weigh without being at the outset, as Cicero says, "dear" (*carus*). The P and S intertwine.

That is, even the character of the purely Prudent, Pleasure-loving person, an apparently Shallow Hal of instrumentalism, depends on character and on love false or true formed somewhere else than on the Profane side of life. The philosopher David Schmidtz (1996:168) puts it this way: "If there was nothing for the sake of which we were surviving, reflection on this fact would tend to undermine our commitment to survival," like an Oblomov or a Bartleby. The "something for the sake of which" is our identity, our faith. It can be as good and profound as a true love for a merciful God or as bad and superficial as an unreflective "love" of Being Cool. But if it is not there, if you have not love, if you lack the striving for the transcendent, you dither—and wither. Harry Frankfurt (2004:16) says, "Suppose we care about nothing. In that case, we would do nothing to maintain any thematic unity or coherence in our desire or in the determination of our will." Such a man "would be uninvolved in his own life" (Frankfurt 2004:22). He would have no identity.

Frankfurt thus describes the deepest problem with a P-Only view of human motivation. Such people would not be human. Without Knight's "final interest," even the business of Prudence would not work. Practical reason does not come with its own motivation. Besides, thinking requires emotion, so the pure rationality of the dream of Descartes is impossible (Damasio 1994). The psychologist Nico Frijda noted that "with cognitive judgments [alone]...there is no reason...to prefer any goal.... Cognitive reasoning may argue that a particular event would lead to loss of money or health or life, but so what?" (Reddy 2001:23). The psychologist Gordon Bower wrote, "Emotion is evolution's way of giving meaning to our lives" (Reddy 2001:23).

Even a "mere" self-regard is not automatic, Schmidtz (1996:167) points out: "It may be standard equipment, so to speak, but even standard equipment requires maintenance." I knew a man once who delighted in exercising the character of the Prudent Man. I was with him when, in Italian, he bargained off and on for an entire hour about the price of a big can of olive oil at a store in Boston's North End. The year was 1966, before the neighborhood was yuppified. (Now the prices are fixed and higher, even accounting for inflation.) My prudent friend had three levels of motivation.

For one thing, he was interested in the prudent saving on the oil, perhaps a dollar or so. But this does not explain much, even in 1966 dollars. More important was his pleasure in enacting so audaciously—to the point of an embarrassing display of intemperance—the character of the Prudent Man. Another P variable? No, S in aid of P. And third, he was keeping faith with the indubitably S-ish variables of his Lago Maggiore Italian speech, birth, and society and the stories that honor such a character. These were his identity, his S variables, his sacred Faith. This identity required main-tenance, and he worked at it. As Hume said, to repeat, "were there no appetite of any kind antecedent to self-love, that propensity could scarcely ever exert itself."

Ralph Waldo Emerson speaks of Napoleon's attachment to the charac-ter of the supremely Prudent Man, which does not mean "cautious" always (which certainly would not characterize Napoleon), but "having know-how, *savoir faire*,"

> that common-sense which no sooner respects any end than it
> finds the means to effect it; the delight in the use of means; in
> the choice, simplification and combining of means; the direct-
> ness and thoroughness of his work; the prudence with which
> all was seen and the energy with which all was done, make him
> the natural organ and head of what I may almost call, from its
> extent, the *modern* party.... [He] showed us how much may be
> accomplished by the mere force of such virtues as all men pos-
> sess in less degrees; namely, by punctuality, by personal atten-
> tion, by courage and thoroughness. "The Austrians," he said,
> "do not know the value of time." (1982:341)

The aristocrats who led the Austrians, in contrast to bourgeois Bonaparte and his ragtag talents, were careless of such an ignoble value as exact cal-culations of time. True, Napoleon was always impatient, which was not bourgeois of him, and he was physically courageous, which the average shopkeeper has little need of. Yet, Emerson says, "I should cite [Napoleon], in his earlier years, as a model of prudence" (1982:352).

Napoleon had pretensions to status among the gentry of his native Corsica. They got him into a military school but not into the regiments of the real aristocrats. Paul Johnson (2002:9) sees the origins of Napoleon's bourgeois behavior in his head for figures and his training in the unfash-ionable but calculating artillery: "Bonaparte began to pay constant atten-tion to the role of calculation in war: distances to be covered; speed and route of march; quantities of supplies and animals' rates at which ammunition was used.... Asked how long it would take to get a siege train from the French fortress of Verdun to the outskirts of Vienna, most officers of the day would shrug bewildered shoulders or make a wild guess. Bonaparte would consult a map and give the answer in exact days and hours." A French historian said of Napoleon that after he abandoned Josephine in pursuit of martial alliances, he became lazy and "bourgeois." No, he became lazy and *aristocratic*. His mad energy was precisely that of the consummate bourgeois engaged on a piece of business—in his case, depending on how you value Napoleon, raping Europe or protecting the Revolution. My Italian American friend was, in these respects, a Napoleon on a little stage, ruthlessly skilled at cards and baseball and coaching girls' basketball, delighting in the exercise of Prudent means. But all was in aid of a Sacred identity, his Faith. No dithering.

Humans live through both P and S. That is to say, a good person is motivated by Prudence, *but also* by other virtues, such as Love, Faith, Courage, Temperance, Justice, and Hope. Michael Novak (1996:4) observes that in the modern world, "a strictly economic, business language has grown up without including within itself the moral, religious, even humane language appropriate to its own activities." Therein lies the problem.

I know a woman with exquisite taste, whose home is full of graceful objects meaningful in her life—a reproduction of a sculpted head from Greece, in honor of her study decades ago of the ancient Greek language; a black abstract painting owned by a dear friend who died too young; numerous books of poetry, which she studies to set a standard for her own. Her home is a temple to Memory. Her possessions are not mere corrupting "consumption," so many bags of Fritos or cases of Coke. Her objects are a species of worship, a touch of transcendence. They are reminders of the love and pain that anchor most women's lives. And yet this woman can remember the *price* of every single thing she owns, every deal she has made since girlhood, and is prudent in other ways as well, saving money, making it with care and courage. She does *both* P and S. Bourgeois people do.

Laurel Thatcher Ulrich (1990:203), in her biography of Martha Ballard—wife of a miller and surveyor, mother of nine children, but especially a midwife who delivered more than eight hundred babies in the Maine of the early national period—reflects on why Martha worked as she did: "What took Martha Ballard out of bed in the cold of night? Why was she willing to risk frozen feet and broken bones to practice her trade? Certainly midwifery paid well." Here is Prudence, and she had no saintly abnegation about it: "Martha cared about her 'rewards,' and she kept her midwifery accounts carefully" (1990:203). Yet, she was not a creature of P-Only. Faith mattered. Her diary is full of conventional, and often more than conventional, praises to God. "She interpreted her work, as all her life, in religious terms," but even more, midwifery "was an inner calling, an assertion of being" (1990:203). "Martha Ballard's specialty brought together the gentle and giving side of her nature [thus, Love] with her capacity for risk and her need for autonomy [thus, Courage]" (1990:203). Both P and S work in bourgeois lives.

Maybe economics ought to acknowledge the fact, beyond any form of P-Only.

Notes

1. This chapter, though revised, draws from my book *The Bourgeois Virtues: Ethics for an Age of Commerce* (2006).

2. Quote from the *Thirty-Nine Articles* of the Church of England.

3. Hoffman and Spitzer (1985), with, for example, Forsythe, Horowitz, Savin, and Sefton (1994), try to find a "rational," that is, a pure prudence, explanation for moral sentiments. The point is that they fail, as, for example, Eckel and Grossman (1996) demonstrate.

4. Compare with page 156, "an owner-entrepreneur engaged in an endless race," and so forth.

5. Jones's (1933) *Increasing Returns* should be better known among economists. A student of Marshall, he anticipated the mathematics of the "residual." He died young, and his work was forgotten except by economic historians.

6. Posner conceded the point but characteristically did not let his concession change his theory or his practice of law.

7. Bob, believe me on this one.

8. Notably, the last book (Nozick 2001) has the same structure as this earlier one: epistemology, metaphysics (especially, free will), and ethics.

9. From http://www.doctorswithoutborders-usa.org/donate/, accessed January 4, 2005.

10. Compare with Gray 1996:63: "We do not charge a consultation fee for listening to our friends' troubles and, if we did, that would signify the death of friendship as a practice among us."

9

The Social Life of "Cash Payment"

Money, Markets, and the Mutualities
of Poverty

James Ferguson

Recent years have seen the emergence of new kinds of welfare states in the global South, a trend that a *Newsweek* (2010) article described as "Welfare 2.0." Advocates have sung the praises of new programs that directly transfer small amounts of cash to the poor—or, as one provocative book title puts it, *Just Give Money to the Poor* (Hanlon, Barrientos, and Hulme 2010). An impressive policy literature has documented the considerable achievements of such programs, among which the most famous are Brazil's Bolsa Familia program and (an instance I discuss at some length here) South Africa's system of pensions and grants. Although narratives of a triumphant neoliberalism might have led us to expect a retreat from programs of social assistance, or even an end to the welfare state, the fact is that new welfare programs are proliferating and expanding across much of the world, most of them based on the appealingly simple device of directly providing poor people with monthly cash payments. Much is unclear about these programs, but they are evidently associated with an important new kind of politics focused, at least in part, on the distributive claims of those excluded from the world of wage labor.

One can easily see why those on the political right, who generally oppose redistribution and disdain state programs of social assistance, would be hostile to the idea of "just giving money to the poor." But proposals to transfer cash into the hands of the poor are often criticized with equal vehemence from the left. Indeed, in making presentations on these issues to a range of audiences in recent years, I have been struck by the fact that most objections to cash transfers, in an academic setting, come from those who position themselves on the left. In an earlier era, such objections might perhaps have been traced to the old antipathy of the revolutionary left to all forms of "reformism." But few on the academic left today are still waiting for the revolution, and my sense is that the real resistance here is based on a more visceral distaste for the very idea of poor people receiving cash.

The concern seems to be that programs of cash transfer ultimately serve the cause of "commoditization" and thus capitalism because people who receive cash are at the same time being "drawn into" a world of market exchange. The idea, which has a long pedigree in socialist thought, is that such participation in markets will "break down" social relationships; the pursuit of money will upend long-established relationships based on meaning and moral obligation in favor of mere egoistic calculations of advantage. Cash, in such a view, is conceived as a universal solvent that dissolves the social glue: "the cash nexus" erodes or displaces all other forms of social and moral relation.

The earliest reference to such a "cash nexus" may be Thomas Carlyle's (1840:58) 1839 essay on Chartism, in which he painted a rather sentimental picture of the social bonds formerly linking the old aristocracy with the lower classes and lamented their destruction, insisting that "*cash payment*" (he italicized the phrase) had become, thanks to capitalism, "the universal sole nexus of man to man." Karl Marx and Frederick Engels (1998:37) would famously extend the argument in *The Communist Manifesto*, charging that the bourgeoisie, in replacing feudalism with capitalism, had "pitilessly torn asunder the motley of ties that bound man to his 'natural superiors', and left remaining no other nexus between man and man than naked self interest, than callous 'cash payment.'" Small wonder, then, if the heirs to this tradition regard with almost instinctive skepticism any social policy, or any substantive politics, that would be based precisely on "cash payment." Cash payment for the poor, in this view, may well alleviate some misery in the short term. But in a longer perspective, it is just another channel through which the corrosive force of money and markets creeps into people's lives, in the process, inevitably destroying a richer and more meaningful world of social connections and obligations. Cash transfers, in this view, may in fact be a Trojan horse. The unsuspecting poor may be quick enough to welcome such payments, thinking only of cash's evident capacity to help them meet their most pressing needs, but they are really being seduced into the "cash nexus" and thus drawn into a capitalist system of monetized exchange that ultimately works against their interests.

Actual studies of how poor people engage with the cash economy, however, reveal a very different connection between money and social relationships, one in which money, meaning, and mutuality are entangled rather than antagonistic. To make sense of this entanglement, we need to rethink the relation between "the cash nexus" and various forms of social connection and mutuality. And this rethinking will entail challenging a whole series of conventional oppositions (interest versus obligation, feeling versus calculation, altruism versus selfishness, etc.) that ground the traditional left's phobic antipathy (as I am increasingly inclined to call it) toward both cash payments and market exchanges.

The southern African poor, as a rule, are both highly social and highly cash oriented. Here I review a rich literature on this topic, drawing conclusions about the way social relations rely on honoring ties of dependence and obligation *and* pursuing the acquisition of cash and the things it can buy. These empirical observations contradict the common tendency to oppose the "logic" of the market to the "logic" of communal solidarity, along with the related view that resources are accumulated in the cash economy (according to one set of rules) and distributed in the moral economy (according to another).

SOCIALISM AND MARKETS

The deeply rooted hostility of the left to markets and processes of commoditization is usefully illustrated by Marxist theorist G. A. Cohen's (2009) eloquent articulation of the first principles of socialism. Cohen exemplifies the virtues of socialism and the moral shabbiness of capitalism by inviting us to consider the way a group of people might organize itself when undertaking a camping trip. The campers have a range of talents and interests, and various facilities and equipment will be used on the trip, but the whole enterprise is structured by a set of mutual understandings and goals, in pursuit of which the campers freely agree to cooperate. Goods are shared and chores distributed in an equitable way. "There are plenty of differences, but our mutual understandings, and the spirit of the enterprise, ensure that there are no inequalities to which anyone could mount a principled objection" (2009:4). Nearly everyone would agree, he suggests, that norms of equality and reciprocity should apply to such a common venture. And he then goes on to invite the reader to imagine situations in which individual campers seek to make egoistic property claims to various talents and discoveries that emerge in the course of the trip. Imagine, he says, that a camper who catches fish ("Harry") comes back to camp and tries to claim a superior share of the catch on the grounds that he "owns" them? What if another ("Sylvia") finds some apples and then tries to exchange them for having fewer chores to do? Would not the others regard these egoistic attempts to profit via exclusion and exchange as outrageous and unacceptable? Such behavior would be seen as greedy, selfish, and contemptible and would quickly be condemned by the other campers. Greedy Harry, for instance, would be rebuked as a "schmuck" and instructed (in language that could only come from a camper who has been dreamed up by a philosopher), "You sweat and strain no more than the rest of us do. So, you're very good at fishing. We don't begrudge you that special endowment, which is, quite properly, a source of satisfaction to you, but why should we reward your good fortune?" (2009:7). Repelled by such selfish advantage-seeking, the group insists on dividing tasks and distributing resources equitably and cooperating in the shared purpose of an enjoyable common experience.

The camping trip, then, is based on a communal solidarity in which sharing and cooperating are accepted as normal, natural, and good. And if we accept such values in the context of small-scale social interaction, as most of us do, Cohen claims, we should also strive for them at the level of society as a whole. He acknowledges that organizing social cooperation and sharing at a large scale is much more difficult than at the scale of a camping trip. But this is a practical obstacle to be worked on, not a reason to abandon the socialist principle of communal solidarity that we rightly value when it comes to small-scale ventures like the camping trip.

An anthropological response might begin by talking about actual camping trips (instead of the made-up kind preferred by philosophers) because one would quickly find that inequalities characterize intimate relations of "communal solidarity" quite as much as they do market situations of exchange. Cohen's analysis is strangely silent about the ways that chores on camping trips are commonly divided unequally, often according to gender (for instance, men catching the fish and women doing the dirty work of cleaning them), or the ways that relations of authority are defined by generation (with parents bossing around children until someone says something like, "I wish I had never come on this stupid trip!"). In fact, the campers in his example seem strangely to have no structured social relations at all with one another. This is hardly a likely scenario for any actual camping expedition and surely an utterly implausible model for communal and cooperative relationships in general.

But Cohen is not really arguing that nonmarket relations are unproblematic or wholly benign, only that they spring from motives less base than that of seeking monetary advantage. For market relations, in his account, unlike those of communal reciprocity and solidarity, are fundamentally based on the seeking of a "cash reward," as he puts it (Cohen 2009:39). The market motive for productive activity is therefore "typically some mixture of greed and fear." It is true that people can engage in market activity for other reasons, but "the motives of greed and fear are what the market brings to prominence" (2009:40). In certain contexts, markets may be a necessary evil, but Cohen (2009:82) is quite clear that they are indeed evil and necessarily so: "Every market, even a socialist market, is a system of predation."

At this point, it is difficult not to recall the long, unhappy history of regimes of the left trying to destroy these so-called systems of predation. State socialism became notorious, of course, for its nonmarket systems of bureaucratic rationing and queuing for basic goods. But such practices were not some Stalinist distortion, for the socialist antipathy to markets runs far deeper and has existed far longer than the Soviet-style central planning state. From the beginning, many early socialists imagined that the revolution would bring with it the end of market exchange and of money itself and that economic life would be organized through either spontaneous nonmarket cooperation or centralized planning. And, of course, even late into the twentieth century, socialist regimes and movements repeatedly pursued disastrous policies that are explicable only in the light of a conviction that markets are evil—the most notorious examples perhaps being the Khmer Rouge's systematic killing of "merchants" or the Peruvian Shining Path's policy of violently attacking rural peasant markets as manifestations of "capitalist exploitation." Less spectacularly but more recent, we have seen Robert Mugabe's regime in Zimbabwe respond to rising bread prices caused by runaway inflation by vilifying "exploitative" bakers who dare to sell their bread at a market price and ordering them to reduce their prices below their production costs, thus effectively driving most bakers out of the business of baking bread and even imprisoning some (BBC 2006).

Anthropologists have often shared traditional socialism's antipathy to market sociality and have sometimes invoked Marcel Mauss's famous essay on the gift in support of a moralistic and nostalgic dualism. As Keith Hart (2007:11) has recently noted, the idea that modern Western capitalist societies have an asocial "commodity economy" and other, radically different societies feature morally inflected "gift economies" has come to be widely circulated, "routinely reproduced in introductory anthropology courses everywhere." Starting with such a binary, we all too easily tell the familiar antimarket story, arguing that whereas precapitalist, traditional societies were built on virtuous things like giving, sharing, and human connection, capitalism and its cash economy have increasingly replaced this full, meaningful world with the cold and inhuman hand of the market.

But as Hart (2007:11) has usefully pointed out, such accounts attribute to Mauss "the very ideology his essay was intended to refute." In tracing the ways that the circulation of objects, across a range of different societies, is always bound up with both social meaning and personal interests, Mauss aimed to show that "human institutions everywhere are founded on the unity of individual and society, freedom and obligation, self-interest and concern for others" (2007:9). His famous examples of the Trobriand kula ring and the Kwakiutl potlatch show that "traditional" gift giving was, in fact, always interested and often involved motives that were both competitive and antagonistic, just as his closing discussion of Western society and its emergent welfare-state institutions (including cooperatives, social insurance programs, and social norms around employment) insists on the continuing relevance of the "prestation" (and related considerations of honor, caring, and solidarity) in the midst of a complex market system.

As David Graeber (2004) has suggested, the essay on the gift should be read with an appreciation both of Mauss's active lifelong commitment to socialism and of his critical response to the Bolshevik experience in the early years of the Soviet revolution. He wrote the gift essay (published in 1924) following his visit to the Soviet Union, and it is best read in conjunction with his extended evaluation of the Soviet "experiment" (Mauss 1983). Mauss's critique of the Bolshevik experience was based precisely on his conviction that markets were both desirable and necessary. What the Bolsheviks had missed or ignored was the fact that socialism had to be founded in society itself, not on abstractions such as the state or the individual. Since markets themselves were social institutions with a central role to play in actual forms of social solidarity and common purpose, socialism would have to work with them, not against them.

As Mauss suggests, market exchange is not the negation of sociality; on the contrary, it forms a vital—even irreplaceable—part of the social life of any modern nation. And any socialism worthy of the name must build on, rather than destroy, such actually existing forms of collective life. Indeed, it is the fact that markets, morality, and sociality are inevitably brought into practical relation in actual social life that surely explains why Peruvian peasants failed to see their cheerful local market days as part of "a system of predation" (as Cohen would have it) but instead recognized them as both a vital sphere of sociality and a valued mechanism of distribution. (And for them, of course, it was not the market vendors seeking a good price for their fruit but the self-righteous guerrillas who were machine-gunning them who appeared as the predators.)

Nonmarket relations, meanwhile, are, as Mauss demonstrated, never based simply on altruism or kinship-based sharing; they contain powerful elements of egoism, self-interest, competitive striving, and antagonism (as he reminded us, the old German word *Gift* means "poison"). In contrast to Cohen's imaginary camping trip, actual "communal solidarity" is not built solely out of egalitarian relations of cooperation and altruism, but just as much out of interested and often competitive relations of exchange. Both a wholly disinterested sharing and a purely asocial calculation are fantasies; real sociality always unites sharing and self-interest in a single act. This state of affairs is sometimes glossed as "reciprocity" but might better (given the unfortunate economistic tendency to reduce complex reciprocal dependencies to tit-for-tat transactions) be expressed as "mutuality."[1] This mutuality is found in the kula and the potlatch or the peasant marketplace, and it is found just as surely in the annual meetings of the modern corporation or the competitive frenzy of the stock market trading floor.

Indeed, in the years since Mauss wrote his groundbreaking account, anthropological scholarship has given us an even clearer picture of the deeply social nature of market-oriented economic action. Nor are passions and sentiments, solidarity and caring, absent from such behavior. A rich recent literature shows that the motives of market participants—even of business professionals in the act of doing business—are suffused with sentiment, affective rationality, social expectations, obligations, and so on.[2]

But not only do the ostensibly "market-oriented" spheres of action reveal social and emotional motives and attachments; relations of intimacy, including those of care, love, sharing, and attachment, are also deeply bound up with market transactions and exchanges. Although an ideology of what Viviana Zelizer (2005) calls "hostile worlds" implies that cash exchanges must contaminate or erode real intimacy, we need only look around our modern societies to see how intimate social relations are combined routinely with monetary transactions. Zelizer (2005:27) observes, "Parents pay nannies or child-care workers to tend their children, adoptive parents pay money to obtain babies, divorced spouses pay or receive alimony and child support payments, and parents give their children allowances, subsidize their college educations, help them with their first mortgage, and offer them substantial bequests in their wills. Friends and relatives send gifts of money as wedding presents, and friends loan each other money. Meanwhile, immigrants support their families back home with regular transmission of remittances."

The presence of cash in these relationships does not render them merely commercial or prevent them from being sites of caring, affection, cooperation, and sharing. Indeed, one main reason people value money in the first place and try so hard to acquire it is precisely so that they can carry out such acts of caring and support for others (sending money home to relatives, saving for a child's education, and so on).

But the insistent linking of asocial self-interest with the very presence of money or market transactions persists. This practice is especially pernicious when we deal with questions of distribution and social assistance, since crudely associating markets and "the cash nexus" with things like selfishness and greed prevents us from seeing two key realities that are central to understanding the contemporary politics of distribution among the southern African poor. The first such reality is that markets are social sites of distribution and coordination and not only of "predation." Recovering the fundamentally social nature of markets helps us to recognize ways that market mechanisms can potentially be turned to progressive distributive ends. The second crucial reality is that in the everyday lives of southern Africa's poor, participation in a cash economy and participation in social relations of care, dependence, and obligation are in practice not contradictory "logics," but mutually enabling practices. The actual solidarities and mutualities that sustain rich lives under adverse circumstances are in fact conditional on, rather than in contradiction with, "the cash nexus." The following two sections take up these two themes in turn. A final section concludes with thoughts about "cash payment" in the context of social assistance.

HOW TO DO THINGS WITH MARKETS

The traditional left's suspicion of "cash payment" tends to be coupled with a general hostility to markets, as noted at the start of this chapter. This hostility has often been shared by anthropologists, who have tended to see market activity as promoting egoistic calculation and destroying or weakening relations of mutuality and community. Yet, if Mauss was right that markets are vital mechanisms of social integration, social coordination, and organized distribution, then those who wish to find ways of reorganizing society to better meet the needs of those who are currently most marginalized or excluded ought to be asking how markets can be used to accomplish this task. It is not a question of replacing markets with something else (which Mauss convincingly argued would be both unworkable and wrongheaded), but of using markets to do socially useful things that would be difficult or impossible to do without them.

What sorts of socially useful things? For one thing, markets make it possible to aggregate and make visible great masses of information—including (something that socialists, of all people, ought to recognize as important) information about the needs of others. G. A. Cohen, for all his hostility to markets, clearly recognizes this capacity. In a complex and highly differentiated economic system, he acknowledges, it would be difficult to know "what to produce, and how to produce it, without market signals: very few socialist economists would now dissent from that proposition" (Cohen 2009:60). As he puts it, prices do two things at once. They provide a "motivation function" (people seeking advantage in their transactions, which Cohen finds morally objectionable), but they also provide an "information function," in which prices send signals about where demand lies and how much people are willing to give for what; in this way, "they show how valuable goods are to people, and thereby reveal what is worth producing" (2009:61). Thus, markets can collect and synthesize information about the wants and needs of huge numbers of consumers and allow goods to be distributed in a way that takes people's preferences into account.

In principle, as economists like to point out, this information function of markets makes it possible for markets to provide a socially coordinated allocation mechanism that takes account of people's needs and values in ways that even the most well-intentioned, centrally planned systems of allocation could never manage. Julian Simon (1994) has presented an especially clear example of such a mechanism: the introduction by airlines of a voucher system for handling overbooking.[3] The old system of arbitrarily picking passengers to be "bumped" was unable to distinguish between different passengers with very different situations. One passenger might be a businessman who flies every week and would just as soon wait for the next plane; the next might be a mother racing to get to her daughter's wedding, for whom any delay would have heartbreaking consequences. Being bumped would have very different "values" to the two passengers, but the officials making the decision lacked the detailed contextual knowledge to make a good (i.e., informed) decision, leading to arbitrary decisions about who would and would not be bumped. A simple regulatory solution (banning the practice of bumping) would give passengers security but at the less-than-optimal cost of airlines flying with more empty seats, which would lead to significantly higher flying costs for all consumers. Instead, by offering a small monetary reward (say, a $200 coupon), the airlines were able to recruit volunteers and avoid bumping those for whom the inconvenience would have the highest "cost." A consciously constructed "market," in this example, allows a group of people, via a kind of self-organization, to identify whose need is greatest and to allocate a good in a way that takes this need into account. As Simon (1994:323) put it, "the people who care least about waiting for the next plane select themselves to get a benefit that they prefer to flying as scheduled."

This example is the kind that economists love, of course—the famous "win-win" scenario, in which everyone is better off (all flyers do better in this system than they would if bumping was arbitrary or outlawed). Since the fliers in the example can freely take or leave the $200 coupon, no one is unjustly forced to give up his or her seat, and those who do not get seats are those who, being most willing to give them up, presumably need them least. Thus, we arrive at a collective decision making, even perhaps justice (allocations are, as Simon [1994:323] puts it, "fair, rather than arbitrary"). Indeed, one can even see here how such a market mechanism can enable sharing, a way of achieving an equitable allocation of a limited good.

But, of course, markets do not just allocate a good based on how much it is needed or desired by the buyer; they also allocate based on the consumer's ability to pay for it. And, in a world of huge inequalities, those with the greatest needs are often those with the least ability to pay. So in the airline bumping example, we might imagine a scenario in which somehow, among the passengers, whom the example seems to presume to be economic equals, a small subclass of desperately poor fliers exists, for whom even a very small voucher would exceed their annual income. Their specific personal circumstances (being in a hurry that day, for example) would immediately pale beside the economic value of the coupon, with the less satisfying result that the one who gives up the seat is now not the one who is least inconvenienced, but the one who is poorest. In such a system, one *class* of passenger will, time and time again, give up its seats for the convenience of the other class (albeit via the mechanism of "free choice"). Critical scholars attentive to such problems of inequality will insist that real-world markets often produce such effects, yielding an allocation principle that is brutally simple and has little to do with either information or justice: the rich get whatever they like, and the very poor get nothing. In the extreme situation of famine, for instance, the "market signal" of high price ensures that all the available food is routed to those who can afford to buy it, leaving the rest to die. For this reason, markets are often bypassed in times of famine as governments move to hand out food directly to those in need—based on justice, not prices.

But new thinking in famine relief questions this practice and suggests ways of combining the information function Cohen acknowledges with the egalitarian goals he advocates. As I (Ferguson 2010) have pointed out elsewhere, recent critics of the conventional use of food aid in response to famine argue that hunger is often best dealt with by boosting the purchasing power of those at risk rather than by distributing food. The current international food aid system involves taking excess grain (produced under subsidized conditions in rich countries) and transporting it to places (largely in Africa) where people are at risk of hunger. Following Amartya Sen (1983a), critics have long noted the perverse effects of this system: depressed producer prices for local farmers and damage to the local institutions for producing and distributing food crops. Often, once food aid has arrived, local food production never recovers, and the "temporary" crisis becomes permanent. As an alternative, Sen's followers have pushed for cash payments to be made directly to those at risk of food deficit. People with money in their pockets, Sen points out, generally do not starve. And the economic chain of events that is set in motion by boosting purchasing power leads (through market forces) to increased capacity for local production and distribution; recipients can use cash flexibly not only to buy food but also to restock or preserve productive assets like livestock and seed (Dreze and Sen 1991; Sen 1983b). Cash transfers in this way work *with* markets (not against them) to enable recipients to achieve relief by deciding for themselves what their most pressing needs are. This strategy allows the information function of markets to operate, even among the desperately poor.

Water provision is a similarly challenging case for markets, and critics of privatization have rightly pointed out that simply treating water as a commodity yields the politically and ethically unacceptable result that poor people are unable to access what ought to be a basic human right. (For a stimulating recent analysis of the South African case, see Von Schnitzler 2008). But simply being against privatization is not an answer to the allocation question. Are people in an undoubtedly water-scarce context such as South Africa simply supposed to take as much water as they like? One well-known antiprivatization activist insisted at a public meeting in Durban in 2009 that metering water is a necessity for progressive public policy: "We don't want the bosses filling their swimming pools at no cost with the public's water." Although a basic minimum allocation of free, or "decommodified," water for the poor has been a key progressive demand in South Africa's water wars, prices also have their place in this politics—for how else will it be possible to soak the overconsuming rich to help cross-subsidize the poor where water is a scarce good to which everyone must have some minimal level of access? Here a progressive pricing mechanism that charges high rates to the rich to cross-subsidize the consumption of the poor can function not as an "instrument of predation" but precisely as an instrument of solidarity.[4] Again, markets are revealed to be tools for coordinating collective affairs and distributing resources in ways that can (by recognizing the artifactual and constructed nature of markets) be brought into accordance with social aims.

Socialists have too often confused cash transactions and market exchanges with the historically much more recent system of production that is capitalism. But markets have no essential attachment to capitalism and have existed (as they undoubtedly will continue to exist in the future) under a much wider set of social and economic systems. If we keep this fact in mind, we may be able to better recognize how markets, as social institutions, can be articulated with other social institutions to produce specific, desired social effects. In addition, we may more easily see the value of some emerging political initiatives (including programs for cash transfers in southern Africa) that rely, as Mauss (1983:353) put it, on "the organization, and not the suppression, of the market." I return to this point in the final section of the chapter.

MONEY AND THE MUTUALITIES OF POVERTY

Notwithstanding a rich anthropological literature on the subject (ably summarized by Maurer [2006]), "most anthropologists," as Keith Hart (2005:1) has observed, "don't like money."[5] It symbolizes "the world they have rejected for something more authentic elsewhere," and "every anthropology student knows that money undermines the integrity of cultures that were hitherto resistant to commerce" (Hart 2005:1). In this rather nostalgic spirit, anthropologists and others engaged with contemporary poverty in Africa still often tell a slightly too familiar story. Once upon a time, Africans lived together in an organic unity, bound by shared values, moral obligations, and ties of kinship. Today, however, capitalism (neoliberalism, modernity, commodification, the world system—the villain changes with the times) tears apart these bonds and replaces them with the heartless logic of "the market." This familiar communitarian framing, tired and clichéd though it is, continues to shape many discussions of the problems of the southern African poor. A recycled modernization theory here conspires with an equally indestructible vernacular critique of "greedy youth" who "nowadays care only about money," and so on. Generosity, in the tragic account that each generation seems determined to tell about the next, has given way to calculation, selfishness, and greed (cf. Cole 2010).

Such moralized accounts, which cast "the market" in the role of demonic archvillain, are increasingly out of touch with the empirical research on the lives of southern Africa's poor, research showing clearly that poor people's livelihoods are bound up with forms of sociality that cut across the divide between nonmarket and market or social obligation versus commoditized exchange. For this reason, understandings of the relations of dependence and mutual assistance with which people are engaged (and on which they depend for their survival) must take account of what David Neves and Andries du Toit (2012) have termed "the sociality of money." Far from being antithetical to relations of sociality and mutuality, the "cash nexus" turns out to be integral to such relations as they actually exist. People seek money and engage in exchanges within the context of dense social relations of mutuality, just as they tend their relationships by fully deploying the powers and potentialities that access to money can enable. Such observations, Neves and du Toit (2012:131) note, "challenge meta-narratives of a 'great transformation' toward socially disembedded and depersonalized relationships in relation to money."

To understand the ways that social relationships and cash exchanges are intertwined, one must return to the old anthropological point that mutuality is not simply altruism, cooperation, or generosity—and not just egoistic advantage-seeking either. As Mauss repeatedly insisted, mutualities normally involve antagonism and generosity at the same time. And such forms of sociality involve people, inexorably, in moral relations of obligation, care, generosity, and obligation *and* various forms of interested exchange. It is not a question of a historical transition from one to the other—the Maussian point is that solidarity and exchange depend upon each other. And this observation is as true in a capitalist market society as it is in any other.

Such mutualities in the southern African context have sustained a large body of high-quality research (especially relevant to my purposes here is a stimulating cluster of recent work from South Africa; see Bank and Minkley 2005; du Toit and Neves 2007, 2009a, 2009b; Harper and Seekings 2010; Hunter 2010; Neves and du Toit 2012; Seekings 2008). Here I offer only a very schematic review of some of the main findings. For the sake of brevity, I discuss just two key sites of intimate sociality where mutualities and the cash economy are constitutively intertwined.

First, the domain of kinship is decidedly not a sphere set apart from money and markets. Kinship, after all, is not something you "have"—it is something you "do." And to "do" it (or at least, to do it right) in today's southern Africa requires cash. Southern Africans have long been in the habit of using cash payments to mark marriages and have long recognized that bridewealth "cattle" are of two kinds: those "with legs" and those "without legs" (i.e., cash; Ferguson 1985; Murray 1981; Sansom 1976). Cash is equally central to that other key ritual passage, the funeral—on which households typically spend the equivalent of a year's income, according to one recent study (Case et al. 2008). And the multiple reciprocities and solidarities with which kinship bonds have long been associated also unfold within (not against) the world of cash. For it is not only those with money who are expected to honor certain claims; needy kin also require access to cash to be able to make strong claims in the first place. Traversing space, for instance, is often key to making successful distributive claims, which means that money for transport is crucial. And the ability of a potential beneficiary to reciprocate (even in very small ways), research has shown, often makes the difference between the sort of kinship claim that will be attended to and the kind that can be ignored (see du Toit and Neves 2007, 2009a, 2009b; Harper and Seekings 2010; Neves and du Toit 2012; Seekings 2008; Turner 2005).

Second, let me mention a very rich literature on the mutualities of sex, love, and money. The topic is, of course, haunted by the specter of prostitution. As Zelizer (2005:124) has noted of discussions of commoditization in general, "the relation between prostitute and patron looms as the ultimate triumph of commercialism over sentiment." But the best scholarship on southern Africa is agreed that sex, love, and money are in fact bound up in ways that the opposition of "real love" versus "prostitution" does more to misunderstand than to clarify. Sexually intimate relations between men and women, in poor and working-class settings across the region, are widely assumed to properly involve relations of economic dependence, and women normally expect their lovers to provide them with a range of gifts, payments, and other forms of material support. Even the most apparently commercial relationships of this kind are normally not without social and emotional content, and relations explicitly based on romantic love, undoubtedly entailing deep emotional attachment, typically also entail trade-offs involving money, which Western observers have long found disturbing. Mark Hunter (2010) has developed the useful concept of "provider love" to capture the way economic provisioning is often understood not to contradict romantic love but to confirm it. Real love, in this conception, should be combined with and given substance by real material care (just as in that other case of provider love—the relation between parent and child). It is not a question of love versus money; both the providing and the love are absolutely real (indeed, the providing is what proves that the love is real). To ask whether a woman in such a relationship is motivated by money or love is therefore to ask the wrong question. The conventional opposition of the material to the sentimental makes no sense since the material is meaningful precisely as the embodiment of the sentiment.

What all of this shows is that, contrary to what generations of social theorists have supposed, intimate social bonds are not eroded or destroyed by the presence of money and markets. What we find is that the most important and highly valued forms of sociality, reciprocity, solidarity, and care among the southern African poor are precisely those that are facilitated by the use of money and participation in markets. Those who are most successful at building social networks of support and care are those who are able to obtain money, and many of the most important ways of obtaining such funds depend on webs of sociality and mutual dependence. The truly isolated and alienated are those who really are, by virtue of utter destitution, outside the "cash nexus"; for the rest, having cash is precisely what enables the myriad mutualities that sustain (what Elizabeth Povinelli [2006] might call) the "thick life" of the southern African poor.

THE SOCIAL LIFE OF CASH PAYMENTS

What are the implications of all this analysis for social assistance? Recent research on cash transfers has emphasized that even very small streams of cash income can both catalyze and stimulate social and economic activities and enable people to better meet their needs as they themselves define them (see Ferguson n.d.). New thinking in social policy emphasizes cash payments to enable low-income people to access goods and participate in livelihood strategies in ways that are responsive to their actual circumstances.

Whereas older thinking saw social assistance as a substitute for "real" sorts of economic activity, like wage labor, the new research emphasizes that cash does not so much compensate for *inactivity* as complement and enable a range of *activities*. Andries du Toit and David Neves (2009b; see also 2007, 2009a), for instance, have provided vivid descriptions of access to social grants enabling poor South Africans both to engage in economic activities (from petty trade to searching for work) and to participate in what du Toit (2007:14) has called "the dance of the relational economy." A major pilot study in Namibia that provided a small, unconditional "basic income grant" to each member of one community found that the insertion of cash not only improved indexes directly related to consumption, like nutrition and health (as one might have expected) but also yielded a surge of new social and economic activity. Grant recipients started businesses and looked for work; they also engaged in new forms of community organization and collective projects and did a better job of caring for their sick (including many suffering from AIDS; Haarmann et al. 2009).

In contrast, the literature paints a very dark picture of those who are so unfortunate as to lack cash entirely. The key to relations of solidarity and mutual assistance, du Toit and Neves (2007, 2009a, 2009b) have argued, is an ability to participate in at least a minimal way in the petty reciprocations of the "relational economy." Those who are unable to reciprocate are also unable to be properly social. Those who are unable to move through space (through lack of money for transport) are at the same time unable to activate and refresh the social relationships they might otherwise be able to depend on. Those who are unable to purchase basic consumer goods are at the same time disabled from coherently marking their social location in a field of signification. If having "style" is a major asset in modern township life (as I [Ferguson 1999] have argued elsewhere), then lacking it is a distinct social disability, implying a withered and diminished personhood. If isolation and alienation exist here, they are not products of being "drawn into" a cash economy, but of having no standing or capacity within it.

The impact of cash transfers needs to be understood in this perspective. Advocates of cash payments are right to insist that such payments can address not only nutritional or physical needs but also social ones. Indeed, the more radical new thinkers about social policy advocate, for just this reason, a universal guaranteed income (or "basic income") for all (see, for example, Haarmann et al. 2009; Standing and Samson 2003; cf. Ferguson n.d.). Some minimum level of ability to engage in consumption and exchange, they argue, should be conceived as a citizenship right. Just as modern systems of water distribution normally recognize a need to provide some minimum amount of "lifeline" water to the poorest citizens (independent of their ability to pay), advocates of basic income insist that some minimum quantum of income must be provided to all citizens—and for the same reason. In a world where cash is nearly as basic to life as water, the provision of at least some basic minimum becomes both a potent political demand and a compelling ethical obligation.

Whatever one might make of such claims, the advocates of basic income are surely right that cash, like water, is more than just a desirable consumer good; it is, under modern conditions, a need so basic that it must be in place before crucial forms of social action and social being can even exist. For, as we have seen, cash in the pocket is related—in a constitutive rather than antagonistic way—to multiple socialities and mutualities that are (quite literally) a matter of life and death.

Implicit in this view is a realization that spending is a productive form of social activity. An older conception of social assistance saw in spending only waste or, at best, "consumption." In this view, there really was (as was often insisted) "no point" in giving money to people who would (as they said) "just spend it!" The idea was that the poor people would, having spent the money, be right back where they were before. And worse, they would have become "dependent." Instead of active and hard-working laborers building something real, they might become, through the hazard of "dependency," passive, demoralized, and inactive. Such conceptions are being displaced, however, by a new perspective on social assistance that has a much more ethnographically informed view of what it means to spend. As one of the innovative "policy intellectuals" working in this vein put it, it is not welfare that makes poor people dependent (Meth 2004). The poor are *always* dependent, and the poorer they are, the more dependent they become. Cash transfers, in this perspective, do not introduce "dependency" into a social world that had been innocent of it; rather, they enable less malevolent dependence to take root and a circuit of reciprocities to unfold within which one-sided relations of dependence can become more egalitarian forms of interdependence (cf. du Toit and Neves 2009b:20). In this perspective, expenditure by the poor is not waste, but a potent form of *activity*, one that stimulates and enables a host of others.

It is true, of course, that the social policies based on cash transfers that are sweeping the globe do not go nearly as far as the "basic income" concept would suggest they should. Both the small size of existing transfers and the conditionalities normally attached to them limit the extent to which they can be associated with far-reaching social transformations (see Ferguson n.d.). But these policies do have the virtue of beginning to accept that people pursue multiple livelihoods that are largely illegible to state planners and to seek governmental strategies that aim to enhance, rather than ignore or demolish, those livelihoods.

I hope to have shown that such policies do not destroy or erode sociality or mutuality. But what about the charge that they help draw people "into" capitalism? In the first instance, the objection seems both naive and anachronistic—as though, if only people were left alone and without any money, they would somehow remain outside capitalism. If there are any places in the world where such a view remains plausible, southern Africa is surely not one of them; any real possibilities of dwelling outside capitalism and the cash economy were extinguished already in the nineteenth century.

But if it is clear that new welfare schemes do not draw people into capitalism (as if from outside it), then it is also true that existing cash transfer programs do seem to take the capitalist system as given and concentrate on ameliorating (rather than overturning) the conditions of extreme poverty and inequality it produces. One can easily argue, for instance, that the new Oxfam-funded cash transfer scheme in Malawi is making a real difference in the lives of the poorest households there. But it is hard to think of this cash as much more than bread crumbs from the table when the benefit on offer is just $3 per person per *month* (Mail and Guardian 2011). President Lula da Silva used to say (in advocating Brazil's cash transfer programs), "It is cheap and easy to care for the poor." But as Perry Anderson (2011:12) has noted when quoting this line, it is difficult to know whether we should regard such a sentiment as "uplifting, or disturbing." Are cash transfer programs the beginning of a potent new left politics? Or just a cheap way of managing the most outrageous deprivation while leaving the system that produces it untouched?

NEW OPENINGS

I suggest, by way of conclusion, that we need to consider the possibility that creating guaranteed incomes, however mild and even feeble they appear in their present form, may indeed have the potential to open up new forms of politics that take us far beyond the limited, technocratic aim of ameliorating poverty that dominates existing cash transfer programs.

Significantly, the program of "basic income" is linked not only to pragmatic discussions in the world of social policy but also to an interesting radical politics. At the leftmost end of the "distributive justice" tradition, for instance, philosopher Philippe van Parijs (Van der Veen and van Parijs 1986; cf. van Parijs 2009) has long advocated an unconditional basic income as a mechanism for achieving what he once called "a capitalist road to communism." Among autonomists, arguments have recently emerged that lodge the source of value in society (rather than in labor) and insist on basic income as the foundation of a new socialist politics (see, for example, Hardt 2009). Such approaches have their problems, but they do point to new sorts of left politics that have been willing to leave behind the widespread nostalgia for the politics of the proletariat (see Barchiesi 2011) and embrace new politics rooted in the needs and demands of what is sometimes called the "precariat" (Frassanito Network 2005; Saul 2011; Standing 2011; cf. Ferguson n.d.).

Other authors have pointed out that cash payments can catalyze a range of economic strategies people are already engaged in to escape capitalist relations of production. J. K. Gibson-Graham (2006) has emphasized the importance of "economic heterogeneity" and the extent to which noncapitalist relations in fact *pervade* economic formations we too easily conceptualize as simply "capitalist" through and through. In the South African context, Franco Barchiesi (2011) has provided a rich account of workers' attempts to exit the capitalist world of work by pursuing projects in the "informal" domain that go far beyond that traditional horizon of conventional left politics, "full employment." Such approaches, by displacing the assumed centrality of wage labor, suggest possibilities for a new politics centered on distribution.

In all of this, we may be able to identify possible points of traction for a radical politics that would start from what people do instead of from some theorist's idea of what they ought to do. Prejudices derived from theoretical deductions (whether the heroization of proletarian wage labor, the disparagement of the "lumpen" classes, or the stigmatization of the "cash nexus") have not well served the left in recent decades. Instead, we might do better to work inductively, watching and listening to what the world's disadvantaged actually do and say and seeking political strategies and social policies that can enhance the cooperation, mutual aid, solidarity, and care already in play. Looking to build upon, rather than destroy or disparage, such actually existing mutualities, as Mauss long ago urged us to do, we may arrive at new ways of thinking about both money and markets and the role they might play in any socialism worth wishing for.

Notes

1. This is a concept recently elaborated by Gudeman (2008), though it should be noted that I use the term here in a slightly different way.

2. Such observations have led Yanagisako (2002), for instance, to suggest that we need an understanding of capitalism that would treat sentiments as being just as central to economic action as interests, and Latour and Lépinay (2009) have recently urged a return to Gabriel Tarde's old insight that economics is first of all about "the passions," rather than rational calculation. See also Ho 2009; Zaloom 2010.

3. I am grateful to Robert Frank for introducing me to this example and explaining its relevance to the topic at hand during a stimulating discussion at the SAR seminar.

4. I am indebted to Patrick Bond for pointing this out to me in a stimulating discussion.

5. Even outside of marriage transactions, money can be semantically set aside from commodity exchange in ways that mark its sociality. For instance, Dlamani (2009:98–103) discusses, in his own family history, the way an envelope of cash to be loaned among friends and family was never described as money, but always as a "package" (Zulu *impahla*), whose transfer was hedged with rules of politeness and indirection.

10

Value Machines and the Superorganic

A Dialogue

Orchestrated by Peter Benson, with James Ferguson, Edward F. Fischer, Robert H. Frank, Stuart Kirsch, Anna Tsing, Bart Victor, and Caitlin Zaloom

Understanding the choices people make is central to both economics and anthropology, although in different ways. Indeed, one could characterize economics as the science of choice, with cost/benefit analysis as the dominant framing. As we see in McCloskey's and Ferguson's chapters (8 and 9, respectively), anthropologists are quick to point out that such choices are not merely material or financial, but social and cultural and emotional as well, meanings not always captured in the tidy figures of a sale price.

In this dialogue, we uncover a key difference between economic approaches to society (individual agents interacting, often discussed in terms of coordination and network effects) and a more anthropological notion of "the social," what Durkheim would have termed the superorganic.

Many economists, including Bob Frank, recognize the limits of assumptions about self-interested, rational actors in models of choice. Yet, in much scholarship, public policy, and popular media, a simplified view of *Homo economicus* and the nature of "free markets" has come to dominate, focusing on rational, self-interested, utility-maximizing individuals to explain why humans behave as they do.

Recent research in behavioral economics and the life sciences presents a new angle of critique of the rational choice paradigm. Neuroeconomics, a burgeoning interdisciplinary field that brings together brain science, behavioral psychology, and economics, uses brain imaging and mapping to understand the biological processes at work in decision making. The field also examines how the brain functions in response to certain stimuli that stage economic situations for research subjects, asking them, for example, to make choices given certain environmental conditions.

The neuroeconomic paradigm tends to portray humans—or at least their brains—as calculating, biomechanical value machines. Caitlin Zaloom's work with neuroeconomics shows how researchers have developed an idea that humans are biologically wired to make certain choices due to the reward structure of the brain, a perspective that seeks to explain what might appear to be irrational "free" choices as the workings of neural networks.

Neural systems are understood to perform ongoing economic evaluations, weighing a range of costs and payoffs to make decisions. An individual system converts diverse, incommensurable rewards into a common scale of valuation shaped both by evolution and by the individual's experience. Aspects of human behavior not typically regarded as economic, including social phenomena such as love and trust, are likewise understood as functions of evaluative computation unfolding along the neural circuitry of the brain.

Yet, biological explanations offered by neuroscience and brain imaging are often in tension with the notions of individual freedom of choice at the heart of market-oriented societies. Further, as this discussion elucidates, the human value machine is always situated and conditioned by social context, a social context greater than the sum of any set of atomized parts.

FRANK: I'm interested in the image of the human as a value calculator that the neuroscientists have in mind. There is the notion that the brain is always faced with choices and has to assign value to this and value to that.

ZALOOM: Actually, the metaphor and model of the brain that anchors neuroeconomics is that the brain is an "information market." Organisms, all kinds of animals, including humans, move through the world constantly processing the kind of values they encounter. The easiest way to think of this is the example of a monkey moving through the forest. This monkey has many kinds of experience in the forest. The monkey thinks, "I might find a stash of bananas over here, or I might find some bananas over there. And now I have to make a decision here. I have to make a choice. I'm going either right or left to find the bananas." The monkey's decision is based on past history. The monkey says, "In my database, going right would be more fruitful." The brain is working on whether expectations were met, whether there is information to add to the database, whether there is information to be updated.

BENSON: Neuroscientists tell us that a machine is essentially a kind of nature, a primate nature or animal nature. Yet, I am skeptical of any essentialist claims about human nature. These scientists know what they are doing, and they are consciously framing choice in terms of machines, and they are stripping off any markers of social context. But are they getting something about human nature?

KIRSCH: They are constructing a model of animal nature that acts like a machine, which, it turns out, looks like traders on the floor.

ZALOOM: A value machine. It is a choice mechanism we have to move through in order to successfully achieve whatever goal we have, whether it is getting bananas or sending our kids to a halfway decent school. This idea gets to something that comes out of Bob Frank's work and Jim Ferguson's work, too. It's actually a *market social*, and it's not exactly the neoliberal model because it's not about the convergence of states and markets and the use of markets by states or the capture of states by markets. There is another vision of the social that comes out of neuroeconomics that I think is really interesting.

FERGUSON: What do you mean by the "market social"?

ZALOOM: There is an information feedback loop between the individual and the environment and also the individual and other individuals. So people become linked together not through draconian forms of solidarity where the individuals add up to a collective that is more than the sum of its parts. Rather, it is through informational feedback loops, which then link together individuals into information sharing systems, which is a market. This information network creates "the social" in what I term the "market social."

　　Choices affect the future trajectory of your life, and so, ideally, you would like to have the ability to actually predict the course of your life (infinitely easier with financial resources). In order to make a choice that looks like a rational one, there is a social apparatus that undergirds the smoothness of the trajectory. So if I make the calculation that I'm going to go to school now because my education will pay off in a better job, to do otherwise would be irrational. The confidence with which one can make those assessments about the future, for anthropologists, is always situated within life courses and social circumstances.

FISCHER: Is this different from just an asymmetrical information issue—if folks had better access to the full information that allowed them to make these predictions?

ZALOOM: The point I'm trying to get at is that it is more about social apparatus than about the individual choice-maker.

Thinking about "the social" from an anthropological perspective is not just thinking about a social contract or coordination problem. Anthropologists tend to see not just individuals with their interests but rather individuals with a given position, part of a system they cannot entirely control and one that has developed over time with particular technologies that diffusely and subtly inform or dictate certain political forms. Durkheim talked about the social as being "superorganic" not in a mystical, metaphysical sense but rather as an acknowledgment of the stickiness and power of the system, the sum over its constituent parts.

FERGUSON: The scientists seem to be able to pose their questions in ways that make no account of the context in which people make calculations or prefer something over another. It is hard for me to believe that they can be as unaware of the issue as they seem to be. Certainly, for anthropologists this is an obvious thing: "Would you like a piece of chocolate?" Well, who is offering it? In what context? Under what circumstance? I will or will not prefer chocolate in a wide variety of ways, depending on the social context. A whole literature of cognitive anthropology shows that even when people are doing literal calculations, their approaches are deeply social and deeply contextual.

ZALOOM: We have been saying that anthropological understanding of choice is contextual. This sounds simple but actually takes a lot of work, a lot of labor on the part of the scientist, to actually denature it in order to put it in a scanner. In fact, when we are attending to these scientific representations of choice, we should be thinking about the denaturing process that allows them to operate within the scientific world.

BENSON: One of the most interesting aspects that has come from this is that the environment is prior to and larger than the individual, and this is the finding of neuroscience. To me, that's incredible because you can go to any number of social theories that will tell you the same thing. But here is neuroscience, which has disciplinary linkages to methodological individualism, nonetheless bearing out that there is a superorganic that is prior to the individual. You can go as far back in evolutionary psychology as you want, but you're going to find an environment. What are the implications of this challenge to methodological individualism?

ZALOOM: The policy angle is the one that's most obvious. We talk a lot about regulating environments. This seems to be a very attractive policy option right now, whether it's in the kind of choice architectures some economists are advocating or in Bob's consumption tax ideas. The consumption tax would produce environments in which the kinds of social feedback loops that are established would be really quite different. The signals about buying a huge 10,000-ft mansion or a beautiful five-bedroom at the high end of the consumption spectrum would be really quite different. It would literally produce different consumption environments in which people operate. That is actually quite different from what we've come to expect from a neoliberal project because it involves engineering environments, possibly through different means but the environment is really critical.

FRANK: The significance is that this model really does highlight several specific ways in which what the individual wants to do won't necessarily be good for the individual or for society as a whole.

VICTOR: Economic theory begins by saying, "Let me simplify choice to atomized self-interest phenomena, and then I can go about my work." These neuroeconomists see this as an opportunity to say that maybe this is or is not true. To take this axiom away and to make it into science, it raises all sorts of implications for what economics means for us as far as information for how we live our lives and what we should be doing with it and the policy that needs to come from it.

FERGUSON: The decision-making model seems to have very little to do with the specificity of the human brain. It sounds like an equally good account of a mouse. Yet, the brain of a mouse or a plant is very different from the brain of a human being. You would think that people who really care about brains in the specificity would have more to say about how human beings make decisions than just that they go where the bananas are.

Getting back to questions about where this science takes us, it seems to imply some superorganic.

TSING: But I thought the point of the market social was that it was methodological individualism. In economics as I understand it, the environment is aggregate individual behavior.

FRANK: Yes, with a complicated feedback from the environment onto the individual.

ZALOOM: There's social feedback from other individuals, but I think what's really interesting to me about it is that, actually, materiality becomes extremely present.

FRANK: Tell me what that means.

Sometimes translation is necessary in academia, especially when you have an anthropologist speaking with an economist. Luckily, these two are already quite conversant in each other's language. Bob Frank brings more of a social sensibility than might be found in other economists. Cait Zaloom has an uncanny ability to speak in the language of economics, partly because of her work on trading floors.

ZALOOM: It means the physical environment, the spaces you move through, the geographical area where you live, and all the ways politics organizes the social geography. All of this becomes really, really important in the conception of the "market social" that comes out of neuroeconomics. The town you live in and the kinds of houses that are there set your benchmarks and influence the decisions you make.

FERGUSON: But the neuroeconomists wouldn't say it's the "social structure" of the town that influences individuals, right?

Here again we have the question of the superorganic. Is the "social" nothing more than the aggregate of individual decisions, or are there social facts, as Durkheim posited, structuring logics of social life that are much greater than the sum of any parts?

FERGUSON: The social structure of the town would matter, too.

ZALOOM: Yes, because this would be all the feedback from other individuals.

FERGUSON: So this would be the approach rather than talking about a thing that has a society that has a structure that can be described through the methods of social science.

We see here a fundamental fissure in the different social science perspectives. Bob Frank says that, of course, the social structure of a town plays a role in influencing individual behavior. Retaining a commitment to methodological individualism, he defines "social structure," as Cait Zaloom points out, as simply the sum of individual behaviors and decisions. For example, a town's structure emerges in so many interactions among individuals, which form the feedback mechanism whereby the structure then informs the very behaviors that continually restructure the town. But, as Jim Ferguson notes, this understanding is different from saying that the "social structure" is an entity in its own right. And this difference is one of the core contrasts in how social scientists of different stripes study the economy.

FERGUSON: So it's not the superorganic? It is really just individuals in an environment?

ZALOOM: In complex feedback loops. This is the question of the superorganic. What I think is missing from the "market social" is what makes it experientially plausible. The account is an analytic one. But the experience of choices actually has to do with forces beyond individual feedback loops. Even if you were going to take this market social, as I'm describing it, on its own terms, it's missing a big chunk.

FRANK: And I still don't feel like I have a clear idea of how this chunk couldn't emerge from the interactions and feedbacks we've been talking about. The idea of God seems totally non-mysterious to me. The moment you have the cognitive ability to project into the future and see that you're going to die and that people you care about are going to die, you have very strong affective ties to them. A narrative that would get you over this hump of constant concern and fretting about it would be a useful distraction.

ZALOOM: But the ethnological and sociological history is that, actually, when people get together, God isn't a fix. God is an entity that comes before the interactions. So it's not just that we need to solve our future problem. The "market social" is missing this sort of basic Durkheimian piece.

The issue is just that the ideas that emerge from social interaction get evacuated of their individual contents. So God actually is a thing. It's not just the sum of our collective ideas. God really is a thing that does stuff in the world.

VICTOR: It is interesting to note here that in [a] normative ethical projects sense, choice is everything. Without choice, there are no ethics and, importantly, there is no responsibility. Acting ethically involves a set of obligations taken by a person who has responsibilities that come from having a position relative to others. Those responsibilities are meaningful only if you have choices. If you don't have choices, there is no meaning to the responsibility: my mind made me do it.

Ethics and morality are, as Victor argues, based on choice. As revealing as the neuroscience is, reducing choice to conditioned synaptic responses diminishes not only individual responsibility but also the complicated social contexts that condition choice. As Zaloom argues, the "market social" goes beyond simply the sum of its parts, the informational feedback loops, to encompass a Durkheimian superorganic sense of social life as lived and experienced.

11

Neuroeconomics and the Politics of Choice

Natasha Schüll and Caitlin Zaloom

Since the late 1990s, a new space of scientific expertise has been emerging in the laboratories of elite universities, at the meetings of scientists and their public policy colleagues, in *Science* and *Nature* and other academic journals, and in the popular media. Located at the intersection of neuroscience, economics, and psychology, the field of neuroeconomics converges around behavioral deviations from the model of the human being as *Homo economicus*, a rational actor who calculates his choices to maximize his individual satisfaction. Neuroeconomists look to the biological substrate of the brain for clues to the puzzles of consumer action—why people often make decisions to buy, sell, invest, and trade in ways that seem to go against their best interests. Going a step further than behavioral economists, who argue that policy designers need to take seemingly "irrational" choices into account, neuroeconomists insist that they need to understand *how* such choices are made in the brain.

In this chapter, we focus on neuroeconomic research into "future discounting," or the tendency to forego future well-being for immediate gratification. This particular puzzle, a long-standing concern of liberal governance, has become a flash point for the young field. In experiments, neuroeconomists design tasks that can isolate and make legible the brain's evaluations of rewards in and over time, operationalizing the future in the form of "intertemporal choice," or a choice between something now and something later. Inside the scanner, the subject weighs her preferences. How long is she willing to wait for a given amount of cash? As she trades off the value of money against time, the scanner takes pictures of her brain activity. In these images, neuroeconomists attempt to discern the neural mechanisms by which human beings value—and often undervalue—the future.

In a historical moment when American policy-makers increasingly link the shortsightedness of citizens' microeconomic decisions to urgent problems—from individual conditions such as addiction and obesity to collective conditions such as the credit crisis and even global warming—probing the neurobiological mechanisms underlying humans' calculations (and miscalculations) about the future has high stakes. Why do Americans spend today when the financial demands of retirement require saving for the future? Why do they keep reaching for candy bars and fried food when they know that heart disease can result from high-calorie diets? Ongoing crises of economy, health, and environment challenge the notion that individuals can be expected to comport themselves according to the tenets of rational action.

Although policy-makers continue to encourage citizens to pursue self-interests as a path to maximizing collective well-being, they have begun to look to neuroeconomics for a model of the human being that can lend conceptual support to economic, social, and health policies designed to address a subject different from the traditional rational actor.[1] By arming themselves with an understanding of citizens as fundamentally calculating but also neurologically ill-suited to the contemporary landscape of choice, lawmakers from Washington's heights to the corridors of state agencies hope to design policy interventions that can accommodate both the capacities and the limitations of human decision making.

But how, exactly, should these capacities and limitations be modeled? Within the field of neuroeconomics, there is heated debate around the mechanisms of future discounting and the kind of model of the brain that best represents those mechanisms. Does future discounting reflect the constitutional myopia of a single value system within the brain or an inner contest between impulsive and rational brain systems? In other words, should the brain be conceptualized as a unified decision-making apparatus or as the site of conflict between an impetuous limbic system at perpetual odds with its deliberate and provident overseer in the prefrontal cortex? Although this debate does not neatly divide the field into its constituent disciplines, with all neuroscientists taking one side and all economists the other, it does fracture along epistemological lines. Whereas neuroscientists trained in the experimental methods of natural science tend to favor a "single system" model that can accommodate the complex morphological and functional constraints of the brain, economists' strong theoretical tradition leads them to favor a "dual systems" model that can reduce the brain and its functions into mathematically manageable formulas. Each model of the biology underlying future discounting endorses a different vision of the human actor, different sites of accountability, and, potentially, different kinds of governance and remediation.

When the neuroeconomics of future discounting is drawn into policy debates, what becomes of its impassioned internal debate? How do differing models of the brain influence thinking about how, and whether, the government should regulate citizens' choices in the long-term interest of individuals and the nation? Does it matter to policy whether choices derive from a unified or split valuation system? In other words, do epistemological politics bear any relationship to wider governmental politics, and if so, what kind of a relationship is it? Scientific debates over choice making in the brain, we argue, are also contests over how to define the constraints on human reason with which governance strategies must contend.

As it turns out, governmental reformers seize upon the model of choice in the brain that they can most readily harness to their pre-existing political agendas, and the other model languishes; in the process, the potential for neuroeconomics to fundamentally reconfigure the choice-making subject of policy founders. We begin our story by laying out the field's ambitious bid to redefine the human choice-maker. Next, we examine the scientific debate around future discounting as it moves through academic conferences, scientific journals, media accounts, and scientific shoptalk. The neuroscientists, psychologists, and economists participating in the new field invoke wide-ranging constituencies for their ideas, from authors and readers of popular accounts of science to interested colleagues in far-flung subfields to policy-makers. Finally, we examine how and why one model of the brain gains traction in discussions of policy reform but the other falls away.

ECONOMICS COMES TO LIFE

"It has become abundantly evident," wrote two neuroscientists in the introduction to a special issue of *Neuron* published in 2002, "that the pristine assumptions of the 'standard economic model'—that individuals operate as optimal decision makers in maximizing utility—are in direct violation of even the most basic facts about human behavior" (Cohen and Blum 2002:197). As Massachusetts Institute of Technology neuro-economist Drazen Prelec put it, "utility maximization has the advantage of being mathematical and precise, but the flaw of being incorrect" (personal communication, 2006). The dissonance between observed human behavior and economic models devised to capture this behavior drove the ascendance of behavioral and experimental economics starting in the late 1970s.[2] Grounding their research in empirical data, either constructed in a laboratory or drawn from more naturalistic settings, researchers in these subfields have documented countless instances when human behavior does not seem to follow the laws of rational economic action; on the contrary, their data have shown that people systematically depart from such laws when they weigh information and judge probabilities.

Nevertheless, the theoretically driven mainstream of economics has continued to dismiss such findings as amounting to an atheoretical and inconclusive "collection" of behavioral anomalies, insisting that existing models can be refined to accommodate such divergences. Over the past decade, the continuing resistance to behavioral and experimental approaches led a group of practitioners to search for scientific partners who could help them explain rather than merely catalog anomalous behaviors. In their eyes, the tools and techniques of neuroscience—particularly, brain imaging—offered the possibility of a unifying theory that could legitimately challenge classical rational actor models. The hope was that neuroscience could link the calculative anomalies they had been documenting for twenty-five years to the biological substrate of the brain. Instead of shoring up existing economic models to account for human departures from rationality, this radical new approach would query life itself as a way to derive alternative models—models based in nature rather than in the self-referential discourse of mathematics.

Neoclassical economics formulates its understandings of human valuation and choice making without attention to psychological and biological processes. The field, which matured at a time when it was impossible to measure such processes at the neural level, instead developed parsimonious mathematical equations to predict choice behavior (Camerer, Loewenstein, and Prelec 2005). Mainstream economics continues to concentrate its efforts on refining such equations, uninterested in the actual mechanisms of choice making because these are assumed to mirror subjects' preferences.

Yet, behavioral economist Colin Camerer, a founder of neuroeconomics, publically insists that the dismissal of neural-level explanation constitutes "brainless economics." Economics, he argues, should overcome its staunch conservatism and explore the choice-making processes that lie behind the skull and precede conscious acts of choice. To this end, the neuroeconomic partnership marries economic experiments that have been honed to solicit aberrant behavior with brain imaging, particularly, functional magnetic resonance imaging (fMRI), a technology that tracks how brain states change in response to real-time experimental stimuli. During the administration of "behavioral probes" that ask subjects to make a series of choices in which they must trade off money and time, fMRI records the intensity of cell firing through the regions of a subject's brain, illuminating the neural pathways involved in each decision.[3]

Like economists, neuroeconomists characterize decision making as a process in which "a system must assign value to each of its available choices" (Montague, Kings-Casas, and Cohen 2006:417). Instead of an abstract calculation, however, value assignment is understood to unfold along the neural circuitry of the brain. Neural tissue performs economic evaluation by means of what Read Montague at Baylor School of Medicine calls "internal currency," translating the money metaphor into the cellular and chemical structures of the brain: "Instead of dollars and cents," the *New York Times* explains, "the brain relies on the firing rates of a number of neurotransmitters—the chemicals, like dopamine, that transmit nerve impulses" (Blakeslee 2003). Levels of neural activation assign value by signaling how a given prospect has lived up to an individual's expectations in the past. In this sense, choice is conceived as a fundamentally temporal process; past and future are essential reference points for every decision. "The brain is a prediction machine," declared the esteemed neuroscientist Wolfgang Schultz at a conference celebrating the publication of the first neuroeconomics textbook.

COMPETING MODELS OF CHOICE IN TIME

If the neural valuation system works by comparing choice outcomes across time, how does it assign worth to time itself? Although it is clear that a reward's nearness or distance in time can amplify or diminish its worth (more proximate rewards, that is, are more highly valued), the rate by which individual brains discount the future is fuzzy at best. Until recently, the most commonly used framework to make sense of this rate came directly from economics. The theory of "discounted utility" proposes that individuals discount future rewards by an amount that increases exponentially as a given reward recedes in time. An example of exponential discounting would be the stable, linear interest rates that banks pay to holders of savings accounts as compensation for delaying their consumption (see Ainslie 2001). This theory leaves the rational actor model intact by assuming that people are unwavering and consistent in their rate of discount, marking down an entity's reward value in accordance with its temporally

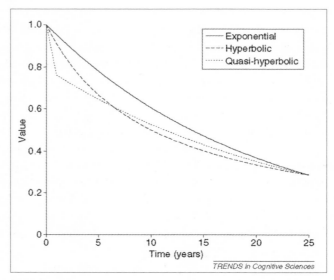

FIGURE 11.1

Graphical renderings of temporal discount functions (Berns, Laibson, and Loewenstein 2007:483).

diminishing objective worth. As a widely read paper in neuroeconomics indicates, "it is well accepted that rationality entails treating each moment of delay equally, thereby discounting according to an exponential function" (McClure et al. 2004:504).

Yet, people "exhibit much steeper devaluation over the near term than is predicted by exponential discounting" (Montague, Kings-Casas, and Cohen 2006:433; see also Lowenstein and Prelec 1992; Montague and Berns 2002:280). With the empirical finding that people sharply overvalue immediate rewards relative to future ones, experimental and behavioral economists began to shift their thinking. Discounting appeared to be hyperbolic rather than exponential, following an inconsistent rate of discount that renders a discount curve in the shape of a hyperbola rather than a gradual slope (fig. 11.1).

What is going on in the brain to render the shape? Neuroeconomists trained in axiomatic methods prefer to explain it by modeling the brain as the site of a conflict between opposing, mathematically representable systems. Those more attuned to the complexities of the biological data prefer to model the brain as a unified system of valuation whose laws we cannot yet mathematically parse. As we will see, only one model of the short-sighted brain is embraced in the policy field.

OF TWO BRAINS

In Aesop's classic fable, the ant and the grasshopper illustrate two familiar but disparate approaches to human intertemporal decision making. The grasshopper luxuriates during a warm summer day, inattentive to the future. The ant, in contrast, stores food for the upcoming winter. Human decision-makers seem to be torn between an impulse to act like the indulgent grasshopper and an awareness that the patient ant often gets ahead in the long run (McClure et al. 2004:503).

The "dual brain hypothesis" represents a variation on the theme of split-selfhood that has been articulated at numerous points in Western thought. Plato famously described reason as a charioteer attempting to steer the twin horses of passion and spirit. Adam Smith wrote of the tension between interests and passions, arguing that coolheaded capitalist calculation could mitigate the dangers of hotheaded affect. Sigmund Freud developed a theory of the ego as the site of a fraught battle between an overseeing superego and a shortsighted, impulsive id. Later theories in the fields of psychology, cognitive science, economics, and political philosophy went on to reiterate the idea of the self as comprising distinct systems of competing tendencies—cold versus hot, deliberative versus impulsive, abstract versus visceral, and the like.

In contemporary neuroscientific versions of this hoary model, an affective system (described as fast, emotional, unconscious, automatic, experiential, associationist, connectionist, and analogical) is understood as rooted in the mesolimbic areas of the brain. A contrasting analytic system (described as slow, logical, conscious, hypothetical, creative, forward looking, and abstract) is rooted in more recently evolved cortical regions that are impervious to the temptations of present rewards and reprise the themes of temperate affect said to emerge from the calculations of enterprise, in early theorists of capitalism (Hirschman 1977). Writing in *Science* in 2004, neuroscientists Samuel McClure and Jonathan Cohen teamed up with economists David Laibson and George Loewenstein to offer a distinctively neuroeconomic spin on split-selfhood, bearing the declarative (and, some would say, argumentative) title "Separate Neural Systems Value Immediate and Delayed Monetary Rewards." The highly influential piece has provided rich soil for the debate over the phenomenon of future discounting. In the experiment on which the article is based, subjects lying in an fMRI scanner were asked to choose between Amazon.com gift certificates of different monetary amounts and delivery delays: $20 now or $30 in two weeks; $5 in two weeks or $10 in four weeks; $20 in four weeks or $40 in six weeks.

The neural data recorded during the experiment's choice trials led the authors to conclude that distinct neural systems appraise near- and far-term rewards (McClure et al. 2004:504). Future discounting, they argued, reflects competition between a midbrain dopamine system activated by immediately available rewards and prefrontal cortical areas activated by all prospective rewards, "irrespective of delay" (2004:503).[4] The phylogenetically "older" limbic system—emotional, impulsive, and myopic in its functioning—overrides the analytical, deliberative, calculating valuation of the "newer" prefrontal cortex. Having begun the article with reference to Aesop's classic fable of the grasshopper and the ant, the authors finish by suggesting that "within the domain of intertemporal choice, the idiosyncrasies of human preferences seem to reflect a competition between the impetuous limbic grasshopper and the provident prefrontal ant within each of us" (2004:506).

In addition to frequent use of metaphor, proponents of the dual-brain hypothesis literalize the competition between the future-focused cortical regions and present-biased mesolimbic challengers. Randy Buckner, a neuroscientist from Harvard University tasked with educating economists on the basics of neuroscience at the 2007 annual meeting of the Society for Neuroeconomics, explained to his charges: "These brain systems are probably competing with each other in non-linear ways.... With fMRI we can see battles between brain systems as they are taking place."

In economics, the idea of internal competition preceded attention to the brain. Two decades before neuroeconomics existed, behavioral economists like Richard Thaler (Thaler and Shefrin 1981) at the University of Chicago constructed a model of competition between internal selves, showing that it was possible to apply game theory–based approaches within a single individual by treating the individual as more than one system. Departures from consistent rationality could then be understood as the result of game interaction between selves—in the case of hyperbolic discounting, between a rational-deliberative self able to consistently rate value over time (identified by economic shorthand as the *delta* parameter) and an emotional-irrational self prone to grab for immediate rewards (identified by economic shorthand as a *beta* parameter) (Elster 1984; Phelps and Pollack 1968). As vulgar as the beta-delta simplification seems, it offers heuristic elegance in the form of a neat equation that accurately predicts the inconsistent rates of temporal future discounting—regardless of whether it accurately depicts their brain mechanisms.

Thaler's student Colin Camerer, along with other game theory–influenced behavioral economists, thus came to neuroeconomics with a ready-made model of split agency in tow and proceeded to map its beta and delta parameters onto the physical brain through scanning technology. Neural regions that appear to be consistently active and exponentially evaluative no matter the time delay of a reward are designated as *delta*, and those that are "activated disproportionately when choices involve an opportunity for near-term reward" are identified as *beta* (Loewenstein 1997:645). The hyperbolic curve of future discounting is reconceived as quasi-hyperbolic, for it reflects two discounting rates operating at the same time, in tension (Laibson 1997; see fig. 11.1); decisions are understood as the vector outcome of competition between planful and impulsive systems.

ONE BRAIN, ONE SELF

Although neuroscientists participating in the new field of neuroeconomics specifically look to economists for the heuristics and behavioral theories with which they can illuminate brain-imaging data, many take umbrage at the cavalier manner in which their collaborators seek to simplify the complexity of the brain's neural system for the sake of explanatory power. Although the field of psychology has developed its own native "dual-systems" and "multi-modal" models of the brain, the beta-delta model that has come to dominate the neuroeconomics of future discounting is one that derives primarily from economics and its tradition of game theory—and one that neuroscientists and psychologists tend to regard as a gross distortion of the human choice-making process. Instead of two selves competing for dominance inside the brain, they believe, the phenomenon of hyperbolic discounting must originate in an integrated set of systems working in concert to produce a value signal.

"We biologists just can't wrap our heads around the idea of split agency, of a non-whole organism," explained Paul Glimcher, a New York University neuroscientist and an early organizer of neuroeconomics (personal communication 2006). Glimcher describes an exchange with economist Laibson: "He told me once, 'If you relax the assumptions, then [the beta-delta model] makes perfect sense.' But wait a minute, David—you aren't allowed to relax the constraints of the brain! It's not just a loose theory. It's a physical entity." Laibson offers his own set of reflections on the epistemological divide Glimcher identifies: "We economists take for granted that the world is complex, and we simplify it to do social science.... Neuroscientists are less willing to crudely simplify. They say, 'Don't tell me two brain[s]. There are billions of neurons. Let's get serious about the neuroanatomy.' But a scientific theory of the world that gets it exactly right is too complicated to be useful" (personal communication 2005).

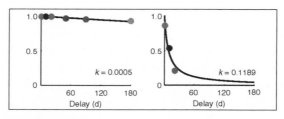

FIGURE 11.2

Discount rates of the most patient subject and the most impulsive subject in Kable and Glimcher's (2007:1627) study.

Laibson casts neuroscientists as mired in biological literalism, incapable of rising above the brain's forest of neurons to think in useful behavioral models. Although he and his fellow behavioral economists argue against the "brainless economics" of their own discipline, they persist in starting from theory and working toward the empirical material, treating the brain as the testing ground and repository of neural evidence for revised models of human behavior. Glimcher moves in the opposite direction: instead of seeking to embed mathematics in the brain, he seeks to biologize choice making. He is convinced that the biology of valuation, choice, and action involves "a unitary system, a convergence of inputs—not a cognitive, multiple self situation, with each side fighting for control over your arm" (Glimcher 2008). His model assumes a single, unified self corresponding to a single, unified brain. He concludes, "There must be a final common path and it looks like we have our finger on it" (2008).

Glimcher and his student Joseph Kable (Kable and Glimcher 2007) propose that a given individual's intertemporal choice behavior reflects her own unique subjective discounting rate; depending on her disposition and past experiences, a subject may display a shallow curve (such as the medical student in the study who saved her earnings from the experiment), a steep curve (such as the drifter who went skydiving with the study money), or anywhere in between (fig. 11.2). Every person expresses a particular style of trading off time and reward that forms the core of his or her decision making in the world, and this style is revealed (much as preferences are revealed in choices, according to standard economics) in the image of an "individual preference curve." This curve matches the behavioral data of the subject's choices and at the same time matches her brain activation; there is a one-to-one correspondence between the two. The slope of her curve may change with experience, but at any given moment, it describes the type of person she is: impetuous and unable to plan or disciplined and skilled at long-term planning.

If the dual-systems model were true, Kable points out, one would expect impulsive subjects to have overactive beta areas, yet both delta and beta brain regions are active across subjects despite marked differences in their degree of impulsivity. This finding supports the case for a unified valuation system in the human brain and advances the idea that future discounting reflects a consistent response to objective changes in amount or delay of rewards rather than inconsistency in rates of discount as a result of competition between distinct inner selves. In other words, there are no impatient or impulsive systems, just impulsive or impatient people. Instead of beta (steep rate of discount) offsetting delta (shallow rate of discount), the data suggest a stable rate of subjective value (neural discount rate). Kable tells us, "From a scientific viewpoint, we haven't found any evidence for multiple competing selves in the brain, where there is one part of your brain that's this impulsive energy source and there's this other part of your brain that's a patient, forward-looking energy source and they're duking it out for control over what you're going to do. Instead, if you're an impulsive person, the neural activity seems to be representing the value of rewards to an impulsive person. And if you're a patient person, the neural activity seems to be representing the value of rewards to a patient person" (personal communication 2006).

THE POLITICS OF MODELS

"At the most general level," write Laibson and his colleagues, "it is important to determine whether the brain has one all-purpose time discounting mechanism or whether the brain draws upon different systems, each with its own occasionally competing time perspective" (Berns, Laibson, and Loewenstein 2007:486). If we can understand the precise mechanisms of future discounting, Laibson paraphrased for a journalist, "we will be in a much better position to design policies that mitigate what can be self-defeating behavior" (Cassidy 2006).

Despite such claims for the importance of neuroeconomics to policy, the question remains, When it comes to guiding people toward decisions that can bring them long-term rewards, does it matter to policy-makers whether self-defeating choices about the future stem from a brain divided by dueling forces or from a brain unified by a common pathway? How does the tension between the data-driven realism of neuroscience and the model-driven mathematics of economics play out at the level of governance and intervention?

Liberal governance seeks to ensure individual and collective well-being through the aggregate of its citizens' self-interested choices—choices assumed to be motivated by a common capacity for rational conduct. This philosophical framework directs individuals to develop an optimal course for their own futures through choice making, faulting those who deviate from the normative social parameters by spending or consuming too much. Neuroeconomists, by locating the problem of shortsighted behavior in the biological substrate of the human brain, suggest that the moral bias of liberal governance is misplaced; future discounting does not indicate deficiencies of an abstract will, but rather the workings of neural circuits. This morally neutral explanation frames humans' shortsighted temporal orientation as an evolutionary endowment that may have carried adaptive value in past contexts but has become non-optimal (and even a liability) in our contemporary decision environment. There is a "massive mismatch," as one neuroeconomist put it, between the template for successful behavior that developed in settings characterized by the day-to-day demands of survival and the long-term investments that success in present-day liberal democracies demands. Although impulsivity may benefit capitalist economies by driving robust consumption, individuals are not well served by the impulsive directives of the shortsighted brain. Nor are they well served by the regulative systems of contemporary capitalism, which are rarely designed in a way that follows "how we are wired," as neuroscientist Hans Breiter explained (personal communication 2008).

The wiring of the neuroeconomic subject thus presents a challenge for policy-makers: If human brains are inclined to overvalue the present or near future, then how to promote the delay of gratification or abstention from consumption? What measures can correct for our nearsighted biology? Neuroeconomics suggests that any adequate answer to these questions must acknowledge the role of human biology in decision making. Rather than proceed in ignorance or denial of this biology, as do policies based on an assumption that rational action is a human universal, regulation should follow the "way we are wired." The new universal that emerges from such an approach is a species-wide frailty of reason located in the brain. The scientific battles we have reviewed can be understood as contests over how to model this frailty. In the different emplotments of the neural pathways involved in future discounting, one- and two-brain models present policy-makers with contrasting visions of human rationality and the synaptic limitations in which to ground applications of liberal philosophy and technique.

Whether in support of existing policies or reform agendas, lawmakers could be said to follow two general models of intervention when it comes to adjusting an individual's future discounting curves. The first seeks remediation at the internal level by changing the person's choice-making tendencies. Addressing the internal drivers of undesirable behavior has a long lineage in liberal governance strategies. From nineteenth-century budgeting instructions for the poor to contemporary head-start programs and courses on parenting skills for welfare mothers, education and training techniques promise to advance the liberal project by boosting individual self-management skills. The second type of policy intervention seeks to remediate future discounting at the external level by reframing environmental cues in a way that can incentivize future-directed choice making—a variation on liberal governance that has taken center stage in the Obama administration.

As it happens, dual- and single-brain models for future discounting lend themselves equally to internal and external governmental approaches. Yet, each model differently renders the object of intervention, and this difference proves critical to their respective policy appeal. The dual-systems model invites policies to buoy the delta function that purportedly lies within every person. The single-system model of the brain, on the other hand, tasks policy-makers with altering specific individuals' subjective valuations (i.e., the preferences that dispose them to skydive today rather than deposit cash in a savings account for growth and future use). Although the dual-systems model allows for the possibility that individuals will have distinct discount rates based on the particular ratio of delta to beta functionality in their brains, the fact that it neatly separates these functions (instead of unifying them, as in the one-brain model) sustains a long-standing tenet of liberal governance, that every member of the polity can be expected to harbor the same essential capacity for rational evaluation. The one-brain model presents a problem for liberal governance by distributing this faculty unevenly across the population and by diluting its potential strength within each person. Unlike the two-brain discounter, the one-brain discounter has no pristine site of rationality to which policy-makers might appeal; the subject does not suffer from an anemia of actuarial capacities that might be remedied with the right policy tools, but from the unconflicted expression of a singular value system. The single-system brain model thus saddles policy-makers with the difficult task of formulating policies whose broad social application could address myopic individuals' discount curves without impinging on the individual freedoms of the rest of the population—freedoms around which liberal governance is organized.

Even as neuroeconomists themselves continue to argue about the mechanisms of future discounting, the two-brain model prevails in policy discussions. Working with this model as a somatic template, policy designers—including those who would alter choice-makers themselves and those who would alter the choice environment—can strategically fashion policies that address the delta regions of the brain, coaxing rationality from citizens and thus guiding them toward both individual and collective good. So-called choice architects, for instance, explicitly invoke the two-brain model to ground an approach that a reporter for the *New Yorker* described as "a new political philosophy based on the idea of saving people from the vagaries of their limbic regions" (Cassidy 2006). In the best-selling policy bible *Nudge: Improving Decisions about Health, Wealth, and Happiness,* Richard Thaler and Cass Sunstein (2008) feature the conflicted human brain as the source of systematic errors in human judgment. They refer to one system alternately as "Automatic" and "Homer Simpson" and set this glutton against the hyper-rational "Mr. Spock" of the "Reflective" system; the trick to regulating, they argue, is to organize decision environments in a way that tips the balance in the Vulcan's favor. Their proposed interventions range from placing fruit instead of cheesecake at the end of a lunch line to requiring that companies automatically set aside a portion of their workers' salaries in a retirement plan (while allowing employees to opt for withdrawing the funds). By transferring a portion of the responsibility for short-term thinking from the choice-maker to the environment, this policy approach seeks to regulate the setting in which a person encounters the conflict between near-term and long-term values.

As financial crises, epidemic obesity, and global warming have raised troubling questions about mainstream economic models of rational action, the work of behavioral economists has attained a new prominence among policy-makers. In a bid to further legitimize their claim that viable economic models must take human irrationality into account, these economists have opened the policy conversation to brain science. Yet, neuroeconomics' endeavor to move beyond the rational actor of classical economics and political philosophy languishes as its dual-systems model recuperates the human subject that liberal governance and its policy technicians have always addressed. Although dual-systems advocates recast this subject as neurological rather than moral and as an incipient, rather than a consistent, rational actor, they preserve intact its essential capacity for rationality—and thus for governability in a liberal framework. In other words, although they demote this capacity from the irreducible and abstract "will" of *Homo economicus* to the material and chemical mechanisms of a "homunculus economicus" in the brain, the dual-systems advocates nevertheless enable the continued command of the rational actor at the helm of liberal governance.

Acknowledgments

Our research was funded by the National Science Foundation Program on Science and Society grant #0621037. For a longer version of the chapter, see Schüll and Zaloom 2011. Thanks are due to the neuroeconomists who shared their work and insights with us, especially Kacey Ballard, Colin Camerer, Paul Glimcher, Julian Jamison, Joseph Kable, Brian Knutson, David Laibson, Kenway Louie, Read Montague, and Antonio Rangel. We also benefited from the counsel of Chris Kelty, Rogan Kersh, Andy Lakoff, and Michael Lynch; Stephen Rosenberg; and the participants in the Harvard workshop "Our Brains Ourselves" and the SAR advanced seminar "Markets and Moralities."

Notes

1. Since the 1990s, an era that President George Bush and the US Congress famously designated as the Decade of the Brain, "notions of what it means to be particular kinds of persons, populations and political subjects are increasingly bound up with the meanings, explanations and theories of contemporary neuroscience" (Vrecko 2010:2). In the past two decades, a growing number of sociologists, anthropologists, and historians of science have begun to study the neurosciences (Beaulieu 2001, 2002; Cohn 2004; Dumit 2003; Harrington 1992; Lakoff 2009; Lynch 1985; Rose 2007; Vidal 2009).

2. Beginning with Kahneman and Tversky's (1979) influential Prospect Theory and extending to Smith's (1991) development of scientific experimentation for economic inquiries, the subfields of behavioral and experimental economics made major strides in destabilizing economics' resistance to empirical models of behavior.

3. Brain-imaging technologies and techniques pose challenging problems for research design, statistical analysis, and the assertion of correlations (between blood flow and behavior). For the purposes of this chapter, however, we describe the process of scientific reductionism in neuroeconomics and fMRI imaging without elaborating a critical position.

4. Lakoff (2009) offers a history of the idea of human rationality in the psychological, physiological, and cognitive sciences, ending with the contemporary assignment of planning and strategizing capacities to functions of the prefrontal cortex. Tracing the shifting epistemic milieus surrounding measures of reasoning capacities, he shows how reason gets shaped as a certain kind of scientific object. The vision of reason in neuroeconomics (i.e., the ability to make goal-oriented decisions under uncertain conditions) maps neatly onto the contemporary endpoint of Lakoff's conceptual history.

12

Ultimatums and Rationalities in Two Maya Towns

Edward F. Fischer and Avery Dickins de Girón

Anthropologists have long questioned the assumptions of self-interest and rational optimization that prevail in neoclassical economics (and in areas of political science, sociology, and law). Granted, utility functions that neatly condense human behavior into a drive to maximize returns in the pursuit of preferences have a certain mathematical beauty. But from an ethnographic perspective, such models fail to account for the complex, often contradictory, motivations stemming from moral values, cultural identities, and all the messy realities of quotidian experience that do not lend themselves to coding as tidy variables.

The burgeoning subfields of behavioral and experimental economics are leading a soft revolution in the discipline, drawing on social psychology and game theory to account for widespread "deviations" from rational-choice expectations and offering an opening for anthropological considerations. Experimental games and scenarios gauge actual behavior against rational-choice assumptions, taking into account proximate knowledge and context-dependent decisions, risk aversion and status quo biases, and cooperative and competitive motivations (e.g., Akerlof and Kranton 2005; Camerer 2003; Güth, Schmittberger, and Schwarze 1982; Shiller 2005; Smith 2000; Thaler 1992). In this chapter, we combine experimental methodologies, in the form of the Ultimatum Game, with ethnographic description to examine the rationalities of cooperation and competition in two Maya communities in Guatemala. The Ultimatum Game offers a robust experimental method for documenting the limits of self-interest and rationality in actual behavior and the competing pulls of competition and cooperation in the context of anonymous game play.

In the Ultimatum Game, two players are anonymously paired with each other, and a sum of money (x) is given in cash to Player A. Player A's sole move is to offer Player B a portion (y) of the total x. Knowing the amount (x) that Player A has received, Player B's one move is then to either accept or reject the offer. If Player B accepts, she keeps the money offered (y), and Player A keeps the rest (x - y). If Player B rejects the offer, the money is returned to the main pot, and neither player receives anything. Thus, the game consists entirely of Player A making an offer and Player B either accepting or rejecting that offer.

In terms of maximizing one's material utility, the most rational move for Player A is to offer the smallest unit of account (10 percent if playing with ten bills) and for Player B to accept the offer (since any amount will have more utility than zero, which is the alternative). In fact, we find that across cultures the modal offer is 50 percent of the total and that average offers usually fall between 40 percent and 50 percent of the total. Hessel Oosterbeek, Randolph Sloof, and Gijs van de Kuilen (2004) conducted a meta-analysis of thirty-two Ultimatum Game experiments from around the world, finding the overall average offer to be 40 percent of the total (and the rejection rate 16 percent), independent of the size of the pie.

Here we report the results of several rounds of the Ultimatum Game played in the Kaqchikel Maya town of Tecpán and the Q'eqchi' Maya community of Chisec. We find unusually high offers in Tecpán, suggestive of a high degree of cooperation, whereas we find relatively low offers and more aggressively competitive moves in Chisec. Our results are consistent with the hypothesis advanced by Joseph Henrich and colleagues (2004), Jean Ensminger (2002), and others that greater market integration results in more cooperative game playing—Tecpán is a booming market town tightly linked to the national economy, whereas Chisec is more remote, marginalized, and impoverished. Although market integration may show a strong correlation with cooperative game behavior, equally important for understanding the Ultimatum Game results from Tecpán and Chisec are vernacular rationalities built upon moral conceptions of equality and fairness, socioeconomic differences between individuals and communities, and local histories of violence and activism.

TABLE 12.1

Ultimatum Game Results from around the World

Group	Mean	Mode	Rejection
Lamalera	.57	.50	n/a
Maya-Tecpán	.51	.50	.05
Ache	.48	.40	.00
Developed countries (average)	.44	.50	n/a
Shona	.44	.50	.08
Maya-Chisec	.43	.40	.29
Tokyo	.42	.50	.24
Jerusalem	.37	.50	.27
Mapuche	.34	.50	.07
Machiguenga	.26	.15	.05

Source: Data come from Roth et al. 1991 and Henrich et al. 2004:20; developed country average from Henrich et al. 2001; see also Hoffman et al. 1994; Oosterbeek, Sloof, and van de Kuilen 2004.

THE ULTIMATUM GAME: CROSS-CULTURAL RESULTS

The Ultimatum Game applies the dilemma of competitive-versus-cooperative behavior to an experimental context of real material stakes. Average offer sizes place a monetary value on players' preferences for cooperation and competition—higher offers reflect greater cooperation. Rejection rates similarly value the utility of punishing noncooperative behavior. Results from the Ultimatum Game played around the world offer a powerful critique of narrowly economic conceptions of self-interest and rationality. Comparing figures from published studies, we see that average offers range from 26 percent of the total (among the Machiguenga of Peru) to 57 percent (among the Lamalera of Indonesia); rejection rates vary between 0 and 29 percent (table 12.1). In between these extremes, we find great variability in game strategies, belying any presumption of universal rationality.

Perhaps the most significant finding to emerge from these studies is that modal offers across cultures tend to be 50 percent of the total, suggesting, if anything, a widespread bias toward cooperation. The deviation from rational expectations (offers of the smallest unit of play and rejection rates of zero) is striking. The most common reason given for higher than minimum offers is the risk of having the offer rejected—a rational choice when taking into account the irrationality of the other player, who might not accept a low offer. Rejection rates, when seen from the perspective of "opportunity costs" (the value of the road not taken), measure the economic value of punishing other players for having offered a minimum percentage (or in economic terms, for acting rationally). Rejecting an offer is equivalent to paying that same amount to punish the other player for not acting fairly.

THE CONTEXTS OF PLAY

Our study compares two rounds of Ultimatum Game experiments. The first was conducted in 2003 with Kaqchikel Maya participants from Tecpán, Guatemala, and the second was carried out in 2004 with Q'eqchi' Maya participants from Chisec. These are two very different Maya communities: one a progressive commercial center with a long history of integration into the national political economy and the other a struggling migrant community on the margins of national life. We call on these circumstances to explain the distinct Ultimatum Game strategies recorded in each town.

Located along the Pan-American Highway about 80 km west of Guatemala City, Tecpán is a relatively affluent Maya town with approximately ten thousand residents. The local economy depends heavily on agriculture—subsistence-oriented milpa plots of maize and beans and, increasingly, export production of broccoli and snow peas (Hamilton and Fischer 2003). But its commercial base sets Tecpán apart from neighboring indigenous communities. Tecpán is home to a large regional market, which takes over the town center on Thursdays, and a thriving manufacturing sector. The areas of greatest growth and opportunity are sweater production and non-traditional agriculture, both of which favor small producers through low barriers to market access and the synergistic network effects of concentrated production (see Fischer and Benson 2006). As a result, we find a strong indigenous bourgeois class that has long supported ethnic consciousness and the value of education. It is increasingly common for Tecpaneco youths to not only complete their secondary education but go also on to attend university in Guatemala City. Our surveys found the average length of education to be 8.6 years, extremely high for a Maya community, and fewer than 3 percent of indigenous respondents were monolingual Kaqchikel speakers.

Tecpán has a reputation in Guatemala as being an especially progressive place, materially, ideologically, and culturally. Kaqchikel residents share a widespread sense of common purpose based on the notion of a Tecpaneco exceptionalism—the feeling that this is no ordinary Maya community. The seat of the pre-Hispanic Kaqchikel empire, the first capital of Guatemala, and long integrated into national life, Tecpán is proudly proclaimed by its residents to be a *pueblo vanguardista* (see Fischer and Hendrickson 2002). A disproportionate number of Maya leaders spearheading the country's pan-Maya movement come from Tecpán, a fact reflected in local organizations to promote Maya culture and the Kaqchikel language.

Located in the relatively remote department of Alta Verapaz in north-central Guatemala, Chisec serves as an urban market center for scores of surrounding villages and hamlets. The municipal population of about eight thousand is composed mostly of Q'eqchi' Maya; most families rely on milpa agriculture for their subsistence, and a sizable portion also grows small plots of cardamom (which will make its way up through layers of middlemen to be exported to the Middle East) and keeps a few head of cattle. The town is home to hardware stores, restaurants, and other small businesses, although the commercial sector here is only a fraction of the size of Tecpán's. Indeed, Chisec is considered to be a relatively affluent community for the area, but in comparison with Tecpán, the poverty is striking. The Chisec region has been historically marginalized from national politics and economics (see King 1974; Wilson 1991) and neglected by the international development programs, which have had a stronger presence in the highlands around Tecpán.

This isolation is reflected in low education levels and high rates of monolingualism, illiteracy, and poverty. Q'eqchi' families in Chisec typically live in wooden homes with earthen floors and thatch roofs; homes located in the central part of town have electricity, but those on the periphery have no electricity or drainage systems. The participants in our study in Chisec had attended an average of 1.76 years of school, less than a second-grade education; 57 percent had never attended school, and 61 percent were monolingual Q'eqchi' speakers. The Q'eqchi' of Chisec and the surrounding area are an immigrant population, having been forced out of their highland homelands over the past 150 years by the expansion of coffee plantations and general land scarcity. In 1981, at the height of Guatemala's civil war, Chisec was converted by the army into a "model development village" and populated by hundreds of families forced to resettle from their remote hamlets into a more easily controlled, urban concentration.

Despite Chisec's greater poverty, lower levels of education, and overall marginalization, respondents there were much more optimistic than those in Tecpán about the economic and political future of Guatemala. More Chisecos see a positive economic future for themselves and their children than do those in Tecpán (69 percent versus 51 percent), but Tecpanecos have significantly lower opinions of both the local and national governments. And whereas only 34 percent of Chisecos believe that postwar democracy in Guatemala is working "well" or "very well," a mere 3 percent of Tecpaneco respondents believe the same. Yet, the optimism of the Chisecos does not translate into greater willingness to cooperate, as we found in the results of our Ultimatum Games.

We attribute the optimism in Chisec to the historical lack of development in the region. The presence of humanitarian aid organizations has dramatically increased in recent years, largely due to the construction of a paved road, completed in 2002. In discussion groups with game participants, many individuals described themselves as having little knowledge or education and few skills. They expressed enthusiasm for the arrival of development programs to the region, implying that in their current situation, they have nothing to lose and everything to gain. Chisecos have a palpable sense that things are changing and for the better.

METHODOLOGY

Borrowing from established methodologies (Camerer 2003; Camerer and Fehr 2004; Güth, Schmittberger, and Schwarze 1982; Kagel and Roth 1995; Smith 2000), we played Ultimatum Games based on a common protocol in Tecpán and Chisec. Local assistants recruited participants through posters put up throughout each town, announcements made in municipal meetings, and word of mouth. Although these are not random samples, we strove for representativeness by recruiting participants from across sectors of the local Indian populations (Chisec's population is more than 91 percent indigenous; Tecpán's is about 70 percent). Only adults over eighteen years of age were allowed to participate, but no eligible volunteers were refused. The average age of participants in Tecpán was thirty-four, and in Chisec it was thirty-seven (with a range of eighteen to eighty for all participants). In Tecpán, 61 percent of the sample was male, compared with 41 percent in Chisec. In total, games were played with seventy-six Tecpanecos and seventy individuals from Chisec. Volunteers were interviewed in the month before the actual experiments took place, and the games were conducted over several days in both towns. Each participant was paid a small stipend for his or her time, and players kept any earnings from the game.

The pot size for the Ultimatum Games we conducted was 10 quetzales (approximately \$1.25). This relatively small stake size is equal to the lowest day wage for unskilled domestic or agricultural labor in both Tecpán and Chisec. (Purchasing power is about the same in Tecpán and Chisec, with lower overhead costs in Chisec offset by higher transport costs.) For some players, the amount involved was significant, and for others it was not, and we must consider the possibility that 10 quetzales was not high enough to invoke more rational behavior on the part of more affluent players. But this supposition itself is revealing: perhaps a certain affluence engenders generosity (and perhaps too much affluence mutes it).

Games were played with groups of between eight and twenty individuals at a time; in both towns, we rented three rooms in a house close to the center. Upon entering the location, participants would pick from a bag a slip of paper that placed them in one of two groups (A or B) and assigned them a number. The two groups were kept in separate rooms throughout the game and were anonymously paired based on their randomly selected numbers (A1 and B1, A2 and B2, and so on). The game was explained to both groups in Spanish and Kaqchikel or Q'eqchi', followed by questions and answers. Immediately before each participant played the game, investigators individually explained the rules to the player and asked her to respond to hypothetical game scenarios (e.g., "If you offer 3 quetzales and the offer is accepted, how many quetzales do you keep?"). Whenever examples were given, a range of hypotheticals was used (e.g., offers of 3, 5, and 7) to avoid influencing participant perceptions of game expectations.

We used 1-quetzal coins to tangibly demonstrate the structure of the game. We would ask each Player A to go through several trial runs in which she made an offer, and then we explained the potential outcomes until we were sure she understood. We repeated the demonstrations and trial runs a sufficient number of times so that particular examples would not affect the individual's strategy in the actual game through imitation. Similar hypothetical trial runs were conducted with each Player B, who could accept or reject the offer made by Player A.

During games, we worked with local assistants who acted as intermediaries between the two anonymously paired players. Offers and the subsequent acceptances or rejections were made by players one-on-one through the investigators who had checked the players' understanding of the game and given them a chance to ask questions. After all offers had been accepted or rejected and accordingly disbursed, we brought all the players together and held a group discussion to debrief the participants and to explore their comments and observations regarding the game.

RESULTS AND INTERPRETATIONS

The most surprising finding is Tecpán's average offer of 51 percent of the total (x), among the highest recorded anywhere in the world (see table 12.1 for comparison), whereas in Chisec, the average offer was 42 percent (table 12.2). In both communities, the modal offer was 50 percent of x, but in Tecpán, 76 percent offered half the pot and in Chisec, only 17 percent offered half. Hyperfair offers (those of more than 50 percent of x) made up 16 percent of offers in Tecpán and only 11 percent in Chisec. More significant, 69 percent of offers in Chisec were below the midpoint, whereas only 8 percent of offers were below midpoint in Tecpán. The high percentage

TABLE 12.2

Ultimatum Game Results from Tecpán and Chisec (with 10-Quetzal Stakes)

	Tecpán	Chisec
Average offer	5.1	4.2
Mode	5.0	5.0
Minimum offer	4.3	3.7
Rejections	5.3%	29.4%
Income-maximizing offer (IMO)	4.85	4.67
Average offer—IMO	0.25	-0.47

of offers below 5 quetzales made by players in Chisec (69 percent) suggests that the participants in Chisec were playing a more aggressive (and rationally maximizing) game.

Yet, in Chisec, rejection rates were much higher (29.4 percent) than in Tecpán (5.3 percent), a presumptively irrational strategy (any percentage of x offers greater material utility than nothing) but consistent with the characterization of Chisecos as employing especially aggressive strategies in the Ultimatum Game. Rejection rates are interesting because they place a monetary value on punishing another player for what is perceived as unfair behavior. In terms of economic opportunity costs, to reject an offer of 3 quetzales is equivalent to paying 3 quetzales in order to deny the other player 7 quetzales to punish her for what is perceived as an inequitable offer. Optimal income-maximizing rational behavior would result in no rejections (any amount is better than none). The rationality of lower offers in Chisec as compared with Tecpán is seemingly offset by the presumptive irrationality of Chisec's high rejection rate. Yet, the overall rejection rate in Chisec is a bit misleading. Disaggregating the 29 percent rejection rate, we find that 58 percent of offers below the median were accepted in Chisec (versus 37 percent in Tecpán). Thus, although we find a higher rejection rate in Chisec compared with Tecpán, players in Chisec were actually more likely to accept low offers (i.e., less than half of the pot size) than players in Tecpán. Although Chisec participants played more aggressively, they were willing to accept lower offers.

Here we encounter the conundrum that Player A may be acting rationally to maximize income, given the anticipated irrationality of Player B (expressed in a willingness to reject an offer seen as insultingly low). To account for this interpretation, we calculate the income-maximizing offer (IMO; see Camerer and Fehr 2004; Paciotti and Hadley 2003). The IMO takes into account the probability of an offer at a given level being accepted. It is determined by ranking the results of each possible offer size (1, 2, 3, 4, 5, etc.) multiplied by 1 minus the percentage of players who said they would reject that offer. (Before revealing the actual offers, we queried each Player B on the minimum amount she would accept, allowing us to determine the probability of rejection for all possible offer amounts.) The IMO in Tecpán is 4.85 and in Chisec 4.67—very close. But when we compare this figure with actual offers (average offers minus IMO), we find that average offers in Tecpán were higher than the IMO (0.25) and in Chisec they were significantly lower (-0.47). Again, we see Chisecos playing much more aggressively in both offers and rejections.

COMMENTARY

Our findings of hyperfair average offers in Tecpán and significantly lower offers in Chisec are consistent with the hypothesis that market integration encourages cooperation between anonymous partners (see Henrich et al. 2004). Yet, this correlation by itself only partly explains the higher average offer size in Tecpán. Following Michael Chibnik (2005), we argue that other sociocultural contextual influences are also at play. In the cases of Tecpán and Chisec, these include personal income and general community affluence (which are hard to separate from market integration), moral values suspicious of inequalities (and particular conceptions of what constitutes fair gains), and the different ways violence, ethnic activism, and the world market have converged in the recent histories of the two towns.

Higher general community affluence and personal wealth (usually associated with degree of market integration) perhaps encourage more cooperative behavior: in this case, Tecpanecos can afford to be more generous and cooperative, whereas the absolute poverty of Chisecos compels them to pursue more immediate self-interest. In Tecpán, cultural traditions reinforce moral values of reciprocity and cooperation—communal harvesting, ritual exchanges of sweet rolls on Maundy Thursday, collective obligations for the town fiesta, and so on. This characterization is not to be romanticized as a subaltern anticapitalist stance—most Tecpanecos value just rewards for hard work and want to better their own material circumstances. At the same time, the Tecpaneco vernacular of capitalist meritocracy (valuing hard work and the fruits of affluence that are honestly come by) is tempered by a deep suspicion of those who get too rich too quickly and are stingy with their resources. Morality tales are told of greedy individuals' Faustian pacts with the devil, hidden chests of gold, and connections to the drug trade.

Tecpán is also home to a number of national leaders of the pan-Maya movement, which seeks to raise the ethnic consciousness of Guatemala's indigenous peoples in pursuit of political recognition and material concessions from the state (see Fischer and Brown 1996; Warren 1998). The movement builds on a long local history of Maya cultural activism and social cohesion founded in a common sense of Kaqchikel identity and Tecpaneco exceptionalism (Fischer 2001). Local activists celebrate reciprocal and cooperative cultural traditions, and the salience of these ideals certainly influenced the higher-on-average offers. When questioned after the games about why they offered what they did, players who offered 50 percent or more of the total told us that they imagined their partner needing the money as much or more than they did and, in this light, they did not feel right taking more than half. Most players who offered less that 50 percent similarly reported that they felt they probably needed the money more than their partner and thus felt morally justified in making a lower offer (and a few invoked a clear income-maximizing rationality to justify low offers). For these reasons, Tecpanecos are inequality-adverse players in the Ultimatum Game.

Paradoxically, because of the town's affluence, Tecpanecos can afford to pursue cultural norms that are inequality adverse. But this impulse is tempered in the trying economic circumstances of Chisec, where offers tend more toward the rationality of self-interest, thus maximizing returns. Although the subsample sizes are very small, the data suggest that even within communities, higher-income individuals tend to exhibit more generosity. Henrich and colleagues (2004) found that the individual attribute of relative wealth did not predict offers when group-level variables (ethnolinguistic group traits) were factored in. At the same time, Henrich and Smith (2004) found that the generally better-off cash-croppers among the Machiguenga tended to make higher offers, although, as the authors point out, this fact could also be consistent with the greater market integration hypothesis.

In comparison with Tecpán, social cohesion in Chisec is weaker, which helps explain the more aggressive game playing (and lesser degree of cooperation). In contrast to Tecpanecos' strong identity and pride rooted in ties to their community's history, Q'eqchi' families living in lowland Alta Verapaz are migrants. In the late nineteenth century, many Q'eqchi' were forced to leave their highland homeland around Cobán due to the presence of foreign investors who rapidly moved in and converted much of the fertile lands there into coffee plantations (Kahn 2001; King 1974; Siebers 1999). They settled in lowland regions of Alta Verapaz, Izabal, El Petén, and Belize, and this process of migration continued into the twentieth century due to population growth and land scarcity. Further displacement occurred during Guatemala's civil war, which reached its height in the early 1980s. At this time, the army established "model villages" in order to control guerrilla activity among primarily indigenous groups living in rural areas. Smaller *aldeas* were destroyed and their inhabitants moved to these settlements, where they were subjected to "ideological instruction" and interrogations, which has had long-lasting impacts on trust (Siebers 1999). Chisec was one of the model villages, and current residents describe being moved from their small, relatively insular communities to Chisec. Model villages fragmented community identity and cohesion because they mixed people from various ancestral villages. In addition, the population of Chisec grew from 651 in 1973 to 1,005 in 1981 and to 5,158 by 1994 (INE 2002), meaning that many families in Chisec have lived in the town for only one or two generations. Similarly, the absence of long-standing civic organizations in Chisec, exacerbated by low educational levels, also diminishes trust and cooperation associated with overall social cohesion. Although a pan-Q'eqchi' awareness is presently emerging in Cobán (the highland homeland of the Q'eqchi' and now departmental capital), most Q'eqchi' identify themselves in terms of their community rather than ethnic group, whether Maya or Q'eqchi' (Siebers 1999; Wilson 1995). In this context, Chisecos displayed a tactical pragmatism in playing the Ultimatum Game that is closer to rational expectations than the cooperative bias found in Tecpán.

Free markets, neoliberal reforms, and the other forces of globalization are often portrayed by politicians and pundits as the "natural" or inevitable way of the world. To the extent that the globalized world is equated with the hegemony of neoclassical economics, individual self-interest and rational optimization often trump social solidarity, placing the individual above the community. Yet, we argue that economic systems cannot be viewed as self-standing institutions but rather are embedded in culturally and historically particular circumstances. Experimental methods such as the Ultimatum Game allow us to get at our interlocutors' future-oriented intentions. Combining these results with ethnographic interpretation of social, cultural, and political-economic contexts gives us a richer understanding of local variation. In the cases of Tecpán and Chisec, we find that economic affluence and the social context of community solidarity (or lack thereof) are key factors, along with market integration, influencing differences in cooperative behavior. Such a bias toward cooperation and social cohesion points the way toward an understanding of community that is based on working together rather than the amalgamation of self-interests.

Acknowledgments

Thanks to Nobert Ross, Pakal B'alam, Ixchel Espantzay, and Marvin Tecum for their helpful comments and assistance in the field.

Part III

Practice

What Is and What Ought to Be

13

Making Moral Markets

A Professional Responsibility Ethic for Business and Poverty

Bart Victor and Matthew Grimes

The market, for all its good and ill, is you and I. We are all economic actors, together. However, in the collective act of creating and sustaining markets, some of us have more prominent roles. The shorthand for these leading economic actors is *businessperson*, and in this chapter, we turn our attention to improving the ethics that guide these actors. Although businesspeople are not members of a profession per se—lacking much of the institutional architecture that binds doctors or lawyers into a shared community, for example—they are recognizable as businesspeople to themselves and others. As managers, entrepreneurs, bankers, advisers, executives, or analysts, their activities are recognizable as business work. Perhaps most critical, their responsibilities are recognizable in that they are tied to a particularly important determinant of our shared destiny. The stake and hope that the world places in the market they make are their special trust.

Given the importance of the market and businesspeople's privileged position, we should have more than ample motive to critically consider the ethics that *ought* to guide the businessperson's decisions and actions. The implications of market making are complex and complicated. In real effects, the making of markets reaches far and deep into human life. In this chapter, we examine the business ethics that popularly offer guidance to the market-making businessperson. We ask whether these ethics are well matched to the real moral challenges and opportunities that confront businesspeople today.

We describe the social and economic embeddedness of the businessperson and couple this description with an emphasis on virtue- or responsibility-based ethics to lay the groundwork for the further construction of the normative ethics of a business professional. Our contribution is a response to the growing strains on the businessperson and the increasing criticality of this professional role—a role that we argue is a function of the individual's agency or creative capacities, stewardship of a civic trust, and thick relational ties. Because the individual's agency, stewardship, and ties extend beyond the boundaries of any particular agreement, contract, or organization, we highlight the particular role and consequential ethical obligations of the businessperson as "market-maker." More specifically, our contribution extrapolates these obligations of the market-maker as follows: accountability for the entire history of one's work, creation of partnerships and an increasing mutuality of interest and ownership between market participants, and net freedom generation for others. Although we develop a case for these obligations in the particular context of market making and the poor, we argue for their relevance to the general ethical problem of market making as well.

THE BUSINESS PERSON AS MARKET-MAKER

The market has an expanding role in our lives. Urbanization (Harvey 1989), globalization (Amin 1997; Dunning 2003), technological change (Schiller 1999), and political transformations (Boisot and Child 1996; Przeworski 1991) are only a few of the forces that have increasingly centered the market as a force in the world. Few corners of the globe remain in which the market is not a determining means, directly and indirectly, for virtually all to meet their needs (Baumol 2002).

Business professionals make and mold this market. Their responsibility for the meaning and consequences of the market requires an ethic that addresses the full range of their moral obligations and opportunities They require an ethic that can constrain and inspire the full range of their decisions and actions and can sustain their solidarity with not only the deed holders to property and direct participants in enterprise but also those who seek to be included, those oppressed or limited by the current state of affairs, and those whose future is opened or closed by the legacy of the market's work (Blowfield and Frynas 2005).

Businesspeople are increasingly urged to engage more directly with the poor in efforts to alleviate poverty (Boyle and Boguslaw 2007; Goddard

2005; Hamann 2006; Leisinger 2007; Noe and Rebello 1994; Rocha 2004; Rosenfeld 1997; Wulfson 2001). These mounting calls are coming from the developing world, from international organizations like the United Nations and World Health Organization, and from traditional business quarters and emerging social business entrepreneurs. Making markets that directly and intentionally engage the poor is particularly challenging work for the business professional. It also puts significant stress on the ethical guidance available to the businessperson.

Most of the world's population (as much as 80 percent by some estimates) live in conditions of significant poverty (Hulme and Shepherd 2003); that is, they lack the basic requirements to create and sustain an acceptable quality of life. Thus, although general economic development is critically important, more targeted, intentional responses are still required to truly alleviate poverty.

By many estimates, traditional aid directed at poverty alleviation is inefficient, dubiously effective, and arguably counterproductive (Easterly 2006). There continues to be a call for new approaches and methods to effectively address poverty and specifically for businesspeople to create markets that are global in their reach and extend into impoverished regions traditionally reserved for aid and relief organizations. For example, C. K. Prahalad (2004) has led much of this advocacy for businesspersons' increased attention to the poor. His book *The Fortune at the Bottom of the Pyramid* (2006) challenges two of the predominant assumptions that have impeded the expansion of the market into impoverished areas. First, he criticizes the assumption that the poor have little to no purchasing power by introducing the idea of the aggregate purchasing power of the poor and the idea that the poor spend according to a different set of consumption priorities. Second, he addresses the assumption that high transaction costs related to distribution access impede market creation and market entry. He discusses trends in the urbanization of the poor and the proliferation of information and communication technologies (ICTs) to expose the possible new markets that exist at the bottom of the "wealth pyramid." Thus, although the logic of market failures presumes that markets are efficient only up to a point, beyond which the state must intervene, Prahalad and many other social entrepreneurs, such as Nobel Prize winner Muhammad Yunus, are not persuaded. They believe that the market's inability to perform well in these geographies is a problem of faulty assumptions about the poor and economic theory (Prahalad 2006; Yunus 2008). For example, Yunus (2008:52) states emphatically that "simply being willing to extend credit to the poor was a revolutionary step in terms of conventional economic thinking. It meant ignoring the traditional belief that loans cannot be made without collateral. This assumption, which the vast majority of bankers hold without analyzing it, questioning it, or even thinking about it, in effect writes off half the human race as being unworthy to participate in the financial system."

Yet, few resources can be found in traditional business ethics to guide businesspersons in this effort to alleviate poverty. According to one fiduciary ethic, the poor by definition are costly risks. As a fiduciary, a businessperson would be warranted in approaching the poor with prudence and caution and perhaps rediscovering the wisdom of leaving this "market" to the government and charity. However, should the fiduciary find levels of risk and reward acceptable enough to commit others' property to this market, he or she would find little guidance from a fiduciary ethic other than to ensure returns in the best way possible.

The institutional ethics of doing business with the poor are richer in implications than the fiduciary ethics but, we argue, still short of what the businessperson needs in order to meet the moral requirements of such a venture. The institutional framework views the poor only intermittently as direct stakeholders and virtually never as shareholders. To the extent that they are customers, they are more often a last-resort market for inferior or excess production (Prahalad 2006). To the extent that they are viewed as producers, they most often serve as a very low-cost means of creating added value (Karnani 2007b). Legitimacy challenges or corporate social responsibility "social" marketing value claims may increase a corporation's potential interest of the corporation in the poor (Endacott 2004). Thus, institutional ethics would clearly bring the interests of the poor to the attention of the socially responsible corporation. However, beyond this general requirement and the implicated justice and due care concerns, institutional ethics would not inherently offer more guidance. These frameworks, though necessary and useful, fall short of providing direct guidance in how to ethically do business with the poor.

Traditional business ethics, therefore, are interested primarily in the mechanisms whereby agents can maximize returns to property or organizations can more efficiently produce goods and services. A utilitarian calculation lies at the heart of such arguments—the economy grows, and individuals, acting as rational utility maximizers, exchange in a free market, all of which leads to a Pareto Optimal outcome (i.e., a market equilibrium in which no one can be made better off without making someone worse off).

EXPANDING BUSINESS ETHICS TO INCORPORATE PROFESSIONAL RESPONSIBILITY

In both of the two primary normative business ethics frameworks in use, the main unit of analysis for the study of business ethics is narrowly drawn. Whether described by the pessimistic axioms of "economic man" or obligations of the fictive corporate person, the subject-in-use of contemporary business ethics has little at stake. Perhaps even more critical, the subject of business ethics is virtually autonomous, embedded in only the most arid of relationships. Consistent criticisms of business and societal distrust of its leaders have fueled scholarly questions of whether business— this fictive person—is in fact not good for real persons (Nielson 2006). In a review of the normative theories of business ethics, Hasnas (1998) ultimately remains partial to the shareholder model but still advances criticisms. He states, "It (1) does not adequately address the limits managers' ordinary ethical obligations as human beings place on the actions they may take in the business environment, and (2) entirely fails to address the managerial obligations that arise out of the actual agreements made with the non-stockholder participants in the business enterprise" (Hasnas 1998:35).

What gets lost in these abstractions is necessary attention to the ethics of the real individuals who operate within and outside the boundaries of their organizations (Solomon 1992; Weaver 2006). Who is the "businessperson"? If markets are directly responsible for the flow and distribution of wealth, for example, and if businesspersons are primarily responsible for making these markets, how might this situation encourage the businessperson to take ethical action? In response to this limitation and in pursuit of ethics that more fully meet the challenges to contemporary business, we join the advocates of reconsidering the role of values and virtues in constructing the businessperson's obligations (Nielsen 2006).

To be a good parent requires a new set of ethical responsibilities not necessarily captured in the moral abstractions found in human rights discussions. Similarly, to be a good businessperson requires more than a reliance on the interests of property rights and organizational transactions to infer the guidelines of ethical action. Importantly, many modern individuals join specific professional communities, and these professional communities often arrive at some evolving consensus as to what ethics should constrain and inspire action (Abbott 1983; Goldman 1980). While the norms or cultural logics embedded in business communities are underdeveloped, as we have noted, our expansion of the businessperson's ethical agency is directed toward a more robust construction of these norms.

And in this charge toward greater responsibility as businesspeople, we step away from a deontological ethical script—one in which a person must deduce both the law and the source of the law. Rather, we assume an ethical script, which requires one to ask what is fitting. Richard Niebuhr (1999:61) argued, "For the ethics of responsibility the *fitting* action, the one that fits into a total interaction as response and as anticipation of further response, is alone conducive to the good and alone is right."

Professional roles—like those of the businessperson—are often assumed to be a way of helping us understand who we are in relation to others and accordingly how we should act. So we refer to roles such as the "good employee" or the "good corporate citizen." We do so with some implicit understanding of the professional responsibilities entailed by such roles. These professional roles then call us to ethically reason and respond in a manner consistent with the fulfillment of our aims, goals, and aspirations (May 1996). And yet, because these roles are entrusted with certain hopes, interests, and expectations of others, they further impel us toward action consistent with these business inter-relationships. Importantly, these "thick" ethical business relationships that we maintain as a function of our socially constituted roles and business communities, unlike strict moral dictums, call for businesspersons to respond in degree rather than absolutely. To refer to someone as a "good" businessperson or "good" patriot, for example, is to draw an ethical distinction rather than a moral one, since it must take into account the degree to which that businessperson or patriot has successfully fulfilled the high normative standards of business or the nation. Essentially, society is making an ethical claim, distinguishing the responsible member of a particular community from an irresponsible one. Niebuhr (1999), for example, offers a set of three ideas that organize the ethics of responsibility: accountability, social solidarity, and response. Each requires a degree of interpretation, but it is precisely in the social process of interpretation and the posture toward others that Niebuhr's ethics of responsibility carry normative weight for human beings as social creatures. In the next section, we construct an image of the businessperson as "market-maker" and account for the increased need for a more robust professional responsibility.

CONSTRUCTING A PROFESSIONAL BUSINESS ETHIC FOR MARKET MAKING AND THE POOR

A. K. Sen (1999:11) coined the term "unfreedom" to describe the conditions of the world's impoverished majority. In Sen's construction of the condition of poverty, income provides some freedom of choice. However, this theoretical freedom of choice can enhance quality of life only through the effective or substantive freedom to choose. Critical capabilities that can constitute substantive freedoms include political and economic participation, social opportunities, security, and liberties of voice, faith, and movement (Sen 1999). For the poor, market making can generate freedom. It can bring needed resources and services within their reach, provide a means for them to create value for themselves, and enable an equal relationship with the nonpoor. But markets can also exploit their vulnerability, deepen their isolation, and put their lives and futures at even greater risk.

Traditionally, businesspeople have been criticized as being uninterested in the potential development of the poor and particularly prone to propagating their exploitation. What is embedded in these criticisms of business and businesspersons is not merely a claim of faulty economic assumptions about the poor, which might lead to missed financial opportunities. Businesspeople are often characterized as being motivated by values ill fit and even hostile to the well-being of the poor. Thus, the charge for businesspeople to take a more direct hand in alleviating poverty not only is novel but also is more poignantly an ethical charge for their greater responsibility as makers of markets. Because the businessperson has been entrusted by society to be a primary figure in the creation of markets, ethical responsibilities follow. Combining the virtue-based, socially derived ethical scripts of the businessperson as a moral agent with the stewardship-based accountability of the businessperson as a global citizen, the ethical market-maker asks, "What is the good market?" and "How might I go about creating the good market?"

Ultimately, the ambition of all who are concerned about poverty is to eliminate it entirely and permanently. To accomplish this goal, the underlying conditions that create and perpetuate the suffering must be transformed. Aid from the nonpoor to the poor with this intention is generally called development. As described previously, development must generate substantive freedom for the poor in order to accomplish its intent (Sen 1999).

The businessperson who assumes the role of ethical market-maker is concerned with transforming how currently existing markets both constrain and enable the freedom of individuals to achieve their desired ends and, more specifically, their capability to lead one type of life versus another type of life. Capabilities have subjective components, and, thus, the normative ethical responsibility of the market-maker is to purposely engage with society, interpreting capability demands and capability constraints and working to create markets that increase or improve those capabilities—in Sen's (1999) terms, moral markets generate and sustain substantive freedom.

Drawing upon these ideas from both Sen and Niebuhr, we can fashion a normative ethical framework for the responsible businessperson who chooses to work among the poor. Market-making work consists of actively connecting people into interdependent transaction-, information-, and resource-rich networks. Through these networks, value is marshaled, transformed, and traded, and the net new value created is distributed, invested, and consumed. These networks, whether or not formally organized as business, can be long lived and dynamically linked to other networks (Rowley 1997). The networks equally generate and sustain meaning, status, and expectations (Granovetter 1983). That is, the work of market making is, importantly, a process of not just production but also social creation and integration.

The following values are consistent with this work:

- Accountability for an entire history of work—seeking to generate freedom, from the initiation of the market through, and after, its dissolution
- Partnerships and integrity—seeking mutuality in interest and reliance in market making
- Generating net freedom—aiming to increase the capabilities of others (the substantive ability of individuals to choose to live as they desire) through market making

Notice that the initial two values, which coincide with Niebuhr's composition of ethical responsibility, are related to the means by which ethical markets are structured. The first accounts for the temporality of the relationship, whereas the second accounts for the procedural content of the relationship. The third—generating freedom—is related directly to the ethical market and its outcomes. Without this third value, the businessperson is not ethically challenged to engage the poor. Alternatively, with this third value, the businessperson is called to engage the poor, and the questions of ethical market making include, "How should the businessperson engage the poor?" and "To what ends should we as businesspeople engage the poor?" In the next section, we examine each of these three values in reference to current examples of businesspersons' market-making activities that engage the poor.

THE RESPONSIBILITY TO BE ACCOUNTABLE IN MARKET MAKING

A central feature of the criticisms of traditional approaches to poverty alleviation has been the evidence that their effects are not only inefficient but also ephemeral (Riddell 2007). Traditional approaches may work well to temporarily ameliorate the conditions of poverty by providing food, shelter, and security. They may also function well to restore what the poor lose due to crisis or catastrophe. However, traditional poverty alleviation efforts have been criticized for failing to transform the conditions that create and maintain poverty (Easterly 2006). In fact, both public and private aid has been charged not only with *not* changing the conditions of poverty but also with even deepening them.

The lives of the poor are precarious, dangerous, and disadvantaged. They are also isolated. Poverty is characterized by the preponderance of strong ties among the poor and weak ties between the poor and nonpoor (Granovetter 1973, 1983). Such isolated strong-tie networks can account for the vulnerability, resource scarcity, and persistence observed in communities of poverty (Venkatesh 2006). Mark Granovetter (1983:213) notes, "The heavy concentration of social energy in strong ties has the impact of fragmenting communities of the poor into encapsulated networks with poor connections between these units; individuals so encapsulated may then lose some of the advantages associated with the outreach of weak ties." This may be one more reason why poverty is self-perpetuating. That is, the impoverished are isolated in their shared scarcity. The criticism of traditional approaches to poverty alleviation and the claims for the advantages of market making can be seen as the potential of the businessperson to transform the embedded economies of poverty that trap the poor (Easterly 2006).

Market making can alleviate suffering by lifting this isolation. Businesspeople occupy a privileged position within and between networks and stores of social capital. They are, to a greater or lesser degree and with more or less centrality, members of market networks. As such, businesspeople have the potential to produce new markets or link other individuals or groups into existing markets (Bourdieu 1980; White 1981). In a sense, responsible market making can build on the ancient Chinese wisdom that giving a man fish feeds him for only a day but teaching him to fish feeds him for a lifetime. Responsible market making would add that teaching a man to fish could feed him and many more for a lifetime if, in addition, he was effectively integrated into networks of other fisherman, bait and tackle suppliers, fishmongers, boat salesmen, bankers, dock workers, experts on fish markets and ecology, and those who can use the labor or products of an experienced fisherman even out of season or when the demand for fish wanes.

And this benefit holds true not only for the direct participant in market making. The economic ties created can also benefit the close network of those in relationships with the poor. "Due to the network effects, improving the status of a given agent also improves the outlook for that agent's connections" (Calvó-Armengol and Jackson 2004:428). The common practice of group-based lending by microfinance institutions has been shown to promote the benefits of this contagion effect (Armendariz and Morduch 2000). When announcing the award of the Nobel Peace Prize to Mohammed Yunus, a self-described "Banker to the Poor," the committee detailed the positive network effect of this particular kind of market making: "The poor people organize themselves into groups, often of five women. It is the group that is granted the loan and is responsible for repayment. The group meets regularly to sharpen each other's perceptions of borrowing, work, repayment and saving. The members undertake to work for food production, pure drinking water, hygiene, health, family planning, economy, discipline, community and motivation in the group and in their families. The groups form networks with other groups. At the grass-roots level the groups thus help to build up communities" (Yunus 1999:23).

Responsible market making among the poor, then, must not only alleviate the suffering associated with poverty; it must effectively and persistently transform the conditions that create and perpetuate poverty. This responsibility implicates much more than any particular agreement or contract and requires attention to far more than the specifics of any particular agreement or contract. Market-making efforts that simply redistribute economic resources or build human capital (e.g., through education or providing health care) without transforming the economy of poverty (Woolcock 1998) are not fully responsible. Market-making efforts that further isolate the poor by saddling them with unpayable debts, crippling them through dangerous or toxic work, or attempting to encourage irrational or socially irresponsible consumption behavior are unethical.

A good example of a product that has been criticized by scholars and social activists for not taking into account histories of social injustices and tensions is Unilever's Fair & Lovely skin-whitening cream. The product maintains a majority share of the skin-whitening market in India and is growing at a rate of 21.5 percent per year (Karnani 2007a). Despite vehement criticism from women's groups, which claim not only that Fair & Lovely perpetuates racist tensions in countries where fair skin is more highly valued but also that it is destructive to the women's movement in East Asia, Unilever continues to run advertisements that many believe exploit a racist market. Indeed, legal bans have been enacted on several of these advertisements. Aneel Karnani (2007a:1354) summarizes the criticism as follows: "This is not empowerment; at best, it is a mirage; at worst, it serves to entrench a woman's disempowerment. The way to truly empower a woman is to make her less poor, financially independent, and better educated; social and cultural changes also need to occur that eliminate the prejudices that are the cause of her deprivations. If she was truly empowered, she would probably refuse to buy a skin whitener in the first place."

How a market-maker brings the poor into the network, how the networks create potential and poverty-alleviating meaning, and how the networks progress or fail all redound on the market-maker. In short, responsible market making leaves the poor increasingly nonpoor. To the extent that this market making is successful, the poor are increasingly capable of participating in economic life on the same terms as the nonpoor. The promise of market making is that the poor can "climb the ladder" of economic development and be integrated into the larger economy (Sachs 2005b). Thus, our first proposition is as follows:

> *Ethical market making demands that businesspeople be accountable for the entire history of their work and seek to generate freedom, from the initiation of the market through, and after, its dissolution.*

THE RESPONSIBILITY FOR PARTNERSHIPS IN MARKET MAKING

One of the critical factors maintaining the poor's isolation and lack of freedom is the indignity of poverty (Poppendieck 1998). This indignity is felt by the poor themselves and is inherent in the relative position of the poor to the nonpoor. The inequality is maintained, and perhaps even deepened, through the traditional processes of charity and aid to the poor. The poor and nonpoor are often brought together over suffering. For the nonpoor, the potential to eliminate specific suffering brings them into a relationship with the poor (Lee and McKenzie 1990). But such aid is always at the discretion of the nonpoor, and only the poor receive such charity. As such, traditional aid is embedded in the differential status identities of the giver and receiver (Schwartz 1967). Accepting aid reconfirms the receiver's social status as "poor" (Bougheas, Dasgupta, and Morrissey 2005).

By giving traditional aid, the nonpoor do not join in partnership with the poor, share a mutual interest with them, or see them as equals. And those are the factors that leave the poor isolated and lacking substantive freedom. So we should not be surprised that, contrary to some popular beliefs, the poor are often loathe to accept such aid (Godelier 1999; Seccombe 2000).

Previously, we cited the Nobel Peace Prize awarded to Muhammed Yunus and the Grameen Bank. This widely lauded award selection represents the growing acceptance of responsible market making among the poor. However, not all market making receives or is deserving of such recognition. Another class of bankers exists whose business is structurally quite similar to the work of the Grameen Bank—payday lenders and pawnbrokers. Such providers of loans to the poor claim to offer a source of needed resources for those outside the traditional banking system. These loans are generally of short maturity and interest bearing. In this way, the payday and pawnshop loans are structurally identical to the loans of the microlenders. However, the impact of payday and pawnshop loans on poverty is far different.

The payday lender does not seek to develop a partnership or mutuality of interest with the poor borrower. Instead, such fringe bankers build a business model that capitalizes on the vulnerability of the poor. Unlike the microlenders, they sell loans primarily for consumptive rather than commercial use. And they charge rates of interest and fees that secure the banks' profits even if the borrower defaults. In fact, a borrower's inability to repay a loan is often an opportunity for the fringe banker to make even more money. "Payday borrowers tend to be repeat customers, with 48 percent taking out seven or more total advances in a year, and 22 percent taking 14 or more. Borrowers also tend to roll over or renew the same loan, postponing final payment and accruing significant interest charges" (Stegman 2001:16) For pawnbrokers, prior possession and a high collateral-value-to loan-value ratio give them an interest in default (Caskey and Zikmund 1990). In the case of fringe banking, the fees, prepaid interest, and high interest rates together create an incentive for the lender to "roll over" the debt. A study by the State of Indiana estimated that "77 percent of payday loans are rollovers, with the average payday customer averaging more than ten loans per year" (Stegman 2001:19). With such rollovers, effective annual percentage rates can readily exceed 400 percent. The use of the loans for consumption and their high default rates deepen the conditions of poverty. The debt not repaid to the lender becomes a visible stain on the borrower's reputation, which further isolates the poor from the nonpoor by reinforcing the identity of the poor person as a bad risk, someone who is unable or unwilling to repay a debt.

In contrast, market making such as that practiced by responsible microlenders can equalize the relationship between the poor and nonpoor. The microlenders' business model is rooted in a shared destiny with the poor, and only through the successful completion of a borrower's debt cycle can a microlender claim success. Microlenders routinely report repayment rates that rival and often exceed comparable rates among the nonpoor (Brau and Woller 2005). And experience is proving that the opportunities for developing mutually beneficial business relationships between the poor and nonpoor are potentially extensive. The recent experience of micro-lenders, for example, has demonstrated that microlending institutions can be grown to significant size and that even a secondary market for the loans can be developed and operated profitably. Our second proposition, there-fore, follows:

> *Ethical market making demands that businesspeople seek partnerships and act with integrity, encouraging participation and mutuality through-out their involvement in the production, distribution, and consumption of goods and services.*

THE RESPONSIBILITY TO CREATE FREEDOM-GENERATIVE MARKETS

Sen (1999) expands the economic concept of market access into a more human concept of capabilities and freedoms. By *capabilities*, Sen (1993) means what a person can do or become, and by *freedom*, he means a person's capacity to choose what he or she will become. As an ethical proposition, then, social arrangements should be evaluated primarily on whether they improve the latter—an individual's freedom to choose the desired life (Sen 1992). By extension, our third proposition follows:

> *Ethical market making demands that businesspeople seek to generate sub-stantive freedoms for those engaged directly and by association with the production, distribution, and consumption of goods and services.*

Moreover, ethical market making aimed at freedom generation among the poor need not be arbitrary, but rather businesspersons can at least par-tially measure, evaluate, and challenge the relative deprivation of these free-doms (Anand and Sen 1994). Addressing this lack of freedom is, of course, no easy ethical or practical task. The consideration of freedom generation in business activity extends well beyond a fiduciary or institutional ethic of business transactions. As such, the approach itself has many degrees of freedom, due to what Sen (1985:176) calls the "plurality of principles," or the diversity of subjective value claims that might define freedom. Greater intersubjectivity and cultural sensitivity is thus required before action can and should be taken. Granted, these evaluations will be "assertively incom-plete" or in need of consistent on-the-ground revisions. Yet, for the busi-nessperson as market-maker—one committed to accountability, integrity, and participatory methods for generating freedom among the poor—such a task of evaluating and responding to the relative deprivation of freedom becomes more feasible.

The freedom-generative capacity of markets highlights, for example, the difference between organizations that are actively transferring knowledge, technology, and ownership of the means of production to local economies and those multinationals that have gone into countries and created labor relations that further enslave the employees to the corporation. As foreign direct investment increased rapidly in the twentieth century, multinational corporations (MNCs) became principal arbiters of capital, technology, and, more recently, knowledge transfer. In many developing economies, within which these MNCs are active, the informal sector (the labor market outside the reach of labor codes) represents a significant proportion of the labor force (Mehmet, Mendes, and Sinding 1999). Unfortunately, the most vulnerable in the society—children, migrants, and women—usually compose the majority of the informal sector. Similar to the informal sector, a number of countries have actually sponsored export processing zones, which provide MNCs with low-rent land and cheap, unorganized labor. Although not all sites and foreign businesspersons employ such labor irresponsibly, these populations are clearly vulnerable. Thus, the distinction between freedom-generative market making and dependency-creating market making is all the more obvious. Those who rely on a vulnerable labor force to drive down the cost of production and who simultaneously constrain workers' rights do so in ways that further a state of dependency among the poor. In contrast, business individuals at Cemex have deliberately instituted programs that attempt to transfer capital, knowledge, and technologies to ensure small retail growth. The Construrama program, for example, provides capital to small retailers for new storefronts, consulting support for scaling their small ventures, and access to Cemex products and services at competitive prices (Singh, Kundu, and Foster 2005). Such practices create market ties that provide not only a distribution of wealth but also capabilities and freedoms for those who are brought into such market arrangements.

CONCLUSION

Markets are "artifactual" in the sense that businesspersons are responsible for their construction (Donaldson and Dunfee 1999). Markets are also the source of great power in our society. Indeed, society has accorded markets with a power exceeding that of the state. When Robert Reich (2007) refers to "supercapitalism," we think of global financial markets, multinationals, and chief executive officers wielding this power, sometimes cautiously, other times carelessly. However, we rarely think of those who work within this system tirelessly creating, re-creating, and sustaining markets. This chapter refocuses attention on those individuals, whom we as a society refer to as "businesspeople," and their embedment within a professional community, as opposed to any particular organization.

Because the business professional has no institutionalized support beyond that offered by law and employer, his or her professional business ethic requires powerful motivation. The corporation clearly has an interest in motivating and enforcing its ethic among its agents and employers. However, individual businesspeople are increasingly mobile across corporations, and corporations themselves are increasingly ephemeral. Further, as entrepreneurs and significant actors in an increasingly networked world, businesspeople's concerns, choices, and actions, as well as their impacts, can hardly be contained within the boundaries of the corporation.

By examining the businessperson's role in market making among the poor, we highlight two critical aspects of responsibility: (1) the consequences of a businessperson's choices and actions are not well bounded by agreements or corporations, nor even broadly conceived but still delimited social contracts, and (2) the responsibilities of a businessperson as market-maker include the potential for, but do not not guarantee, profoundly positive impacts on the world. We delineate three values that emerged from our examination of this responsibility: accountability, partnership, and the generation of substantive freedom. These values carry particular importance in the course of a businessperson's professional work with the poor. It was critical in our analysis to describe these values not as simply extensions of the responsibilities of citizenship but as particular values relevant to the businessperson's special position in such work. As evidence of their relevance, we apply the values to distinguish between market making and other forms of poverty alleviation work and between responsible and irresponsible market making for the alleviation of poverty.

Beyond the specific case of market making and the poor, we contend that these values and the professional responsibility of the businessperson have general relevance. Because our collective interests are increasingly tied to the efficient functioning of markets, society trusts that those responsible for their creation are acting as responsible stewards. This trust demands a business ethic that has yet to be encompassed by the two primary normative ethical views: fiduciary and institutional ethics. To remain relevant and challenging to a business world in desperate need of reclaiming its ethics, this chapter offers a more expansive view of business ethics.

Most important, we argue for an expansion of the businessperson's ethical agency and ethical stewardship. In this vein, we believe that future scholarship on business ethics will remain relevant to the extent that it continues to re-examine and specify the *ethical boundaries* of the businessperson, the *ethical prioritization* given to proximate relationships, and the *ethical content* of those relationships. In other words, if the businessperson's ethics are not derived merely from the organizational contracts related to employment, then we must continue to show which additional relationships matter, why they matter, and to what extent they matter. Such questioning has led us to advocate that businesspersons assume the role of ethical market-maker—a role that requires the businessperson to reason through answers to the following questions: "What is the 'good' market?" "How might one go about creating and sustaining such a market?" The stakes could hardly be higher.

14

Corporate Social Responsibilities or Ruses?

A Dialogue

Orchestrated by Stuart Kirsch, with Peter Benson, James Ferguson, Robert Frank, and Bart Victor

Corporate social responsibility (CSR) has become one of the most important buzzwords of our time. Under its banner, energy companies are repositioning themselves as green in response to debates about climate change. The mining industry is making questionable claims about sustainability and environmental values. Major food and beverage companies, such as Coca-Cola and Pepsi fund youth health programs in public schools even as they market products that contribute to an obesity epidemic. Even the tobacco companies say that they want you to quit smoking.

One of the topics on the table at our seminar in Santa Fe was the question of how much traction these claims have. Do they constitute a new sort of capitalism or just a ruse? The idioms of ethics, health, environmentalism, and corporate responsibility may conceal the contradictions of capitalism and hide negative human and environmental consequences. At the same time, there may be something more substantive and real in corporate efforts to improve public health and the environment.

Theoretical perspectives on CSR center on the question of how best to structure global enterprise to produce economic development that is consistent with raising labor standards and encouraging environmental protection. In practice, however, CSR can involve paradoxes that belie these admirable goals.

KIRSCH: One of the key cover terms and new strategies of the mining industry is to promote something they call "sustainable mining." They are using the language of "sustainable development" in new ways. It is also a term that sounds reasonable. Why would anyone object to business becoming more sustainable? But that's part of how the term works as a strategy. These corporate oxymorons do not get unpacked.

If we look historically at how the term *sustainability* has been used, sustainable development was concerned with not degrading an environment beyond the point that it can reproduce itself. Yet, in its use by the business community and in particular the mining industry, the term has been progressively redefined so that the link to the environment and ecology has largely disappeared.

How did the mining industry get from sustainable development to sustainable mining? If you remove the environmental referent from the term, you end up focusing only on economic returns. This requires moving from a notion of strong sustainability in which human and natural capital are not interchangeable to a notion of weak sustainability in which the only goal is to increase the total stock of capital.

The fallacy of the shift is that if you keep investing in fishing boats, you do increase the total stock of capital, but eventually you'll destroy the fishery. You end up with a tragedy of the commons scenario. That's where the notion of sustainable mining takes us, too.

BENSON: We need to be very careful about the slogans being used and the kind of reasonableness corporations advocate. It is well known that the tobacco industry long produced faux science to raise doubts about smoking and health. There was a controversial article in the *New England Journal of Medicine*, later retracted by the journal. Apparently, the industry had covertly funded the study, which showed that preventative screening for lung cancer reduces the mortality rate by something like 80 percent. Well, this is true. The article went through the journal's rigorous peer review process. Why would the industry want to fund this study? Because if lung cancer death can be prevented, then smoking perhaps becomes more socially acceptable.

The journal retracted the article because it said that it will never publish anything funded by the tobacco industry. But was the science wrong? It is not like the old days when it was clear that the tobacco industry's science was junk, as compared with what public health researchers were doing.

This is just one example that leads me to say that CSR is not a ruse. It involves a full-fledged engagement with a repertoire of strategies, scientific research, and social policy.

FRANK: I would still call that a ruse, based on your account. You have to ask what their economic prospects would have been if they had adopted the other strategy. The tobacco industry's options were pretty bleak unless they took this proactive ethical posture about smoking and the regulation of it and were more receptive about attempts to control it in various ways. Against their own vision of what their alternatives were, this keeps more people smoking longer. It's a ruse.

FERGUSON: Let me throw in another example that goes beyond public relations. On the Zambian copper belt, the government always used to do malaria control, so there was no malaria in the towns. And in the late eighties, things really started getting bad. The price of copper was down, the state was falling apart. They stopped the disease control program, and malaria came back. For years, you had a situation where you were getting malaria in the towns in which you never used to get it. What's happened in the last few years is that the mining companies decided, as part of corporate social responsibility, to do malaria eradication campaigns, and the copper belt is malaria free again. One interpretation is that they did it so that people would think they are good guys and it's just public relations. The other interpretation is that they thought, "There is a public good here that really ought to be provided, and we have states that no longer are doing the types of things we expected states to do for us." Corporations are taking on some of the functions that we have historically associated with states.

KIRSCH: About the Zambian copper belt, it's my understanding that the royalty rate that the mining companies have negotiated with the country is now one of the lowest in the world. The threat is that those companies can go find copper elsewhere. They use that leverage power to negotiate the contract. Yes, it looks like corporate social responsibility to eradicate malaria, but this expenditure also covers up the exploitative relationship between corporation and the state.

VICTOR: We've put on the table the very important issue of corporations doing things that are extra-corporate in their impact but that may have nothing to do with responsibility. We have seen an important move in the context of how corporations have effects well beyond their narrow interests, maybe in pursuit of those interests. Then there is this subset of that, which is now labeled corporate responsibility, which makes more positive moral claims. This looks like a reaction to advocacy and social movements.

Indeed, new levels of awareness about social justice issues in a globalized world spur the booming CSR industry, which includes for-profit and nonprofit organizations, academic journals, standards, and prizes. Theoretical perspectives on corporate social performance and stakeholder management have been developed in business schools. Many kinds of actors, including politicians, activists, celebrities, and academics, are involved in promoting and monitoring the social responsibilities of corporations.

Kirsch: When Rachel Carson published *Silent Spring,* the chemical industry
had a huge negative reaction. But she tapped into a strong sensibility
emerging at the time that corporations lacked sufficient governance
or regulatory oversight and were, in fact, doing things that were really
harmful. Carson brought science out of the laboratory and the corporations
into public view. The public became an actor in scientific decision making
in a way it hadn't been before. Carson's work led to the creation of the
EPA [Environmental Protection Agency] and new forms of environmental
regulation.

There's also a connection to the story about malaria eradication and
mining that Jim mentioned. After DDT was banned, you no longer could
use it for malaria control. And now there are people saying that banning
DDT has had deleterious outcomes for people in developing countries
because of increased malaria. There are scientists on both sides of this
question, some of whom are asking whether bringing DDT back is such a
good thing. But who is behind bringing DDT back, and why? The NGO
[nongovernmental organization] Africa Fighting Malaria, which promotes
DDT use, has strong ties to the conservative American Enterprise Institute
and support from several of the largest mining companies. Why are these
companies funding this organization? Is it corporate responsibility? Is it
a ruse?

The biggest challenge faced by the mining industry comes from public
advocacy groups, which did not really exist as effective political actors
until recently. What the mining industry wants to do is put the genie back
in the bottle, to return science back into the hands of the scientists, the
technicians, and the corporations so that they will not have to defend
themselves against their opponents all the time. What could be better than
to go back to where it all began and show that Rachel Carson was wrong
about DDT?

Victor: We have talked a lot about global capitalism, but there is also
another story, which is the NGO response and how they were working and
responding and changing. This is the globalization of civil society, such
as the globalizing environmental movement. This globalizing civil society
might have resources and mechanisms to show how regulation can have
promising impacts that are multilateral in nature.

Here we see Victor, a business school professor with a focus on ethics within organizations, suggest that the work of NGOs can establish a
feedback loop between society, CSR, and regulatory practices. In contrast,
Stuart, an anthropologist who has studied mining company interactions
with NGOs and indigenous communities, emphasizes corporations' ability
to adapt to critique and evade pressure to reform their practices. In fact,
these are not mutually exclusive positions.

KIRSCH: What we see in the mining industry is not only shopping for the richest ore bodies but also shopping for places where they can operate with the least interference. This refers not only to regulation but also to the resources of the local communities in terms of posing a threat to the company's operation. The companies benefit from the fact that communities might not have a high literacy rate or scientific education.

So, many large mining projects are being located where people have certain characteristics. We can call them "indigenous." The indigenous themselves mobilize that term for political reasons. The companies go to a place where there's a really steep learning curve for these communities. They don't know how to access the levers of power. They don't know how to effectively protest.

As these groups become more effective political actors, the mining industry isn't just passive in response. It develops strategic responses. "Okay, the natives are getting restless. Why don't we throw some small-scale development projects at them?" This looks good in public relations brochures. Part of the deception is that these communities generally want some form of development. The companies realize that mining won't really bring development, so they offer this limited alternative.

FERGUSON: That links back to Anna's concept of supply chain capitalism. Big companies exert control with these strategies. What we see in the proliferation of subcontracting, certainly in the mining industry and in many other industries as well, makes it very hard to bring a company to accountability. The mining that is being done, say, in the Congo right now in really irresponsible ways is being done by small start-up companies. I know how to go after BHP Billiton. I don't know how to go after these small operations. They are only going to be here for a few years, and I don't know where they sell their ore, but they sell it somewhere and probably not to the same people this week as they did last week. We need regulatory approaches that can get at the subcontracting disavowal of responsibility.

KIRSCH: A colleague once compared big mining companies to dinosaurs, huge beasts with tiny brains. You can poke them with a stick over and over, and they barely get the message. The little mining companies are more like pythons that are in and out of your chicken house, taking all your eggs before you even realize that they are there.

BENSON: In response to litigation against the tobacco industry, the major tobacco companies signed on to the Master Settlement Agreement and now pay into an escrow account. Subsequently, hundreds of small tobacco companies popped up, and they avoid the cost of paying for the litigation. And so they sell cigarettes at discounted rates, and this leads to more smoking. One of the reasons why Philip Morris has so vigorously pursued regulation is to get these little guys, who cannot afford the attendant administrative costs. There are always these two sides.

KIRSCH: This comes back to the question of social responsibility and whether it's a ruse or not. I think both Pete and I want to step out of the language of motivation and look at strategies and tactics. What we are seeing is that you have civil society trying to bring about a certain change through critique. Then you have the corporate response. They are in a dialectical relationship. Corporate social responsibility is usually presented as an ethically motivated act, but in practice it involves a response to threats to corporate legitimacy. They undertake these measures, which make it look like they are accommodating critique, but, again, the impetus is not to change the mode of production, not to change the process that was causing harm and outrage. It is only when corporations reach the point that their legitimacy and continued access to the market [are] jeopardized that they are willing to accept a more robust regulatory framework.

VICTOR: Both of you describe this moment very well. Do we fight against pythons and dinosaurs? Do we get on the side of the dinosaurs and fight the pythons? Do we get on the side of the pythons and fight the dinosaurs?

BENSON: The major public health groups in the United States stood alongside Philip Morris in supporting FDA [Food and Drug Administration] legislation that benefits smokers but also benefits the corporation and perhaps secures its long-term viability as a tobacco manufacturer.

FERGUSON: Michael Watts said, "We'd have no problem if Shell ran all the oil wells in the Niger Delta, right? But the problem is, they don't." Shell responds to pressure. You can put pressure on Shell. They're branded. They have a gas station on every corner. You can actually enforce certain codes of conduct on Shell. But, to the extent that you've done that successfully, the business has gone elsewhere, and so you have all these pythons.

BENSON: As Stuart said earlier, I'm not really interested in the motivations of the company—is it a ruse or not—but on the effects of particular actions. I don't like to talk about strategies and tactics in the language of motivation. You can see what a company's official position is, and then you can put that into a context of who are its competitors, what are the outcomes, and so on. I don't know what is in the hearts of the people creating those strategies.

FRANK: Let me come back to this critique of regulation. It resembles the critique that comes from the right side of the political spectrum. It's the idea that government regulation is all well and good in principle but that when we get down to the nitty-gritty, when government is empowered by regulators, you get regulators captured by industry interests and they do the bidding of industry. So their conclusion is, don't regulate.

FERGUSON: Which makes it worse.

FRANK: I don't think anyone is saying, just because corporations are influencing the regulatory process, "Therefore, don't regulate at all, and rely on corporate social responsibility." That, to my ear anyway, doesn't sound like a very attractive path to take in responding to these problems. It's probably worth focusing on where the capture occurs, how it is that regulators end up promoting industry interests rather than the public interest. The main place I would focus is the campaign nexus in this country. For example, there is a lot of pressure about who gets appointed to the FCC [Federal Communications Commission] and who gets appointed to the FDA, and this comes from who's contributing to whose campaigns.

BENSON: There are different angles to analyze regulation. We need to go beyond the all-or-nothing way of thinking. We need to analyze regulation in terms of what it does but also what it does not do and what alternative frameworks are eclipsed or downplayed. And this is where research feeds into the forms of critical awareness and understanding in the civil society. Coming back to something Stuart said, part of the labor of being in a society—being part of a civil society—involves the dissemination of information and the expression of ideas. Any regulation is going to need to undergo constant analysis and critique. Regulation is often promoted as a solution, as sort of an end point. So it seems we have resolved the problem. But a role of academic research, linked up to NGOs, social movements, and public intellectualism, is constant critique of the forms of regulation and their relationship to business practices.

We have previously looked at how markets function as techniques or conventions, and this discussion brings out another key aspect of markets and moralities. Here we get at the sort of micropolitics Anna Tsing calls for in chapter 4, namely, how different sorts of actors influence markets, including corporations and consumers, as well as civil society and NGOs. We have seen how corporations justify their behavior in the language of ethics and responsibility, but we still have outstanding questions about whether their strategies are driven primarily by the bottom line or represent a new sort of engagement with society. The anthropologists and the economist and business school professor suggest that a healthy skepticism of corporate claims is warranted, even if they disagree over where the line is between self-interested and maximizing behavior and moral regard for a greater good.

15

Mining Industry Responses to Criticism

Stuart Kirsch

The relationship between corporations and their critics plays an important role in contemporary capitalism. The popularity of neoliberal economic policies has led the state to neglect its regulatory responsibilities, shifting the task of monitoring international capital from the state to NGOs and social movements. Corporations employ a variety of "corporate social technologies" (Rogers 2012) designed to manage these relationships, including discursive forms that borrow or co-opt the language of their critics. Studying these interactions provides a different perspective on markets and morality than tracking commodity and supply chains (Tsing, chapter 4, this volume) or conducting ethnographic research on stockbrokers (Zaloom 2006).

Consider the mining industry. For decades, mining companies managed to maintain a low profile. The industry's lack of visibility is related to the way that most metals are sold to other companies rather than directly to consumers. This practice can be contrasted with branding in the petroleum industry, in which consumers engage directly with corporations at the pump.[1] The remote location of most mining projects also historically afforded them relative freedom from oversight or interference.

But during the 1990s, sustained critical attention from NGOs and increasingly effective strategies and tactics of resistance by indigenous peoples took the industry by surprise. The widespread nature of these conflicts is another consequence of the spread of neoliberal economic policies, including the promotion of foreign direct investment, which opened up new regions of the world to minerals extraction. Many of these new projects are located in marginal areas in which indigenous peoples have retained control over lands not previously seen to have economic value and where development has historically been limited or absent. Suzana Sawyer (2004) argues that the neoliberal dismantling of the state ironically transforms corporations operating in rural areas into new sites of governmentality and indigenous peoples into transgressive subjects. Activists and NGOs now regularly collaborate with indigenous political movements, exploiting new technologies ranging from the Internet and cell phones to satellite imaging that enable them to monitor corporate activity in approximately real time wherever it occurs (Kirsch 2007).

The unexpected rise of indigenous opposition provoked a "crisis of confidence" in the mining industry (Danielson 2006:7). At the 1999 World Economic Forum in Davos and in subsequent meetings in London, executives from the world's largest mining companies met to discuss these issues. They identified their strained relationship with indigenous peoples as their greatest challenge (Mining Journal 2001:268). They acknowledged that "non-governmental organizations were becoming more powerful and vocal" and that "the rapid transfer of information [about] impacts and regulatory developments" had facilitated NGOs "in driving the agendas... of concern to the mining industry" (Mining Journal 2001:267, 268). They were forced to concede that "despite the industry's best efforts...[their] message had failed to get through, leaving them 'too often on the defensive'" (Mining Journal 2001:267).

Since the late 1990s, the mining industry has devoted increasing attention to its critics. This chapter examines some of the industry's primary strategies in responding to its critics, including discussion of the three phases of corporate response to critique (Benson and Kirsch 2010a). One key strategy is to co-opt the discourse of their critics. For example, mining companies increasingly draw on the language of corporate social responsibility to represent their practices (Rajak 2011). This chapter focuses on how the mining industry promotes itself as sustainable. The corporate oxymoron *sustainable mining* represents the industry's response to criticism of its environmental impacts (Benson and Kirsch 2010b; Kirsch 2010). I show how the concept of sustainability has undergone a progressive shift in definition from its original emphasis on the environment to current use of the term, in which profits and development have become paramount, all but obscuring reference to the environment. Corporations benefit from strategies that persuade or neutralize their critics, but investigation and analysis of these strategies reveal new opportunities for political activism and reform.

PHASES OF CORPORATE RESPONSE

The initial phase of corporate response to critique entails denial that the criticism is valid or that legitimate problems exist (Benson and Kirsch 2010a). The objective is to limit corporate liability for negative externalities, those costs for the environment, society, or human health that are not taken into account by the project. For example, mining companies rarely pay the full costs of the water they use, including opportunity costs for other users, such as farmers. Mining companies also fail to pay the total economic costs of the pollution that results from mineral extraction. In the United States alone, more than 156 abandoned hard-rock mining sites have been targeted for federal cleanup. This intervention will cost the US government an estimated $15 billion, which is more than ten times the annual Superfund budget for all large-scale environmental problems (Office of the Inspector General 2004).[2] Requiring payment for the externalized costs of mining would not only erode profitability but would also make many existing mining projects no longer economically viable. Full disclosure of the environmental legacies of mining could also erode the industry's legitimacy. To avoid accountability for the negative externalities of mining, denial that serious problems exist and refusal to engage with critics are the status quo for the industry.

A key strategy of phase 1 is the sowing of doubt about the extent or severity of the negative impacts. This approach was pioneered by the tobacco industry, which for many years argued that the link between smoking and disease had not been scientifically established (Brandt 2007). Until recently, the petroleum industry continually denied the link between fossil fuel consumption, the accumulation of carbon dioxide, and global climate change. The artificial promotion of uncertainty has become standard practice across a wide range of industries (Davis 2002; Michaels 2008).[3] This frequently includes promotion of counter-science that supports the interests and claims of industry (see Beck 1992:32).

Consider the following example of a phase 1 response by Ok Tedi Mining Ltd., which operates a large gold and copper mine in Papua New Guinea. Since the mid-1980s, the mine has discharged more than 1 billion metric tons of tailings, the finely ground material that remains after the valuable metal has been extracted, and waste rock into the Ok Tedi and

FIGURE 15.1

Ok Tedi Mining public relations poster from the late 1980s.

Fly Rivers. Pollution from the Ok Tedi Mine has caused extensive defor-estation downstream, the collapse of local fisheries, loss of biodiversity, and potential threats to human health (Kirsch 2006, 2007, 2008). Yet, in response to early concerns about the environmental impacts, in the late 1980s the mining company distributed a public relations poster denying that the mine posed a threat to the environment (fig. 15.1).

The Melanesian Tok Pisin text for the poster reads "Environment: The company protects the river, forest, and wildlife. No harm will come to you when the waste material from the gold and copper is discharged into the river." A blue sky soars over green fields, an orange butterfly, and an orange and red flower, suggesting that all is well. This reassuring message

FIGURE 15.2
Deforestation along the Ok Tedi River.

is contradicted by a photograph of deforestation on the Ok Tedi River taken by the author in 1996, in which the destruction caused by the Ok Tedi Mine is abundantly clear (fig. 15.2).

When problems become too great to deny and the opposition too effective to ignore, companies may shift to a phase 2 corporate response: acknowledgment that problems exist, that something is harmful or defective, and that the critique has some scientific validity or ethical merit. Until the people living downstream from the Ok Tedi Mine filed a lawsuit against the parent company BHP (Broken Hill Proprietary Ltd.), the company actively promoted its image as a responsible steward of the environment. Consider the advertisement published by BHP in the *Mining Environmental Journal* in February 1997, shortly after the lawsuit against the company was settled out of court: the caption reads "Leaving Our Environment the Same Way We Found It" (fig. 15.3). The advertisement depicts BHP's Island Copper Mine in British Columbia, Canada, after mine closure.[4] Like the optimistic cartoon produced by the Ok Tedi Mine (see fig. 15.1), this image is also deceptive. Although the ad appears to depict a healthy freshwater lake, the mining pit has been filled with ocean water to prevent the development of acid mine drainage (Poling 2002). Like other salt lakes, the water in the mining pit at the Island Copper Mine does not support organic life.

FIGURE 15.3

"Leaving Our Environment the Same Way We Found It" (BHP ad, 1997).

The advertisement reflects BHP's pursuit of a phase 1 corporate response that seeks to conceal the company's impact on the environment.

After the out-of-court settlement of the lawsuit against BHP and the Ok Tedi Mine, the company was forced to acknowledge its impacts on the environment. The settlement was initially valued at $500 million in compensation and commitments to tailings containment (Tait 2006; see Banks and Ballard 1997). After the settlement, Ok Tedi Mining Ltd. admitted that the environmental impacts were "far greater and more damaging than predicted" (OTML 1999:1), leading BHP to conclude that the project was "not compatible with [its] environmental values" (Economist 1999). The cover of BHP's environment and community report for 1999 conveyed a very different message than the Island Copper Mine advertisement published two years earlier (fig 15.4). Instead of attempting to reassure the public that the

FIGURE 15.4

"There's No Question Our Business Has an Impact" (BHP report, 1999).

company would restore the environment to its original state, BHP acknowledged its impact on the landscape with an image of a coal seam being exploded by dynamite. The caption "There's No Question Our Business Has an Impact" illustrates BHP's shift to a phase 2 corporate response to critique.

Despite acknowledging that problems exist, phase 2 responses to corporate critique are generally limited to symbolic gestures such as the payment of compensation or small-scale improvements. The goal is to avoid paying the full cost of eliminating negative impacts. In the Ok Tedi case, the mining company installed a dredge in the lower Ok Tedi River, which lowers the riverbed and reduces flooding and deforestation but removes only 40 percent of the tailings discharged into the river system and 20 percent of the total waste material produced by the mine. Meanwhile, deforestation along the river corridor continues to spread downstream and now affects more than 2,000 square kilometers.

Whereas in phase 2 the threats posed to the corporation are limited, in phase 3 they are critical and call for crisis management. Phase 3 is defined by the risk that the problems will become financially and socially too great to manage. The threat of catastrophic loss, bankruptcy, industry collapse, or the complete loss of legitimacy motivates corporations to shift to a phase 3 response: the corporation actively engages with its critics and participates in the shaping of politics that lead to the regulation and management of industry-related problems. For example, after it was established that exposure to asbestos causes lung cancer and other respiratory ailments, legal action against the industry led to bankruptcy proceedings. Paint manufacturers faced similarly catastrophic costs due to the effects of lead on children's nervous systems. However, the threat of financial insolvency posed by the costs of cleanup and compensation resulted in the negotiation of novel agreements that allowed corporations to continue operating so that they could make partial restitution for the harms they caused. Other costs from asbestos and lead were socialized by their transfer to the government or the individuals affected, including consumers made responsible for cleaning up properties affected by these toxic materials (Brodeur 1985; Warren 2001).

The phase 3 corporate response to critique takes many forms. It can involve the development of certification programs that provide problematic processes of production and consumption with the stamp of public approval (Szablowski 2007). Corporations may also assimilate critics within corporate structures by forming partnerships with NGOs or recruiting activists to join corporate boards, reducing their ability and motivation to bring about radical restructuring and change. Conversely, other critics may be portrayed as radical and impractical, a strategy of divide-and-rule that can have disruptive consequences for NGOs and civil society. Another phase 3 corporate response is the institution of what has been called "audit culture" (Power 1994; Strathern 2002), the development of regimes of monitoring and accountability that avoid the imposition of significant structural change (Szablowski 2007).

The core of phase 3 corporate response is the strategic management of critique and the establishment of a new status quo. Corporations may also envision the possibility of competitive advantage and the achievement of a new kind of legitimacy through their participation in regulatory processes. For example, support for the Kimberly Process, which restricts the trade of "blood diamonds" from conflict zones in Africa, was financially beneficial to De Beers, which controls the lion's share of the world's diamond trade and benefits from the reduction in supply, keeping prices high.

Corporations and industries move back and forth through the different phases of response. Particular corporations within a given industry may respond differently to critique and thus may be located in a different phase than their competitors, and all three phases exist across capitalism at the same moment. In general, phase 1 is the most profitable position for corporations to occupy because they are able to avoid financial liability for costly externalities. Corporations generally resist the move to phase 2 because of the costs added by negotiation with their critics. However, in some cases it may be strategically advantageous for corporations to move preemptively into a phase 2 posture in order to manage their critics. This strategy is promoted by the public relations industry, which encourages corporations to meet and educate their critics before conflict arises or the public even realizes that a problem exists (see Deegan 2001; Hance, Chess, and Sandman 1990). Corporations can then achieve positive recognition for being responsible corporate citizens without engaging in confrontational relationships that would require them to modify production or undertake actions that might reduce their profitability. The phase 3 corporate response to critique is typically the last resort, in which the possibility of collapse, bankruptcy, or illegitimacy threatens the future of the corporation or the industry.

CORPORATE OXYMORONS

One strategy for neutralizing critical discourse is the deployment of corporate oxymorons (Benson and Kirsch 2010b). Such figures of speech seek to disable the critical facilities of the consumer or shareholder with claims that require one to simultaneously subscribe to two contradictory beliefs, an example of what George Orwell (2003) famously called "doublethink" in his novel *Nineteen Eighty-Four*. A prominent example of a corporate oxymoron is *clean coal*, which is promoted as the solution to the energy crisis even though it does not exist (fig. 15.5). Although there are technologies that scrub sulfuric acid from the emissions of power plants that burn coal, no one has devised an economical means of preventing the resulting carbon dioxide, the greenhouse gas most responsible for global climate change, from being released into the atmosphere. Yet, the reassuring sound of the corporate oxymoron *clean coal* implies that such technology is already available or at least within reach. The objective is to limit criticism of the coal industry by promoting an illusion, that coal can be used to generate electricity without exacerbating the problems caused by

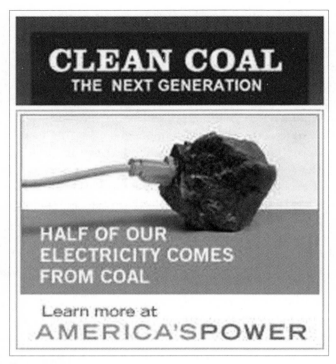

FIGURE 15.5
"Clean Coal: The Next Generation" (Cleancoalusa.org, 2008).

global climate change.[5] The example of clean coal shows how corporate oxymorons conceal harmful practices.

Corporate oxymorons represent a particular type of branding that conveys a political message intended to ease the minds of otherwise critical observers. The pairing of a positive cover term with the description of a harmful product or process, such as *clean coal* or *sustainable mining*, involves a tacit acknowledgment that a problem exists. Corporate oxymorons seek to limit critique through repetition of the conjoined phase, making the terms seem familiar and plausible despite the inherent contradiction. Analysis of corporate oxymorons helps to reveal how corporations manage critique. In the final section of the chapter, I describe how the mining industry promotes the corporate oxymoron *sustainable mining* (Kirsch 2010).

SUSTAINABLE MINING

In 1999 the nine largest mining companies decided to respond collectively to the threat from their indigenous and NGO critics (Danielson

2002:7), resulting in unprecedented collaboration between companies that previously regarded one another as fierce competitors.[6] According to one NGO observer of the process, their goal was to "divert attention away from specific corporate misdeeds by involving the industry...in civil discourse about sustainability and corporate social responsibility" (Moody 2007:257). The resulting campaign created and promoted the corporate oxymoron of *sustainable* mining.

The concept of sustainability has been publically shaped through a series of multilateral conferences. Pressure from different constituencies has progressively redefined the term so that a key component of its original formulation, the need to protect the environment, has been almost completely obscured. This redefinition permits the concept of sustainability to circulate widely by increasing the number of contexts in which it can be applied, although the resulting changes should not be seen as politically innocent. Contemporary use of the term *sustainability* has its origins in the 1972 United Nations Conference on the Human Environment, in Stockholm, which focused on what was needed "to maintain the earth as a place suitable for human life not only now but for future generations" (Ward and Dubos 1972, cited in Danielson 2002:19). The emphasis was on human activities that cause environmental degradation, especially pollution due to industrialization (Adam 2001:55). When the International Union for the Conservation of Nature (IUCN 1980:1) published the World Conservation Strategy in 1980, it linked concerns about sustainability to the concept of development: "For development to be sustainable, it must take account of social and ecological factors, as well as economic ones; of the living and nonliving resource base; and of the long term as well as short term advantages and disadvantages of alternative actions." This "conservation-centered" approach to development sought to balance economic and environmental concerns (Reed 2002:206).

The 1987 World Commission on Environment and Development, now known as the Brundtland Commission, adopted a more "human-centered" approach to these questions (Reed 2002:206). Responding to concerns that imposing environmental restrictions on southern countries would impede their ability to catch up to the North, the commission placed greater emphasis on meeting the needs of people living in developing countries, including future generations. The resulting definition of sustainability has been described as "equity-centered" (Reed 2002:206). The Brundtland Commission formulated the definition that remains in popular parlance: sustainable development "meets the needs of the present without compromising the ability of future generations to meet their own needs" (Brundtland 1987:15).

In the 1990s, the discourse of sustainable development underwent further modification. The 1992 UN Conference on Environment and Development, in Rio de Janeiro, commonly known as the Earth Summit, promoted a "growth-centered" approach to development while setting aside prior concerns about equity (Reed 2002:206). It favored the preservation of biodiversity through the protection of small, relatively pristine sites as conservation areas. This trade-off opened the remainder of the world to virtually unimpeded development. The mining industry capitalized on the new consensus by funding conservation projects that offset the environmental impacts of new mining projects (BBOP 2009; Shankleman 2010). The mining industry regularly collaborates with many of the world's largest and most influential conservation organizations, including the World Wild Fund for Nature (WWF), Conservation International, and the International Union for the Conservation of Nature (IUCN), displacing earlier alliances between conservationists and indigenous peoples (Kirsch 1997; West 2005).[7]

The corporate oxymoron *sustainable mining* follows the growth-centered approach advanced by the Rio Earth Summit. The concept of sustainability has undergone progressive redefinition that obscures the original reference to ecology, so the mining industry's use of the term *sustainability* refers primarily to economic variables. The contribution made by particular mining projects to sustainable development is presented in terms of royalties and taxes that can be used to support development and business opportunities projected to continue after mine closure (Crook 2004; Welker 2009). One of the first mining companies to integrate sustainability into corporate audit culture was the Canadian firm Placer Dome, which in 1999 began to issue annual sustainability reports for all of its major projects (fig. 15.6).[8] These reports identify the primary objective of sustainability as the capacity "to maintain profitability for the shareholders," although they also seek to "develop closer integration as a partner and contributor to community development" and "to leave an environment that offers no loss of opportunities to future generations after mine closure" (Placer Dome Asia Pacific 2000). Less than a decade later, all the major mining companies had enacted similar policies on sustainability.

The original definition of *sustainability* focused on the relationship between economy and ecology, but the balance between the two has shifted over time, culminating in the complete elision of references to ecology or biology in the way the term is now deployed by the mining industry. This process was facilitated by a conceptual shift from strong to weak sustainability (Daly 1996:76–77; see Danielson 2002:22). The two competing notions of sustainability differ with respect to the relationship between natural

FIGURE 15.6
Placer Dome Asia Pacific sustainability reports, 1999.

capital and human or manufactured capital. The concept of weak sustainability refers to the argument that natural capital and manufactured capital are interchangeable and that sustainability is achieved when the total value of capital remains constant or increases. According to this formula, a mine that pollutes a river and causes extensive deforestation may be regarded as sustainable if the profits from the project are successfully converted into manufactured capital with an economic value that equals or exceeds the value of what has been consumed or destroyed in the process. From this perspective, a mine is considered sustainable as long as the "total stock" of capital remains the same or increases. In contrast, strong sustainability acknowledges the interdependence of human economies and the environment without treating them as interchangeable. From this perspective, weak sustainability, to which the mining industry subscribes, is a category error (Daly 1996:78). The economist Herman Daly (1996:77) illustrates his critique of weak sustainability by pointing out that the complete replacement of fishing stock (natural capital) with fishing boats (manufactured capital) is a recipe for a tragedy of the commons.

Whereas the concept of sustainability may previously have been used to critique the environmental impacts of the mining industry, it has now become a means to promote mining. BHP Billiton (2009) claimed, "Sustainable development is about ensuring our business remains viable

FIGURE 15.7
BHP Billiton logo on University of Michigan solar car.

and contributes lasting benefits to society." Despite its responsibility for the environmental disaster downstream from the Ok Tedi Mine, BHP Billiton was appointed to the external advisory board at the University of Michigan's new institute for environmental sustainability (Blumenstyk 2007). The interim director of the institute, a professor of business administration, defended his rationale in inviting BHP Billiton to participate: "'There's no pure company out there,' he says. 'I have no reason to doubt that this company has really screwed a lot of people,' just as nearly every other company is 'unjust to people' at one point or another. 'These organizations are part of the problem, and they're also part of the solution'" (Blumenstyk 2007). Ironically, the logo for the mining company responsible for the Ok Tedi mining disaster is now prominently displayed on the University of Michigan's solar car (fig. 15.7).

Similarly, the Anglo-Australian mining company Rio Tinto (2009) asserts that its "contribution to sustainable development is not just the right thing to do": "We also understand that it gives us business reputational benefits that result in greater access to land, human and financial resources." Rio Tinto subsidiary Alcan also sponsors an annual US$1-million prize for NGOs working to "advance the goals of economic, environment, and social sustainability" (Rio Tinto 2009). The meaning of *sustainability* increasingly depends on how it is deployed and by whom and no longer has any necessary relationship to the environment.

The mining industry's appropriation of the discourse of sustainability seeks to cover up the fact that there have been few significant reforms in how mining is practiced, nor overall reduction of its harmful impacts, as the term *sustainable* would imply.[9] The promotion of mining as sustainable development also makes it more difficult for critics of the industry to increase public recognition of its externalized costs.[10] The appropriation of their critics' discourse is one of the key strategies used by corporations to conceal harm and neutralize critique.

CONCLUSION

When corporations are successful in silencing their critics, they are able to promote a sense of resignation about one's ability to make a difference or change the status quo (Benson and Kirsch 2010a). The corporate strategies and tactics described in this chapter and the general feelings of disempowerment and cynicism that pervade contemporary political life are directly linked. Corporations actively cultivate and benefit from the politics of resignation, contributing to the illusion that corporate power is either inevitable or largely immovable. However, it is possible to pierce the veil; the examination of how corporations seek to achieve legitimacy and contain liability reveals significant vulnerabilities and contingencies. The success of these corporate strategies is by no means certain or guaranteed. Showing how corporations work to conceal the harm they produce provides an opportunity for people to rethink their relationships to corporations. Tracking corporate responses to critique can reveal strategic opportunities for calling corporations to account for their actions, mobilizing political discontent around the evasion of corporate responsibility, and forging stronger standards for legitimacy.

Notes

1. The events following the 2010 BP oil spill in the Gulf of Mexico challenged some of these assumptions. Although outrage against BP was high, consumers had limited means of putting pressure on the company. Boycotting BP gas stations had little impact on the company's bottom line because these stations are independent franchises, and given the fungibility of crude oil, they do not necessarily sell BP gas. More generally, consumers have limited options when it comes to ethically and environmentally sound choices of petroleum companies: Exxon had its *Valdez*, Shell its Niger Delta, Texaco its Ecuadorian oil spill and Chevron-Texaco its refusal to clean it up, BP its Gulf

of Mexico, and so forth. Clearly, petroleum companies do not compete for consumers based on their environmental performance.

2. This figure does not include extensive cleanup at abandoned coal mines in the United States.

3. A recent study attributes public skepticism regarding environmental problems to conservative think tanks that seek to defend corporations against regulation (Jacques, Dunlap, and Freeman 2008). More than 90 percent of conservative think tanks are involved in promoting skepticism about environmental problems, often referring to the scientific research they seek to discredit as "junk science" (Jacques, Dunlap, and Freeman 2008:349).

4. Island Copper used controversial submarine tailings disposal, discharging mine wastes directly into the ocean. Submarine tailings disposal is banned in the United States, and only a small number of mines employ this technology, most of which are located in Southeast Asia and the Pacific.

5. The clean coal campaign has also been the subject of satire (http://greeninc .blogs.nytimes.com/2009/02/26/the-coen-brothers-do-clean-coal/, accessed June 15, 2009); "subvertisements" like this one also challenge corporate oxymorons (Sawyer 2010).

6. Luke Danielson (2006:26) notes that "it is hard to identify any industrial sector (with the possible exception of nuclear power) that features such low levels of trust and such a history of division, strife and anger as the extractive industries."

7. Anthropologist Mac Chapin (2004:18) criticizes these NGOs for "partnering with multinational corporations directly involved in pillaging and destroying forest areas belonging to indigenous peoples."

8. Placer Dome followed the lawsuit against the Ok Tedi Mine very closely and commissioned these reports not long after the case was settled out of court in 1996. Barrick Gold purchased Placer Dome in 2006.

9. Andy Whitmore (2006) aptly compares the mining industry's attempt to represent itself as sustainable to the story of the emperor's new clothes.

10. An interesting example of how corporations manipulate the media can be seen in Chevron's response to the news that the American investigative television program *Sixty Minutes* planned to report on pollution from the oil company's operations in the Ecuadorian Amazon. Chevron hired a former journalist to represent its side of the story and then purchased Google ads to ensure that its website about the lawsuit, including its own fourteen-minute video, would appear at the top of any search as a sponsored link (Stelter 2009).

16

Philip Morris, the FDA, and the Paradoxes of Corporate Social Responsibility

Peter Benson

Tobacco has been a visible part of daily life in large parts of the world for hundreds of years. Profound changes in tobacco's prevalence and effects occurred in the twentieth century. The modern commercial cigarette and multinational tobacco corporations proliferated to the extent that smoking is now the single greatest cause of preventable disease and death worldwide. One hundred million tobacco-related deaths occurred over the past century. Although smoking declined and tobacco-control measures took hold in several countries over the past few decades, it is now widely recognized that the unabated global demand for cigarettes will kill one billion people in the current century (Proctor 2001). The majority of these deaths will be in developing countries, where the industry continues to infuse smoking with positive social meanings, recruit adolescent smokers, maintain free-market environments for this harmful product, and leverage political influence to limit public health efforts, including implementation of the World Health Organization's international Framework Convention on Tobacco Control (WHO 2008).

In the United States, however, the tobacco industry now engages with public health critique and policy through different strategies. Leading the way is Philip Morris USA, which has adopted a corporate social responsibility platform in the past decade. Its company website boldly claims, "There is no safe cigarette" (Philip Morris USA 2007). The website is part of a broader media campaign that includes television and print ads aimed at publicizing information about smoking risks. Why would the biggest of Big Tobacco, the world's largest, most powerful cigarette-maker, insist to the public that its product is unsafe?

On one level, this insistence is about public image: Philip Morris's makeover into a "responsible corporate citizen" (Brandt 2007:444). Hence, the website also attests, "Our goal is to be the most responsible...manufacturer and marketer of consumer products" (Philip Morris USA 2007). The firm is pursuing image-enhancement strategies to overturn decades of delegitimization and deception that have made the tobacco industry a symbol of corporate wrongdoing. For example, Philip Morris has aligned itself with the leading public health groups (e.g., Campaign for Tobacco-Free Kids, American Lung Association, American Heart Association, and American Cancer Society) in the United States in supporting sweeping tobacco-control measures, namely, legislation granting the Food and Drug Administration (FDA) authority to regulate cigarettes and other tobacco products. But this image-control strategy is also a means of limiting corporate liability and deflecting risk assumption for smoking disease and death onto consumers.

In this chapter, I explore some of the economic and ethical paradoxes that define this contentious policy change and Philip Morris's newfound commitment to corporate social responsibility. I am interested in what these transformations reflect about contemporary capitalism and the effects of corporate power and strategy on public policy and on populations of consumers and producers. I discuss the politics around the FDA legislation, highlighting the dangerous role of a particular corporate oxymoron—the safe cigarette—in Philip Morris's strategic engagement with public health and consumer markets. Although Philip Morris admits on its website that there is "no safe cigarette," the firm is banking on the expectation that FDA regulation will inadvertently sustain the company's continued promotion of the profitable illusion of a "safer" cigarette.

MOST ADMIRED COMPANY

Motorists driving up and down Interstate 95 pass Philip Morris's headquarters outside Richmond, Virginia. In 2004 I passed the behemoth corporate campus on my drive from Boston, where I was a graduate student at the time, to North Carolina to conduct one year of anthropological fieldwork with tobacco growers and workers. Between the highway shoulder and the parking lots is a tall metal obelisk (it looks like a giant cigarette) wrapped with the logos of the company's most popular cigarette brands: Marlboro, Virginia Slims, Parliament, L&M, and Basic. Many motorists probably roll their eyes, thinking about this company's public relations, which they have seen in print or on television, and the perversity of Philip Morris now fashioning itself as something of a public health advocate.

But the company's image has improved, according to internal and independent polls. In the mid-1990s, Americans had a very negative view of Philip Morris, giving it an average favorability rating of about 33 percent (only slightly higher than the smoking rate at the time). By 2004, nearly 60 percent of all Americans (more in the young adult age group) said that Philip Morris was acting more responsibly than in the past, and they distinguished it as more responsible than other tobacco companies (McDaniel, Smith, and Malone 2006:219–220).

In 2008, *Fortune* magazine ranked Philip Morris as the tobacco industry's "most admired" company. The company's overall "admiration" ranking (8.4 out of 10) reflected the magazine's evaluation of such factors as social responsibility, people management, financial soundness, global competitiveness, and product quality. Incredibly, this rating is the highest score of any company on *Fortune*'s lists. Although this rating would appear to make Philip Morris the most admired company in the world, in fact, it is not included in *Fortune*'s overall list of the Top 50 most admired companies (which does include such icons as Apple, Berkshire Hathaway, Google, Johnson & Johnson, Coca-Cola, Walt Disney, and McDonald's). Nor, in the case of Philip Morris, does *Fortune* provide an extended commentary about "Why It's Admired," a blurb included for all non-tobacco companies. However, the company does appear in the alphabetized list of the Top 363 most admired companies and quite near the top, because one of Philip Morris's strategic responses to critique was to change its name to the Altria Group.

THE TOBACCO PROBLEM

The science of smoking-related disease that arose in the early twentieth century did not identify a problem never before recognized as requiring sociopolitical intervention. In the famous "A Counterblaste to Tobacco," published in 1604, King James I declared that tobacco is "a custom loathsome to the eye, hateful to the nose, harmful to the brain, dangerous to the lung." Subsequent centuries saw various social movements critique tobacco consumption and seek prohibition. Perhaps the most forceful was the temperance movement in the early twentieth-century United States, which placed tobacco alongside alcohol as the main source of moral ruination in modern society (Brandt 2007:45–48).

In the past half century, anti-tobacco politics were radically amplified and distinctively transformed in parts of the world. These changes certainly have to do with the biosciences' mounting interrogation of smoking and the new alliances between science, government, and civil society, as well as the sheer magnitude of the public health catastrophe that has increasingly been linked to tobacco consumption. A watershed was the landmark 1964 US surgeon general's report, which helped publically solidify the scientific and medical consensus about smoking and health. The tobacco industry responded with various strategies, including redoubling marketing campaigns to legitimize the smoking habit and secretly funding pseudoscience to foment public debate and doubts about even the most basic facts of tobacco's toxicity (Brandt 2007).

To understand what it means for tobacco to be a problem today entails apprehending, among many other things, the forms of political calculation and intervention that have evolved in relation to tobacco; the development of official government approaches, as well as criticism and advocacy work; and the responses and engagements of the tobacco industry and its political supporters (Benson 2012). More than the increase in scientific evidence linking smoking to disease or the simple fact that government regulation of tobacco has increased in the past half century, new and different kinds of institutional and societal arrangements define and act upon tobacco as a problem. My concern is with how corporations respond to critique or increased public awareness about the environmental and health problems related to their business. Far from being opposed to governments, corporations are often actively involved in shaping regulation as both an intellectual space linked to normalized ethical and cultural values and an institutional space defined by dominant approaches and concerns. This perspective is broadly appropriate to the study of many health problems because claims to corporate social responsibility are evident across many industries, including the food and beverage companies marketing the products that significantly contribute to chronic disease conditions.

Anthropologists are increasingly studying the adoption of corporate social responsibility (CSR) in various industries, the economic strategies and political valences that usually define these trends, and the implications for public health, the composition of markets, and the welfare of affected environments and populations (Benson and Kirsch 2010; Welker, Partridge, and Hardin 2011). For example, anthropologists examine how biotech and pharmaceutical firms hype the life-saving potential of their products (Sunder Rajan 2006). In Stuart Kirsch's contribution to this volume (chapter 15), he shows how anthropologists are looking at the role of CSR claims in facilitating extractive industries and mediating conflicts between indigenous communities and these industries in various parts of the world (Kirsch 2010; Sawyer 2010; Welker 2009). Much of my own work explores the adoption of CSR in the tobacco industry as a strategic response to concerns about not only smoking but also labor conditions and environmental issues related to tobacco manufacturing and industrial tobacco agriculture (Benson 2008, 2010). My goal is to open up the crucial role of corporations in modern public health to more rigorous analysis and to critically reflect on both the inadequacies of contemporary public health approaches that do not attend to the harm caused by industry and the role of corporations in their social management of harm (Benson and Kirsch 2010b).

Tobacco companies never simply responded to a problem that existed, apart from their involvement in shaping the terms of debate. The tobacco problem was constructed from the back-and-forth between the intensified criticism of the industry in the past half century and the responses and justifications provided by the industry. In contrast to the temperance movement's somewhat religious focus, the regulatory approaches since the postwar decades were more secular. The emphasis on sin and moral ruination shifted to a concern with health. Not health in the vague sense referenced by early monarchs and the temperance activists, who were aware of smoking-related ailments, but rather a scientific understanding of health in terms of epidemiological risk factors (Brandt 1990).

Regarding smoking as gravely threatening to the nation would have been a plausible response to the scientific evidence about smoking and health in the 1950s. However, tobacco's legitimacy and legality were not questioned, even though tobacco killed more Americans in the past century than all of the country's military operations combined. The federal government was not going to take bold action against the tobacco products that were ubiquitous in the culture; thus, the surgeon general's report did not lead to a call for prohibition or even the wholesale restructuring and regulation of the tobacco industry. The report instead led to new government interventions designed to enhance public awareness of risk and improve individual decisions, including a mandate that warning labels be printed on cigarette packs and the regulation of tobacco advertisements. The project of eliminating tobacco from society, an approach characteristic of the prohibition movement, was replaced by a biopolitics linking accumulated knowledge about smoking risk to the development of techniques for managing risk at the population level and promoting behavior management and modification at the individual level.

Hence, the modern anti-tobacco movement has been and remains premised on the idea that more and more scientific information about smoking risk is essential to improving public health. In addition, this epistemological and organizational framework of tobacco control has determined in large measure how other chronic disease problems, like obesity, are conceptualized and managed. Although prevention has been part of the official public health response to the epidemiological transition—the increased chronic disease burden and disease-related problems linked to consumption and lifestyle—the dominant approach has favored health promotion over prevention, making consumers the locus of intervention (as in the case of warning labels) and upholding distinctive American beliefs in individual autonomy and responsibility and the cultural framing of freedom in terms of the marketplace (Brandt 2007:442–445).

In the 1960s and 1970s, the tobacco industry and the federal government worked collaboratively to develop potentially reduced-risk tobacco products. The US Department of Agriculture funded studies in search of less toxic tobacco leaf varieties. The American Cancer Society and the American Heart Association pushed for the removal of "high-tar" cigarettes from the market. Leading public health officials formed the Less Hazardous Cigarette Working Group (later renamed the Tobacco Working Group to appease the industry) and contracted with scientific laboratories and industry scientists to develop less risky products. Meanwhile, the federal Public Health Service cautioned that the promotion of supposedly reduced-risk products "might lull the consumer into believing that he could smoke this kind of cigarette without *any* accompanying risk" (Fairchild and Colgrove 2004:193–195). The relationship between government and industry does not seem so adversarial, however, if one considers the institutional complicities that influenced how tobacco was reckoned a problem and drove responses that were, frankly, quite nonchalant given their public health impact.

While hiding clear knowledge of the dangers of smoking, as in the excerpt from an internal tobacco company document seen in figure 16.1, the tobacco industry introduced a series of products, such as filtered cigarettes, that were purported to be safer than conventional cigarettes. These new products were marketed as a form of what one company called "health protection" (Brandt 2007:244), which implicitly acknowledged that tobacco products were causing harm. Subsequent advertising used misleading product descriptors like "light" or "low-tar" to allay consumer anxieties (Pollay and Dewhirst 2002). However, it was well known within the industry that these new products provided a false sense of security. Tobacco companies chose not to divulge their knowledge that these products delivered as much

Arthur D. Little, Inc

CONFIDENTIAL
LIMITED

March 15, 1961

L & M - A PERSPECTIVE REVIEW

. There are biologically active materials present in cigarette tobacco.

These are:
a) cancer causing
b) cancer promoting
c) poisonous
d) stimulating, pleasurable, and flavorful.

FIGURE 16.1

Excerpt from internal tobacco company document. Source: Tobacco Documents Online. Anne Landman Collection, Bates no. 2021382496/2498. http://tobaccodocuments.org/landman /176632.html.

tar and nicotine as conventional cigarettes. Aggressive marketing perpetuated dependence on tobacco as smokers switched to the new products en masse in the mistaken belief that they were less risky (Fairchild and Colgrove 2004). The market share for light cigarettes increased from 4 percent in 1970 to 50 percent in 1990 and, with aggressive advertising campaigns, to 80 percent in 1998. People "believed, and still do, that these products pose less risk to health than other cigarettes" (Institute of Medicine 2001:26).

PROJECT SUNRISE

In the late 1980s, Philip Morris considered quitting the cigarette business because mounting legal pressures threatened the company's food and beverage subsidiaries (namely, Kraft, General Foods, and Nabisco). Industry consultants began to speak of a "litigation time bomb" (Smith and Malone 2003b:208). Institutions such as universities divested from tobacco stock. Public image and legal liability were impacting the market value of tobacco companies, and tobacco control was gaining ground as a movement, with several strong national organizations, a widespread network of public health activists and researchers, and an approach that now included the more forceful strategies of litigation, excise taxes on cigarettes, and clean air ordinances and other public health regulations (McDaniel, Smith, and Malone 2006:216).

However, executives used focus groups to guide a strategic repositioning campaign and remake the company's image around concepts like trustworthiness, caring about consumer safety and health, and notions of community commitment, along with providing choice, which tested particularly well, boosting company likability by thirty percentage points. Public relations experts created a media campaign—Project Sunrise—to publicly associate these values with the newly formed Altria Group, a more pharmaceutical-sounding name for Philip Morris. A legal shelter was created by incorporating the tobacco businesses as separate entities (Smith and Malone 2003a, 2003b).

Most of what the public has seen of this campaign involves $1 billion of corporate investment in a youth smoking prevention department, which creates communications and resources aimed at encouraging parents to "talk to their kids about not using tobacco products," according to the company's website. The department provides schools and youth organizations with grants to support the development of "healthy lifestyles" and funds programs to inform tobacco product retailers about smoking laws. This selective public health focus is strategic. Internal company documents reveal that Philip Morris executives have long believed that philanthropic engagement with youth health issues is an especially effective way of demonstrating that the company is "acting reasonably and responsibly," as one internal executive memo states, while shaping the public debate about health behaviors to focus on parents and kids rather than industry (Philip Morris USA 2010).

In one memo from the early 1990s, corporate officials strategized about how to influence the balance of "youth smoking versus prohibition trends in public health" (McDaniel, Smith, and Malone 2006:217). The narrowing of tobacco governance to focus on adult choice, law enforcement, and family matters is a choreographed effect of what appear on the surface simply to be noble investments in public health on the part of a responsible corporate actor. Why should corporations be held accountable for smoking disease when the responsibility lies with law enforcement officers, convenience store clerks, high school educators, and parents?

Other less visible aspects of Project Sunrise are likewise notable. Behind the scenes, Philip Morris conducts social research on smoking and smokers with the aim of tailoring products and programs to promote social acceptability and reinforce smoking rituals. The company makes an effort to ensure that smoking remains permitted in public places through cigarette-butt litter-reduction programs; research to promote the use of ventilation systems in restaurants, bars, and other public places as an alternative to smoking bans; and the design of cigarettes said to be less toxic or emit less secondhand smoke.

Project Sunrise also involves what the company has called the "Fair Play" strategy, researching tobacco-control advocates and organizations, with the aim of gaining leverage within the public health community and promoting a moderate agenda for tobacco control. The company amasses a database on the composition and objectives of different tobacco-control groups, as well as their relationships to one another and to funding sources. According to internal documents, company executives believed that this "competitive intelligence" would improve the company's ability to respond in "proactive and offensive" ways to the tobacco-control movement. The identification of more "moderate" groups would facilitate efforts to "disrupt" the movement's "cohesion," officials with Philip Morris have stated (McDaniel, Smith, and Malone 2006).

The simple point is that the investment in youth smoking prevention as a basis for claims about social performance and social responsibility coevolved alongside efforts to augment the social acceptability of smoking and undermine the two scientifically validated methods of substantially reducing smoking prevalence: smoke-free legislation to prohibit smoking in public places and increased excise taxes on tobacco products.

Motorists might think that Philip Morris has been headquartered in Richmond forever. The building does blend in nicely with the brickwork of the city's old tobacco warehouses and cigarette factories, which are now either boarded up or have been redeveloped. In fact, only in 2004 did Philip Morris decide to relocate from a posh Manhattan tower—the Philip Morris Building at 120 Park Avenue—that had been its main office for decades. The company publicly described its relocation as a cost-cutting measure, the somewhat less metropolitan but more tobacco-friendly Southern town having offered millions in tax incentives. The explanation was a neat way to make this enormously profitable company seem strapped, victimized by the financial fallout from lawsuits and tobacco-control efforts. But the move may have also been a strategic retreat to a place where its operations would receive more favorable media coverage. In addition, around the time of the move, New York City required all buildings to be smoke free, but the behemoth that motorists pass on the Virginia highway has a powerful ventilation system to accommodate smokers, a more "reasonable" public health approach, the company claims. Although the health benefits of smoke-free legislation and the inadequacies of ventilation systems are well documented (Barnoya and Glantz 2006), the tobacco industry uses financial support of legislators and sideways lobbying through chambers of commerce and trade associations to obstruct the passage of such legislation in the United States and around the world.

Meanwhile, the \$100-million television campaign launched by the youth smoking prevention department in the early 2000s, called "Think. Don't smoke," is the largest anti-tobacco campaign ever undertaken by the tobacco industry. Public health research finds that effective youth smoking prevention programs must include comprehensive information about smoking disease and the nature of addiction, as well as critical anti-industry perspectives that discuss how tobacco companies market products to underage populations and prey upon young people in order to turn a profit (Thrasher et al. 2004). Not surprisingly, Philip Morris's television and print media steer clear of these issues and favor an emphasis on parenting. The ads convey the idea that smoking is for adults, which may actually instigate smoking behavior. As studies show, regular viewers of this campaign believe that tobacco companies are "more responsible" socially than in the past and are not culpable for smoking harms (see Friedman 2007; Szczypka et al. 2007).

FDA REGULATION

Since the 1980s, major public health groups have sought to include cigarettes under the FDA's regulatory mandate, which covers foods, drugs, pharmaceuticals, and cosmetic products, partly to control the tobacco industry's deceptive marketing practices. In recent years, Philip Morris has joined these groups in supporting the regulation, and the company played an active role in crafting the public debate and the legislation's language up through its final passage in 2009.

The bill authorizes larger cigarette pack warning labels, allows the FDA to restrict advertising and promotions that appeal to children, and requires the publication of an annual list of the harmful constituents in each brand. It allows the FDA to use clinical and public health science as a basis for mandating changes in tobacco product design and the ingredients to potentially minimize nicotine levels and toxicity. It also prevents manufacturers from using terms such as *low-tar* and *light* (Shatenstein 2004).

Although all these changes sound positive, certain segments of the public health field raised critical questions about the legislation. The bill forbids the FDA from banning tobacco sales to adults or requiring that nicotine yields be substantially reduced, and warning labels and ingredient disclosures—the core tenets of the bill—are legal apparatuses that safeguard corporations from liabilities related to consumption and underwrite individual risk assumption (Givel 2007; Siegel 2004). Philip Morris, unlike other tobacco companies, supported the bill because the legislation disadvantages competing firms that are less capable of adhering to new quality-control standards and tobacco product safety mandates within their more limited supply chains. Hence, other firms have called the bill a "Marlboro Monopoly Act," referring to Philip Morris's main brand, Marlboro, which controls half of the US market and is the most popular cigarette globally (Hsu 2001).

Public health researchers have also criticized the FDA bill for promoting a dangerous harm-reduction approach. Tobacco companies have introduced a spate of new tobacco products that claim to reduce risk for consumers who do not want to or cannot quit, including products that supposedly yield less secondhand smoke, products with a modified tobacco or nicotine content, and "smokeless" cigarettes that use chambers to scorch rather than burn tobacco as a way of reducing some toxins. Tobacco companies have also become aggressive in marketing new oral tobacco products. Because these are smokeless products, companies imply that they are safer than cigarettes, even though all tobacco products entail health risks. In contrast to the plain packaging of older varieties of spit or chewing tobacco, the new oral products are marketed as clean and refreshing, with colorful packaging and the use of flavors, which makes them seem more like bubblegum or candy.

What worries segments of the public health community is that tobacco companies will be able to market these new products as being approved by the FDA to help smokers reduce risk, even though they contain addictive levels of nicotine and involve substantial health risks. The link between reduced toxin exposure and ingredient control and health outcomes remains extremely complex and poorly understood. Far from clearing the air, critics worry that the FDA legislation might "institutionalize the problem of unsubstantiated health risk claims by cigarette marketers" (Siegel 2004:439). Tobacco companies might be able to continue to treat risk as a selling point by promoting different products or improved product design, using anxieties about health to enhance the marketability of their products, and encouraging smokers who are thinking about medicinal nicotine (e.g., nicotine gum) to instead purchase a modified tobacco product, thus protecting the company's share of the nicotine-dependence market from pharmaceutical companies. Philip Morris's position was that the FDA bill will allow companies to pursue types of tobacco products that are less harmful than traditional cigarettes.

Rather than abandon a risky product, Philip Morris has crafted a strategy that capitalizes on health risks to create an image of itself as a caring and innocent company that promotes lawful behavior, respects consumer autonomy, and works for the public health. A dominant cultural model of the consumer as a rational chooser is central to the alignment of certain corporate tobacco interests and certain public health policy interests around the FDA bill. The Campaign for Tobacco-Free Kids (2003:1), a leading anti-tobacco advocacy group and the bill's most vocal proponent, emphasizes at the beginning of a fact sheet about the legislation, "Adults are free to choose to use tobacco, which, despite the health risks involved, remains a legal product for adults to purchase and use. The bills advocated by the public health community...enhance adult choice by providing consumers with the information they currently do not have access to on what is in the tobacco products they use and the health risks associated with any of the ingredients in the product or the chemicals contained in tobacco smoke. As a result, under the bills advocated by the public health community, adult choice is an informed choice."

In the context of the growing societal burden of chronic diseases, various industries are developing business plans and marketing strategies to take into account public health concerns and take advantage of a dominant governmental approach that emphasizes corporate and consumer agency rather than industry regulation. Multinational corporations like Philip Morris claim to operate for the public good and address problems of human life more efficiently and effectively than the state, and in adopting governmental rationales and goals, they are working to hold back state power, contain the momentum of social movements that are an important source of critique and adversarial politics, and positively influence the social meanings of products and consumption.

A MORASS OF PARADOXES

Emergent and enduring complicities, rather than a simple opposition between the tobacco industry and public health, continue to define how tobacco is governed. Some form of prohibition or very tight regulation would seem to be the only response that lives up to the government's constitutional mandate to protect the general welfare. Tobacco is the only legal consumer product that is harmful when used as intended. "In a perfect world, we'd ban all cigarettes," acknowledged Representative John D. Dingell, a Michigan Democrat, when speaking about the proposed FDA legislation. "But the hard fact of the matter is that there are a lot of jobs depending on this. And more importantly, there are a lot of people out there who are addicted to this and they've got to have their fix" (Saul 2008). Our tacit acceptance of tobacco's legality is the direct result of the tobacco industry's decades of influence in the culture. Perhaps the most enduring of the tobacco industry's strategies has been the argument that individual consumers are aware of smoking risks and are therefore responsible agents, an ideology that is powerfully recapitulated when Philip Morris disseminates information about smoking and health in its public relations.

The tobacco industry and its political supporters in tobacco farm states have claimed that tobacco ought to remain legal and that tobacco-control measures ought to be restrained because rural farming communities and tobacco-processing towns are dependent on tobacco revenues (see Benson 2012). The use of this justification intensified during the 1980s and 1990s as the industry faced increasing scrutiny from the national anti-tobacco movement and extensive litigation. Although tobacco has long provided an important source of livelihood in the South—in the 1960s, nearly half a million tobacco farm families spread across more than a dozen states—this justification was strategically misleading. The appeal on behalf of Southern farmers ignored the mass exodus of farmers from tobacco agriculture in the 1980s and 1990s due to economic hardships associated with the globalization of tobacco production and liberalization policies pursued by a seemingly protectionist industry, which undermined the very small-scale family farm units promoted as the rationale for protecting the tobacco industry. The romanticized image of the threatened family farm also covered over the realities of race and class differentiation within rural communities. The tobacco industry used support for tobacco farmers as a way to secure its own legitimacy, discounting the fact that government programs could have facilitated a transition away from their dependency on tobacco revenues.

Elsewhere, I (Benson 2008) have explored the complex impact of the FDA bill on rural communities in North Carolina's tobacco-producing region. The FDA bill coincided with a new era of vertical integration on tobacco farms, and tobacco companies now directly contract with growers and mandate stringent quality-control measures to give the appearance that tobacco leaf is cleaner and safer for consumers and the environment. This model of liberalized, health-driven production fosters contextual factors that promote social and health problems at the farm level. At the same time that contracting contributes to local patterns of job loss and dislocation—year after year, more and more growers lose their contracts, leaving fewer and fewer in business—it puts financial pressure on farms, individualizes production risks, and deepens dependency on an illegal labor system characterized by the squalid housing conditions and various health problems that affect migrant workers.

These complex ethnographic dimensions were lost in the debates leading up to the recent passage of FDA legislation. The Congressional Budget Office estimates that the legislation will reduce youth smoking by 10 percent and adult smoking by 2 percent in the 2010s (Wilson 2009). But the FDA regulation does nothing to address economic instability and conditions of exploitation in tobacco-farming regions, worldwide smoking prevalence, and the ongoing redistribution of leaf production to the developing world. Research at the farm level reveals important contradictions on which enhanced consumer health and safety measures are established. Such research also suggests a need for assessment of FDA legislation in all its complexity and on multiple levels because the legislation stands to benefit tobacco corporate interests and contributes to uneven spheres of risk and vulnerability.

At the international level, the tobacco industry portrays the World Health Organization's attempts to globalize tobacco-control measures as extreme, working in legislatures around the world to instead construe the tobacco business as an engine of economic development and promote the adoption of regulations that focus on consumer education and choice. One key way that the WHO's landmark Framework Convention on Tobacco Control seeks to control the spread of tobacco involves recommendations concerning tobacco agriculture. The WHO encourages countries to develop economically sustainable alternatives to tobacco agriculture and to address the social and environmental costs related to tobacco farming. Developing countries where tobacco leaf is now widely grown (e.g., Brazil, India, and Malawi) are experiencing widespread deforestation, soil depletion and erosion, water table pollution, and, in the environment and the workforce, pesticide and nicotine poisoning. Tobacco companies, concerned with economic performance, often negotiate such low prices for tobacco leaf that production requires child labor and debt servitude (Otañez and Glantz 2009).

The public is becoming increasingly aware of these issues as a result of scholarship and field reporting, as well as advocacy, like that of the Human Rights and Tobacco Control Network, a group formed in 2008 by researchers and activists from many countries and fields to propel the anti-tobacco movement beyond a focus on consumer health to a holistic consideration of environmental health and labor issues. In response, the tobacco industry has integrated these issues into its CSR claims, mainly through public relations, philanthropy to states and institutions to fund ecology and agronomy projects, and the creation of friendly nongovernmental agencies.

For example, Philip Morris and British American Tobacco—the global cigarette giants—together recently created a nongovernmental organization called the Eliminating Child Labour in Tobacco Growing Foundation. The mission statement claims that the group is guided by "a new understanding that tobacco production is not just about products and the marketing, but also about corporate citizenship and about the whole value chain" (see www. eclt.org). The group makes infrastructural investments in tobacco-producing regions—in primary education, vaccination and screening programs, and sewage and water systems—and frames child labor as a problem of access to education and vaccines rather than industrial design and political economy. The group also invests in microcredit loans to tobacco growers to help them mechanize, become more efficient, and grow their businesses as a means of alleviating child labor. However, this dynamic only makes tobacco growers deeply dependent on the tobacco industry for basic livelihood, infrastructural, and health-care needs (Otañez and Glantz 2009).

To further foment loyalties and dependencies and expand political influence in poor countries, tobacco companies are helping to train future cohorts of ministries of agriculture by funding agronomy programs at major universities around the world. They are also establishing nongovernmental organizations in southern Africa and in Asia to focus on reforestation projects that do not challenge or displace tobacco agriculture but instead serve its needs. Nearly all of the tobacco industry's reforestation projects introduce non-native trees that grow more rapidly than native trees. Although these projects impact water table ecology and environmental sustainability issues, the number of trees replanted serves as a simple index of social responsibility and masks the hidden economic calculus of optimizing leaf curing and economies of scale in reforested areas. All of these processes deepen tobacco industry power in developing countries and make it more difficult for public health advocates and officials to argue for crop diversification and alternative livelihoods for tobacco farmers. National and local officials have become reluctant to criticize the tobacco industry out of fear of disrupting the cash flow and external funding for economic and environmental projects (Otañez and Glantz 2009).

CONCLUSION

The ethical consumerism of recent decades has driven new markets for "business care, where social and environmental investments pay economic dividends as more responsible businesses become the 'companies of choice' for consumers, investors, governments, and civil society partners" (Welker 2009:145). Social movements have sought to hold industries and corporations accountable for externalities and environmental, social, and public health impacts. Given this scenario, corporations are engaging with and reconfiguring scientific practices and objectives, the social meanings of human biology, and the cultural expectation that private businesses participate in public works. An entire CSR industry of consultants, organizational and marketing experts, academic journals and researchers, conferences and workshops, and evolving guidelines and standards is booming.

This parallel industry helps corporations in their efforts to develop repositioning concepts and confront new levels of criticism and concern regarding the potentially harmful and costly effects of industrial production and mass consumption.

Walmart now makes public claims about its efforts to maintain chronically low prices while improving the nutritional quality of its food products by pressuring its suppliers to reduce levels of fat, sodium, and sweeteners, an act of corporate social responsibility praised by the US federal government (Stolberg and Stolberg 2011). This shift presumably arose in direct response to public health research showing that Walmart's food sales alone account for 10 percent of the increase in obesity in the United States (Courtemanche and Carden 2011). Meanwhile, the retail giant's adoption of health values may also reflect a powerful economic strategy to foreshorten public criticism and further disadvantage competitor firms that will likely be less capable of simultaneously changing product offerings and containing costs within their more limited supply chains.

These claims—like all claims about social performance and values—must be scrutinized in light of the backstage intentions of corporations revealed by internal documents and anthropological research with key stakeholders who are within or are impacted by industry. We are likely to find important discrepancies between what companies say they are doing and what their activities actually do to populations and environments. However well-intentioned corporate actors may be or claim to be, their social responsibility agendas are secondary to the fiduciary responsibility of executives and managers, who are required by their shareholders to constantly maximize profits. This profit seeking often entails legitimizing and expanding industrial processes that are harmful in one way or another. Anthropologists can scrutinize the exact ways that corporations claim to resolve health and human problems in light of alternative approaches, and they can explicate why companies choose to focus their humanitarian endeavors on certain issues while often opposing other efforts to improve life conditions, such as Philip Morris's focus on youth smoking and parenting. Not only is such research helpful for understanding how the politics of health and civic virtue shapes capitalism, but it also reveals the underappreciated role of corporations in shaping what the ethics and politics of life mean, how significant health and social problems are strategically structured and governed, and how supply chains that bring harm to humans and environments are maintained even in the face of substantial criticism.

17

The Libertarian Welfare State

Robert H. Frank

I think of myself as a libertarian.

When my libertarian friends hear me say this, they often laugh, because they think I favor a much too expansive role for government to qualify for membership in their club. I believe, for example, that our current tax system should be more progressive and that government should coerce us to save more and take fewer risks on the job. No real libertarian, my friends say, could support such positions.

It is a position they should reconsider. As John Stuart Mill argued in *On Liberty* (1869), governmental restraint of individual behavior is legitimate only when necessary to prohibit undue harm to others. Mill was not a libertarian, but libertarians are quick to cite his harm principle as a reason for opposing regulations. In this chapter, I adopt Mill's statement of the libertarian position as my own and argue that it is consistent with a far broader range of regulation than most libertarians suppose.

Where my libertarian friends and I part company is in how we think about what constitutes harm to others. We all agree that it is legitimate for government to restrain people from stealing others' property or from committing violence against them. The difficult cases concern more indirect forms of harm.

For example, although a sprinter who consumes anabolic steroids may make no physical contact with his closest rival, he nonetheless imposes heavy costs on him. The rival can either abstain from taking steroids, thereby losing the race and forfeiting any return on his substantial investment of time and effort, or restore the competitive balance by consuming steroids himself, thereby courting serious long-term health risks. Either way, the original sprinter's action will have caused him greater harm than if he had been physically assaulted or had his bicycle stolen. Yet, many self-described libertarians insist that a sprinter should have the right to take performance-enhancing drugs if he chooses. Why should that right trump the right of others to escape the resulting harm? Why should harm not count merely because it is indirect?

My answer is that for Mill's harm principle to have any coherent meaning, indirect forms of harm must count. My conception of what constitutes harm to others will strike some libertarians as expansive. It is, however, a conception that honest libertarians will find difficult to challenge in their own terms. If they had complete liberty to join others in forming any sort of society they pleased, they would find compelling reasons for joining one that gave indirect harm equal footing with direct harm. Confusion about this point arises because indirect harm is often harder to measure than direct harm. But direct harm is sometimes hard to measure, too, and in those cases, we usually have no debate about whether it should count.

The basic claim I defend, then, is this: If one adopts any reasonable conception of what constitutes harm to others, the regulatory apparatus of the modern welfare state becomes completely consistent with—and is indeed even dictated by—Mill's statement of the libertarian position.

My second aim in this chapter is to breathe more life into the true libertarian position in public policy debates. In practice, many self-described libertarians do not even pay lip service to Mill's harm principle. For convenience, I will call them movement libertarians. Their impulse is to insist that they have a right to do whatever they please, irrespective of what harm or risk their behavior might impose on others. Speed limits? Illegitimate! Banking regulations? Illegitimate! Rules against fireworks at backyard barbeques? Illegitimate!

Movement libertarians also insist that mandatory taxation is theft, never bothering to explain how any government could possibly function in the absence of mandatory taxation. With no government, you have no army, and without an army, your country will eventually be invaded by some country that has one, whereupon you will pay mandatory taxes to its government. Through their support of such transparently absurd positions, movement libertarians have almost completely marginalized the genuine libertarian position in serious public policy discussions.

It is a voice that will be sorely missed as government's role expands in the years ahead. In many cases, people can be prevented from causing undue harm to others in multiple ways. Provided the state discharges its obligation to protect others from undue harm, its respect for personal autonomy dictates making choices that preserve the broadest possible latitude for individuals to do as they please. Yet, credible advocates for this libertarian position have almost vanished from the debate.

The choice between different methods of curtailing pollution provides a clear illustration of why such advocates are needed. Suppose, for example, that factory emissions cause health problems that could be alleviated at a reasonable cost in either of two ways: by requiring each factory to cut its emissions by half or by charging producers sufficiently high emissions fees to achieve the same aggregate result. If, as will almost always be true, some producers can reduce their emissions more cheaply than others, the far better approach will be to charge emissions fees.

For one thing, this approach lets firms decide for themselves how much pollution to eliminate. Given this freedom, those that can limit emissions cheaply will choose to cut back a lot, and others will find it cheaper to continue polluting and pay higher fees. As a result, we achieve the aggregate emissions target at lowest possible cost. With firms, of course, there is less reason than with individuals to worry that someone's feelings might be ruffled by being told what to do. But the analogy is nonetheless instructive.

Rules that restrict individual freedom impose greater psychological burdens on some people than on others. Instead of adopting flat prohibitions of harmful behavior, we could impose fines or other disincentives. The latter approach will generally achieve our aggregate harm-reduction goal at the lowest possible total cost and in the most equitable manner. Those who can reduce harm cheaply will alter their behavior, and others will continue to cause harm and be penalized accordingly.

By insisting that restrictions on individual behavior are almost never legitimate, movement libertarians have earned their reputation as cranks who can safely be ignored in policy debates. By diminishing the credibility of those who would argue most forcefully for governance with a light touch, they have imposed high costs on all of us.

SHOULD THE MERE DESIRE NOT TO BE RESTRICTED COUNT?

The movement libertarian's impulse is to say that taking steroids should be allowed because the sprinter *wants* to take steroids and would experience a violation of his personal autonomy if he were prevented from doing so. Well, yes. But most people do not like being told what to do, and simply having that preference does not grant them license to do whatever they please. You cannot drive 100 miles per hour in a school zone simply because you want to.

But this does not mean that the libertarian's objection should be ignored. Libertarians *really* do not like being told what to do. Indeed, an exaggerated preference for personal autonomy is surely the single personality trait that best predicts which people will end up calling themselves libertarians, faux or genuine. If we assume for the moment that libertarians are not free simply to abandon that preference, then restricting their behavior imposes real costs on them, even when what they are prevented from doing has little intrinsic value. They are not just posturing.

Mill's harm principle does not imply that it is legitimate to restrict individual behavior whenever failure to do so would result in harm to others. We permit harmful behavior all the time. Unkind remarks, for example, cause harm to others, yet we permit them within limits because the harm from curtailing free speech would be even greater. Similarly, a firm is permitted to cut its price and thereby harm its rivals because failure to allow this practice would cause even greater harm to consumers.

For the harm principle to make any sense at all, it must be understood to mean that the legitimacy of a restriction must be decided by weighing its cost to those being restricted against the harm others would suffer if the behavior were not restricted. An immediate practical question, then, is how we might measure the cost of being told what to do.

In economics, the time-honored approach to measuring the strength of a preference is the so-called hedonic pricing model. If we want to measure how strongly people feel about peace and quiet, for example, we can compare the price of a house in a noisy neighborhood with that of a similar one in a quiet neighborhood. If we want to know how strongly people feel about avoiding risks to life and safety, we can compare wages for risky jobs with those for otherwise similar safe ones. In like manner, by comparing the wages for similar jobs that offer different degrees of autonomy, we can get at least a rough idea of how much autonomy is worth to people.

Shortly before my first sabbatical, a personal experience suggested that, for me at least, this price is steep. At the invitation of a former colleague, I visited New York City to interview for a temporary position in an economic consulting firm in which he had become a principal. One of my duties, he explained, would be to appear as an expert witness before various regulatory commissions. My former colleague thought that I would find it exciting to test my wits under hostile cross-examination from some of the most talented attorneys in the nation. I had done this a few times on a freelance basis and had in fact enjoyed it. The kicker, though, was that my salary would be almost ten times what I was earning at Cornell.

It sounded tempting. But as my friend was taking me on a guided tour of the firm's plush Midtown headquarters, showing off its stunning views, one of the senior partners barked at him from an open office doorway. My friend had better have the XYZ report finished by noon the next day, the partner said in a threatening tone. At exactly this moment, I knew I could never work there.

I am hardly alone. A like-minded colleague, for example, once explained that being a professor was the best possible job: "I work for no one, and no one works for me." Each year, millions of people attempt to launch their own businesses, most of them with full knowledge that the overwhelming majority of new ventures fail within the first several years. Many willingly take this risk not with any expectation that they will get rich, but simply because they want to be their own boss.

There is nothing perverse or illegitimate about desiring autonomy. We know that autonomy is of great value to many people because of the enormous costs they are willing to incur to acquire or protect it. So if people experience significant costs when the government tells them that they cannot do what they want to do, this reaction merits consideration in decisions about whether to restrict them. But it does not trump others' claims for protection against undue harm.

LIBERTARIAN PATERNALISM, BROADLY UNDERSTOOD

Before going further, I want to forestall possible confusion by saying something about what my argument in this chapter is *not* about. In 2008 the economist Richard Thaler and his former colleague the law professor Cass Sunstein published *Nudge*, a book offering sensible advice about how choices can be framed in ways that improve people's decisions about their health, wealth, and happiness. The authors were quick to disavow any notion that they were trying to impose their personal vision of the good life on others. Rather, they described themselves as "libertarian paternalists," whose goal was to help people make choices that the choosers themselves view as better. I, too, am advocating a libertarian paternalism, but it is different from the one advocated by Thaler and Sunstein.

Their argument rests on the premise that people are prone to a variety of cognitive errors that lead to bad choices. They urge policy-makers to become "choice architects," people who design environments with an eye toward increasing the likelihood of good decisions. For example, school cafeteria managers should put the most healthful foods early in the line and at eye level. "Nudging" people in this way, they argue, is completely consistent with respect for individual rights.

A good illustration of the contrast between their message and mine is how we treat the issue of workplace safety. Thaler and Sunstein believe that bad job choices are rooted largely in faulty reasoning. In deciding whether to accept a riskier job at higher pay, for example, one would obviously want to take into account the degree of additional risk the job entails. For such estimation problems, people often use simple heuristics. One is the availability heuristic, which says that the more likely a type of event, the easier it is to summon examples of it from memory. Thus, according to this heuristic, one occupation is more dangerous than another if it is easier to think of examples of workers in the first occupation getting injured or killed.

The availability heuristic works well much of the time. But if relevant examples from one category happen to be particularly vivid or salient, it can be misleading. Most people, for instance, would reckon that being a roofer is more dangerous than being a driver/sales worker, when in fact the reverse is true. The judgment error occurs because deaths caused by falls from high places are salient and hence easy to remember. In many such cases, the authors argue, simple disclosure requirements may be a sufficient remedy for poorly informed job choices.

Thaler and Sunstein (2008:252) see libertarian paternalism as a potential solution to the partisan bickering that has plagued the American political system in recent decades: "We hope that the general approach might serve as a viable middle ground in our unnecessarily polarized society. The twentieth century was pervaded by a great deal of artificial talk about the possibility of a 'Third Way.' We are hopeful that libertarian paternalism offers a real Third Way—one that can break through some of the least tractable debates in contemporary democracies." But given their relatively narrow interpretation of what is permissible under libertarian paternalism, this hope seems unrealistic. The question of whether government should try to help people avoid making foolish decisions is surely not a major source of the bitter partisan discourse that the authors decry. I believe that all their proposals should be adopted right away, but even if they were, an enormous range of contested political issues would remain.

Historically, the main mission of government has been not to prevent people from making stupid decisions but to resolve collective action problems—to maintain public goods like roads, schools, and national defense; to provide a social safety net; to protect the environment; and, of special relevance here, to prevent undue harm to others. Political polarization is rooted in disputes about the proper scope of such activities and how to pay for them. Many of these disputes directly involve mandates of one form or another. Mandates will not go away. Paying taxes will continue to be mandatory, for example, and movement libertarians will continue to object. Disputes over such issues will not stop just because government starts nudging citizens to make better decisions.

But if the authors' hopes for libertarian paternalism are in this specific sense too high, there is a sense in which the concept has the potential to embrace a far broader range of issues than they appear willing to include under their rubric. It is this broader conception of libertarian paternalism that is my focus here.

On the question of workplace safety regulation, Thaler and Sunstein (2008:251) note that current occupational safety and health laws go beyond paternalism: "They impose flat bans, and they undoubtedly do hurt some people. Such laws do not permit individual workers to trade their right to (what the government considers to be) a safe work environment in return for a higher salary, even if sophisticated and knowledgeable people might like to do that." Without insisting that safety laws are completely without merit, they are clear that their own program does not embrace such further excursions "down the paternalistic path" (2008:251).

Indeed, if our only objective were to protect people from the consequences of their own bad decisions, it is hard to see how mandates could ever be justified. Because the problems addressed in *Nudge* fall into this category, their decision to denounce mandates seems a natural strategic choice. But not every bad outcome is the consequence of a bad individual decision. Errors in judgment, for example, may lead some workers to choose jobs that are too risky for their own good, but people often take excessive risks even when their judgment is beyond reproach. In these cases, mandates may be the only practical solution. And they are perfectly consistent with the broader construal of libertarian paternalism I develop here.

THE CHALLENGE POSED BY COLLECTIVE ACTION PROBLEMS

In the economist Thomas Schelling's celebrated example, hockey players who are free to choose for themselves invariably skate without helmets, yet when they are permitted to vote in a secret ballot, they unanimously support rules that require these. Because skating without a helmet confers a small competitive edge—something athletes care deeply about—players eagerly accept the additional risk. The rub, of course, is that when every player skates without a helmet, neither team gains a competitive advantage.

As Schelling's diagnosis makes clear, the problem confronting hockey players has nothing to do with imperfect information or lack of self-control or poor cognitive skills. It is a garden-variety collective action problem. Players favor helmet rules because this is the only way they are able to play under reasonably safe conditions. A simple nudge—say, a sign in the locker room reminding players that helmets reduce the risk of serious injury—just will not solve their problem. They need a mandate.

What about the libertarian's complaint that helmet rules deprive individuals of the right to choose? This objection is absurd on its face. It is akin to objecting that a military arms control agreement robs the signatories of their right to choose for themselves how much to spend on bombs. Of course, but this is the whole point of such agreements! Parties who confront a collective action problem often realize that the only way to get what they want is to constrain their own ability to do as they please.

Again, as John Stuart Mill made clear in *On Liberty*, it is permissible to constrain the individual's freedom of action to prevent undue harm to others. The hockey helmet rule appears to meet this test. By skating without a helmet, a player imposes harm on rival players by making them less likely to win the game, an outcome that really matters in their eyes. If the helmet rule itself somehow imposed even greater harm, it would not be justified. But this is a simple practical question, not a matter of deep philosophical principle. Mandates like hockey helmet rules are thus completely in harmony with the broader construal of libertarian paternalism I am advocating.

A MANDATE FOR STRICTER SAFETY RULES?

Workplace safety regulation can also be viewed as the solution to a collective action problem. Because making the workplace safer costs money, there is an inverse relationship between how safe a job is and how much it pays. Each individual worker can thus earn additional income by accepting employment that entails greater risks to health and safety. But even with complete information and high mobility in perfectly competitive labor markets, I see no reason to expect that free individual choice will result in the optimal level of workplace safety.

The problem is that in life, as in hockey, many important rewards depend on relative performance. Most parents, for example, wish to send their children to the best possible schools. By accepting a riskier job at higher pay, any parent can plausibly expect to purchase a house in a neighborhood with better schools. But a "good" school is a relative concept: a school that is better than other schools. When all parents respond to the same incentive, they succeed only in bidding up the prices of houses in the better school districts. As in the familiar stadium metaphor, all stand to get a better view, yet none see more clearly than if all had remained seated.

It does not follow that because mandates like safety regulations go beyond purely voluntary libertarian paternalism, they are undesirable. Mandates are sometimes objectionably paternalistic, yes. But on other occasions, they are merely devices that enable people to achieve outcomes that they themselves desire. Mandates in these cases are precisely analogous to interventions meant to rectify cognitive errors. It is misleading to characterize them as heavy-handed attempts by do-gooders to impose their own values on others. Mandates are just a broader form of libertarian paternalism.

A MANDATE TO SAVE MORE?

Failure to save adequately is sometimes a consequence of bad individual decisions. But savers also confront an important collective action problem. Most parents earning the median income could save enough to preserve a comfortable standard of living in retirement, but if they did so, they might have to send their children to a school whose students score in the thirtieth percentile in reading and math. By saving much less, they could buy a house in a better school district, one whose students score in the fiftieth percentile. Most parents would feel compelled to choose the second option and worry later about how to get by during retirement. But here, too, when all save less to bid for houses in better school districts, the effect is merely to bid up the prices of those houses. As before, half of all children are destined to attend bottom-half schools.

Changing the default minimum contribution to 401(k) savings plans does not solve the collective action problem confronting these families. But it is easy to see why they might favor government-sponsored retirement accounts financed by (mandatory!) additional taxes on their own income. To be sure, such a program would limit the freedom of individuals to spend those dollars as they saw fit. Yet, without the program, they might feel compelled to spend the same money on a fruitless bidding war for houses in better school districts.

THINKING MORE SYSTEMATICALLY ABOUT HARM TO OTHERS

The question of whether to restrict actions that cause harm to others requires a careful weighing of the harm caused by the actions themselves against the harm that would be caused by restricting the freedom to act. Ronald Coase won the Sveriges Riksbank Prize in Economic Sciences in

1991 largely on the strength of his contribution to our way of thinking about this delicate balancing act.

Before Coase, policy discussions of activities that cause harm to others were commonly couched in terms of perpetrators and victims. A factory that created noise, for example, was a perpetrator, and an adjacent physician whose practice suffered as a result was a victim. Coase's insight was that externalities like noise or smoke are purely reciprocal phenomena. The factory's noise harms the doctor, yes, but to invoke the doctor's injury as grounds for prohibiting the noise would harm the factory owner. The factory owner's intent is not to harm the doctor. Nor is it the doctor's intent to impede the workings of the factory. Their proximity to each other and the nature of their specific activities creates a mutual problem to be solved. Both the factory owner and the doctor, Coase argued, have a shared interest in finding the least costly solution to this problem. He concluded that if they were able to negotiate freely with each other, they would resolve it efficiently, regardless of whether the government held the factory owner liable for noise damages.

But the deeper message of Coase's paper was a different one—namely, that when negotiation is for some reason impractical, the state should assign the burden of adjusting to externalities to whichever party can accomplish it at lower cost. For example, if the doctor and the factory owner cannot negotiate, the government should hold the factory liable for noise damage if it is less costly for the factory to reduce its noise than it is for the doctor to move to a more sheltered location. But if the reverse is true, then the government should not hold the factory liable. This posture, Coase reasoned, would induce the doctor to relocate, which under the circumstances would be the efficient solution.

What does Coase's reasoning have to say about the problem of consumption choices that cause harm to others? To help frame the ideas, I begin with a simple example whose details echo many of the issues that arise in the analysis of free speech. Suppose that some in the population enjoy wearing purple shirts but others are offended by the sight of them. Let us imagine that those who like them would collectively pay up to $1,000 for the privilege of wearing them and that those who dislike them would pay up to $2,000 to avoid having to see them. If negotiation between the two groups were practical, opponents could compensate those who favor purple shirts for agreeing not to wear them. But suppose negotiation is impractical. Should the state then prohibit the wearing of purple shirts? Since the shirts generate larger costs than benefits by assumption, a prohibition might appear to be the efficient outcome.

But this reasoning alone is insufficient to justify a prohibition. If it were, the laws of free speech would prohibit most personal insults, which typically impose greater costs on the one who is insulted than bestow benefits on the insulter. In the free speech case, the right to insult others may be defended on at least two other grounds that appear relevant to the purple shirt example. First, as suggested earlier, the right to speak freely appears to have general value above and beyond the value one might assign to speaking freely on any given occasion. By the same token, the right to choose clothing according to one's whims of the moment may have general value beyond what one would be willing to pay for the right to wear a purple shirt.

A second concern is the need to anticipate the extent to which affected parties might adjust over time to the injuries in question. In a climate in which personal insults are permissible as a matter of right, for example, potential victims of insults might gradually learn to tune them out or perhaps even alter their behavior and social circumstances to avoid them. Similarly, in a climate that defends the individual's right to wear colors of her own choosing, those who are initially offended by purple shirts might eventually get used to them or might tailor their environments to limit exposure to them.

Defending any given right entails both costs and benefits. In the end, questions regarding which specific rights to defend are quintessentially practical ones. Having the right to insult others and the right to choose the color of one's clothing permits one to cause harm to others. These rights nonetheless appear defensible because the alternatives seem likely to generate greater harm than good. It is in this spirit that I frame my discussion about the extent to which we should defend the individual's right to spend her income in whatever ways she chooses, even if some forms of spending impose costs on others.

No one familiar with the relevant evidence would deny that spending decisions are heavily influenced by social context. The economist Richard Layard (1980:741) has written, "In a poor society a man proves to his wife that he loves her by giving her a rose, but in a rich society he must give a dozen roses." For the past three decades, virtually all income gains in the United States have gone to top earners. Recipients have spent most of their extra income on positional goods, things whose value depends heavily on how they compare with similar things bought by others. Like mutually offsetting weapons in a military arms race, consumption of this sort is largely wasteful. When the wealthy all build larger mansions, for example, the primary effect is to raise the bar that defines a suitable mansion for people in their circle.

Although we have little evidence that middle-income families in America resent the spending of top earners, they are nonetheless affected by it in tangible ways. Additional spending by the rich shifts the frame of reference that defines what the near rich consider necessary or desirable, so they, too, spend more. In turn, this spending shifts the frame of reference for those just below the near rich, and so on, all the way down the income ladder. Such expenditure cascades help explain why the median new house built in the United States is now about 50 percent larger than its counterpart from thirty years ago, even though the median real wage has risen little since then.

Higher spending by middle-income families is driven less by a desire to keep up with the Joneses than by the simple fact that the ability to achieve important goals often depends on relative spending. Because of the link between housing prices and neighborhood school quality, for example, the median family would have to send its children to below-average schools if it failed to match the spending of its peers on housing.

Although additional outlays for positional consumption goods—such as houses beyond a certain size—do not accomplish much, they crowd out forms of spending that would produce real improvements in the quality of life. If houses grew less rapidly, for example, we could invest in mass transit systems that would yield shorter, less stressful commutes, which would free up more time to spend with friends and family. Or we could support medical research and safety investments that would reduce premature death. The list goes on.

Wasteful positional arms races occur because people take too little account of the costs that certain types of consumption impose on others. When one job applicant spends more on an interview suit, for example, others must spend more as well or else accept lower odds of getting a callback. Yet, when all spend more, no one's odds of landing the job are any higher than before.

Is it permissible for society to attempt to limit the consumption expenditures of top earners in the interest of constraining the expenditure cascades that impose heavy costs on families farther down the income scale? For illustrative purposes, I focus again on housing expenditures, although virtually the same issues would arise for many other goods. Are the losses to top earners from having their expenditures on housing restricted likely to outweigh the gains to middle-class families from such restrictions?

If the only costs associated with expenditure cascades were psychological, middle-income families might in time find means of adjusting to the discomfort they initially experience from living in houses that appear diminished by the increased housing expenditures of others. But even if the capacity to adjust to psychological costs were limited, the burden of adjustment might still be best placed on those who experience these costs, since the alternative might be interpreted as a tacit invitation to complain.

As noted, however, expenditure cascades in the housing market also entail far more tangible costs; most notably, failure to keep up with community spending patterns means having to send one's children to schools of below-average quality. The scope for accommodation to such costs seems far more limited. For many families, the best response will be to match the housing expenditures of other families with similar incomes. To do so, they may have to save less, work longer hours, accept riskier jobs, carry more debt, and commute longer distances. All of those responses take a toll.

What about the costs to top earners of spending less on housing? In light of evidence that, beyond some point, the capacity of a house to confer utility depends predominantly on its relative size, top earners would experience little harm if all had slightly smaller houses. On the contrary, if the primary reason for buying large houses is to meet social expectations, top earners might well feel better off if all lived in smaller houses. It is a hassle, after all, to recruit and supervise the staff required to run a mansion.

Of course, people might experience more general costs from the mere fact of having their spending options restricted. Such costs would depend, of course, on the specific instruments by which the restrictions were implemented. A regulatory commission assigned to micromanage the building plans of high-income households might be a costly intrusion indeed. But expenditures can also be restrained in other, far less intrusive ways through the tax system.

REDISTRIBUTION

One of the most controversial actions of the modern welfare state is to tax the well-to-do and distribute the proceeds to people of more modest means. All contemporary governments do this, and libertarians almost always complain. If it is theft to take someone's income by force to build a road, they say, it is *really* theft to take someone's income and give it to a poor person.

But such pronouncements do not provide a reliable guide for the actual economic choices we face. These choices are always best made pragmatically—by carefully weighing the relevant costs and benefits of competing options. In a choice between two mutually exclusive programs, for example, the better choice is always the one whose benefit outweighs its cost by the larger margin, even when that option requires income transfers.

Consider, for instance, the choice between two methods for reaching a given air quality target in Los Angeles. Program A would require all cars, new and old, to meet reasonably strict emissions standards. Program B would exempt cars more than fifteen years old from these standards but would require much stricter standards for newer vehicles. Both programs would yield the same overall air quality, but because program B's stricter standards for new vehicles are extremely costly, it is more expensive overall than program A.

The cost-benefit test identifies program A as the better option. But supporters of program B argue that despite its higher cost, it is still the better choice, since imposing the burden of meeting emissions standards on the mostly poor drivers who own older vehicles would be unacceptable.

This argument makes no sense. More than 80 percent of the smog in Los Angeles now comes from exempt older vehicles. The money saved by eliminating the exemption and adopting less strict standards for newer vehicles would have been more than enough to give every owner of an older vehicle a voucher sufficient to buy a compliant late-model used car. To do this, however, it would be necessary to tax the rich and transfer money to the poor. Would movement libertarians continue to object if they realized that preventing such transfers would make everyone poorer, themselves included?

When discussing the proper weight to assign to indirect harm, I suggested earlier that it is instructive to imagine the regulations libertarians might agree to live under if they had the opportunity to persuade others to join them in forming a new society of their own design. The same thought experiment sheds light on the distributional arrangements libertarians might embrace. Even the most eloquent libertarian would be hard pressed to persuade anyone to join a state that lacked the kinds of redistributive programs that have become staples in the modern welfare state.

IS BIG-BROTHER-KNOWS-BEST PATERNALISM EVER PERMISSIBLE?

Restricting individual behavior to solve collective action problems is not really paternalism as the term is understood in everyday language, since those affected by the restrictions often endorse them enthusiastically. More traditionally, paternalism is understood to mean government prohibitions of specific behavior in order to prevent people from making unwise choices. But even restrictions of this generally more objectionable sort are sometimes permissible under John Stuart Mill's harm principle.

When one of my sons was fourteen, he took a serious spill on his bike, landing violently on his head and shoulder. Fortunately, he suffered only a broken collarbone. But the emergency room doctor who treated him told me that he probably would have been killed had he not been wearing his helmet, the right side of which was shattered when he struck the ground.

The main reason he was wearing a helmet was that New York State has a law requiring all bicyclists under the age of sixteen to wear them. Some parents object to this law, saying that it should be their responsibility, not the state's, to prescribe safety standards for their children.

But even before my son's accident, I and many other parents I know were grateful for the requirement. Many boys display their willingness to incur risks as a badge of honor, and those who wear helmets in the absence of a requirement are often derided by their peers. In an ideal world, parents would successfully condition their children to ignore such pressures. But we do not live in an ideal world. What is clear, in any event, is that if helmets were not required, substantially fewer children would wear them, notwithstanding the best efforts of their parents.

Does New York State's helmet requirement meet John Stuart Mill's test? That is, does it restrict someone's behavior in order to prevent undue harm to others? That the requirement prevents enormous harm is beyond dispute. Except for it, many more children, perhaps including my son, would be dead today. Quite apart from this potential loss is the loss suffered by parents and others who care about these children. Even without precise estimates of the magnitude of these losses, surely no one can doubt their enormity. The question, then, is whether the considerable harm prevented by the helmet requirement outweighs the harm experienced by those who are forced to wear them.

Of course, many people who are subject to the requirement would have worn a helmet anyway. Even so, many of them are quietly grateful for the requirement because they find it socially less awkward to wear one when everyone else does. For the same reason, many others who would not have worn helmets without a requirement are pleased about being required to do so. For these groups, the requirement causes no harm at all. But inevitably, a minority will be offended by the mandate, and the injury suffered by this group must be weighed against the harm prevented.

A strict application of Mill's criterion would require defensible estimates of the dollar-equivalent magnitudes of the harms on both sides of the equation. The New York State legislature passed its helmet law in the absence of such estimates, perhaps because most lawmakers thought that the obvious harm it would prevent vastly outweighed any possible harm it might cause.

Libertarians who oppose the helmet rule should be prepared to argue that the annoyance of those who are offended by it constitutes greater harm than the pain and suffering that the requirement prevents. Few libertarians, however, seem prepared to argue in these terms. Instead, they appear content merely to assert that helmet rules should not be permitted, because the state does not have the right to tell people how to conduct their lives. But unless they are willing to abandon Mill's harm principle completely, this simply will not do. If libertarians have the power to block the majority's desire to implement a helmet rule for children, they have the power to inflict enormous harm on parents and others. By what right might they claim such an entitlement?

Some libertarians will object that the example is unfair, that of course the state should have the right to enact helmet requirements for children, who, after all, often lack the necessary judgment and experience to make prudent decisions about risky behavior. It is a reasonable objection. But evidence suggests that nothing magical happens when a child morphs into an adult. Myopia, naive optimism, and vulnerability to social pressure may diminish with chronological age, but these traits are still present in ample measure in most adults. And like children, the typical adult has many people who love him, people who will suffer greatly if he is seriously injured or killed.

During a recent sabbatical in Paris, I had a conversation with a colleague who biked to the office daily through forty-five minutes of heavy traffic. Although bicycle accidents are common in Paris, this intelligent, emotionally mature woman never wore a helmet. I told her about my son's accident and urged her to consider wearing one. When she demurred, I teasingly suggested that her reluctance was rooted in her fear of looking unfashionable. She protested vigorously, and I believe, truthfully, that she had little interest in fashion. A few weeks later, however, she sheepishly admitted that she had tried on some helmets over the weekend and just could not imagine herself appearing in public with one. Indeed, I cannot recall seeing a female cyclist wearing a helmet during the year I spent in Paris.

Nor can I imagine the French passing a law requiring helmets. But libertarians who accept Mill's harm principle cannot categorically oppose such laws, even when they apply to adults. Because the social environment profoundly affects individual decisions, many individuals are simply in no position to escape the effects of what others do. Some people will be harmed whether or not we require helmets. In such cases, our shared interest is in minimizing total harm.

Over the violent objections of libertarians, many states have passed laws requiring even adult motorcyclists to wear helmets. My son who suffered the bicycle injury is an adult now. He is not a motorcyclist, but if he were, I would be grateful that New York is among the states with a helmet requirement. But too often missing from public debates about such requirements are forceful advocates for alternative strategies that would be less costly to the people who are most deeply offended by outright prohibitions.

Consider, for example, a helmet requirement that would allow exceptions for the people who most keenly desire to ride without helmets. The department of motor vehicles could sell special medallions to these people for an annual fee of, say, $300. A cyclist who felt strongly about riding with the wind in his hair could then legally do so simply by purchasing a medallion and affixing it to his license plate. People who did not feel strongly about this issue would save the $300 and wear helmets. Because the vast majority of cyclists would belong to the second group, individuals would no longer experience the social pressures that might have otherwise dissuaded them from wearing helmets.

By refusing even to consider the possible legitimacy of helmet requirements, most libertarians have essentially dropped out of the debate. They have forfeited their seemingly natural role as advocates for more flexible methods of accommodating their desire not to be regulated.

CONCLUDING REMARKS

In the frontier days, the public made relatively few demands for government to restrict individual behavior. Because people did not bump into their neighbors nearly as often, they had fewer opportunities to cause harm to one another. Society is not only much denser now but also much more highly interactive. Opportunities to cause harm to others are far more abundant. These opportunities will continue rising sharply and will generate demands for additional regulation.

Self-described libertarians would do well to reconsider their insistence that restrictions of individual freedom are permissible only to prevent direct forms of harm to others, such as theft or physical assault. The case for limiting individual action arises most forcefully in the context of collective action problems but is also compelling in any context in which failure to regulate will result in undue harm to others, direct or indirect. On close examination, the libertarian position to the contrary is utterly indefensible. This position has greatly weakened the influence of genuine libertarians, who understand that preserving individual freedom often requires curtailing what we permit ourselves to do.

18

German Eggs and Stated Preferences

Edward F. Fischer

Buying eggs may be one of life's more mundane tasks, something most of us do without much thought beyond occasionally comparing prices. But egg shopping in Germany compels one to make an explicit moral decision with every purchase, to lay bare the price one puts on certain values. Of course, economic choices are always laden with moral consequences. And as much as we may try to segregate the study of economic science from moral philosophy, the two are intimately interwoven in practice. Adam Smith and Karl Marx, to name but two, saw themselves as moral philosophers as much as economic observers. But today the dominant model of economics is more about math than philosophy, and the allure of mathematical precision can divert us from the moral ambiguities of real life. At the same time, as consumers, we are increasingly faced with explicit moral choices—to buy fair trade coffee or Folgers, to shop at the corner grocery or the Walmart Supercenter, to go local or to go global.

In this chapter, I make a simple point: although economic modeling focuses almost exclusively on "revealed" preferences (that is, observable behavior), we can learn a lot from "stated" preferences (what folks say). This idea is nothing new to ethnographers, who take seriously what people say they want, as well as what they actually do. Stated preferences give greater emphasis to long-term goals and moral projects, common goods and the common good; revealed preferences are more embedded in market logics of immediate material maximization. In the consumer realm, stated preferences are more likely to be concerned with the "moral provenance" of goods—positive and negative externalities, the impact of commodity chains on the environment, social relations, and our views of a just world.[1] Stated preferences are fundamental to understanding the aspirations and trade-offs that inform socially embedded (i.e., all) market transactions. Stated preferences may well contradict revealed preferences, but it does not automatically follow that revealed preferences are any more real or important. Indeed, we must take into account the hopes and desires of stated preferences to understand well-being.[2] I conclude by arguing that, given the desires expressed in stated preferences, regulations and norms that reduce choice may not only act to protect common goods in certain contexts but may also improve individual overall well-being.

My argument is based on a very particular ethnographic case. I look at middle-class supermarket shoppers in the Südstadt neighborhood of Hannover, Germany. In particular, I focus on the eggs they buy and the discourses around their selection. In Germany, we find a broad concern with the provenance of eggs, facilitated by mandatory labeling. Shoppers often explain their choices by valuing a nebulous environmental commons and frequently invoke a salient notion of social "solidarity." We also find an anomaly between stated and revealed preferences, one that speaks to the delicate balance of individual choice and regulatory constraints in promoting well-being along multiple dimensions.

SHOPPING IN SÜDSTADT

To the casual visitor, Hannover in many ways looks like an unexceptional German city. With a population of 520,000 (1.1 million in the metropolitan area) in 2006, it is about the same size as my home city of Nashville. Indeed, I often describe Hannover as much like Nashville in that Nashville is a pretty typical American city and Hannover can be said to be a pretty typical German city.

The Südstadt section of town was not razed during the war, and its layout and architecture reflect the 1920s and 1930s style more than that of any other part of the city. All around Südstadt are oddly winding streets lined with contiguous and continuous rows of reddish-brown brick buildings. They are charming, kempt, and Art Deco–ish in design, with an occasional whimsical element (a gargoyle or a jutting balcony). But the knowledge that they were built mostly in the 1930s also invokes a sense of stark, scary, Third

Reich minimalism, as with the quaint little cheese shop displaying a sign that proudly proclaims, "Since 1933."

Today—as in the 1930s—Südstadt is a working-class neighborhood, although it is gentrifying. I lived there in 2005–2006 and have returned every year since for a month or two of follow-up fieldwork. In our Südstadt neighborhood are two *Reformhäuser* and a small *öko* (organic) supermarket,[3] in addition to the growing selection of *bio* and öko (organic, "green," environmentally friendly) products in the regular supermarkets.

In Germany, the market for bio and öko goods has been growing at well over 15 percent per year for the past few years. In 2007, sales reached €5.45 billion; although this figure is still less than 5 percent of the total German food market, it is the largest organic market by far in Europe.

Here we should remember that although we often speak of "capitalism" (or "globalization") in the singular, a multitude of capitalisms, or varieties of capitalism, actually exist and thrive. Germany's version of compassionate capitalism—the *Soziale Marktwirtschaft* (social market economy), the Rhenish model, ordoliberalism, or the stakeholding model—differs in important ways from Anglo-American capitalism (see Streeck 2009; also Beckert 2011; Hall and Soskice 2001; Thelen 2001; Turner 1998). The German model tends to be more "coordinated" than the "liberal" Anglo-Saxon market economies; Germany has strong unions and workers' rights in corporate governance, and the capital market structure favors long-term horizons. For shoppers, this model means much more regulation: laws govern store-opening hours and the terms of sales; butchers, bakers, and even clerks in bookstores have to be trained and certified by their trade guilds; in a number of categories, such as books, items must be sold at their suggested retail price, favoring small operations.

In June and July 2008, assistants and I conducted 114 interviews on the sidewalk in front of the Edeka supermarket on Stefansplatz in Südstadt.[4] The store is located next door to the neighborhood post office and Post Bank, which draws a wide range of the area's socioeconomic groups. Half a block away is a park, usually inhabited by groups of unemployed men drinking beer or schnapps and kids playing soccer or scrambling on the monkey bars. On Fridays, the park is taken over by the weekly market, with farmers, butchers, and other vendors filling the Stefansplatz. Within the radius of a few blocks are a public school, a library, businesses, and apartment houses. In terms of income, our sample reflects the range of standard income categories for Germany, tilted slightly toward the lower end of national averages (a majority of our sample earned less than €21,600 per year).

TABLE 18.1
Factors in Buying Decisions

Quality	4.11
Price	3.67
Environmentally friendly	3.66
Origin	3.42
Social conditions of production	3.16
Quality seal	3.15
Convenience	2.64

Germans have a deserved reputation for prudence and frugality ("Frugality Is Hot" was one large retailer's successful tagline for a while), and one might expect price-conscious consumers to be frugal. But the German case offers an odd twist predicated on a valuation of quality. Respondents were also asked to rank several qualities in terms of overall importance in their buying decisions on a 1–5 scale. Table 18.1 shows the average responses.

The conventional wisdom of US marketing holds that price, quality, and convenience are the most important factors in consumer decisions (roughly in that order). In our Hannover sample, quality clearly trumps price,[5] and price just barely edges out environmental friendliness as the second most important factor. Price is clearly important to many consumers, and decisions usually rest on a delicate and subtle balance between price, quality, and other factors. Nonetheless, the preference for quality over price is remarkable. This German preference for quality has also been observed by Wolfgang Streeck (1997:40), who notes that "price competition is mitigated by socially established preferences for quality." Such a preference for quality may, in fact, be consistent with prudent frugality—as in buying small amounts of high-quality products (e.g., cured meats measured in grams) or investing for the long term (a BMW, say, to last for ten or twenty years).

Convenience was not a major factor for our Hannover sample. Indeed, we had difficulty translating *convenience* (as, for example, *Komfort* or *Bequemlichkeit*); German simply does not have a term that adequately glosses American-style "convenience." This is not to say that folks do not take into account factors we would categorize under "convenience." German shoppers do weigh expediency and efficiency in their decisions, but the lack of a neat gloss for *convenience* points to the concept's lack of saliency as a quick, uncontested justification of first resort.

Many consumers in the Hannover sample explicitly privileged quality over price by invoking a long time horizon and explicit moral projects in their explanations of preferences. Joachim, a married insurance salesman in his midforties, stated, "We have to change this idea that everything has to be cheap. We are wealthy enough that we can afford to buy more expensive foods. We need for folks to be better informed. With as little income as we spend on food, we can pay more. I rarely eat meat, for example, but when I do, I buy quality meat. *We can buy less but have better quality*" (emphasis added). This sentiment was common in our interviews, and it holds not just for grocery products. People also prefer to buy more expensive cars and keep them for a long time.

Discourses around "quality" are also used to convey feelings of national pride, which have long been frowned upon in post–World War II polite society. In our survey, a number of respondents expressed a clear quality preference for specifically German products—and these were often contrasted to "Chinese products" (which represent cheap goods produced by exploited labor and a vague fear of China as it becomes stronger and stronger and takes over more and more of the German export market). Claudia, a woman in her early thirties, explained, "We can see our country like a family, and so it is better to buy German and help the family stay strong." But when pressed, Claudia, and others, would back away from claiming any sort of inherent German superiority, cloaking an incipient nationalism in terms of specific quality attributes and environmental impacts.[6]

So it is with complex moral projects. They take on endless idiosyncratic variations and shades of meaning as people espouse values ranging from prudence to nationalism. And yet, at times they converge, as with the German consumer concern with quality. Linked to concerns about quality, 60 percent of our sample stated that it was "important" or "very important" to buy organic (and more broadly, environmentally friendly bio) products, and 61 percent said the same for the conceptually linked fair trade products.

We found among many consumers in our sample a willingness to assume the costs of negative externalities. For example, Barbara, a married woman in her forties, told us, "I pay more because the price for bio is the price that it really costs. Sustainability and ecological costs are not included in the price of regular products. I pay more and therefore can have an influence on society and on the next generation." Here we see a recognition of the external effects of consumption and a willingness to pay for them. Barbara's views were not shared by all. Thomas, a man in his forties who worked for an advertising agency, asserted dismissively that consumption is not a political position ("Konsum ist keine Politik")—that political battles should be fought in the political arena and not degraded in the marketplace. Many respondents invoked a moral argument of "solidarity" to justify ethical consumer choices. Said one young woman, "I am ready to pay more to help make the world economy more just." Significantly, a clear majority of consumers in our sample showed a tolerance for higher prices in the service of certain moral projects linked to notions of "solidarity" and a common good. Such moral projects, informed by a broad sense of stakeholding, reflect stated preferences that value a sometimes vague notion of environmental and social obligations.

MORAL PROVENANCE AND EGGS

Nowhere is the effect of moral values on German consumer choices so clear as with eggs. Since 2004 the European Union (EU) has required all eggs to carry a code: a number that denotes how the chicken was raised, two letters that record the country of origin (*DE* for Germany), and a unique identifying number for the farm and packing company. The designations for how the eggs were handled are 0 (organic and free range), 1 (free range), 2 (cage free), and 3 (battery-cage raised, also sometimes pejoratively termed "KZ eggs," or concentration camp eggs, a strong analogy indeed for Germans, who tend not to joke about the Holocaust). These designations are posted over the display shelves, putting details front and center describing the conditions of production that force a morally laden decision about how much to pay for the social values embodied in different sorts of eggs. It is a decision one has to make every time one buys eggs.

In the 2008 Hannover surveys, more than 60 percent of the supermarket shoppers we interviewed reported buying free-range (1) or organic and free-range (0) eggs. Almost 9 percent bought eggs from a farmer at a local market (also a socially conscious purchasing), and 5 percent did not eat eggs (table 18.2). Given the significant price differences, these data are surprising. They reveal an apparent willingness of German consumers to pay a big premium for moral preferences—up to €2.40 more (or almost three times as much) for organic compared with battery-cage raised. And this pattern holds true across socioeconomic groups.

One shopper, a woman in her thirties who works at a law firm, noted that although the price difference is big, even so, "€3 or €4 isn't so much money. So this may be expensive compared with other eggs, but eggs overall aren't expensive."

The egg example captures the structural/institutional design element and the cultural norms and intentionalities of individual actors. The choice here is structured: the alternatives are made explicit, and one has to choose. Further, the numeric code provides more information than had been

TABLE 18.2

Egg Preferences and Prices

Egg Type	Reported Purchasing (%)	Average Price (in euros per 10)
0 = organic, free range	26.5	3.79
1 = free range	33.6	1.99
2 = cage free	12.4	1.39
3 = battery-cage raised	13.3	1.39
by farmers in market	8.8	2.50

previously easily accessible about the eggs' provenance. And the choices we documented in our Hannover sample reflect a strong concern with what James Foster and I have termed "moral provenance," or the unseen social conditions embedded in goods—the social externalities, economic relations, and environmental impact of an item's production.

The concern with moral provenance has been growing in the United States and Europe in recent years. Moral provenance manifests itself in consumer behavior as a willingness to pay a premium for positive externalities, such as just working conditions, and to punish companies for (perceived and actual) negative externalities. The values of moral provenance stem from a number of areas, including fair trade practices and ecological concerns. The growing market segment concerned with moral provenance is often assumed to represent an affluent demographic, but it is rapidly expanding into lower socioeconomic brackets as well.

In our Hannover sample, many consumers stressed the quality and positive externalities of öko products. One man reported that öko bread "stays fresh longer and tastes better." Others related quality (and environmental friendliness) to health: "Bio products are healthier, and this is more important for children and young people. These products taste better, better quality."

Eggs produced under different conditions taste different. But for many of our respondents, this difference was not an overriding factor: they reported being more motivated by an explicitly ethical/moral stance, a concern for how chickens are treated. (A surprising number of respondents cited a particular television special on industrial chicken production.) One man in his late thirties explained, "When I buy the more expensive— bio—eggs, I feel good about myself because I am eating healthy, and this is important to me. Maybe the bio eggs taste a little better, but that's not really why I buy them."

It is impossible to disentangle the choice here between quality and moral provenance, for both are at work, and the discourses around quality converge with those around morality, the commons, and, at times, a covert nationalism.

Most consumers in our sample were able to articulate a conscious balance they sought between moral values and economic expediency, which was remarkable in its explicitness and, further, demonstrates the ways stakeholding values permeate quotidian life. Gerda, a middle-aged professional woman, remarked, "I buy free-range eggs because if the hens' lives are better, the eggs taste better. They are more expensive, but more expensive is sometimes worth it because the quality is better. It costs more, but I buy these products. The world is going downhill—not only the environment but humanity as well—so it is important to do what we can." To some extent, this consumer choice is wrapped up with self-interested pursuits and self-congratulation, as with Christian, who states, "I buy only German eggs—in order to be socially responsible, to support good living conditions for everyone, and it makes me as a consumer feel good." Again, we see the complexities and idiosyncrasies of moral projects—here a commitment to a perceived greater good and yet a recognition, as well, of the vicarious pleasure and self-regard such responsibility may bring. Immediate preferences and long-term preferences are often held in such a tension.

WORD AND DEED IN THE EGG MARKET

What we say is not always what we do. With this in mind, let us return to our survey of Hannover supermarket shoppers. Over 60 percent of our sample reported buying either organic or free-range eggs; however, in national sales data, we find that just over 30 percent of eggs sold are organic or free range. Taking our sample as broadly representative, we see that twice as many people say they buy organic or free-range eggs than actually do. So what is their preference? Their revealed preferences presumably value price over moral provenance and quality (more battery-cage raised and cage-free eggs are bought), yet their stated preferences are just the opposite (for organic and free-range eggs). Both tell us something important about consumer values (table 18.3).

We have found a clear disconnect here, a dissonance between what folks say they want and what they actually do. But we should not take their revealed preferences to be self-evident, as representing what they *really* want. They also really want what they say they want, and this truth reveals much about their ideals and values, the sorts of persons they imagine themselves to be and the sort of world they would like to live in. Such aspirational values orient our long-term goals, yet we often also succumb to short-term

TABLE 18.3
Reported and Actual Purchases

Egg Type	Reported Purchasing (%)	National Sales (%)[a]
0 = organic, free range	26.5	7.0
1 = free range	33.6	23.5
2 = cage free	12.4	40.2
3 = battery-cage raised	13.3	29.3
from farmers in market	8.8	—

[a] From the GfK-Haushaltpanel, reported on www.animal-health-online.de/lme/2009/09/10/mehr-eier-im-juli-gekauft/3788/, accessed February 15, 2010.

gratification at the expense of longer-term aspirations or feel compelled to pursue individual versus collective interests so that we do not fall behind in relative terms because of collective action problems.

Indeed, behavioral economists such as Richard Thaler (1992) have found a surprising propensity among most of us to systematically discount the future and overvalue immediate rewards. Natasha Schüll and Caitlin Zaloom (chapter 11, this volume) show how neuroeconomists map this characteristic onto short-sighted beta systems (as opposed to the more rational delta systems) of our brain. Although future discounting clearly provides immediate utility, it can also erode the welfare of our future selves. In preferring one dollar now over five dollars next month or eating and drinking too much and regretting it later, we almost unwillingly subvert long-term stated preferences, which undermines long-term goals, especially of the sort Deirdre McCloskey (2006) calls Prudence. On the other hand, Robert Frank (2004) shows that some character traits, such as trustworthiness, have clear advantages that lead individuals to forgo immediate rewards (to not pick up someone else's tip, for example) in pursuit of a larger goal (to be a trustworthy person).

Our Hannoverian shoppers want to buy premium eggs—indeed, they see themselves so much as the sort of people who buy organic eggs that they say they do even when evidence suggests that they do not. We may assume, then, that they *want* to buy the higher-priced, morally provenanced eggs but at the moment of the financial decision, where the rubber hits the road and the money changes hands, the 200+ percent premium is too much to bear.

This conundrum raises an intriguing possibility: reducing consumer choice might increase overall well-being by enforcing long-range stated preferences.

STATED PREFERENCES AND MORAL PROVENANCE

Economists distinguish between "stated preferences" (the things people say they do or would like to do) and "true" or "revealed preferences" (what they actually do, usually understood to be the choice revealed when money changes hands). And, going back to Paul Samuelson's classic *Foundations of Economic Analysis* of 1947, economists tend to privilege revealed preferences (after all, these are what can be observed and measured; see Samuelson 1938, 1948).

On the one hand, this approach is empirically rigorous because "true" preferences are revealed through documented behavior such as purchases made or votes cast. On the other hand, the laser focus on revealed preferences discounts the importance of the cultural and institutional contexts of decisions—the fact that choices are delimited by structural conditions, as in the all too common scenario we are faced with in the grocery store aisle and in the voting booth of choosing the lesser of two (or more) evils. What if stated preferences are not attended to by the market? What if competition diverts preferences toward goals with less overall utility? In such cases, there may be real value (if not cash) on the table that can be realized only through regulatory structures designed to solve collective action problems uncovered ethnographically.

By their very nature, stated preferences may take a long-term, big-picture view, less constrained by logistics, finances, and collective action problems and more cognizant of both positive and negative externalities (see Wilk 1993). It is not that revealed preferences do not reflect loftier long-term values—they must if we are to ever realize our stated preferences—but they are also much more sensitive to the hedonistic impulse and material maximization of immediate, short-term desires. Revealed preferences are more heavily influenced by what Stephen Gudeman (2008) terms "calculative reasoning," a drive toward market efficiency and short-term maximization. Stated preferences are also shaped by maximization and material aspirations, but they are more sensitive to the pull of social solidarity and mutuality (see Stout 2010). Anthropologists are especially sensitive to stated preferences, taking seriously what folks say that they want to do, which helps us understand their values and ideals, hopes and dreams of the future. These stated preferences tell us a lot not only about the way things are but also the way things could be, the aspirations that inform life projects.

Perhaps, then, revealed preferences do not capture just "true" preferences, but also myriad hedonistic impulses; in such cases, folks might well say that their stated preferences are more "true" and more fully capture who they want to be. We may then ask whether there are cases in which laws, regulations, and social norms that reduce our range of choice and individual freedom might make us better off—not just physically or financially, but in terms of a greater sense of self-defined well-being, a feeling of being the sort of people we want to be, even approaching an Aristotelian *eudaimonia*.

The nexus of stated and revealed preferences provides a productive site for anthropological analysis. Stated and revealed preferences are not dichotomous frames invoked in discreet contexts. Rather, they are coexisting modalities that variously converge and diverge, informing economic behavior and the construction of moral subjectivity. They represent two different cultural logics at work, both being meaningful and important (see Fischer 2001). Gudeman (2008:150) remarks, "Everyone is both a socially embedded or conjoint actor who is constituted by social relationships and ideas, and a disjoint chooser with aspirations, hopes, desires, and wants." In the German context, Dominic Boyer (2005) sees this tension as one between *Geist* (spirit) and *System*, between creative subjectivity and external forms. Such tensions between what is stated and what is revealed point to the often competing pulls of market rationalities of material maximization and the reflexive bonds of mutuality and solidarity.

As the German data show, the stated preferences expressed in our sample place great value on an abstracted idea of a common good, often glossed as "solidarity." Many in our sample clearly described long-term moral projects that involved protecting the environment, eradicating unfair work practices, and otherwise safeguarding common resources in the name of "solidarity." In thinking about the German concept of solidarity, we should recall Amartya Sen's (1982) analysis of what he terms "commitment." Commitment is marked by "counter-preferential choice," which is to say, making oneself worse off (materially) in support of a larger project, be this a sense of identity, religious belief, or other sorts of locally meaningful moral values. Cindy Isenhour (2010:521) describes a similar situation among "sustainable consumers" in Sweden, who use their buying power to "attempt to rein in what many middle-class Swedes see as immoral, irresponsible, and rampant materialism among the world's wealthiest citizens."

Among our sample of Hannover supermarket shoppers, we find a wide range of consumers willing to pay a significant premium for certain "green" and fair trade products. They usually explain their actions by calling on broad notions of fairness and social solidarity, environmental concerns, and civic obligations, all of which blur together into a sense of a common good that is expressed through their concern with the moral provenance of goods.[7]

STATED PREFERENCES, REGULATED CHOICES, AND HAPPINESS

Does more choice make us happier? The instinctive American response would likely be yes, but a growing body of literature suggests otherwise. In *The Paradox of Choice*, Barry Schwartz (2004) reviews a range of studies showing that too many choices actually decrease satisfaction. This effect is due in large part to "regret aversion," because choosing forecloses the unknown bounties of those paths not taken, and to informational overload, there simply being too many variables to consider when choosing a product even as simple as jam or chocolate.

German supermarkets differ from their US counterparts. The carts are smaller, like overgrown children's wagons, the aisles are narrower, and the selection is dramatically smaller. You would be lucky to find a dozen types of breakfast cereal in a Südstadt grocery, whereas the aisles of my Nashville grocer look like Andreas Gursky's photograph *99 Cent II Diptychon*. But are the Nashvillians happier with their choices?

Sheena Iyengar and Mark Lepper (2000:1003) report on three studies that show "the provision of extensive choices, while initially appealing to choice-makers, may nonetheless undermine choosers' subsequent satisfaction and motivation." Their subjects reported that having a more extensive array of choices was "simultaneously more enjoyable, more difficult, and more frustrating" and that they felt "burdened by the responsibility of distinguishing good from bad decisions" (2000:1003–1004).[8]

Starting January 1, 2010, new regulations forbade German farmers from selling conventional battery cage–raised eggs. (Stores may continue to sell such eggs imported from other EU countries until the end of 2011.) To many Americans, this government intrusion would seem unwarranted, analogous to EU regulations on banana shapes and sizes. But we have seen that more German consumers *say* they want to buy free-range and organic eggs than actually do—suggesting that the temptation of immediate monetary savings trumps ideal preferences. Perhaps, then, this case is one in which regulation could best help individuals effectively pursue their long-term stated preferences.[9]

The new German regulation prohibits certain choices in order to remove temptations to act against a perceived greater good and to presumably fulfill the stated preferences of the majority of our sample. A recent trend in behavioral economics looks at how research can influence public policy in precisely such areas. Richard Thaler and Cass Sunstein's (2008) *Nudge* advocates "choice architecture," a paternalistic libertarianism that seeks to protect the freedom of choice while channeling paths of least resistance and default option.

In Robert Frank's contribution to this volume (chapter 17), he moves beyond gentle nudges to propose a "libertarian welfare state." Following John Stuart Mill, Frank holds that behaviors can be legitimately regulated when they cause harm to others. Frank is able to square this view with the apparent contradiction of a "welfare state" by taking an expansive view of what constitutes "harm to others." He deals with some classic "externalities," such as pollution and secondhand smoke, but also takes into account collective action problems and competition driven by positional goods. (Positional goods' value derives in large part from how much they are desired and consumed by others; status symbols are the iconic example.) He concludes that a highly progressive consumption tax would not only divert resources away from positional goods and toward more productive ends but would also increase the felt utility and well-being of those same high-income households. Perhaps the invisible hand works best not flailing about and gesticulating by itself, but firmly ensconced in the grip of social norms and legal regulations.

In Südstadt, we find a range of individuals improvising a multitude of personal moral projects that converge around certain salient themes of solidarity and ecological conscientiousness, as well as material self-interest and frugality. These develop through a dialectical engagement with political structures, such as regulations concerning store opening hours, vacation time, and other conditions imposed upon daily life. They also emerge from cultural flows and personal concerns and are expressed, among other ways, through consumer choices. In our sample of the Hannoverian middle class, we found a pronounced preference for "quality" over price and an overt concern for environmental and social externalities and moral provenance. These concerns evidence stakeholding norms based on a sense of moral community and shared responsibility, a tolerance for higher prices in pursuit of a perceived greater good.

Yet, German shoppers are not a sort of *Homo communitarius*; individuals are constantly working out complex and contextually dependent algorithms of costs and benefits. Indeed, German shoppers often pride themselves on being *günstig*, which translates as *cheap* but with the morally positive connotations of *fair, favorable,* and *auspicious,* in other words, *prudent.* Such cultural dispositions are encouraged by institutional structures and the genealogies of power they reflect, and decisions are formed as part of the ongoing moral projects that are folks' lives. Moral projects converge at times around salient themes, sometimes vague ("being a 'good' person," expressing "solidarity") and sometimes with clear behavioral mandates (as with prudence). We have documented how these themes play out in consumer decisions, a form of what Dan Ariely and Michael Norton (2009) term "conceptual consumption." The valences are not always clear cut or consistent, however—the comfort of "solidarity" entails the exclusion of certain others in an imagined community, and the material virtues of "quality" can convey a sublimated nationalism.

CONCLUSIONS

Economists make a clear distinction between revealed and stated preferences while privileging the former. Anthropology—ethnography, at least—speaks most directly to stated preferences, taking seriously what people say, their hopes and dreams and aspirations, which often elide the constraints of what is possible. We create the world in which we live, and, thus, we should take seriously the imaginings of what that world might look like under different circumstances. It is from such desires that the future is forged.

Stated and revealed preferences may be understood as two distinct framings for understanding market decisions, in line with Erving Goffman's (1974) seminal work and Amos Tversky and Daniel Kahneman's (1981) application to rational choice. Yet, these are more than rhetorical frames; they are modalities of thought, what I (Fischer 2001) have elsewhere termed cultural logics. In many ways, they reflect the tension between calculative maximization and other virtues (such as solidarity), which Deirdre McCloskey (2010) describes.

Revealed preferences tend to be framed by the cost/benefit analysis of perceived utility as represented in a dollar-and-cents value. The symbolic (and sacred, McCloskey's S variables, including the solidarity of social obligations and convictions of moral values) is often undervalued in such monetary conversions. Revealed preferences are highly sensitive to contextual and structural constraints, a necessary and pragmatic concern with what is possible. They are also influenced by what behavioral economists term "hyperbolic discounting," a bias for immediate and short-term rewards expressed by discounting future values (see Schüll and Zaloom, chapter 11, this volume).

Stated preferences, on the other hand, are less bounded by the practicalities of time horizons and collective action problems. They take into consideration "what if" possibilities: what kind of person one would like to be, what sort of world one would like to live in.

We can find an analogy in the burgeoning field of happiness studies (see Easterlin 2004; Layard 2005). Researchers who study these things generally distinguish between two types of happiness. One is "hedonic" happiness, that everyday contentment (and the cheeriness the term calls to mind in common American usage). Close to the gritty practice of everyday life, such happiness is related to revealed preferences. But we also experience a broader sense of "life satisfaction," judged by the criteria of "well-being" and "the good life"—Aristotle's "meaningful life" (eudaimonia). I suggest that such overall life satisfaction is most closely aligned with long-term, stated preferences. This makes sense: we adjust our daily expectations to what is "reasonable" for us and our circumstances and adapt our mundane happiness to that norm. But when we look back (or forward) over the broad sweep of possibilities, of what was obtainable and what was not in terms of life paths, we are struck more by what could have been.[10]

In the German case, we find a strong stated preference for "quality" and "solidarity" yet revealed preferences that value material maximization (frugality) over these qualities. We might expect supermarket decisions to be especially susceptible to hyperbolic discounting: money will shortly change hands in the checkout line (most often a cash transaction in Hannover, underlining the fiduciary impact); one must decide the value of an immediate savings versus perhaps more distant preferences for quality and solidarity. Potential free-rider and collective action problems are also at play. If everyone else is supposed to be supporting a commons (such as environmental consciousness or social solidarity) and, given what most folks say, this would be a reasonable supposition, then a bit of individual backsliding appears not so significant. In this case, regulatory structures that reduce choice, such as those being implemented in Germany, could improve individual and collective well-being by coordinating and aligning revealed with stated preferences.

In any case, we should not ignore the importance of stated preferences as we seek to understand what motivates economic behavior. These tend to value broad, long-range ideals and unveil a concern for common goods that often remains hidden in the immediacy of revealed preferences. As the case of the moral provenance of German eggs suggests, we might do well to promote economic structures that help us realize our stated preferences and not just cater to the quick buck made from indulging our hedonistic, revealed preferences.

Acknowledgments

Thanks to Peter Benson, Jens Beckert, Bart Victor, Stephen Gudeman, James Carrier, Peter Mancina, Bob Frank, James Foster, Rudi Colloredo-Mansfeld, and the participants in the SAR advanced seminar "Markets and Moralities" for useful suggestions. Thanks to Tilman Sattler and Johannes Fischer for their assistance in coducting surveys and interviews. This research was funded by the Alexander von Humboldt Foundation.

Notes

1. James Foster and I are developing the concept of "moral provenance" elsewhere.

2. By "well-being," I refer to a holistic sense of quality of life, the objective and subjective component of overall life satisfaction (which is being measured with increasing accuracy, most notably, using the Alkire/Foster metrics of multidimensional poverty; see Alkire and Foster 2009; Alkire and Santos 2010; Foster 2010).

3. The Reformhaus movement began in the early twentieth century to promote natural foods; it was consolidated into a national cooperative structure in the 1930s. Today, Reformhäuser offer a range of all-natural foodstuffs, herbal supplements, and homeopathic treatments.

4. Our sampling strategy was simply to ask every sixteenth passerby to consent to an interview, with counting starting at the end of the preceding interview or rejection of request (approximately 35 percent refused). Although not designed to be a stratified random sample, based on my ethnographic understanding of the context, built up over years of fieldwork, I believe the results to be broadly representative.

5. Some previous market surveys in Germany have found that low prices are the most important factor for consumers; in one GfK (2005) report, 50 percent of the sample reported that price was more important than any other consideration.

6. It is interesting to compare such intense skepticism toward nationalism tempered by the obligations of a secular social contract in the former East with the West (see Berdahl 1999; Borneman 1992).

7. Shariff and Norenzayan (2007) report on experiments in which subjects play the dictator game (unilaterally deciding how an amount of money should be split with another player); those primed with religious or civic words tend to be much more generous in their offers. In this light, it seems likely that invoking an idea of the commons might also act to prompt generosity (on the philanthropic side) or a willingness to pay a premium for externalities that benefit a notion of "the commons" (on the market side). We find this in the discourses of "solidarity" of our German sample.

8. The *Economist* (2010) reports that, unlike Americans, German shoppers

are not put off by more choice, something they chalk up to the "sheer dreariness" of German grocery stores.

9. We might also consider the caring aspect of shopping—the love, devotion, and sacrifice that are expressed through shopping, as Miller (1998a) describes (see also McCloskey 2006 on the role of love in economic rationalities).

10. Whereas Easterlin, Layard, and others have pointed out that income above a certain level does not seem to affect hedonic happiness proportionately, new research does show that income plays a big role in overall life satisfaction (see Kahneman and Deaton 2010).

19

Misfits or Complements?

Anthropology and Economics

Stephen Gudeman

Why do anthropologists and economists have such trouble talking to each other? Economists talk to political scientists. Anthropologists talk to geographers. Both talk with sociologists and psychologists, but their talk with each other is filled with thoughts of "wrong," "ignorant," and worse. Even bridging moves, such as the new institutionalism, do not seal the gap.

Do most anthropologists not really understand economics, and most economists not grasp the project of anthropologists? In the terms of Karl Polanyi, is one looking at "embedded" and the other at "disembedded" economies—different data, different theories? Does one side come back again and again to the importance of reciprocity, and the other look at how individuals maximize their preferences? Does one group consider social relationships and their moralities, whereas the other focuses on competitive exchanges and their moralities? Sometimes the two fields appear to have different methodologies, different epistemologies, and different ontologies that make them irreconcilable. These and other ways of framing the differences, as well as some mediating positions, are put on display in stimulating ways by the authors in this volume. But what are we to make of the disjuncture? Why does it exist, why do so many try to blur its edges or deny it, and who is right?

I think that the two sides are responding to the fact that people are both connected and disconnected. We are the products of others and are in others through social interaction, and we are separate beings with our own personal volition. Economies are built on both of these human faces in varying ways. I disagree with economists and the conventional idea that economy means markets, because anthropologists have shown that it is also much more, and I disagree with anthropologists who think that markets lack morality, because they are pervaded by a morality, and not always a bad one.

I favor the idea that economies are built on the dialectic of social relationships and self-interest, which yields separation, opposition, and shifts in dominance, as well as veiling or mystification of one by the other. Anthropologists traditionally have looked at one side of material life, and economists at the other. If anthropologists have sometimes had difficulty reconciling acquisitiveness with their prized idea of reciprocity, economists have had difficulty justifying and explaining social welfare and sociality through the lens of individual choice. Both have been caught in the dialectical argument.

Many of the contributors to this volume confirm this perspective through their studies, even if they do not voice it. On one point, all are in agreement: markets are contrivances. They are socially constructed arenas with regulations about entry, expectations about interactions, and rather porous borders. Markets do not exist without a social framing on the outside and regulations on the inside. They are not "natural" occurrences. Most of the contributions also illustrate my dialectical view of material life. For example,

- Jonathan Shayne (chapter 3) argues that money—the supreme instrument and sign of markets—is founded on social trust. This trust, to expand his suggestion, grows in bubbles and scams to the extent that it can be likened to what Émile Durkheim (1995) called "collective effervescence," which forms the basis of sociality and relationships.

- Anna Tsing (chapter 4), who harbors reservations about markets, shows us the tension between price-as-value in the consumer market and local models of value in supply chains. She brings a degree of transparency to the local models in the face of the dominant value-in-exchange model or market price.

- Jonathan Friedman (chapter 6) explores the contradictions of social morality and markets to illuminate economic crises and to ask whether the terms of this critique are, themselves, embedded in the local language being critiqued.

- Deidre McCloskey (chapter 8) offers a general opposition of P (prudence) and S (sacred) moralities, which can be seen in the difference between Adam Smith's volumes of 1759 (1982) and 1776 (1976), a point to which I shall return.

- James Ferguson (chapter 9) illustrates how cash giving and mutuality may be combined rather than opposed.

- Natasha Schüll and Caitlin Zaloom (chapter 11) in their discussion of neuroeconomics explore the contrast of *Homo economicus* as a short-term and long-term calculator. I wonder how the relational or connected person would appear in the neuroeconomic models?

- Ted Fischer and Avery Dickins de Girón's (chapter 12) comparison of the Ultimatum Game as played in two Mexican towns illustrates the dialectic between self-interest and mutuality.

- João Biehl (chapter 7) shows how people struggle to improve the welfare of AIDS survivors within the context of, and by combining care with, market relations and neoliberal policies.

- The several contributions on business ethics, corporate advertising, best practices, and linked topics (by Bart Victor and Matthew Grimes [chapter 13], Stuart Kirsch [chapter 15], and Peter Benson [chapter 16]) deal precisely with the problematics of bringing together economy's two faces, sometimes with ease and sometimes by way of mystifications.

- Robert Frank (chapter 17) expands a market fundamentalist or libertarian position to include the impact and importance of social relationships; he also illustrates the dialectic of economy's two sides.

- Ted Fischer's (chapter 18) study of preferences for "green" eggs in Germany precisely brings out the tension between calculative reason, which is bolstered by markets, and social sharing, which evinces mutuality and community.

In these and other ways, this volume illustrates the two aspects of material life that together compose economy. The tension between them exemplified by the unending conflict between the values of efficiency and equity is played out in real practices around the world. One or the other value is integral to the principal perspectives of economics and anthropology, and one or the other is employed in its different analyses and explanations. Even if we cannot bring the two disciplines together, can we gain a better understanding of their relation by exploring this divide? Is it a difference in theories or within economy itself?

WELFARE?

Known as the first, fundamental, or welfare theorem, Pareto efficiency is a central concept in economics, at least for beginning students. In layman's terms, which are the ones I use, Pareto efficiency is achieved when one person cannot be made better off through trade without worsening the condition of another. If someone can realize a better position without making someone else worse off, further exchanges take place, and a more efficient distribution of the available resources, or a Pareto improvement, will be achieved. Pareto efficiency, realized through market exchange, is an important, if not the central, benchmark by which economic systems can be judged. For example, central planning does not achieve efficiency. But for Pareto efficiency to be attained, certain market conditions must hold: all goods must be tradable, markets must be perfectly competitive, and transaction costs must be negligible. When these and other stipulations are met and Pareto efficiency is obtained, the market reaches a settling point or equilibrium.[1]

This theorem about welfare has held great appeal to economists for its elegance and justification of free markets and because it promises the best result given the available resources. Rendering no opinion about the fairness of the distributional outcome, the theorem gives a technical result, which is termed "welfare." Any other technique of distribution must be judged against this gold standard of efficiency, which is said to be value free. Or so it seems, because I observe that market efficiency is also a value or an ideal for many economists and others outside the field. The mystification of a value as being value free forecloses discussion about the consequences of and justifications for efficiency.

Let us consider the consequences of a market that is Pareto efficient. The first theorem says nothing about the distributional equity of market exchange. If some people have more capital or resources to bring to the bar of exchange, they will end up with more; those who have few resources cannot expect more, only a rearrangement of what they possess. Perfect markets help produce growth through efficiency, and they reproduce the wealth positions that separate people and that help to reproduce family, class, ethnic, gender, race, and other differences. The positions, distinctions, and identities of persons are not exchanged or necessarily changed in the process. We have everyday justifications for the results of efficiency, such as "A rising tide lifts all boats," "Sink or swim," and "Wealth trickles down," but these are watery justifications for exalting efficiency. Despite the name of the first theorem, welfare is produced in the context of persisting wealth divisions, which are only integrated more efficiently.

Our economists now insist on joining the discussion because they provide a subtle answer to the equity question through the second welfare theorem. It states (roughly) that after efficient market exchanges take place, the overall outcome can be redistributed among participants to change their endowments; then, with new competitive exchanges, the market can again be Pareto efficient with a different (and desired) distributional outcome, depending on how the redistribution is enacted. Economists observe that such "lump sum" (all-at-once) distributions are difficult to enact and that they may distort the economy by changing the prices of productive factors. We might add that if this practice were put in place, then welfare as some of us may conceive of it—as equity, equality, and other values—would occur only through operationalizing the second theorem and that the first theorem is not really about welfare.

But now we reach a gap between the theorems. In the first Pareto theorem, people are assumed to be individuals or disconnected persons whose preferences are independent of everyone else's. They are isolates who trade out of self-interest. The story of the first theorem shows that this self-interest leads to a beneficial result for all in terms of the highest return, given everyone's self-interests. The first theorem neither presumes nor produces sociability.

Use of the second theorem contradicts the assumptions of the first. In form, it is like the first, but its application presumes that participants have redistributed the goods or shifted their initial resources, presumably because they care about the welfare of those with whom they trade. Otherwise, why redistribute the gains from the first round of exchanges? In the first situation, people are disconnected, competitive individuals; then they redistribute their returns as connected persons-within-community in order to act as disconnected individuals in another round of trade. The shift from use of the first theorem to the second assumes that people transform themselves from one identity to another and then back to the first. Individuals start as self-interested transactors or rational choosers in the market; after exchanging, they agree to redistribute their wealth outside the market; then, with a different array of resources, they try again to maximize what they have through market trade. People continually shift from the disconnected to the connected to the disconnected way of life. Economists offer no explanation for this shifting personhood because they assume that only one type of person exists—the separate individual. Anthropologists often hold the opposite position: they assume that we are persons-within-community, who sometimes trade in competitive markets in order to sustain a community. In my view, whichever way it is read, this dialectic makes up the tension in an economy, although one side or the other is often effaced in academic discussions.

For some economists, the two welfare or Pareto theorems, with their justification of free markets, reach back to Adam Smith's famous declaration about the "invisible hand" through which we are led to promote the good of all even while seeking only our personal gain: "By pursuing his own interest he frequently promotes that of the society more effectually than when he really intends to promote it. I have never known much good done by those who affected to trade for the public good" (Smith 1976:477–478). The Pareto theorems elaborate Smith's claim in *The Wealth of Nations* that self-interest leads to the common benefit whereas intended good, as in the shift and redistribution between them, does not. How are we to justify and explain practices of sharing in face of Smith's declaration about the invisible hand and its frequent evocation by economists?

SHARING

For most people, markets are spaces for the anonymous and competitive exchange of goods and services. Self-interest, expressed as rational choice, is the propelling motive, and profit in currency is the goal. In this model, sharing takes place outside markets and outside the economy. By contrast, I suggest that the domain of mutuality in an economy is built around sharing characterized by three transactions: allotment, for the ways of distributing an immovable or permanent holding; apportionment, for the flows or returns from material endeavors; and reciprocity, for extending identity and connection to others through goods and services. We build and sustain connections through material goods, and we reciprocate to blur our differences and to have relationships. These transactions make up a part of economy.

With this brief, I return to the contrast of the two disciplines. Sharing as varied modes of allocation and as reciprocity constitutes anthropology's "fundamental finding," as opposed to the "fundamental theorems" of economics. The two basic positions are opposed. For example, economists do not often speak about reciprocity, but when they do, they mean a one-off, tit-for-tat, self-interested trade; for them, a market exchange is a reciprocal act. The anthropologists say, however, that a market exchange does not produce or sustain society, nor does it produce reciprocity or caring; instead, it sustains the differences that separate people. Anthropologists do not concur that sharing and reciprocity can be reduced to self-interest.

But how do anthropologists explain sharing? With tongue in cheek and a glance at our helpful economists, I might begin with Adam Smith. Modern economics may start with *The Wealth of Nations* (Smith 1976), published in 1776, but I shall begin with Smith's (1982) volume that was published seventeen years earlier, *The Theory of Moral Sentiments*. The Pareto theorems may or may not represent a working out of Smith's notion in *The Wealth of Nations* that an "invisible hand" leads our self-interest to promote the public good, but he first invoked the image of an invisible hand in *The*

Theory of Moral Sentiments, where he used it differently. The divergence neatly reflects the tension between market and mutuality or self-interest and sharing. I draw on Adam Smith neither to suggest that anthropology should begin with the founder of economics nor to argue that the invisible hand is all that is needed or even accepted in economics. I offer a line of thought that might have led to a more encompassing view, which economics might have incorporated, and to indicate its relation to Rousseau, who is an ancestor of Durkheim (1960).[2]

Let us begin with Rousseau, who preceded Smith. In the *Discourse on the Origin and Foundation Of Inequality Among Men*, which was published in 1755, Rousseau (1994:45) speaks of pity as the "one natural virtue." This sentiment moderates self-love or self-interest. Pity, Rousseau (1994:47) offered, "becomes stronger as the animal looking on more closely identifies itself with the animal suffering," and it is most powerful in the state of nature.

Smith was well acquainted with Rousseau's *Discourse* and apparently could describe it without recourse to the text.[3] For Smith, as for Rousseau, identification with and compassion for others became a central theme. His initial sentence in *The Theory of Moral Sentiments* is arresting in light of his later book: "How selfish soever man may be supposed, there are evidently some principles in his nature, which interest him in the fortune of others, and render their happiness necessary to him, though he derives nothing from it except the pleasure of seeing it. Of this kind is pity or compassion... this sentiment, like all the other original passions of human nature, is by no means confined to the virtuous or the humane" (Smith 1982:9).

Smith (1982:9) continues, "As we have no immediate experience of what other men feel, we can form no idea of the manner in which they are affected, but by conceiving what we ourselves should feel in the like situation.... By the imagination, we place ourselves in his situation." Smith (1982:10) uses the word *sympathy* for this "fellow-feeling" that humans have. Today we label it "empathy." To follow Smith's line of thought, we have the ability to project ourselves into the place of others, even though we do not know how they feel and experience the world. Empathy rests on the symbolic capacity by which we imagine ourselves in others' positions. We change places with them in thought. Smith (1982:10) states, "Whatever is the passion which arises from any object in the person principally concerned, an analogous emotion springs up, at the thought of his situation, in the breast of every attentive spectator."

Smith (1982:112) advances the argument by suggesting that just as we empathize with others, we imagine that they empathize with us, which leads us to examine our actions in light of how others may perceive us.[4] Through the empathic capacity, we see ourselves as others would see us. The argument brings in imagination, projection, the symbolic capacity, and reflexivity, or the ability to reflect on our feelings and thoughts through our ability to understand others. These ideas are central to the anthropological project. So two disciplines, two books, one author. But this is not all.

Later in the volume, Smith invokes the invisible hand, which seems to be his only other use of the famous image. But here it refers to the social redistribution of the product and not—as in *The Wealth of Nations*—to the market allocation of resources. Observing that self-interest, rapacity, and insatiable desires propel the industry of man, he argues that the rich also share their returns with the poor: "They are led by an invisible hand to make nearly the same distribution of the necessaries of life…had the earth been divided into equal portions among all its inhabitants, and thus without intending it…advance the interest of the society" (Smith 1982:184–185).

In *The Theory of Moral Sentiments*, Smith recognizes self-interest but says that the wealthy share their good fortune with others. In market allocation and then in redistribution of the rewards, the invisible hand benefits society without conscious intent on the part of participants. The actions are opposed, but the result is the same. Through self-interest and sympathy, the invisible hand leads to market allocation and to communal sharing. The sympathetic invisible hand, which is fundamental to anthropology, fills the gap between the two fundamental theorems of economics, which are based on the self-interested invisible hand.[5]

I present Smith's narrative about moral sentiments in condensed form.[6] Even so, this is an account of sharing as it is linked to communication, reflexivity, and what Giambattista Vico might have termed *fantasia*, or understanding the position of others. Sharing is a product of the human capability to place oneself in the position of others. But if we have this capacity, realized or fulfilled in varying degrees, then we understand that others have this same capability. And if we can realize that others understand us, then we also understand that others understand that we empathize. This recursive process provides a foundation for sharing and reciprocity. Through the capability and impulse of empathy—this "one natural virtue"—we share and reciprocate. We share rules and expectations; we form communities; and we pass on again and again goods, services, and ideas, for many reasons—for pleasure, to know others, to help, for prestige, for care—all of which help frame and are part of an economy built on both self-interest and empathy.

The two realms are in tension, however, for the market way of acting, which is generated by competitive transactions, expands market borders and cascades over them into communal spaces. Spreading through many domains of life, from neighborly relations to friendship to kinship, and converting them to its behavioral design, calculative reason not only debases its needed companion but often mystifies it as a product of private interest because it cannot incorporate caring, concern for the welfare of others, and reciprocity.

Yet, we do offer care to individuals and communities. Through care, we provide what is necessary for someone's health, well-being, maintenance, or protection. In times of emergency, we offer food, medicine, loans and gifts of money, housing, and counseling to others. We offer care to children, the aged, partners, friends, acquaintances, communities, villages, nation-states, and strangers, as well as the unfortunate, impoverished, and diseased. These relationships can be up close, as in the family, or far distant, as in packages sent to remote lands. Feeling empathy or concern, we want to help meet others' needs that are not fulfilled through markets.

Even if sharing lies outside market practices, it does not emerge after them, because sharing is necessary to establish markets and equip the participants. Markets take place in arenas set up by sociality and sustained by communal agreements. These agreements are not contracts because their formation would require a larger framework of commitments, and so on, infinitely. Market agreements are not reducible to the players' volitions (although often the players try to make them so). Mutuality is constitutive of markets, as our contributors agree.

THE DOUBLE CHALLENGE

Orthodox economists cannot explain the existence of sharing, mutuality, and reciprocity without reducing them to the premise of individual, optimizing choice. They may justify giving low-interest loans to other countries in order to fill an investment gap, and some economists allow that "safety nets" should be erected for those who temporarily fall from a market's competitive arena (Stiglitz 2002). But this sharing covers a market's short-term failures, and any broader justification for it falls outside this perspective. Anthropologists have shown the pervasiveness of sharing and have developed concepts to explain it, but we need to expand both sides, especially in the context of globalization, rapid capital flows between economies that disrupt ordinary lives, porous borders of national economies, and regional trading agreements.

The Environment

Drawing on such devices as cap and trade (as Frank describes in chapter 17 of this volume) to control carbon emissions or calculating the costs of negative externalities to assign costs of damage by one party to another only reinstates the centrality of calculative reason, whose extent must be subjected to further calculated reasons. Environmental degradation is not new, but it has reached new levels with the onset of global warming and disasters of enormous dimensions. In 1967 the *Torrey Canyon* supertanker produced the first major oil spill, off the coast of Great Britain, and the world was shocked; it was succeeded by the larger *Exxon Valdez* spill off the coast of Alaska in 1989, which was followed by the Prudhoe Bay, Alaska, spill in 2006. These disasters were dwarfed by the explosion of British Petroleum's oil rig in the Gulf of Mexico, which caused the death of eleven persons and massive oil spillage into the Gulf. Pollution and irreparable damage to humans, wildlife, land, and oceans have been the results of these disasters, which seem to grow in magnitude. Damage claims against parties judged responsible and the requirment of increased insurance coverage in the future are not remedies, and the use of auctions and trading of pollution credits is only one part of the solution to environmental degradation. We need to consider again that markets are set up by shared norms and moralities and that society must also assign their limits.

Finance and Business

The period between 1990 and 2009 witnessed a rise in the unequal distribution of wealth in the United States, partly fueled by tax changes but also because the margins on takings were expanding. In addition to the Bernie Madoff scam that Shayne (chapter 3) and Friedman (chapter 6) look at, this period saw an increase in backdating stock options, of accounting irregularities, of expanding corporate perks (in the face of increased corporate pollution), and of executive remuneration, loudly claimed to be deserved. These trends became even more pronounced with the expansion of the abstract tools of exchange that emerged from the asset allocation and derivatives revolutions. Can we establish a better case for the way sharing both builds (via innovation and copying) and must constrain financial takings? Victor and Grimes (chapter 13) suggest ways of instilling a culture of responsibility in business executives, but Kirsch (chapter 15) and Benson (chapter 16) show the limits of relying on corporate responsibility. The long-term solution will require rethinking the entire system and not just tinkering with its parts.

Humans

In tandem with the expansion of calculative reason in the service of commercial and financial returns, the regard for human welfare in the broadest sense has stagnated, whether in the form of promoting safety in consumer products and conditions of production, setting up welfare nets, providing gainful jobs, or sharing an economy's wealth.

The commoditization of the material world with its abstraction into the financial world has grown, but the significance of human relationships in the economy has shrunk. Do we need to rethink the "fundamentals" of economy—not its possible form as in capitalism versus socialism but its presuppositions? What would it mean to think in terms of the disconnected and connected person who treats others as anonymous competitors through markets and also relates to them through sharing as it is locally defined? Both take part in moralities: one stretches into global markets; the other brings these connections to immediate contexts. Each adds elements of freedom and constraint—the freedom to choose, to optimize, to be unencumbered by the rigidities of communities, and the freedom to set limits on the freedoms of others as they pursue individual ends. I would expand Frank's version of libertarianism, already expanded from a focus on John Stuart Mill, to include the contrasting visions of freedom offered by Isaiah Berlin and by Amartya Sen (see Gudeman 2009).

Markets need communities of people in order to persist and to have capacitated persons who make and change markets. But market participants pay little heed to this necessity, especially when the prevalent ideology denigrates support for public education, infrastructure, health plans, the unemployed, and the aged. Today more than ever, market participants are receiving a free good, partly donated from the past. But what do they owe in return? The response cannot be calculated as a market payment because this construction would convert the service to a market resource that can be priced within the market, which would obviate what it does. I am not advocating a return to distribution by central planning or to calculating exactly what markets owe for the education, health care, or retraining that its participants receive, although the numbers are useful.

We need to see the connection between economy's two domains as a relationship. Anthropologists have terms for this connection: sharing and reciprocity. This take-and-give-and-take is not a constraint on markets, but an enhancing of both market and mutual freedoms. Today, sharing is found in up-close relations and among strangers, but the supply is short for lack of market concern and resistance, as well as support in popular ideology. Anthropologists and economists need to elaborate their theories of sharing, show how sharing and reciprocity are built in diverse economies, link them imaginatively in new ways, use them to show how national economies are connected in this age of globalization and inequities, and tie our small-scale observations to macro perspectives. If socialism is a failed ideal and markets are failing us, can we develop a different morality of economy for the future? The chapters in this volume suggest this possibility in a variety of ways, and we would do well to cultivate the ground tilled here.

Notes

1. I try in this chapter to use in an accessible way the technical language, about which I do not claim expertise. The literature on this subject is enormous. See Hurwicz 1973 for a sophisticated discussion of the complexities and Blaug 2007 for an interesting discussion.

2. This strand of thought could have influenced Lévi-Strauss by way of Durkheim instead of his dialectical use of binary oppositions drawn from structural linguistics.

3. According to Raphael and Macfie (1982:10), "In his 'Letter to the Editors of the *Edinburgh Review*'…Smith could describe, from his own reading…Rousseau's *Discourse on Inequality*."

4. Here he introduces the idea of the "impartial spectator," which is rather like the "understanding anthropologist" who also distances himself from the morality of others.

5. Smith (1982:83) does say that everyone "naturally prefers himself to all mankind" but others "do not enter into that self-love by which he prefers himself " and "indulge it so far as to allow him to be more anxious about, and to pursue with more earnest assiduity, his own happiness than that of any other person." We might say that the disjoint individual is socially constituted or that markets are framed through mutuality.

6. For a different and interesting treatment of the invisible hand image, see Lubasz 1992.

References

Abbott, Andrew

1983   Professional Ethics. American Journal of Sociology 88(5):855–885.

Ackerly, Brooke

2008   Universal Human Rights in a World of Difference. Cambridge: Cambridge University Press.

Adam, William M.

2001   Green Development: Environment and Sustainability in the Third World. New York: Routledge.

Adams, Vincanne

In press Evidence-Based Global Public Health: Subjects, Profits, Erasures. *In* When People Come First: Critical Studies in Global Health. João Biehl and Adriana Petryna, eds. Princeton, NJ: Princeton University Press.

Adams, Vincanne, T. Novotny, and H. Leslie

2008   Global Health Diplomacy. Medical Anthropology 12(4):315–323.

Ainslie, George

2001   Breakdown of the Will. Cambridge: Cambridge University Press.

Akerlof, George A.

2005   Explorations in Pragmatic Economics. Oxford: Oxford University Press.

2007   The Missing Motivation in Macroeconomics. American Economic Review 97(1):5–36.

Akerlof, George A., and Rachel E. Kranton

2000   Economics and Identity. Quarterly Journal of Economics 115(3):715–753.

2004   Identity and the Economics of Organizations. Journal of Economic Perspectives 19(1):9–32.

2005   Identity and the Economics of Organizations. Journal of Economic Perspectives 19(1):9–32.

Alkire, Sabina, and James Foster

2009   Counting and Multidimensional Poverty Measurement. OPHI Working Paper, 32. Oxford: Oxford Poverty and Human Development Initiative.

Alkire, Sabina, and Emma Maria Santos

2010   Acute Multidimensional Poverty: A New Index for Developing Countries. OPHI Working Paper, 38. Oxford: Oxford Poverty and Human Development Initiative.

Amin, Samir

1997   Capitalism in the Age of Globalization: The Management of Contemporary Society. Atlantic Highlands, NJ: Zed Books.

REFERENCES

Anand, Sudhir, and Amartya K. Sen
1994   Human Development Index: Methodology and Measurement. Oxford: Oxford University Press for UNDP.

Anderson, Perry
2011   Lula's Brazil. London Review of Books 33(7):3–12.

Appadurai, Arjun
1996   Modernity at Large: Cultural Dimensions of Globalization. Minneapolis: University of Minnesota Press.

Appiah, Kwame A.
2008   Experiments in Ethics. Cambridge, MA: Harvard University Press.

Ariely, Dan
2008   Predictably Irrational: The Hidden Forces That Shape Our Decisions. New York: HarperCollins.

Ariely, Dan, and Michael Norton
2009   Conceptual Consumption. Annual Review of Psychology 60:475–499.

Aristotle
1934[ca. 330 BCE] Nicomachean Ethics. H. Rackham, trans. Cambridge, MA: Harvard University Press.

Armendariz de Aghion, Beatriz, and Jonathan Morduch
2000   Microfinance beyond Group Lending. Economics of Transition 8:401–420.

Arrighi, Giovanni
1994   The Long Twentieth Century: Money, Power, and the Origins of Our Times. New York: Verso.

Arrow, Kenneth
1974   The Limits of Organization. New York: Norton.

Banerjee, Abhijit V.
2005   "New Development Economics" and the Challenge to Theory. Economic and Political Weekly, October 1, 4340–4344.
2007   Making Aid Work. Cambridge, MA: MIT Press.

Bank, Leslie, and Gary Minkley
2005   Going Nowhere Slowly? Land, Livelihoods and Rural Development in the Eastern Cape. Social Dynamics 31(1):1–38.

Banks, Glenn, and Chris Ballard, eds.
1997   The Ok Tedi Settlement: Issues, Outcomes and Implications. Pacific Policy Paper, 27. Canberra: National Centre for Development Studies and Resource Management in Asia-Pacific, Australian National University.

Barchiesi, Franco
2011   Precarious Liberation: Workers, the State, and Contested Social Citizenship in Postapartheid South Africa. Albany: State University of New York Press.

Barnoya, Joaquin, and Stanton A. Glantz
2006   Cardiovascular Effects of Secondhand Smoke Help Explain the Benefits of

Smoke-Free Legislation on Heart Disease Burden. Journal of Cardiovascular Nursing 21(6):457–462.

Baumol, William J.
2002   The Free-Market Innovation Machine: Analyzing the Growth Miracle of Capitalism. Princeton, NJ: Princeton University Press.

BBC (British Broadcasting Corporation)
2006   Zimbabwe Jail over Bread Prices. BBC News, December 1. http://news.bbc .co.uk/go/pr/fr/-/2/hi/africa/6199516.stm.

BBOP (Business and Biodiversity Offsets Programme)
2009   Compensatory Conservation Case Studies. Washington, DC: BBOP. http:// content.undp.org/go/cms-service/stream/asset/?asset_id=2469112.

Beaulieu, Anne
2001   Voxels in the Brain: Neuroscience, Informatics and Changing Notions of Objectivity. Social Studies of Science 31(5):635–680.
2002   Images Are Not the (Only) Truth: Brain Mapping, Visual Knowledge, and Iconoclasm. Science, Technology, & Human Values 27(1):53–86.

Beck, Ulrich
1992   Risk Society: Towards a New Modernity. New York: Sage.

Becker, Gary S.
1996   Accounting for Tastes. Cambridge, MA: Harvard University Press.

Becker, Gary S., and Guity Nashat Becker
1996   The Economics of Life. New York: McGraw Hill.

Becker, Uwe
2009   Open Varieties of Capitalism: Continuity, Change and Performances. New York: Palgrave Macmillan.

Beckert, Jens
2002   Beyond the Market: The Social Foundations of Economic Efficiency. Princeton, NJ: Princeton University Press.
2011   The Transcending Power of Goods: Imaginary Value in the Economy. *In* The Worth of Goods: Valuation and Pricing in the Economy. Jens Beckert and Patrik Aspers, eds. Pp. 106–128. Oxford: Oxford University Press.

Bellah, Robert
2003   Imagining Japan: The Japanese Tradition and Its Modern Interpretation. Berkeley and Los Angeles: University of California Press.

Benedict, Ruth
1989[1946] The Chrysanthemum and the Sword: Patterns of Japanese Culture. Boston: Houghton Mifflin.

Benson, Peter
2008   Good Clean Tobacco: Philip Morris, Biocapitalism, and the Social Course of Stigma in North Carolina. American Ethnologist 35(3):357–379.

REFERENCES

2010   Safe Cigarettes. Dialectical Anthropology 34(1):49–56.

2012   Tobacco Capitalism: Growers, Migrant Workers, and the Changing Face of
         Global Industry. Princeton, NJ: Princeton University Press.

Benson, Peter, and Stuart Kirsch

2010a   Capitalism and the Politics of Resignation. Current Anthropology
         51(4):459–486.

2010b   Corporate Oxymorons. Dialectical Anthropology 34(1):45–48.

Berdahl, Daphne

1999   Where the World Ended: Re-unification and Identity in the German
         Borderland. Berkeley: University of California Press.

Berlant, Lauren

2011   Cruel Optimism. Durham, NC: Duke University Press.

Berns, G. S., D. Laibson, and G. Loewenstein

2007   Intertemporal Choice—Toward an Integrative Framework. Trends in
         Cognitive Sciences 11(11):482–488.

BHP Billiton

2009   Our Approach to Sustainability. http://www.bhpbilliton.com/bb/Sustainable
         Development/OurApproachToSustainability.jsp.

Biehl, João

2005   Vita: Life in a Zone of Social Abandonment. Berkeley: University of
         California Press.

2007   Will to Live: AIDS Therapies and the Politics of Survival. Princeton, NJ:
         Princeton University Press.

2008   Drugs for All: The Future of Global AIDS Treatment. Medical Anthropology
         27(2):1–7.

Biehl, João, Byron Good, and Arthur Kleinman

2007   Subjectivity. Berkeley: University of California Press.

Biehl, João, and Peter Locke

2010   Deleuze and the Anthropology of Becoming. Current Anthropology
         51(3):317–351.

Biehl, João, and Ramah McKay

2012   Ethnography as Political Critique. Anthropological Quarterly
         85(4):1211–1230.

Biehl, João, and Amy Moran-Thomas

2009   Symptom: Subjectivities, Social Ills, Technologies. Annual Review of
         Anthropology 38:267–288.

Biehl, João, and Adriana Petryna, eds.

In press When People Come First: Critical Studies in Global Health. Princeton, NJ:
         Princeton University Press.

Biehl, João, Adriana Petryna, Alex Gertner, Joseph J. Amon, and Paulo D. Picon

2009   Judicialisation and the Right to Health in Brazil. Lancet 373:2182–2184.

Blakeslee, Sandra
2003   Brain Experts Now Follow the Money. New York Times, June 17. http://www
.hnl.bcm.tmc.edu/cache/Brain%20Experts%20Now%20Follow%20the%20
Money.htm, accessed January 11, 2011.

Blaug, Mark
2007   The Fundamental Theorems of Modern Welfare Economics, Historically
Contemplated. History of Political Economy 39(2):185–207.

Blowfield, Michael, and Jedrzej G. Frynas
2005   Setting New Agendas: Critical Perspectives on Corporate Social
Responsibility in the Developing World. International Affairs 81(3):499–513.

Blumenstyk, Goldie
2007   Mining Company Involved in Environmental Disaster Now Advises
Sustainability Institute at University of Michigan. Chronicle of Higher
Education 54(15):A22.

Boisot, Max, and John Child
1996   From Fiefs to Clans and Network Capitalism: Explaining China's Emerging
Economic Order. Administrative Science Quarterly 41(4):600–628.

Borneman, John
1992   Belonging in the Two Berlins: Kin, State, Nation. Cambridge: Cambridge
University Press.

Bougheas, Spiros, Indraneel Dasgupta, and Oliver Morrissey
2005   Tough Love or Unconditional Charity? CREDIT Research Paper.
Nottingham: Centre for Research in Economic Development and
International Trade, School of Economics, University of Nottingham.

Bourdieu, Pierre
1977   Outline of a Theory of Practice. Cambridge, MA: Harvard University Press.
1980   The Production of Belief: Contribution to an Economy of Symbolic Goods.
Media, Culture and Society 2:261–293.

Boyer, Dominic
2005   Spirit and System: Media, Intellectuals, and the Dialectic in Modern German
Culture. Chicago: University of Chicago Press.

Boyle, Mary-Ellen, and Janet Boguslaw
2007   Business, Poverty and Corporate Citizenship: Naming the Issues and
Framing Solutions. Journal of Corporate Citizenship 26:101–120.

Brandt, Allan
1987   No Magic Bullet: A Social History of Venereal Disease in the United States
since 1880. New York: Oxford University Press.
1990   The Cigarette, Risk, and American Culture. Daedalus 119(4):155–176.
2007   The Cigarette Century: The Rise, Fall, and Deadly Persistence of the Product
That Defined America. New York: Basic Books.

REFERENCES

Brau, James, and Gary Woller

2005   Microfinance: A Comprehensive Review of the Existing Literature and an Outline for Future Financial Research. Journal of Entrepreneurial Finance and Business Ventures 9(1):1–26.

Braudel, Fernand

1977   Afterthoughts on Material Civilization and Capitalism. Baltimore, MD: Johns Hopkins University Press.

1979   Civilisation matérielle, économie et capitalisme: XVe–XVIIIe siècle. Paris: A. Colin.

1984   The Perspective of the World. New York: Harper & Row.

Brodeur, Paul

1985   Outrageous Misconduct: The Asbestos Industry on Trial. New York: Pantheon.

Brundtland, Gro Harlem, ed.

1987   Our Common Future: The World Commission on Environment and Development. http://conspect.nl/pdf/Our_Common_Future-Brundtland_Report_1987.pdf.

Butler, Bishop Joseph

1736[1725] Fifteen Sermons. In The Analogy of Religion and Fifteen Sermons. Pp. 335–528. London: The Religious Tract Society.

Calvó-Armegnol, A., and Matthew O. Jackson

2004   The Effects of Social Networks on Employment and Inequality. American Economic Review 94(3):426–454.

Camerer, Colin F.

2003   Behavioral Game Theory: Experiments in Strategic Interaction. Princeton, NJ: Princeton University Press.

Camerer, Colin F., and Ernst Fehr

2004   Measuring Social Norms and Preferences Using Experimental Games: A Guide for Social Scientists. In Foundations of Human Sociality: Economic Experiments and Ethnographic Evidence from Fifteen Small-Scale Societies. Joseph Henrich, Robert Boyd, Samuel Bowles, Colin Camerer, Ernst Fehr, and Hebert Gintis, eds. Pp. 55–95. Oxford: Oxford University Press.

Camerer C., G. Loewenstein, and D. Prelec

2003   Major Issues & Questions About FDA Legislation. September 12. http://www.tobaccofreekids.org/research/factsheets/pdf/0189.pdf.

2005   Neuroeconomics: How Neuroscience Can Inform Economics. Journal of Economic Literature 43(1):9–64.

Campaign for Tobacco-Free Kids

2003   Major Issues & Questions About FDA Legislation. September 12. http://www.tobaccofreekids.org/research/factsheets/pdf/0189.pdf.

Carlyle, Thomas
1840   Chartism. London: James Fraser.

Carrier, James G.
1998   Abstraction in Western Economic Practice. *In* Virtualism: A New Political Economy. James G. Carrier and Daniel Miller, eds. Pp. 25–48. Oxford: Berg.

Carrier, James G., ed.
1997   The Meanings of the Market: The Free Market in Western Culture. Oxford: Berg.

Carrier, James G., and Daniel Miller, eds.
1998   Virtualism: A New Political Economy. Oxford: Berg.

Carter, John R., and Michael D. Irons
1991   Are Economists Different, and If So, Why? The Journal of Economic Perspectives 5(2):171–177.

Case, Anne, Anu Garrib, Alicia Menendea, and Analia Olgiati
2008   Paying the Piper: The High Cost of Funerals in South Africa. NBER Working Paper No. 14456. Washington, DC: National Bureau of Economic Research.

Caskey, John P., and Brian J. Zikmund
1990   Pawnshops: The Consumer's Lender of Last Resort. Economic Review—Federal Reserve Bank of Kansas City, March/April, 5–18.

Cassidy, John
2006   Mind Games: What Neuroeconomics Tells Us about Money and the Brain. New Yorker, September 18. http://www.newyorker.com/archive/2006/09/18/060918fa_fact.

Castley, Robert
1997   Korea's Economic Miracle: The Crucial Role of Japan. New York: St. Martin's Press.

Chapin, Mac
2004   A Challenge to Conservationists. Worldwatch 17(6):17–31.

Chibnik, Michael
2005   Experimental Economics in Anthropology: A Critical Assessment. American Ethnologist 32(2):198–209.

Cicero, Marcus Tullius
1938[44 BCE]   De amicitia [Concerning Friendship]. W. A. Falconer, trans. Loeb edition. Cambridge, MA: Harvard University Press.

Cohen, G. A.
2009   Why Not Socialism? Princeton, NJ: Princeton University Press.

Cohen, J., and K. Blum
2002   Reward and Decision. Neuron 36(2):193–198.

Cohn, Simon
2004   Increasing Resolution, Intensifying Ambiguity: An Ethnographic Account of Seeing Life in Brain Scans. Economy and Society 33(1):52–76.

REFERENCES

Cole, Jennifer

2010   Sex and Salvation: Imagining the Future in Madagascar. Chicago: University of Chicago Press.

Collier, Stephen J., and Aihwa Ong

2005   Global Assemblages, Anthropological Problems. *In* Global Assemblages: Technology, Politics, and Ethics as Anthropological Problems. Aihwa Ong and Stephen J. Collier, eds. Pp. 3–21. Malden, MA: Blackwell.

Comaroff, Jean

2007   Beyond Bare Life: AIDS, (Bio)Politics, and the Neoliberal Order. Public Culture 19(1):197–219.

Comaroff, Jean, and John Comaroff

1991   Of Revelation and Revolution, vol. 1: Christianity, Colonialism, and Consciousness in South Africa. Chicago: University of Chicago Press.

2000   Millennial Capitalism: First Thoughts on a Second Coming. Public Culture 12(2):291–343.

Coombe, Rosemary J.

1998   The Cultural Life of Intellectual Properties: Authorship, Appropriation and the Law. Durham, NC: Duke University Press.

Correa, Carlos M.

2000   Intellectual Property Rights, the WTO and Developing Countries. London: Zed Books.

Courtemanche, Charles, and Art Carden

2011   Supersizing Supercenters? The Impact of Walmart Supercenters on Body Mass Index and Obesity. Journal of Urban Economics 69(2):165–181.

Cowen, Tyler

2007   Discover Your Inner Economist: Use Incentives to Fall in Love, Survive Your Next Meeting, and Motivate Your Dentist. New York: Dutton Adult.

Crook, Tony

2004   Transactions in Perpetual Motion. *In* Transactions and Creations: Property Debates and the Stimulus of Melanesia. Eric Hirsch and Marilyn Strathern, eds. Pp. 110–131. Oxford: Berghahn.

Cueto, Marcos

2007   Cold War, Deadly Fevers: Malaria Eradication in Mexico, 1955–1975. Washington, DC: Woodrow Wilson Center.

Daly, Herman E.

1996   Beyond Growth: The Economics of Sustainable Development. Boston: Beacon.

Damasio, Antonio

1994   Descartes' Error: Emotion, Reason and the Human Brain. New York: Grosset / Putnam.

Danielson, Luke

2006   Architecture for Change: An Account of the Mining Minerals and

Sustainable Development Project. Berlin: Global Public Policy Institute. http://info.worldbank.org/etools/library/view_p.asp?lprogram=107& objectid=238483, accessed March 15, 2008.

Danielson, Luke, ed.

2002   Breaking New Ground: Mining, Minerals and Sustainable Development. International Institute for Environment and Development. London: Earthscan. http://www.iied.org/mmsd/finalreport/index.html.

Das, Veena

2006   Life and Words. Berkeley: University of California Press.

Davis, Devra

2002   When Smoke Ran like Water: Tales of Environmental Deception and the Battle against Pollution. New York: Basic Books.

Deaton, Angus

2010   Instruments, Randomization, and Learning about Development. Journal of Economic Literature 48:424–455.

Deegan, Denise

2001   Managing Activism: A Guide to Dealing with Activists and Pressure Groups. Institute of Public Relations, PR in Practice Series. London: Kogan Page.

Deleuze, Gilles

2006   Desire and Pleasure. *In* Two Regimes of Madness: Texts and Interviews, 1975–1995. Pp. 122–134. New York: Semiotext(e).

Dlamani, Jacob

2009   Native Nostalgia. Cape Town: Jacana.

Donaldson, Thomas, and Thomas W. Dunfee

1999   Ties That Bind: A Social Contracts Approach to Business Ethics. Cambridge, MA: Harvard Business School Press.

Donaldson, Thomas, and Lee E. Preston

1995   The Stakeholder Theory of the Corporation: Concepts, Evidence, and Implications. Academy of Management Review 20:65–91.

Dreze, Jean, and Amartya Sen

1991   Hunger and Public Action. New York: Oxford University Press.

Duflo, Ether, Rachel Glennerster, and Michael Kremer

2008   Using Randomization in Development Economics Research: A Toolkit. *In* Handbook of Development Economics, vol. 4. T. Paul Schultz and John Strauss, eds. Pp. 3895–3962. Amsterdam: Elsevier.

Duménil, Gérard, and Dominique Lévy

2004   Capital Resurgent: Roots of the Neoliberal Revolution. Cambridge, MA: Harvard University Press.

2010   The Crisis of Neoliberalism. Cambridge, MA: Harvard University Press.

Dumit, J.

2003   Picturing Personhood: Brain Scans and Biomedical Identity. Princeton, NJ: Princeton University Press.

REFERENCES

Dunn, Elizabeth
2004   Privatizing Poland: Baby Food, Big Business, and the Remaking of Labor. Ithaca, NY: Cornell University Press.

Dunning, John H.
2003   Making Globalization Good: The Moral Challenges of Global Capitalism. Oxford: Oxford University Press.

Durkheim, Émile
1960   Montesquieu and Rousseau. Ann Arbor: University of Michigan Press.
1995[1912]   The Elementary Forms of Religious Life. Karen E. Fields, trans. New York: The Free Press.

du Toit, Andries
2007   Poverty Measurement Blues: Some Reflections on the Space for Understanding "Chronic" and "Structural" Poverty in South Africa. Paper presented at the "Workshop on Concepts and Methods for Analysing Poverty Dynamics and Chronic Poverty," Manchester, October 23–25, 2006. Revised draft, January 2007.

du Toit, Andries, and David Neves
2007   In Search of South Africa's "Second Economy": Chronic Poverty, Economic Marginalisation and Adverse Incorporation in Mt Frere and Khayelitsha. Working Paper, 1. Bellville, South Africa: Programme for Land and Agrarian Studies (PLAAS), University of the Western Cape.
2009a   Informal Social Protection in Post-apartheid Migrant Networks. Working Paper, 2. Bellville, South Africa: Programme for Land and Agrarian Studies (PLAAS), University of the Western Cape.
2009b   Trading on a Grant: Integrating Formal and Informal Social Protection in Post-apartheid Migrant Networks. Working Paper, 3. Bellville, South Africa: Programme for Land and Agrarian Studies (PLAAS), University of the Western Cape.

Dworkin, Ronald
1980   Is Wealth a Value? Journal of Legal Issues 9(2):191–226.

Easterlin, Richard A.
2004   The Economics of Happiness. Daedalus 133(2):26–33.

Easterly, William
2006   The White Man's Burden: Why the West's Efforts to Aid the Rest Have Done So Much Ill and So Little Good. New York: Penguin.

Eckel, Catherine, and Philip J. Grossman
1996   Altruisim in Anonymous Dictator Games. Games and Economic Behavior 16:181–191.

Economist
1999   Mea Copper, Mea Culpa. Australia's Broken Hill Proprietary May Pull Out of New Guinea. August 21, 58.
2010   The Tyranny of Choice: You Choose. December 16, 124.

Ekholm, Kasja, and Jonathan Friedman

1980   Towards a Global Anthropology. *In* History and Underdevelopment. L. Blussé, H. L. Wesseling, and G. D. Winius, eds. Pp. 61–76. Leyden: Center for the History of European Expansion, Leyden University.

Eliade, Mircea

1959[1957]   The Sacred and the Profane: The Nature of Religion. W. R. Trask, trans. New York: Harcourt, Brace & World.

Elster, Jon

1984   Ulysses and the Sirens. New York: Cambridge University Press.

1989   The Cement of Society: A Study of Social Order. Cambridge: Cambridge University Press.

Emerson, Ralph Waldo

1982[1850]   Napoleon; Or, the Man of the World. *In* Selected Essays. L. Ziff, ed. Pp. 337–359. New York: Viking Penguin.

Endacott, R. W. J.

2004   Consumers and CRM: A National and Global Perspective. Journal of Consumer Marketing 21(23):183–189.

Ensminger, Jean

2002   Experimental Economics: A Powerful New Tool for Theory Testing in Anthropology. *In* Theory in Economic Anthropology. Jean Ensminger, ed. Pp. 59–78. Walnut Creek, CA: AltaMira.

2004   Market Integration and Fairness: Evidence from Ultimatum, Dictator, and Public Goods Experiments in East Africa. *In* Foundations of Human Sociality: Economic Experiments and Ethnographic Evidence from Fifteen Small-Scale Societies. Joseph Henrick, Robert Boyd, Samuel Bowles, Colin Camerer, Ernst Fehr, and Herbert Gintis, eds. Pp. 356–381. Oxford: Oxford University Press.

Epstein, Helen

2007   The Invisible Cure: Africa, the West, and the Fight against AIDS. New York: Farrar, Straus and Giroux.

Escobar, Arturo

1995   Encountering Development: The Making and Unmaking of the Third World. Princeton, NJ: Princeton University Press.

Fairchild, Amy, and James Colgrove

2004   Out of the Ashes: The Life, Death, and Rebirth of the "Safer" Cigarette in the United States. American Journal of Public Health 94(2):192–204.

Fama, Eugene

1970   Efficient Capital Markets: A Review of Theory and Empirical Work. Journal of Finance 25:383–417.

Farmer, Paul

2001   Infections and Inequalities: The Modern Plagues. Berkeley: University of California Press.

REFERENCES

2004   Pathologies of Power: Health, Human Rights, and the New War on the Poor. Berkeley: University of California Press.

2008   Challenging Orthodoxies: The Road Ahead for Health and Human Rights. Health and Human Rights 10(1):5–19.

2010   Partner to the Poor: A Paul Farmer Reader. Haun Saussy, ed. Berkeley: University of California Press.

Fassin, Didier

2007   When Bodies Remember: Experiences and Politics of AIDS in South Africa. Berkeley: University of California Press.

2008   Beyond Good and Evil? Anthropological Theory 8(4):333–344.

2011   Humanitarian Reason: A Moral History of the Present. Berkeley: University of California Press.

Ferguson, James

1985   The Bovine Mystique: Power, Property and Livestock in Rural Lesotho. Man, n.s., 20(4):647–674.

1990   The Anti-Politics Machine: "Development," Depoliticization, and Bureaucratic Power in Lesotho. Cambridge: Cambridge University Press.

1999   Expectations of Modernity: Myths and Meanings of Urban Life on the Zambian Copperbelt. Berkeley: University of California Press.

2006   Global Shadows: Africa in the Neoliberal World Order. Durham, NC: Duke University Press.

2010   The Uses of Neoliberalism. Antipode 41(1):166–184.

N.d.   Give a Man a Fish: Reflections on the New Politics of Distribution. Unpublished manuscript, Stanford University.

Fidler, David

2007   Architecture amidst Anarchy: Global Health's Quest for Governance. Global Health Governance, 1–17. http://diplomacy.shu.edu/academics/global-health/journal/PDF/Fidler-article.pdf, accessed February 15, 2011.

2008   Global Health Jurisprudence: A Time of Reckoning. Georgetown Law Journal 96(2):393–412.

Fischer, Edward F.

1999   Cultural Logic and Maya Identity: Rethinking Constructivism and Essentialism. Current Anthropology 40(4):473–499.

2001   Cultural Logics and Global Economies: Maya Identity in Thought and Practice. Austin: University of Texas Press.

Fischer, Edward F., and Peter Benson

2006   Broccoli and Desire: Global Connections and Maya Struggles in Postwar Guatemala. Stanford, CA: Stanford University Press.

Fischer, Edward F., and McKenna R. Brown, eds.

1996   Maya Cultural Activism in Guatemala. Austin: University of Texas Press.

Fischer, Edward F., and Carol Hendrickson
2002   Tecpán Guatemala: A Modern Maya Town in Local and Global Contexts. Boulder, CO: Westview.

Fodor, Jerry
1998   The Trouble with Psychological Darwinism. London Review of Books 20(2):11–13.

Fogel, Robert W.
2000   The Fourth Great Awakening and the Future of Egalitarianism. Chicago: University of Chicago Press.

Forsythe, R., J. L. Horowitz, N. E. Savin, and M. Sefton
1994   Fairness in Simple Bargaining Experiments. Games and Economic Behavior 6:347–369.

Foster, James
2010   Freedom, Opportunity, and Wellbeing. OPHI Working Paper, 35. Oxford: Oxford Poverty and Human Development Initiative.

Foucault, Michel
1980   The History of Sexuality, vol. 1. New York: Vintage Books.
2007   Security, Territory, Population: Lectures at the Collège de France, 1977–1978. New York: Palgrave Macmillan.
2008   The Birth of Biopolitics: Lectures at the Collège de France, 1978–1979. New York: Palgrave Macmillan.

Fourcade, Marion, and Kieran Healy
2007   Moral Views of Market Society. Annual Review of Sociology 33:285–311.

Fox, Richard G., ed.
1991   Recapturing Anthropology. Santa Fe, NM: School of American Research Press.

Frank, Robert H.
1988   Passions within Reason: The Strategic Role of the Emotions. New York: W. W. Norton.
2004   What Price the Moral High Ground? Ethical Dilemmas in Competitive Environments. Princeton, NJ: Princeton University Press.

Frank, Robert H., Thomas Gilovich, and Dennis T. Regan
1993   Do Economists Make Bad Citizens? Journal of Economic Perspectives 10(1):187–192.

Frankfurt, Harry G.
1971   Freedom of the Will and the Concept of a Person. Journal of Philosophy 68(1):5–20.
2004   The Reasons of Love. Princeton, NJ: Princeton University Press.

Frassanito Network
2005   Precarious, Precarization, Precariat? http://precariousunderstanding. blogsome.com/2007/01/05/precarious-precarization-precariat/, accessed August 10, 2011.

REFERENCES

Freedman, Lynn

2005   Achieving the MDGs: Health Systems as Core Social Institutions. Development 48(1):19–24.

Freyre, Gilberto

1987   Masters and Slaves. Berkeley: University of California Press.

Friedman, Jonathan

1992   General Historical and Culturally Specific Properties of Global Systems. Review (Fernand Braudel Center) 15(3):335–372.

1994   Cultural Identity and Global Process. Thousand Oaks, CA: Sage.

2000   Globalization Class and Culture in Global Systems. Special issue, "Fetschrift for Immanuel Wallerstein," Journal of World-Systems Research 6(3):636–656.

2004   Champagne Liberals and the New Dangerous Classes: Reconfigurations of Class, Identity and Cultural Production in the Contemporary Global System. *In* Globalization: Critical Issues. Allen Chun, ed. Pp. 49–82. Critical Interventions, 2. New York: Berg.

Friedman, Lissy S.

2007   Philip Morris's Website and Television Commercials Use New Language to Mislead the Public into Believing It Has Changed Its Stance on Smoking and Disease. Tobacco Control 16(6):e9.

Fullbrook, Edward, ed.

2004   A Guide to What's Wrong with Economics. London: Anthem.

Galbraith, John Kenneth

1954   The Great Crash, 1929. Boston: Houghton Mifflin.

1998[1958]   The Affluent Society. New York: Mariner Books.

Geertz, Clifford

2000   The World in Pieces: Culture and Politics at the End of the Century. *In* Available Light: Anthropological Reflections on Philosophical Topics. Pp. 218–263. Princeton, NJ: Princeton University Press.

Geschiere, Peter

2009   The Perils of Belonging: Autochthony, Citizenship, and Exclusion in Africa and Europe. Chicago: University of Chicago Press.

GfK

2005   Price Is More Important Than Quality. http://www.gfk.de.

Gibson-Graham, J. K.

2006   The End of Capitalism (As We Knew It): A Feminist Critique of Political Economy. Minneapolis: University of Minnesota Press.

Giddens, Anthony

1984   The Constitution of Society: Outline of the Theory of Structuration. Cambridge: Polity.

Givel, Michael

2007   FDA Legislation. Tobacco Control 16:217–218.

Glimcher, P.

2008   From Value to Choice. Paper presented at the conference "Neuroeconomics: Decision Making and the Brain," New York University, New York, January 11–13.

Goddard, Trevor

2005   Corporate Citizenship and Community Relations: Contributing to the Challenges of Aid Discourse. Business and Society Review 110:269–296.

Godelier, Maurice

1999   The Enigma of the Gift. Cambridge: Polity.

Goffman, Erving

1974   Frame Analysis: An Essay on the Organization of Experience. New York: Harper & Row.

Goldman, Alan H.

1980   The Moral Foundations of Professional Ethics. Lanham, MD: Rowman & Littlefield.

Graeber, David

2004   Fragments of an Anarchist Anthropology. Chicago: Prickly Paradigm.

Granovetter, Mark

1973   The Strength of Weak Ties. American Journal of Sociology 78(6):1360.

1983   The Strength of Weak Ties: A Network Theory Revisited. Sociological Theory 1:201–233.

Gray, John

1996   Isaiah Berlin. Princeton, NJ: Princeton University Press.

Greenblatt, Stephen J.

2004   Will in the World: How Shakespeare Became Shakespeare. New York: W. W. Norton.

Gudeman, Stephen

2001   The Anthropology of Economy: Community, Market, and Culture. Oxford: Blackwell.

2008   Economy's Tension: The Dialectics of Community and Market. Oxford and New York: Berghahn Books.

2009   Economy's Tension. New York: Berghahn.

Gupta, Akhil, and James Ferguson

1992   Beyond Culture. Cultural Anthropology 7(1):6–23.

Güth, Wener, Rolf Schmittberger, and Bernd Schwarze

1982   An Experimental Analysis of Ultimatum Bargaining. Journal of Economic Behavior and Organization 3(4):367–388.

REFERENCES

Haarmann, Claudia, Dirk Haarmann, Herbert Jauch, Hilma Shindondola-Mote, Nicoli Nattrass, Ingrid van Niekirk, and Michael Sampson
2009   Making the Difference! The BIG in Namibia. Basic Income Grant Pilot Project Assessment Report, April. Windhoek, Namibia: BIG (Basic Income Grant) Coalition.

Hacking, Ian
2000   The Social Construction of What? Cambridge, MA: Harvard University Press.

Hahn, Robert, and Marica Inhorn
2008   Anthropology and Public Health: Bridging Differences in Culture and Society. New York: Oxford University Press.

Hall, Peter A., and David Soskice, eds.
2001   Varieties of Capitalism: The Institutional Foundations of Comparative Advantage. Oxford: Oxford University Press.

Hamann, Ralph
2006   Can Business Make Decisive Contributions to Development? Towards a Research Agenda on Corporate Citizenship and Beyond. Development Southern Africa 23:175–195.

Hamilton, Sarah, and Edward F. Fischer
2003   Non-traditional Agricultural Exports in Highland Guatemala: Understandings of Risks and Perceptions of Change. Latin American Research Review 38(3):82–110.

Hammett, Dashell
1984[1929]   The Maltese Falcon. New York: Vintage.

Hance, B. J., Caron Chess, and Peter M. Sandman
1990   Industry Risk Communication Manual: Improving Dialogue with Communities. Boca Raton, FL: Lewis.

Hanlon, Joseph, Armando Barrientos, and David Hulme
2010   Just Give Money to the Poor: The Development Revolution from the Global South. Sterling, VA: Kumarian.

Hardt, Michael
2009   The Politics of the Common. Z-Net document. http://www.zcommunications .org/politics-of-the-common-by-michael-hardt.

Harford, Tim
2007   The Undercover Economist. New York: Random House.

Harper, Sarah, and Jeremy Seekings
2010   Claims on and Obligations to Kin in Cape Town, South Africa. CSSR Working Paper, 272. Cape Town: Center for Social Science Research, University of Cape Town.

Harrington, Anne
1992   So Human a Brain: Knowledge and Values in the Neurosciences. Basel: Birkhauser.

Hart, Keith

2001   Money in an Unequal World: Keith Hart and His Memory Bank. New York: Texere.

2005   Notes toward an Anthropology of Money. Kritikos 2(June). http://intertheory.org/hart.htm, accessed August 16, 2011.

2007   Marcel Mauss in Pursuit of the Whole: A Review Essay. Comparative Studies in Society and History 49(2):1–13.

Harvey, David

1989   From Managerialism to Entrepreneurialism: The Transformation in Urban Governance in Late Capitalism. Geografiska Annaler. Series B, Human Geography 71(1):3–17.

2005   A Brief History of Neoliberalism. Oxford: Oxford University Press.

Hasnas, John

1998   The Normative Theories of Business Ethics: A Guide for the Perplexed. Business Ethics Quarterly 8:19–42.

Hayek, Friedrich von

1944   The Road to Serfdom. Chicago: University of Chicago Press.

Heilbroner, Robert

1999[1953]   The Worldly Philosophers: The Lives, Times, and Ideas of the Great Economic Thinkers. 7th edition. New York: Simon and Schuster.

Henrich, Joseph, Robert Boyd, Samuel Bowles, Colin Camerer, Ernst Fehr, Herbert Gintis, and Richard McElreath

2001   In Search of *Homo economicus*: Behavioral Experiments in 15 Small-Scale Societies. AEA Papers and Proceedings 91(2):73–78.

2004   Overview and Synthesis. *In* Foundations of Human Sociality: Economic Experiments and Ethnographic Evidence from Fifteen Small-Scale Societies. Joseph Henrick, Robert Boyd, Samuel Bowles, Colin Camerer, Ernst Fehr, and Herbert Gintis, eds. Pp. 8–54. Oxford: Oxford University Press.

Henrich, Joseph, and Natalie Smith

2004   Comparative Experimental Evidence from Machiguenga, Mapuche, and American Populations. *In* Foundations of Human Sociality: Economic Experiments and Ethnographic Evidence from Fifteen Small-Scale Societies. Joseph Henrich, Robert Boyd, Samuel Bowles, Colin Camerer, Ernst Fehr, and Herbert Gintis, eds. Pp. 125–167. Oxford: Oxford University Press.

Herzfeld, Michael

2005   Political Optics and the Occlusion of Intimate Knowledge. American Anthropologist 107(3):369–376.

Hirschman, Albert O.

1977   The Passions and the Interests: Political Arguments for Capitalism before Its Triumph. Princeton, NJ: Princeton University Press.

REFERENCES

Ho, Karen
2009   Liquidated: An Ethnography of Wall Street. Durham, NC: Duke University Press.

Hoffman, Elizabeth, Kevin A. McCabe, K. Sachat, and Vernon L. Smith
1994   Preferences, Property Rights, and Anonymity in Bargaining Games. Games and Economic Behavior 7:346–380.

Hoffman, Elizabeth, and Matthew Spitzer
1985   Entitlements, Rights and Fairness: An Experimental Examination of Subjects' Concepts of Distributive Justice. Journal of Legal Studies 14(2):259–298.

Holanda, Sergio Buarque de
1956   Raízes do Brazil. Rio de Janeiro: J. Olympio.

Holland, D., and J. Lave, eds.
2001   History in Person. Santa Fe, NM: School of American Research Press.

Hsu, Spenser S.
2001   Davis's Bill on Tobacco Is Criticized; Philip Morris Stands to Benefit, Foes Say. Washington Post, June 22.

Hulme, David, and Andrew Shepherd
2003   Conceptualizing Chronic Poverty. World Development 31:403–423.

Hume, David
1751   An Enquiry Concerning the Principles of Morals. London: A. Millar.

Hunter, Mark
2010   Love in the Time of AIDS: Inequality, Gender, and Rights in South Africa. Bloomington: Indiana University Press.

Hurwicz, Leonid
1973   The Design of Mechanisms for Resource Allocation. American Economic Review 63(2):1–30.

INE (Instituto Nacional de Estadística)
2002   Censos nacionales de población y habitación. Guatemala City: INE.

Institute of Medicine
2001   Clearing the Smoke: The Science Base for Tobacco Harm Reduction. Washington, DC: Institute of Medicine.

Isenhour, Cindy
2010   Building Sustainable Societies: A Swedish Case Study on the Limits of Reflexive Modernization. American Ethnologist 37(3):511–525.

IUCN (International Union for Conservation of Nature)
1980   World Conservation Strategy: Living Resource Conservation for Sustainable Development. Gland, Switzerland: IUCN, UNEP, and WWF.

Iyengar, Sheena S., and Mark R. Lepper
2000   When Choice Is Demotivating: Can One Desire Too Much of a Good Thing? Journal of Personality and Social Psychology 79(6):995–1006.

Jackall, Robert
1988   Moral Mazes: The World of Corporate Managers. Oxford: Oxford University Press.

Jacques, Peter J., Riley E. Dunlap, and Mark Freeman
2008   The Organisation of Denial: Conservative Think Tanks and Environmental Skepticism. Environmental Politics 17(3):349–385.

Johnson, Paul
2002   Napoleon. New York: Viking.

Jones, G. T.
1933   Increasing Returns. Cambridge: Cambridge University Press.

Kable, Joseph, and Paul Glimcher
2007   The Neural Correlates of Subjective Value during Intertemporal Choice. Nature Neuroscience 10(12):1625–1633.

Kagel, John H., and Alvin E. Roth
1995   The Handbook of Experimental Economics. Princeton, NJ: Princeton University Press.

Kahn, Hilary
2001   Respecting Relationships and Día de Guadalupe. Journal of Latin American Anthropology 6(1):2–29.

Kahneman, Daniel
2011   Thinking, Fast and Slow. New York: Farrar, Straus and Giroux.

Kahneman, Daniel, and Angus Deaton
2010   High Income Improves Evaluation of Life but Not Emotional Well-Being. Proceedings of the National Academy of Sciences. http://www.pnas.org/cgi /doi/10.1073/pnas.1011492107.

Kahneman, Daniel, and Richard H. Thaler
1991   Economic Analysis and the Psychology of Utility: Applications to Compensation Policy. American Economic Review 81(2):341–346.

Kahneman, Daniel, and Amos Tversky
1979   Prospect Theory: An Analysis of Decision under Risk. Econometrica 47(2):263–292.

Karnani, Aneel
2007a   Doing Well by Doing Good—Case Study: "Fair & Lovely" Whitening Cream. Strategic Management Journal 28:1351–1357.
2007b   The Mirage of Marketing to the Bottom of the Pyramid: How the Private Sector Can Help Alleviate Poverty. California Management Review 49(4):90–111.

Kim, Jim Yong, and Michael E. Porter
N.d.   Redefining Global Health Care Delivery. Unpublished manuscript, Harvard Business School.

REFERENCES

King, Arden

1974   Coban and the Verapaz: History and Culture Process in Northern Guatemala. New Orleans, LA: Tulane University Middle American Research Institute.

Kirsch, Stuart

1997   Regional Dynamics and Conservation in Papua New Guinea: The Lakekamu River Basin Project. Contemporary Pacific 9(1):97–121.

2006   Reverse Anthropology: Indigenous Analysis of Social and Environmental Relations in New Guinea. Stanford, CA: Stanford University Press.

2007   Indigenous Movements and the Risks of Counterglobalization: Tracking the Campaign against Papua New Guinea's Ok Tedi Mine. American Ethnologist 34(2):303–321.

2008   Social Relations and the Green Critique of Capitalism in Melanesia. American Anthropologist 110(3):288–298.

2010   Sustainable Mining. Dialectical Anthropology 34(1):87–93.

Kleinman, Arthur

2006   What Really Matters: Living a Moral Life amidst Uncertainty and Danger. Oxford: Oxford University Press.

Knight, Frank

1997[1935]   Economic Theory and Nationalism. *In* The Ethics of Competition. Pp. 268–351. New Brunswick, NJ: Transaction.

Kondo, Dorinne K.

1990   Crafting Selves: Power, Gender and Discourses of Identity in a Japanese Workplace. Chicago: University of Chicago Press.

Kremer, Michael, and Edward Miguel

2007   The Illusion of Sustainability. Quarterly Journal of Economics 122(3):1007–1065.

Kristof, Nicholas D.

2007   Attack of the Worms. New York Times, July 2.

Krugman, Paul

2000   Thinking about the Liquidity Trap. Journal of the Japanese and International Economies 14:221–237.

2008   Macro Policy in a Liquidity Trap (Wonkish). The Conscience of a Liberal blog, November 15. http://www.nytimes.com.

Laibson, David I.

1997   Golden Eggs and Hyperbolic Discounting. Quarterly Journal of Economics 112(2):443–477.

Lakoff, A.

2009   Memory of the Future: Object Sorting and the Neural Science of Decision. Paper presented at the workshop "Neurocultures," Max Planck Institute for the History of Science, Berlin, February 20–22.

Lamont, Michèle

2000   The Dignity of Working Men: Morality and the Boundaries of Race, Class, and Immigration. Cambridge, MA: Harvard University Press.

Latour, Bruno, and Vincent Antonin Lépinay

2009   The Science of Passionate Interests: An Introduction to Gabriel Tarde's Economic Anthropology. Chicago: Prickly Paradigm Press.

Layard, Richard

1980   Human Satisfactions and Public Policy. Economic Journal 90:737–750.

2005   Happiness: Lessons from a New Science. New York: Penguin.

Lee, Dwight, and Richard B. McKenzie

1990   Second Thoughts on the Public-Good Justification for Government Poverty Programs. Journal of Legal Studies 19(1):189–202.

Leisinger, Klaus M.

2007   Corporate Philanthropy: The Top of the Pyramid. Business and Society Review 112:315–342.

Lepore, Jill

2008   The Creed: What Poor Richard cost Benjamin Franklin. The New Yorker, January 28. http://www.newyorker.com/arts/critics/atlarge/2008/01/28/080128crat_atlarge_lepore?currentPage=all.

Levitt, Steven D., and Stephen J. Dubner

2005   Freakonomics. New York: William Morrow.

Loewenstein, George

1997   Exotic Preferences: Behavioral Economics and Human Motivation. Oxford: Oxford University Press.

Loewenstein, George, and Drazen Prelec

1992   Anomalies in Intertemporal Choice: Evidence and an Interpretation. Quarterly Journal of Economics 107(2):573–597.

Lubasz, Heinz

1992   Adam Smith and the Invisible Hand—of the Market? In Contesting Markers. Roy Dilley, ed. Pp. 37–56. Edinburgh: Edinburgh University Press.

Lynch, Michael

1985   Discipline and the Material Form of Images: An Analysis of Scientific Visibility. Social Studies of Science 15(1):37–66.

Macfarlane, Alan

1987   The Culture of Capitalism. New York: Blackwell.

MacIntyre, Alasdair

1981   After Virtue. South Bend, IN: University of Notre Dame Press.

1988   Whose Justice? Which Rationality? South Bend, IN: University of Notre Dame Press.

REFERENCES

Mail and Guardian

2011   Oxfam's Cash Trickle Goes a Long Way in Malawi. May 20. http://mg.co.za/article/2011-05-20-oxfams-cash-trickle-goes-a-long-way-in-malawi, accessed May 21, 2011.

Marwell, G., and R. Ames

1981   Economists Free Ride, Does Anyone Else? Journal of Public Economics 15:295–310.

Marx, Karl, and Frederick Engels

1998[1848]   The Communist Manifesto: A Modern Edition. New York: Verso.

Maurer, Bill

2005   Mutual Life, Ltd: Islamic Banking, Alternative Currencies, Lateral Reason. Princeton, NJ: Princeton University Press.

2006   The Anthropology of Money. Annual Review of Anthropology 35:15–36.

Mauss, Marcel

1983   A Sociological Assessment of Bolshevism (1924–25). Economy and Society 13(3):331–374.

2001[1924]   The Gift: The Form and Reason for Exchange in Archaic Societies. London: Routledge.

May, Larry

1996   The Socially Responsive Self: Social Theory and Professional Ethics. Chicago: University of Chicago Press.

McClay, Wilfred

1993   The Strange Career of *The Lonely Crowd*; or, The Antinomies of Autonomy. *In* The Culture of the Market: Historical Essays. T. L. Haskell and R. F. Teichgraeber III, eds. Pp. 397–440. Cambridge: Cambridge University Press.

McCloskey, Deirdre N.

1991   Voodoo Economics. Poetics Today 12(2):287–300.

1998   The Rhetoric of Economics. 2nd edition. Madison: University of Wisconsin Press.

2002   The Secret Sins of Economics. Chicago: Prickly Paradigm.

2006   The Bourgeois Virtues: Ethics for an Age of Commerce. Chicago: University of Chicago Press.

2008   Adam Smith, the Last of the Former Virtue Ethicists. History of Political Economy 40(1):43–71.

2010   Bourgeois Dignity: Why Economics Can't Explain the Modern World. Chicago: University of Chicago Press.

McClure, S. M., D. I. Laibson, G. Loewenstein, and J. D. Cohen

2004   Separate Neural Systems Value Immediate and Delayed Monetary Rewards. Science 306(October 15):503–507.

McDaniel, Patricia A., Elizabeth A. Smith, and Ruth E. Malone

2006   Philip Morris's Project Sunrise: Weakening Tobacco Control by Working with It. Tobacco Control 15:215–223.

McKay, Ramah

2012   Afterlives: Humanitarian Histories and Critical Subjects in Mozambique. Cultural Anthropology 27(2):286–309.

Mehmet, Ozay, Errol Mendes, and Robert Sinding

1999   Towards a Fair Global Labour Market: Avoiding a New Slave Trade. London: Routledge.

Melo Neto, João Cabral de

2005   Education by Stone. New York: Archipelago Books.

Meth, Charles

2004   Ideology and Social Policy: "Handouts" and the Spectre of "Dependency." Transformation 56:1–30.

Michaels, David

2008   Doubt Is Their Product: How Industry's Assault on Science Threatens Your Health. Oxford: Oxford University Press.

Mill, John Stuart

1869   On Liberty. London: Longman, Roberts, & Green.

1874[1844]   Essays on Some Unsettled Questions of Political Economy. 2nd edition. London: Longmans, Green, Reader, and Dyer.

1909[1871]   Principles of Political Economy, with Some of Their Applications to Social Philosophy. London: Longmans, Green.

Miller, Daniel

1998a   A Theory of Shopping. Cambridge: Polity.

1998b   A Theory of Virtualism. *In* Virtualism: A New Political Economy. James G. Varrier and Daniel Miller, eds. Pp. 187–215. Oxford: Berg.

2008   The Comfort of Things. Cambridge: Polity.

Mining Journal

2001   Industry in Transition. April 13, 267–268.

Mitchell, Timothy

2005   The Work of Economics: How a Discipline Makes Its World. European Journal of Sociology 45(2):297–320.

Montague, P. R., and G. S. Berns

2002   Neural Economics and the Biological Substrates of Valuation. Neuron 36:265–284.

Montague, P. R., B. Kings-Casas, and J. Cohen

2006   Imaging Valuation Models in Human Choice. Annual Review of Neuroscience 29:417–448.

Moody, Roger

2007   Rocks & Hard Places: The Globalization of Mining. London: Zed Books.

Murray, Colin

1981   Families Divided: The Impact of Migrant Labour in Lesotho. New York: Cambridge University Press.

REFERENCES

Nakamoto, Michiyo, and David Wighton
2007   Citigroup Chief Stays Bullish on Buy-Outs. Financial Times, July 9. http://
        www.ft.com/intl/cms/s/0/80e2987a-2e50-11dc-821c-0000779fd2ac.
        html#axzz1MuTW9eeR.

Nelson, Robert H.
2001   Economics as Religion. University Park: State University of Pennsylvania
        Press.

Neves, David, and Andries du Toit
2012   Money and Sociality in South Africa's Informal Economy. Africa
        82(1):131–149.

Newsweek
2010   Welcome to Welfare 2.0 for the World's Poor. December 27. http://www
        .thedailybeast.com/newsweek/2010/12/27/welfare-for-the-developing
        -world-s-poor.html.

Nguyen, Vinh-Kim
2005   Antiretroviral Globalism, Biopolitics, and Therapeutic Citizenship. *In* Global
        Assemblages: Technology, Politics, and Ethics as Anthropological Problems.
        Aihwa Ong and Stephen J. Collier, eds. Pp. 124–144. Malden, MA: Blackwell.
2010   The Republic of Therapy: Triage and Sovereignty in West Africa's Time of
        AIDS. Durham, NC: Duke University Press.

Niebuhr, H. Richard
1999   The Responsible Self: An Essay in Christian Moral Philosophy. Westminster:
        John Knox.

Nielsen, Richard P.
2006   In Search of Organizational Virtue: Moral Agency in Organizations.
        Introduction to special issue, Organization Studies 27(3):317–321.

Noe, Thomas H., and Michael J. Rebello
1994   The Dynamics of Business Ethics and Economic Activity. American
        Economic Review 84(3):531–547.

Novak, Michael
1996   Business as a Calling: Work and the Examined Life. New York: The Free Press.

Nozick, Robert
1981   Philosophical Explanations. Cambridge, MA: Harvard University Press.
1989   The Examined Life: Philosophical Meditations. New York: Simon and
        Schuster.
2001   Invariances: The Structure of the Objective World. Cambridge, MA:
        Harvard University Press.

Nye, John V. C.
1997   Thinking about the State: Property Rights, Trade, and Changing Contractual
        Arrangements in a World with Coercion. *In* The Frontiers of the New
        Institutional Economics. John Drobak and John Nye, eds. Pp. 121–142. New
        York: Academic Press.

Office of the Inspector General
2004   Nationwide Identification of Hardrock Mining Sites. Evaluation Report 2004-P-00005. Washington, DC: United States Environmental Protection Agency. http://www.epa.gov/oig/reports/2004/20040331-2004-p-00005.pdf.

Ong, Aihwa
1999   Flexible Citizenship: The Cultural Logics of Transnationality. Durham, NC: Duke University Press.
2006   Neoliberalism as Exception: Mutations in Citizenship and Sovereignty. Durham, NC: Duke University Press.

Oosterbeek, Hessel, Randolph Sloof, and Gijs van de Kuilen
2004   Cultural Differences in Ultimatum Game Experiments: Evidence from a Meta-analysis. Experimental Economics 7:171–188.

Orwell, George
2003[1949]   Nineteen Eighty-Four. New York: Plume.

Otañez, Marty, and Stanon Glantz
2009   Trafficking in Tobacco Farm Culture: Tobacco Companies' Use of Video Imagery to Undermine Health Policy. Visual Anthropology Review 24(1):1–24.

OTML (Ok Tedi Mining Ltd.)
1999   OTML Releases Environmental Impact Options Reports. Ok Tedi Mining Ltd. media release, August 11.

Owen, Stephen
1996   An Anthology of Chinese Literature, Beginnings to 1911. New York: W. W. Norton.

Paciotti, Brian, and Craig Hadley
2003   The Ultimatum Game in Southwestern Tanzania: Ethnic Variation and Institutional Scope. Current Anthropology 44(3):427–432.

Pahl, Ray
2000   On Friendship. Malden, MA: Polity Press.

Peterson, Christopher, and Martin E. P. Seligman
2004   Character Strengths and Virtues: A Handbook and Classification. Oxford: Oxford University Press.

Petryna, Adriana
2009   When Experiments Travel: Clinical Trials and the Global Search for Human Subjects. Princeton, NJ: Princeton University Press.

Pfeiffer, James, and Rachel Chapman
2010   Anthropological Perspectives on Structural Adjustment and Public Health. Annual Review of Anthropology 39:149–165.

Phelps, E. S., and R. A. Pollak
1968   A Second-Best National Saving and Game-Equilibrium Growth. Review of Economic Studies 35(2):185–199.

REFERENCES

Philip Morris USA

2007   Philip Morris USA website. http://www.philipmorrisusa.com/en/home.asp.

2010   Helping Reduce Underage Tobacco Use. Philip Morris USA website. http://www.philipmorrisusa.com/en/cms/Responsibility/Helping_Nav/Helping_Reduce_Underage_Tobacco_Use/default.aspx?src=top_nav.

Placer Dome Asia Pacific

2000   Porgera Mine Sustainability Report 2000: Towards a Sustainable Future. http://www.placerdome.com.

Polanyi, Karl

1944   The Great Transformation. Boston: Beacon.

Poling, George Wesley

2002   Postclosure Rehabilitation and Assessment of Inlet System. *In* Underwater Tailing Placement at Island Copper Mine: A Success Story. George W. Poling, Derek V. Ellis, James W. Murray, Timothy R. Parsons, and Clem A. Pelletier, eds. Pp. 161–165. Littleton, CO: Society for Mining, Metallurgy, and Exploration.

Pollay, R. W., and T. Dewhirst

2002   The Dark Side of Marketing Seemingly "Light" Cigarettes: Successful Images and Failed Fact. Tobacco Control 11:18–31.

Poppendieck, Janet

1998   Sweet Charity: Emergency Food and the End of Entitlement. New York: Penguin.

Porter, Michael E.

2009   A Strategy for Health Care Reform—Toward a Value-Based System. New England Journal of Medicine 361(2):109–112.

Porter, Michael E., and Elizabeth O. Teisberg

2006   Redefining Health Care: Creating Value-Based Competition on Results. Cambridge, MA: Harvard Business School Press.

Povinelli, Elizabeth

2006   The Empire of Love: Toward a Theory of Intimacy, Genealogy, and Carnality. Durham, NC: Duke University Press.

2011   Economies of Abandonment: Social Belonging and Endurance in Late Liberalism. Durham, NC: Duke University Press.

Power, Michael

1994   The Audit Explosion. London: Demos.

Prahalad, C. K.

2004   The Blinders of Dominant Logic. Long Range Planning 37:171–179.

2006   The Fortune at the Bottom of the Pyramid. Upper Saddle River, NJ: Wharton School.

Proctor, Robert N.

2001   Tobacco and the Global Lung Cancer Epidemic. Nature Reviews Cancer 1:82–86.

Przeworski, Adam

1991   Democracy and the Market: Political and Economic Reforms in Eastern Europe and Latin America. Cambridge: Cambridge University Press.

Rajak, Dinah

2011   In Good Company: An Anatomy of Corporate Social Responsibility. Stanford, CA: Stanford University Press.

Ramiah, Ilavenil, and Michael R. Reich

2005   Public-Private Partnerships and Antiretroviral Drugs for HIV/AIDS: Lessons from Botswana. Health Affairs 24(2):545–551.

Raphael, D. D., and A. L. Macfie

1982   Introduction. *In* The Theory of Moral Sentiments, by Adam Smith. Pp. 1–52. Indianapolis, IN: Liberty Classics.

Reddy, William M.

2001   The Navigation of Feeling: A Framework for the History of Emotions. Cambridge: Cambridge University Press.

Reed, Darryl

2002   Resource Extraction Industries in Developing Countries. Journal of Business Ethics 39:199–226.

Reich, Robert B.

2007   Supercapitalism: The Transformation of Business, Democracy, and Everyday Life. Illustrated edition. New York: Knopf.

Reynolds Whyte, S., M. Whyte, L. Meinert, and B. Kyaddondo

In press   Therapeutic Client-ship: Belonging in Uganda's Mosaic of AIDS Projects. *In* When People Come First: Critical Studies in Global Health. João Biehl and Adriana Petryna, eds. Princeton, NJ: Princeton University Press.

Riddell, Roger C.

2007   Does Foreign Aid Really Work? Oxford: Oxford University Press.

Rio Tinto

2009   Corporate website. http://www.riotinto.com.

Robins, Steven

2006   From "Rights" to "Ritual": AIDS Activism in South Africa. American Anthropologist 108(2):312–323.

Rocha, Hector O.

2004   Entrepreneurship and Development: The Role of Clusters. Small Business Economics 23:363–400.

Rogers, Douglas

2012   The Materiality of the Corporation: Oil, Gas, and Corporate Social Technologies in the Remaking of a Russian Region. American Ethnologist 39(2):284–296.

Rose, Nikolas

2007   The Politics of Life Itself: Biomedicine, Power, and Subjectivity in the Twenty-first Century. Princeton, NJ: Princeton University Press.

REFERENCES

Rosenberg, Daniel, and Susan Harding

2005   Histories of the Future. Durham, NC: Duke University Press.

Rosenfeld, Stuart A.

1997   Bringing Business Clusters into the Mainstream of Economic Development. European Planning Studies 5:3–23.

Roth, Alvin E., Vesna Prasnikar, Mashiro Okuno-Fujiwara, and Shmuel Zamir

1991   Bargaining and Market Behavior in Jerusalem, Ljubljana, Pittsburgh, and Tokyo: An Experimental Study. American Economic Review 81(5):1068–1095.

Rousseau, Jean-Jacques

1994[1755]   Discourse on the Origin and Foundation Of Inequality Among Men. Oxford: Oxford University Press.

Rowley, Timothy

1997   Moving beyond Dyadic Ties: A Network Theory of Stakeholder Influences. Academy of Management Review 22:887–910.

Sachs, Jeffrey

2005a   The End of Poverty: Economic Possibilities for Our Time. New York: Penguin.

2005b   The End of Poverty: How We Can Make It Happen in Our Lifetime. London: Penguin.

Sahlins, Marshall

1972   Stone Age Economics. New York: Aldine Transaction.

2008   The Western Illusion of Human Nature. Chicago: Prickly Paradigm.

Samsky, Ari

2012   Scientific Sovereignty: How International Drug Donation Programs Reshape Health, Disease, and the State. Cultural Anthropology 27(2):310–332.

Samuelson, Paul

1938   A Note on the Pure Theory of Consumer Behavior. Economica 5(17):61–71.

1947   Foundations of Economic Analysis. Cambridge, MA: Harvard University Press.

1948   Consumption Theory in Terms of Revealed Preference. Economica 15(60):243–253.

1965   Proof That Properly Anticipated Prices Fluctuate Randomly. Industrial Management Review 6:41–49.

1976   Economics. 10th edition. New York: McGraw-Hill.

Sansom, Basil

1976   A Signal Transaction and Its Currency. *In* Transaction and Meaning. Bruce Kapferer, ed. Pp. 143–161. Philadelphia, PA: Institute for the Study of Human Issues.

Saul, John

2011   Proletariat and Precariat: Non-transformative Global Capitalism and the African Case. Paper presented at the conference "Beyond Precarious Labor: Rethinking Socialist Strategies," CUNY Graduate Center, New York, May 12–13.

Saul, Stephanie

2008   Bill to Regulate Tobacco Moves Forward. New York Times, April 2. http://www.nytimes.com/2008/04/02/business/02cnd-tobacco.html.

Sawyer, Suzana

2004   Crude Chronicles: Indians, Multinational Oil, and Neoliberalism in Ecuador. Durham, NC: Duke University Press.

2010   Human Energy. Dialectical Anthropology 34(1):67–77.

Sayer, Andrew

2000   Moral Economy and Political Economy. Studies in Political Economy 61(Spring): 79–103.

2006   Approaching Moral Economy. Cultural Political Economy Working Paper Series, 6. Lancaster: Institute for Advanced Studies in Social and Management Sciences, University of Lancaster.

2011   Why Things Matter to People: Social Science, Values and Ethical Life. Cambridge: Cambridge University Press.

Schiller, Dan

1999   Digital Capitalism: Networking the Global Market System. Cambridge, MA: MIT Press.

Schiller, Robert J.

2001   Irrational Exuberance. New York: Broadway Books.

Schjeldahl, Peter

2004   Dealership: How Marion Goodman Quietly Changed the Contemporary-Art Market. New Yorker, February 2, 36–41.

Schmidtz, David

1996   Reasons for Altruism. *In* The Gift: An Interdisciplinary Perspective. Aafke E. Komter, ed. Pp. 164–175. Amsterdam: University of Amsterdam Press.

Schüll, Natasha, and Caitlin Zaloom

2011   The Shortsighted Brain: Neuroeconomics and the Governance of Choice in Time. Social Studies of Science 41(4):515–538.

Schwartz, Barry

1967   The Social Psychology of the Gift. American Journal of Sociology 73(1):1–11.

2004   The Paradox of Choice: Why More Is Less. New York: Ecco.

Scott, James

1977   The Moral Economy of the Peasant. New Haven, CT: Yale University Press.

1985   Weapons of the Weak. New Haven, CT: Yale University Press.

Seccombe, Karen

2000   Families in Poverty in the 1990s: Trends, Causes, Consequences, and Lessons Learned. Journal of Marriage and Family 62(4):1094–1113.

Seekings, Jeremy

2008   Beyond "Fluidity": Kinship and Households as Social Projects. CSSR Working Paper, 237. Cape Town: Center for Social Science Research, University of Cape Town.

REFERENCES

Sen, Amartya

1979   Rational Fools: A Critique of the Behavioral Foundations of Economic
        Theory. *In* Scientific Models and Man. H. Harris, ed. Pp. 87–109. Oxford:
        Oxford University Press.

1982   Choice, Welfare, and Measurement. Oxford: Blackwell.

1983a   Development: Which Way Now? Economic Journal 93(372):745–762.

1983b   Poverty and Famines: An Essay on Entitlement and Deprivation. New York:
        Oxford University Press.

1985   Well-Being, Agency and Freedom: The Dewey Lectures 1984. Journal of
        Philosophy 82(4):169–221.

1987   On Ethics and Economics. Oxford: Blackwell.

1992   Inequality Reexamined. Cambridge, MA: Harvard University Press.

1993   Capability and Well-Being. *In* The Quality of Life. Martha Nussbaum and
        A. Sen, eds. Pp. 30–54. Oxford: Clarendon.

1997   On Ethics and Economics. Malden, MA: Blackwell.

1999   Development as Freedom. Oxford: Oxford University Press.

2006   Identity and Violence: The Illusion of Destiny. New York: W. W. Norton.

Sennett, Richard

2008   The Craftsmen. New Haven, CT: Yale University Press.

Shankleman, Jill

2010   Going Global: Chinese Oil and Mining Companies and the Governance
        of Resource Wealth. Woodrow Wilson International Center for Scholars.
        http://www.wilsoncenter.org/topics/pubs/DUSS_09323Shnkl_rpt0626.pdf.

Shariff, Azim F., and Ara Norenzayan

2007   God Is Watching You: Priming God Concepts Increases Prosocial Behavior
        in an Anonymous Economic Game. Psychological Science 18(9):803–809.

Shatenstein, Stan

2004   Food and Drug Administration Regulation of Tobacco Products:
        Introduction. Tobacco Control 13:438.

Shiller, Robert J.

2005   Behavioral Economics and Institutional Innovation. Cowles Foundation
        Discussion Paper, 1499. New Haven, CT: Cowles Foundation for Research in
        Economics, Yale University.

Siebers, Hans

1999   "We are children of the mountain": Creolization and Modernization among
        the Q'eqchi'es. Amsterdam: Center for Latin American Research and
        Documentation.

Siegel, Michael

2004   Food and Drug Administration Regulation of Tobacco: Snatching Defeat
        from the Jaws of Victory. Tobacco Control 13:439–441.

Silk, Joan B.

2005   The Evolution of Cooperation in Primate Groups. *In* Moral Sentiments and Material Interests: On the Foundations of Cooperation in Economic Life. H. Gintis, S. Bowles, R. Boyd, and E. Fehr, eds. Pp. 43–73. Cambridge, MA: MIT Press.

Simon, Julian L.

1994   The Airline Oversales Auction Plan: The Results. Journal of Transport Economics and Policy 28(3):319–323.

Singer, Merrill, and G. Derrick Hodge, eds.

2010   The War Machine and Global Health. Lanham, MD: AltaMira.

Singer, Peter

2009   The Life You Can Save: Acting Now to End World Poverty. New York: Random House.

Singh, Anupama, Sudarshana Kundu, and William Foster

2005   Corporate Social Responsibility through the Supply Chain: MNCs to SMEs. New York: School of Public and International Affairs, Columbia University.

Smith, Adam

1776   An Inquiry into the Nature and Causes of the Wealth of Nations. Dublin: Whitestone.

1976[1776]   The Wealth of Nations. Chicago: University of Chicago Press.

1982[1759]   The Theory of Moral Sentiments. Glasgow edition. D. D. Raphael and A. L. Macfie, eds. Indianapolis, IN: Liberty Classics.

Smith, Elizabeth A., and Ruth E. Malone

2003a   Altria Means Tobacco: Philip Morris's Identity Crisis. American Journal of Public Health 93(4):553–556.

2003b   Thinking the "Unthinkable": Why Philip Morris Considered Quitting. Tobacco Control 12:208–213.

Smith, Vernon

1991   Introduction. In Papers in Experimental Economics. Pp. 3–7. New York: Cambridge University Press.

2000   Bargaining and Market Behavior: Essays in Experimental Economics. New York: Cambridge University Press.

Solomon, Robert C.

1992   Ethics and Excellence. New York: Oxford University Press.

Standing, Guy

2011   The Precariat: The New Dangerous Class. New York: Bloomsbury Academic.

Standing, Guy, and Michael Samson, eds.

2003   A Basic Income Grant for South Africa. Cape Town: University of Cape Town Press.

Stark, Rodney

2001   One True God: Historical Consequences of Monotheism. Princeton, NJ: Princeton University Press.

Stegman, Michael

2001   The Public Policy Challenges of Payday Lending. Popular Government 66(3):16–22.

REFERENCES

Stelter, Brian

2009 When Chevron Hires Ex-reporter to Investigate Pollution, Chevron Looks Good. New York Times, May 10. http://www.nytimes.com/2009/05/11/business/media/11cbs.html?_r=1.

Stiglitz, Joseph

1993 Market Socialism and Neoclassical Economics. *In* Market Socialism: The Current Debate. P. Bardhan and J. Roemer, eds. Pp. 21–41. Oxford: Oxford University Press.

2002 Globalization and Its Discontents. New York: W. W. Norton.

2010 Freefall: America, Free Markets, and the Sinking of the World Economy. New York: W. W. Norton.

Stolberg, V., and V. Stolberg

2011 Policies Regulating Tobacco, U.S. *In* Encyclopedia of Drug Policy. M. Kleiman and J. Hawdon, eds. Pp. 650–653. Thousand Oaks, CA: Sage.

Stout, Lynn

2010 Cultivating Conscience: How Good Laws Make Good People. Princeton, NJ: Princeton University Press.

Strathern, Marilyn

1988 The Gender of the Gift: Problems with Women and Problems with Society in Melanesia. Berkeley: University of California Press.

2002 Audit Cultures: Anthropological Studies in Accountability, Ethics and the Academy. New York: Routledge.

Streeck, Wolfgang

1997 German Capitalism: Does It Exist? Can It Survive? *In* Political Economy of Modern Capitalism: Mapping Convergence and Diversity. Colin Crouch and Wolfgang Streeck, eds. Pp. 33–54. Thousand Oaks, CA: Sage.

2009 Re-forming Capitalism: Institutional Change in the German Political Economy. Oxford: Oxford University Press.

Streeck, Wolfgang, and Kozo Yamamura, eds.

2001 The Origins of Nonliberal Capitalism: Germany and Japan. Ithaca, NY: Cornell University Press.

Sunder Rajan, Kaushik

2006 Biocapital: The Constitution of Postgenomic Life. Durham, NC: Duke University Press.

Szablowski, David

2007 Transnational Law and Local Struggles: Mining Communities and the World Bank. Oxford: Hart.

Szczypka, Glen, Melanie A. Wakefield, Sherry Emery, Yvonne M. Terry-McElrath, Brian R. Flay, and Frank J. Chaloupka

2007 Working to Make an Image: An Analysis of Three Philip Morris Corporate Media Campaigns. Tobacco Control 16:344–350.

Szwarcwald, Célia Landmann, Aristides Barbosa Júnior, Paulo Roberto Borges de Souza-Júnior, Kátia Regina Valente de Lemos, Paulo Germano de Frias, Karin Regina Luhm, Marcia Moreira Holcman, and Maria Angela Pires Esteves
2008   HIV Testing during Pregnancy: Use of Secondary Data to Estimate 2006 Test Coverage and Prevalence in Brazil. Brazilian Journal of Infectious Diseases 12(3):167–172.

Tait, Nikki
2006   Ok Tedi Copper Mine Damage Claim Settled. Financial Times, June 12, 19.

Thaler, Richard
1992   The Winner's Curse. Princeton, NJ: Princeton University Press.

Thaler, Richard H., and Hersh M. Shefrin
1981   An Economic Theory of Self-Control. Journal of Political Economy 89(2):392–406.

Thaler, Richard H., and Cass R. Sunstein
2008   Nudge: Improving Decisions about Health, Wealth, and Happiness. New Haven, CT: Yale University Press.

Thelen, Kathleen
2001   Varieties of Labor Politics in the Developed Democracies. In Varieties of Capitalism: The Institutional Foundations of Comparative Advantage. Peter A. Hall and David Soskice, eds. Pp. 71–103. Oxford: Oxford University Press.

Thompson, E. P.
1971   Moral Economy of the English Crowd in the Eighteenth Century. Past and Present Society 50(1):76–136.

Thrasher, J. F., J. Niederdeppe, M. C. Farrelly, K. C. Davis, K. M. Ribisl, and M. L. Haviland
2004   The Impact of Anti-tobacco Industry Prevention Messages in Tobacco Producing Regions: Evidence from the US Truth Campaign. Tobacco Control 13:283.

Tocqueville, Alexis de
1954[1840]   Democracy in America, vol. 2. Phillips Bradley, trans. New York: Vintage.

Todd, Petra E., and Kenneth I. Wolpin
2006   Assessing the Impact of a School Subsidy Program in Mexico: Using a Social Experiment to Validate a Dynamic Behavioral Model of Child Schooling and Fertility. American Economic Review 96(5):1384–1417.

Tronto, Joan
1993   Moral Boundaries: A Political Argument for an Ethic of Care. London: Routledge.

Tsing, Anna
2009   Beyond Ecological and Economic Standardization. Australian Journal of Anthropology 20(3):347–368.

Turner, Lowell
1998   Fighting for Partnership: Labor and Politics in Unified Germany. Ithaca, NY: Cornell University Press.

REFERENCES

Turner, Stephen J.

2005   Livelihoods and Sharing: Trends in a Lesotho Village, 1976–2004. Research Report, 22. Bellville, South Africa: Program for Land and Agrarian Studies (PLAAS), University of the Western Cape.

Tversky, Amos, and Daniel Kahneman

1981   The Framing of Decisions and the Psychology of Choice. Science 211:453–458.

Ulrich, Laurel Thatcher

1990   A Midwife's Tale: The Life of Martha Ballard, Based on Her Diary, 1785–1812. New York: Vintage / Random House.

Van der Veen, Robert J., and Philippe van Parijs

1986   A Capitalist Road to Communism. Theory and Society 15(5):635–655.

van Parijs, Philippe

2009   Marxism Recycled. New York: Cambridge University Press.

Veblen, Thorsten

1899   The Theory of the Leisure Class: An Economic Study of Institutions. New York: Macmillan.

Velthuis, Olav

2005   Talking Prices: Symbolic Meanings of Prices on the Market for Contemporary Art. Princeton, NJ: Princeton University Press.

Venkatesh, Sudhir Alladi

2006   Off the Books: The Underground Economy of the Urban Poor. Cambridge, MA: Harvard University Press.

Vidal, Fernando

2009   Brainhood, Anthropological Figure of Modernity. History of the Human Sciences 22(1):5–36.

Von Schnitzler, Antina

2008   Citizenship Prepaid: Water, Calculability, and Techno-Politics in South Africa. Journal of Southern African Studies 34(4):899–917.

Vrecko, Scott

2010   Neuroscience, Power and Culture: An Introduction. History of the Human Sciences 23(1):1–10.

Wallerstein, Immanuel

1991   Braudel on Capitalism, or Everything Upside Down. Special issue on modern France, Journal of Modern History 63(2):354–361.

Ward, Barbara, and Rene Dubos

1972   Only One Earth: The Care and Maintenance of a Small Planet. New York: W. W. Norton.

Warren, Christian

2001   Brush with Death: A Social History of Lead Poisoning. Baltimore, MD: Johns Hopkins University Press.

Warren, Kay B.

1998   Indigenous Movements and Their Critics: Pan-Maya Activism in Guatemala. Princeton, NJ: Princeton University Press.

Weaver, Gary R.

2006   Virtue in Organizations: Moral Identity as a Foundation for Moral Agency. Organization Studies 27(3):341–368.

Weber, Max

1958[1905]   The Protestant Ethic and the Spirit of Capitalism. T. Parsons, trans. New York: Scribner's.

1978[1914]   Economy and Society. Berkeley: University of California Press.

Welker, Marina

2009   "Corporate Security Begins in the Community": Mining, the Corporate Social Responsibility Industry, and Environmental Advocacy in Indonesia. Cultural Anthropology 24(1):142–179.

Welker, Marina, Damani J. Partridge, and Rebecca Hardin

2011   Corporate Lives: New Perspectives on the Social Life of the Corporate Form. Supplement, Current Anthropology 52(S3):S3–S16.

West, Paige

2005   Conservation Is Our Government Now: The Politics of Ecology in New Guinea. Durham, NC: Duke University Press.

White, Harrison

1981   Where Do Markets Come From? American Journal of Sociology 87(3):517–547.

White, James Boyd

1990   Justice as Translation: An Essay in Cultural and Legal Criticism. Chicago: University of Chicago Press.

Whitehead, Alfred North

1978[1929]   Process and Reality: An Essay in Cosmology. David Ray Griffin and Donald W. Sherburne, eds. New York: The Free Press.

Whitmarsh, Ian

2008   Biomedical Ambiguity: Race, Asthma, and the Contested Meaning of Genetic Research in the Caribbean. Ithaca, NY: Cornell University Press.

Whitmore, Andy

2006   The Emperor's New Clothes? Sustainable Mining. Journal of Cleaner Production 14:309–314.

WHO (World Health Organization)

2008   WHO Report on the Global Tobacco Epidemic, 2008: The MPOWER Package. Geneva: World Health Organization.

Wilk, Richard

1993   Altruism and Self-Interest: Towards an Anthropological Theory of Decision Making. Research in Economic Anthropology 14:191–212.

REFERENCES

1996   Economies and Cultures. Boulder, CO: Westview.

Wilson, Duff

2009   Senate Approves Tight Regulation over Cigarettes. New York Times, June 11. http://www.nytimes.com/2009/06/12/business/12tobacco.html.

Wilson, Richard

1995   Maya Resurgence in Guatemala: Q'eqchi' Experiences. Norman: University of Oklahoma Press.

1991   Machine Guns and Mountain Spirits: The Cultural Effects of State Repression among the Q'eqchi' of Guatemala. Critique of Anthropology 11(1):33–61.

Woolcock, Michael

1998   Social Capital and Economic Development: Toward a Theoretical Synthesis and Policy Framework. Theory and Society 27(2):151–208.

Wulfson, Myrna

2001   The Ethics of Corporate Social Responsibility and Philanthropic Ventures. Journal of Business Ethics 29:135–145.

Yanagisako, Sylvia Junko

2002   Producing Culture and Capital: Family Firms in Italy. Princeton, NJ: Princeton University Press.

Yoshihara, Kunio

1994   Japanese Economic Development. Oxford: Oxford University Press.

Yoshiro, Michael Y., and Thomas Lifson

1986   The Invisible Link: Japan's Sogo Shosha and the Organization of Trade. Cambridge, MA: MIT Press.

Yunus, Muhammad

1999   Banker to the Poor: Microlending and the Battle against World Poverty. New York: PublicAffairs.

2008   Creating a World without Poverty: Social Business and the Future of Capitalism. New York: PublicAffairs.

Zaloom, Caitlin

2006   Out of the Pits: Traders and Technology from Chicago to London. Chicago: University of Chicago Press.

2010   Out of the Pits: Traders and Technology from Chicago to London. Chicago: University of Chicago Press.

Zelizer, Viviana

2005   The Purchase of Intimacy. Princeton, NJ: Princeton University Press.

Index

School for Advanced Research Advanced Seminar Series

PUBLISHED BY SAR PRESS

CHACO & HOHOKAM: PREHISTORIC
REGIONAL SYSTEMS IN THE AMERICAN
SOUTHWEST
 Patricia L. Crown & W. James Judge, eds.

RECAPTURING ANTHROPOLOGY: WORKING
IN THE PRESENT
 Richard G. Fox, ed.

WAR IN THE TRIBAL ZONE: EXPANDING
STATES AND INDIGENOUS WARFARE
 *R. Brian Ferguson &
 Neil L. Whitehead, eds.*

IDEOLOGY AND PRE-COLUMBIAN
CIVILIZATIONS
 *Arthur A. Demarest &
 Geoffrey W. Conrad, eds.*

DREAMING: ANTHROPOLOGICAL AND
PSYCHOLOGICAL INTERPRETATIONS
 Barbara Tedlock, ed.

HISTORICAL ECOLOGY: CULTURAL
KNOWLEDGE AND CHANGING LANDSCAPES
 Carole L. Crumley, ed.

THEMES IN SOUTHWEST PREHISTORY
 George J. Gumerman, ed.

MEMORY, HISTORY, AND OPPOSITION
UNDER STATE SOCIALISM
 Rubie S. Watson, ed.

OTHER INTENTIONS: CULTURAL
CONTEXTS AND THE ATTRIBUTION OF
INNER STATES
 Lawrence Rosen, ed.

LAST HUNTERS–FIRST FARMERS: NEW
PERSPECTIVES ON THE PREHISTORIC
TRANSITION TO AGRICULTURE
 *T. Douglas Price &
 Anne Birgitte Gebauer, eds.*

MAKING ALTERNATIVE HISTORIES:
THE PRACTICE OF ARCHAEOLOGY AND
HISTORY IN NON-WESTERN SETTINGS
 Peter R. Schmidt & Thomas C. Patterson, eds.

CYBORGS & CITADELS: ANTHROPOLOGICAL
INTERVENTIONS IN EMERGING SCIENCES
AND TECHNOLOGIES
 Gary Lee Downey & Joseph Dumit, eds.

SENSES OF PLACE
 Steven Feld & Keith H. Basso, eds.

THE ORIGINS OF LANGUAGE: WHAT
NONHUMAN PRIMATES CAN TELL US
 Barbara J. King, ed.

CRITICAL ANTHROPOLOGY NOW:
UNEXPECTED CONTEXTS, SHIFTING
CONSTITUENCIES, CHANGING AGENDAS
 George E. Marcus, ed.

ARCHAIC STATES
 Gary M. Feinman & Joyce Marcus, eds.

REGIMES OF LANGUAGE:
IDEOLOGIES, POLITIES, AND IDENTITIES
 Paul V. Kroskrity, ed.

BIOLOGY, BRAINS, AND BEHAVIOR: THE
EVOLUTION OF HUMAN DEVELOPMENT
 *Sue Taylor Parker, Jonas Langer, &
 Michael L. McKinney, eds.*

WOMEN & MEN IN THE PREHISPANIC
SOUTHWEST: LABOR, POWER, & PRESTIGE
 Patricia L. Crown, ed.

HISTORY IN PERSON: ENDURING
STRUGGLES, CONTENTIOUS PRACTICE,
INTIMATE IDENTITIES
 Dorothy Holland & Jean Lave, eds.

THE EMPIRE OF THINGS: REGIMES OF
VALUE AND MATERIAL CULTURE
 Fred R. Myers, ed.

CATASTROPHE & CULTURE: THE
ANTHROPOLOGY OF DISASTER
 *Susanna M. Hoffman &
 Anthony Oliver-Smith, eds.*

URUK MESOPOTAMIA & ITS NEIGHBORS:
CROSS-CULTURAL INTERACTIONS IN THE
ERA OF STATE FORMATION
 Mitchell S. Rothman, ed.

REMAKING LIFE & DEATH: TOWARD AN
ANTHROPOLOGY OF THE BIOSCIENCES
 Sarah Franklin & Margaret Lock, eds.

TIKAL: DYNASTIES, FOREIGNERS,
& AFFAIRS OF STATE: ADVANCING
MAYA ARCHAEOLOGY
 Jeremy A. Sabloff, ed.

GRAY AREAS: ETHNOGRAPHIC
ENCOUNTERS WITH NURSING HOME
CULTURE
Philip B. Stafford, ed.

PLURALIZING ETHNOGRAPHY: COMPARISON
AND REPRESENTATION IN MAYA CULTURES,
HISTORIES, AND IDENTITIES
John M. Watanabe & Edward F. Fischer, eds.

AMERICAN ARRIVALS: ANTHROPOLOGY
ENGAGES THE NEW IMMIGRATION
Nancy Foner, ed.

VIOLENCE
Neil L. Whitehead, ed.

LAW & EMPIRE IN THE PACIFIC:
FIJI AND HAWAI'I
Sally Engle Merry & Donald Brenneis, eds.

ANTHROPOLOGY IN THE MARGINS
OF THE STATE
Veena Das & Deborah Poole, eds.

THE ARCHAEOLOGY OF COLONIAL
ENCOUNTERS: COMPARATIVE
PERSPECTIVES
Gil J. Stein, ed.

GLOBALIZATION, WATER, & HEALTH:
RESOURCE MANAGEMENT IN TIMES OF
SCARCITY
Linda Whiteford & Scott Whiteford, eds.

A CATALYST FOR IDEAS: ANTHROPOLOGICAL
ARCHAEOLOGY AND THE LEGACY OF
DOUGLAS W. SCHWARTZ
Vernon L. Scarborough, ed.

THE ARCHAEOLOGY OF CHACO CANYON:
AN ELEVENTH-CENTURY PUEBLO
REGIONAL CENTER
Stephen H. Lekson, ed.

COMMUNITY BUILDING IN THE TWENTY-
FIRST CENTURY
Stanley E. Hyland, ed.

AFRO-ATLANTIC DIALOGUES:
ANTHROPOLOGY IN THE DIASPORA
Kevin A. Yelvington, ed.

COPÁN: THE HISTORY OF AN ANCIENT
MAYA KINGDOM
E. Wyllys Andrews & William L. Fash, eds.

THE EVOLUTION OF HUMAN LIFE HISTORY
Kristen Hawkes & Richard R. Paine, eds.

THE SEDUCTIONS OF COMMUNITY:
EMANCIPATIONS, OPPRESSIONS,
QUANDARIES
Gerald W. Creed, ed.

THE GENDER OF GLOBALIZATION: WOMEN
NAVIGATING CULTURAL AND ECONOMIC
MARGINALITIES
*Nandini Gunewardena &
Ann Kingsolver, eds.*

NEW LANDSCAPES OF INEQUALITY:
NEOLIBERALISM AND THE EROSION OF
DEMOCRACY IN AMERICA
*Jane L. Collins, Micaela di Leonardo,
& Brett Williams, eds.*

IMPERIAL FORMATIONS
*Ann Laura Stoler, Carole McGranahan,
& Peter C. Perdue, eds.*

OPENING ARCHAEOLOGY: REPATRIATION'S
IMPACT ON CONTEMPORARY RESEARCH
AND PRACTICE
Thomas W. Killion, ed.

SMALL WORLDS: METHOD, MEANING,
& NARRATIVE IN MICROHISTORY
*James F. Brooks, Christopher R. N. DeCorse,
& John Walton, eds.*

MEMORY WORK: ARCHAEOLOGIES OF
MATERIAL PRACTICES
Barbara J. Mills & William H. Walker, eds.

FIGURING THE FUTURE: GLOBALIZATION
AND THE TEMPORALITIES OF CHILDREN
AND YOUTH
Jennifer Cole & Deborah Durham, eds.

TIMELY ASSETS: THE POLITICS OF
RESOURCES AND THEIR TEMPORALITIES
*Elizabeth Emma Ferry &
Mandana E. Limbert, eds.*

DEMOCRACY: ANTHROPOLOGICAL
APPROACHES
Julia Paley, ed.

CONFRONTING CANCER: METAPHORS,
INEQUALITY, AND ADVOCACY
Juliet McMullin & Diane Weiner, eds.

PUBLISHED BY SAR PRESS

DEVELOPMENT & DISPOSSESSION: THE
CRISIS OF FORCED DISPLACEMENT AND
RESETTLEMENT
Anthony Oliver-Smith, ed.

GLOBAL HEALTH IN TIMES OF VIOLENCE
Barbara Rylko-Bauer, Linda Whiteford,
& Paul Farmer, eds.

THE EVOLUTION OF LEADERSHIP:
TRANSITIONS IN DECISION MAKING FROM
SMALL-SCALE TO MIDDLE-RANGE SOCIETIES
Kevin J. Vaughn, Jelmer W. Eerkins, &
John Kantner, eds.

ARCHAEOLOGY & CULTURAL RESOURCE
MANAGEMENT: VISIONS FOR THE FUTURE
Lynne Sebastian & William D. Lipe, eds.

ARCHAIC STATE INTERACTION: THE
EASTERN MEDITERRANEAN IN THE BRONZE
AGE
William A. Parkinson &
Michael L. Galaty, eds.

INDIANS & ENERGY: EXPLOITATION
AND OPPORTUNITY IN THE AMERICAN
SOUTHWEST
Sherry L. Smith & Brian Frehner, eds.

ROOTS OF CONFLICT: SOILS, AGRICULTURE,
AND SOCIOPOLITICAL COMPLEXITY IN
ANCIENT HAWAI'I
Patrick V. Kirch, ed.

PHARMACEUTICAL SELF: THE GLOBAL
SHAPING OF EXPERIENCE IN AN AGE OF
PSYCHOPHARMACOLOGY
Janis Jenkins, ed.

FORCES OF COMPASSION: HUMANITARI-
ANISM BETWEEN ETHICS AND POLITICS
Erica Bornstein & Peter Redfield, eds.

ENDURING CONQUESTS: RETHINKING THE
ARCHAEOLOGY OF RESISTANCE TO SPANISH
COLONIALISM IN THE AMERICAS
Matthew Liebmann &
Melissa S. Murphy, eds.

DANGEROUS LIAISONS: ANTHROPOLOGISTS
AND THE NATIONAL SECURITY STATE
Laura A. McNamara &
Robert A. Rubinstein, eds.

BREATHING NEW LIFE INTO THE EVIDENCE
OF DEATH: CONTEMPORARY APPROACHES
TO BIOARCHAEOLOGY
Aubrey Baadsgaard, Alexis T. Boutin, &
Jane E. Buikstra, eds.

THE SHAPE OF SCRIPT: HOW AND WHY
WRITING SYSTEMS CHANGE
Stephen D. Houston, ed.

NATURE, SCIENCE, AND RELIGION:
INTERSECTIONS SHAPING SOCIETY AND
THE ENVIRONMENT
Catherine M. Tucker, ed.

THE GLOBAL MIDDLE CLASSES:
THEORIZING THROUGH ETHNOGRAPHY
Rachel Heiman, Carla Freeman, &
Mark Liechty, eds.

KEYSTONE NATIONS: INDIGENOUS PEOPLES
AND SALMON ACROSS THE NORTH PACIFIC
Benedict J. Colombi & James F. Brooks, eds.

REASSEMBLING THE COLLECTION:
ETHNOGRAPHIC MUSEUMS AND
INDIGENOUS AGENCY
Rodney Harrison, Sarah Byrne, & Annie
Clarke, eds.

IMAGES THAT MOVE
Patricia Spyer & Mary Margaret Steedly, eds.

VITAL RELATIONS: MODERNITY AND THE
PERSISTENT LIFE OF KINSHIP
Susan McKinnon & Fenella Cannell, eds.

ANTHROPOLOGY OF RACE: GENES,
BIOLOGY, AND CULTURE
John Hartigan, ed.

STREET ECONOMIES IN THE URBAN
GLOBAL SOUTH
Karen Tranberg Hansen, Walter E. Little,
& B. Lynne Milgram, eds.

TIMELESS CLASSICS FROM SAR PRESS

Participants in the School for Advanced Research advanced seminar "Markets and Moralities" co-chaired by Peter Benson and Edward F. Fischer, May 3–7, 2009. *Standing, from left*: Bart Victor, James Ferguson, Anna Tsing, Robert Frank; *seated, from left*: Caitlin Zaloom, Edward F. Fischer, Peter Benson. Photograph by Jason S. Ordaz.